After Authoritarianism

Transitional justice – the act of reckoning with a former authoritarian regime after it has ceased to exist – has direct implications for democratic processes. Mechanisms of transitional justice have the power to influence who decides to go into politics, can shape politicians' behavior while in office, and can affect how politicians delegate policy decisions. However, these mechanisms are not all alike: some, known as transparency mechanisms, uncover authoritarian collaborators who did their work in secret while others, known as purges, fire open collaborators of the old regime. *After Authoritarianism* explores these mechanisms in depth and shows their contrasting effects on the quality and stability of new democracies. While transparency mechanisms, such as truth commissions and lustrations, enhance democratic processes, mechanisms firing open collaborators such as purges frequently hurt new democracies. Using a highly disaggregated global transitional justice dataset, the book shows that mechanisms of transitional justice are far from being the epilogue of an outgoing authoritarian regime, and instead represent the crucial first chapter in a country's democratic story.

MONIKA NALEPA is the Professor of Political Science at the University of Chicago. Her first book, *Skeletons in the Closet: Transitional Justice in Post-Communist Europe*, received the Best Book Award from the Comparative Democratization section of APSA and the Leon Epstein Outstanding Book Award from the Political Organizations and Parties section of APSA. With a focus on postcommunist Europe, her research interests include transitional justice, parties, and legislatures, and the political economy of regime change.

POLITICAL ECONOMY OF INSTITUTIONS AND DECISIONS

Series Editors

Jeffry Frieden, *Harvard University*
John Patty, *Emory University*
Elizabeth Maggie Penn, *Emory University*

Founding Editors

James E. Alt, *Harvard University*
Douglass C. North, *Washington University of St. Louis*

(*Continued after the Index*)

After Authoritarianism

Transitional Justice and Democratic Stability

MONIKA NALEPA

The University of Chicago

CAMBRIDGE
UNIVERSITY PRESS

University Printing House, Cambridge CB2 8BS, United Kingdom

One Liberty Plaza, 20th Floor, New York, NY 10006, USA

477 Williamstown Road, Port Melbourne, VIC 3207, Australia

314–321, 3rd Floor, Plot 3, Splendor Forum, Jasola District Centre,
New Delhi – 110025, India

103 Penang Road, #05–06/07, Visioncrest Commercial, Singapore 238467

Cambridge University Press is part of the University of Cambridge.

It furthers the University's mission by disseminating knowledge in the pursuit of
education, learning, and research at the highest international levels of excellence.

www.cambridge.org
Information on this title: www.cambridge.org/9781316513439
DOI: 10.1017/9781009072540

© Monika Nalepa 2022

First published 2022

A catalogue record for this publication is available from the British Library.

Library of Congress Cataloging-in-Publication Data
Names: Nalepa, Monika, 1976– author.
Title: After authoritarianism : transitional justice and democratic stability /
Monika Nalepa.
Description: Cambridge : Cambridge University Press, 2022. |
Series: Peid political economy of institutions and decisions |
Includes bibliographical references and index.
Identifiers: LCCN 2022019317 (print) | LCCN 2022019318 (ebook) |
ISBN 9781316513439 (hardback) | ISBN 9781009073714 (paperback) |
ISBN 9781009072540 (epub)
Subjects: LCSH: Authoritarianism. | Transitional justice. | Democratization. |
Political purges. | BISAC: POLITICAL SCIENCE / General
Classification: LCC JC480 .N36 2022 (print) | LCC JC480 (ebook) |
DDC 320.53–dc23/eng/20220701
LC record available at https://lccn.loc.gov/2022019317
LC ebook record available at https://lccn.loc.gov/2022019318

ISBN 978-1-316-51343-9 Hardback
ISBN 978-1-009-07371-4 Paperback

Pamięci Mojej Babci, Józefy Nalepy

Contents

Figures

Tables

Acknowledgments

Writing a book as an associate professor means incurring debts to everyone – from your students to your advisors, from your parents to your pets.

I will start with thanking students who worked with me in the Transitional Justice and Democratic Stability Lab over the years, but especially Milena Ang, Genevieve Bates, and Ipek Cinar. Without their constant input, diligent work, and at times unrelenting criticism, the vision that I had in graduate school of collecting data on all transitional justice events in the world would never have materialized.

These three founding members of the lab trained more graduate and undergraduate students, showing them the same attention and respect showing them the same attention and respect whether they worked with us for a month or a year. It is thanks to the community that the Transitional Justice and Democratic Stability Lab has become that this project continued uninterrupted through the pandemic months. Special thanks are due also to Hope Dancy and Zikai Li, who joined the lab while it was entirely virtual and not only stuck with it but took on leadership roles.

Among the undergraduate students, I am especially grateful to Viivi Jarvi, Karen "Ken" Krmoyan, Moksha Sharma, and Jordi Vasquez.

Alas, even at the University of Chicago, researchers cannot sustain themselves on ideas alone. None of these hardworking individuals would have been supported for their efforts were it not for the generous sponsors from within the University of Chicago and beyond. Among the latter, my sincerest gratitude goes to Brian Humes, the National Science Foundation Program Director for Political Science, who steered the project toward funding in 2017 and answered countless questions along the way. I am also grateful to Tim Nokken for helping me revise and spend my budget.

At the University of Chicago, I am grateful first and foremost to the Center of International Social Science Research (CISSR), and especially its director, Jenny Trinitapoli. CISSR under Trinitapoli was about so much more than funding research: She created a community of scholars united in their pursuit of truth in social science and offered friendship and support for this project, including babysitting a second-grader in the final stretch of manuscript preparation. The Pearson Institute and the College Curriculum Innovation Fund – both at the University of Chicago – also funded the students working in the lab over multiple years. Equally critical for the project's success was the support of my two writing buddies – Anne Meng and Jennifer Gandhi.

Beyond these two, I am grateful to Scott Gehlbach, Scott Gates, John Huber, and Krzysztof Krakowski for reading the manuscript in its entirety at an early stage for a book manuscript workshop in June 2019. I also appreciate greatly feedback on early chapter drafts from participants in the Center for the Study of Democracy, the Committee for Quantitative Methodology Colloquium, and the Political Economy Lunch Group at the University of Chicago, the Political Science Colloquium at Washington University in St. Louis, the Comparative Politics Workshop at Vanderbilt University, and the Asian Online Political Science Seminar Series. I am especially grateful for comments to Jeff Statton, Pablo Montagnes, Noam Lupu, John Brehm, Anthony Fowler, Susan Stokes, Aziz Huq, and Tim Ginsburg.

At some level, I feel as if I started writing this book twenty years ago as a student and research assistant of Jon Elster. Jon's role was critical in two regards. The first was theoretical by questioning how any transitional justice mechanism could possibly do new democracies any good. Having arrived from a country suddenly intoxicated with the desire to settle scores with its past, this seemed a very provoking thought. Jon's second input was empirical. While working on his *Closing the Books: Transitional Justice in Historical Perspective*, Jon asked me to collect data on transitional justice in several East European countries. When I asked him how he would like the data organized, he replied "frankly, I was hoping you would propose something, Monika." And so the adventure began – thinking of what is the best way to summarize transitional justice procedures in a way that is practical for a comparativist. Years later, that strategy of tracking down transitional justice became the Global Transitional Justice Dataset.

Sara Doskow at Cambridge University Press made the publishing process as smooth as it could possibly be and found thoughtful and constructive reviewers. I am grateful for their insights that made the manuscript considerably stronger.

I could not have written this book at a better place than the University of Chicago, among what I believe is the strongest group of political economists in the world. I am particularly grateful to Maggie Penn, Konstantin Sonin, Robert Gulotty, John Patty, Austin Wright, and Justin Grimmer, some of whom no longer work here but with whom I was lucky to interact while at the University of Chicago.

As intellectually stimulating as the University of Chicago is, its intensity can be crushing to the soul without the respite of family life. In marrying Suyash Agrawal ten years ago, I won the relationship lottery. There is nobody else I would rather come home to. He is always the first and last to hear my ideas. The harshest critic is of course my daughter, Maja, but she also gives the warmest hugs. Finally although she will never let me sleep past 5:30 am, I would be one grumpy professor without the goofiness of Geneva. If only every author had such a tight pack.

I

Letting Sleeping Dogs Lie?

Chair of Vetting Commission: *Do you swear to faithfully serve the new Polish Republic?*
Franz Mauer: *I do, to the very end, be it mine or hers.* (Wladyslaw Pasikowski, *Psy* [*Dogs*])

    After Generalissmo Francisco Franco died, the elites who succeeded him resolved on behalf of the Spanish people to let bygones be bygones. Formally, in 1977, they passed an Amnesty Law; informally, they agreed to a "Pact of Forgetting." The rationale offered for this deliberate decision was to chose democracy over justice. Although the Francoist regime had committed numerous atrocities during the civil war of 1936–1939 as well as after the Nationalists' victory, Spanish elites decided to "seal the archives" of the *Guardia Civil* and the *Policia Armada* (Franco's secret police)[1] and not attempt any reckoning with the past. Even private conversation concerning the civil war and the authoritarian regime that succeeded it was rendered taboo. This "Pact of Forgetting" was shared widely by all sides of the political spectrum, including the communists against whom Franco's Nationalists had fought in the civil war. For instance, Santiago Carillo (general secretary of the Spanish Communist Party at the time of transition) was quoted as saying: "In our country, there is but one way to reach democracy, which is to throw out anyone

---

[1] Both were security agencies designed to preserve the power of the Spanish dictator. The Guardia Civil was mainly active in rural areas, whereas the Policia Armada patrolled cities and metropolitan areas.

who promotes the memory of the Civil War. We do not want any more wars, we have enough of them already."[2]

The informal pact became so entrenched that when, in 2007, a socialist government tried to revisit the past by proposing the mildest of transparency measures, victim rehabilitation, it was met with staunch criticism.[3] The Spanish example stood in contrast with its geographic and temporal neighbors, Greece and Portugal, both of which thoroughly purged their former authoritarian leadership and its agencies. To see this contrast, one need only to look at Figures 1.1 and 1.2. Both are based on data from the Global Transitional Justice Dataset.[4] Figure 1.1 shows the removal of leaders associated with the *ancien régime* in eighty-four countries that had such leadership purge events. Most notably, since zeroes have been omitted from these figures, Spain is not even listed among the countries that underwent such purges. Figure 1.2 shows thorough purge events, that is, instances of shuttering entire former authoritarian agencies. Spain had no such events either.

Incidentally, neither Greece nor Portugal fared as well recovering from their authoritarian pasts as Spain. By the early 1990s, Spain had risen to be come one of the leading nations in the European Community, with a GDP per capita of almost 68 percent of that of the United States in 1991 (based on purchasing power parity according to the International Monetary Fund, IMF)[5] and a Polity IV score of 10. Scholars of comparative democratization, a popular and growing field of political science in the twentieth century, overwhelmingly agreed that Spain consolidated because of letting bygones be bygones rather than despite it. Regardless of what kind of authoritarian or post-conflict legacy a country was recovering from, transitional justice (TJ) was believed to jeopardize, not facilitate democratization (Huntington 1991; Linz et al. 1978; O'donnell et al. 2013; Przeworski 1991).

It is then hardly surprising that when twenty years later, a wave of democratization spread across Eastern Europe, Spain's approach to reckoning with the authoritarian past was used as a model for (not) dealing with the legacies of communism. In Poland, this approach was

---

[2] See *Europe: Painful memories; Spain's civil war* (2006).
[3] See *Europe: A Rude Awakening; Spain's Past* (2007).
[4] The details on how this dataset was prepared are explained later in this chapter as well as in Chapter 4.
[5] As a point of comparison, Portugal's GDP per capita relative to that of the United States for the same year was 56 percent, barely higher than the 52 percent recorded in 1982, and Greece's was 60 percent, down from 72 percent in 1980.

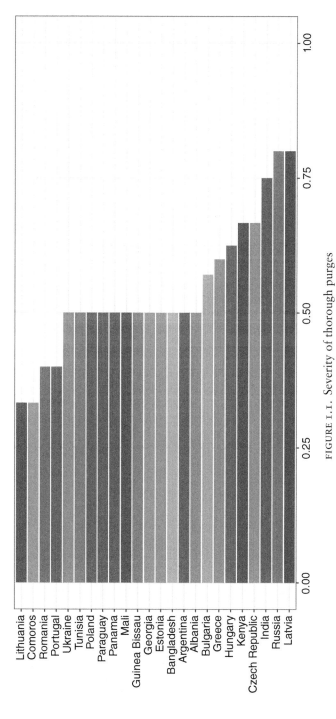

FIGURE 1.1. Severity of thorough purges

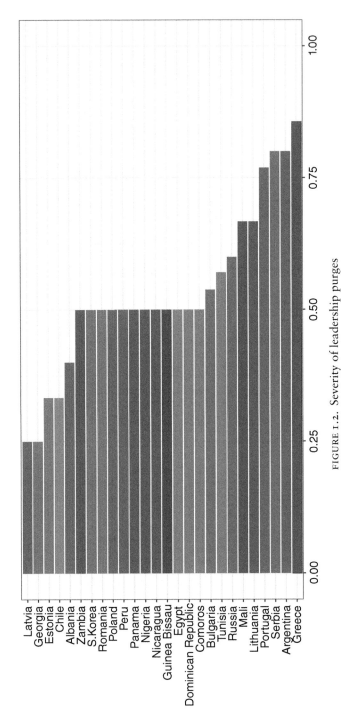

FIGURE 1.2. Severity of leadership purges

summarized with the term *"gruba kreska"* ("thick line"). Although originally intended to represent the idea of a clean slate for the new noncommunist cabinet, which would only be held accountable for policies implemented after assuming office, it quickly came to represent the idea of forgiving the communists for all human rights violations committed during their 45-year-long tenure in Poland.[6]

In his 1989 inaugural speech to parliament as the first non-communist prime minister in 45 years, Tadeusz Mazowiecki announced *I present to you a cabinet that bears no responsibility for the mortgage it is inheriting today. Even though it affects the circumstances in which we must operate, we are separating ourselves from the past with a **thick line*** (Gostkiewicz 2013).

The international community of scholars largely applauded this decision. Jack Snyder argued that "the prosecution of perpetrators of atrocities according to universal standards risks causing more atrocities than it would prevent, because it pays insufficient attention to polit-ical realities" (Snyder & Vinjamuri 2004, p. 5). Samuel Huntington maintained that sometimes "amnesty...is necessary to establish a new democracy on a solid basis" (Huntington 1993, p. 214) and that "even if a moral and legal argument could be made for prosecution, this would fall before the normative imperative of creating a stable democracy."

This policy was also widely endorsed by a group of social scientists formed around the law journal *The East European Constitutional Review* published in the 1990s; first, at the University of Chicago and later at New York University. Jon Elster and Stephen Holmes spearheaded this move-ment and used Spain's most benign way of dealing with former author-itarian collaborators to build their case that "doing nothing" is the best approach for new democracies to deal with past authoritarian regimes (Elster 2004). "Gruba kreska" and the "Pact of Forgetting" in contrast to "witch hunts" and "ritual sacrifices," they argued, allow typical political cleavages of left and right to form without the development of a "regime divide" where opponents of the previous regime overlook their ideological differences and maintain a united front against successor autocrats, even when these members of the opposition actually share ideological identities with the successor autocrats.[7] Delayed democratic consolidation due to

---

[6] These violations included torture, despite Poland signing the Geneva Convention Against Torture and Other Cruel, Inhuman or Degrading Treatment or Punishment.

[7] In the context of post-communist Europe, for reasons explained later, "gruba kreska" failed and a regime divide did emerge (Grzymala-Busse 2001). Concretely, Grzymala-Busse defines the regime divide as the persisting conflict between the successors

a party system that fails to develop programmatically is but one of the possible costs of making TJ central to political debates.

Poland and Hungary, which transitioned in short succession, both refrained at least initially from harsh decommunization. In Poland, President Wałęsa and his supporters from the Citizens' Committee prevented any decommunization bills spontaneously passed on the legislative floor from being implemented.[8] Latter attempts were halted by the Constitutional Tribunal, a constitutional court established a few years before the transition. In Hungary, the Constitutional Court was also responsible for first halting and then significantly delaying attempts to deal with the past.

Borrowing the Spanish Model and applying it to countries with completely different authoritarian legacies seemed like a perfectly legitimate thing to do. Scholars had not yet started to appreciate that how dictatorship operated has critical implications for the types of TJ that can and should be used. This is one of the misconceptions I will address in this book.

The key difference between Eastern Europe on the one hand, and Spain on the other, is that propping up communist regimes for more than four decades required a skilled and powerful secret police apparatus that collaborated with tens of thousands of secret informers whose identity at the time of the transition to democracy was unknown.

Some of those offering support to the regime were open collaborators, such as communist party functionaries and top-echelon workers of the state. Even salaried cops of the secret police, to the extent that they did not hide their policing activity were open collaborators. Others such as the informers and agents recruited by the secret police conducted their activity in secret. Procedures dealing with open collaborators are not only descriptively but analytically different from those that deal with secret collaborators. The latter, as painful as this may be, ought to be exposed. Failing to do so risks damage to the fledging democracy. The open collaborators, on the other hand, sometimes must be purged but sometimes should be kept on.

---

to the pre-1989 communist parties and the parties emerging from the communist era opposition. The deeper this divide, the lower the chances of coalition formation between the communist successors and their opposition counterparts based on shared policy goals.

[8] In a spectacular takedown of legislation, aiming to reveal the identities of secret police agents by the Polish Minister of Interior, Wałęsa and his allies brought down the entire cabinet and replaced it with one that vowed to stay clear of dealing with the past.

1.1 NEITHER RETRIBUTION, NOR RECONCILIATION

The opening quote to this book features a policeman of the secret enforcement apparatus, Franz Mauer, during such a moment of reckoning. He is being interviewed by a vetting commission set up to decide whom among the communist law enforcement the new democratic state should rehire. Franz Mauer's file contains more red flags than honors, so in the end, the commission's chair asks Mauer directly if he will "faithfully serve the new Polish Republic." Mauer's cynical reply indicating that he is committed to the mission until the end, be it his or hers, does not dissuade the chair from rehiring him. Hence, a former communist cop is left unscathed by the purge. In contrast, many informers recruited by the likes of Franz Mauer will be exposed and sometimes prevented from holding public office.

This book will show that paradoxically, it is more important to expose the nonprofessional agents and informers than to purge the state of open members and administrators of former dictatorships. Though purging the former authoritarian state depends on the specific traits of the authoritarian regime, exposing collaborators who supported the *ancien régime* in secret is critical.

Secret authoritarian legacies have a way of undermining successor regimes even years after the transition. For instance, collaborators of the former regime may have engaged in acts that under a new democratic regime could tarnish their reputation. If these acts remain secret while former collaborators rise to positions of power, they may be blackmailed by those who threaten to release their "skeletons in the closet."

To illustrate this point, consider the following case from Poland. In February of 2016, the widow of Czesław Kiszczak, the former chief of communist Poland's secret police, discovered a thick secret police file containing evidence that Lech Wałęsa, Nobel Peace Prize Laureate and former Solidarity leader, had collaborated with the communist secret police between 1970 and 1976. The revelation raised serious concerns about the quality of Wałęsa's presidency, which had ended before Poland implemented its lustration law.[9] Although Wałęsa's collaboration preceded his career as Solidarity trade union organizer, Kiszczak could have pressured him to avoid implementing certain policies by threatening to release the compromising file. This left many questioning the extent to which he

---

[9] A lustration program would have vetted Wałęsa for connections to the communist secret police. Had it been in effect when Wałęsa ran for or held office, his political career could have ended had he falsely maintained his innocence.

represented interests of the electorate instead of those of the former secret police. More generally, it left scholars wondering about the prevalence of such acts of blackmail. How often did former authoritarian elites pressure their former spies into following their policy preferences over those of the voters? To the extent that one considers representing voters' wishes as a marker of high-quality representative democracy, the revelation left many wondering just how representative Polish democracy was of its electorate.

The arguments in support of the "Pact of Forgetting" and "gruba kreska" assume that TJ – the combined set of mechanisms designed to deal with past authoritarian legacies – cannot be democracy enhancing. The widely held belief is that TJ can at most promote reconciliation,[10] though any brooding in the past comes at the cost of delaying normal democratic processes, normal political cleavage formation, and party system institutionalization. In this book, I challenge the belief that one can and must choose between democracy and justice. First, I argue that democracies do not emerge in a vacuum. Legacies of former authoritarian states permeate the new polity through unsettled scores of human rights abuses, staff of former security agencies, and archives of the former secret police that list the names of collaborators of the authoritarian security apparatus.

Without TJ mechanisms that reveal ties of politicians to agents of the *ancien régime*, voters cannot recall from office dishonest politicians. The ability to recall such "bad" representatives is a key characteristic of representative democracy. Blackmailed politicians keep their true identity secret and respond to demands of blackmailers, threatening to expose *kompromat* instead of their own constituents. According to the argument I present in this book, revealing evidence of human rights violations and collaboration with members of the *ancien régime* prevents former authoritarian elites from influencing policy in new democratic polities. Where transparency is lacking, former authoritarian elites can pressure politicians into policy concessions by threatening to reveal compromising information that could jeopardize these politicians' careers.

Not all forms of authoritarian dominance are as transparent as repression (King et al. 2013; Mattingly 2019; Nugent 2019; Tyson 2018). In many instances, the very acts that sustained the authoritarian regime were secret collaboration (Blaydes 2010), cooptation (Magaloni 2006), and

---

[10] However, see criticisms of the reconciliation goal that hold that it is too ambitious and imposes a collectively shared belied about the truth of past events instead of allowing competing, conflicting narrative of that past Muller (2002).

sabotage (Dragu & Przeworski 2019). A key aspect of dealing with the secret acts of supporting the *ancien régime* is the disclosure of such actions and the revelation of the identities of collaborators, spies, and saboteurs. This transparency class of TJ mechanisms, revealing who among persons holding public office collaborated with the secret police to the detriment of the antiauthoritarian opposition are often left out of classical critiques of TJ, but they ensure the honesty of politicians and the ability of parties to be broadly representative. This book will show that transparency mechanisms (lustration and truth commissions) have a critical impact on who selects to enter politics and how well they are able to perform once in office. Such transparency mechanisms can improve the quality of representation by bringing policy proposals closer to the preferences of the median voter than keeping skeletons in the closet would. When transparency mechanisms reach deeper into society, they can help curb wide-scale political corruption.

Because transparency regimes regulate when and how skeletons in the closet are released, they have implications for the quality of democracy and the success of the democratization project. If democracy survives, damaging information collected by the former authoritarian secret police for the benefit of authoritarian elites may, if kept secret, turn elected politicians into clients of blackmailers who threaten to reveal their skeletons in the closet (Nalepa 2010*b*). Forgiving and forgetting may sabotage elected politicians' capacity to represent voters, a phenomenon that is hard to pick up on by studies focusing on the immediate aftermath of a transition. That is why in this book, I adopt a long time horizon to evaluate if mechanisms of dealing with the past are indeed working. The empirical span of my analysis reaches even decades into the democratization project.

In sum, there is no "gruba kreska:" New democracies do not have the luxury of separating themselves from the past with a "thick line" and starting with a blank slate. There are cobwebs of former authoritarian regimes everywhere. Some of them are secret and these must be, as this book will argue, exposed. What about the other legacies that are perfectly transparent?

The old regime relied on an enforcement apparatus and staff of the state administration. These networks are not secret, but dealing with them is no less consequential. The opening quote of this book underscores the dilemma of the administrative crisis that new democracies face: Who should run their state? On one hand, there are both normative and practical cases to be made for removing the Franz Mauers, the agents of the *ancien régime*. On the other hand, there is a clear trade-off to purging the state and replacing existing actors with new agents: inexperienced people, lacking expertise. How can new democracies, emerging out of recent authoritarianism, construct a government that will be accountable and yet proficient?

For a different context, consider the case of Tunisia- until recently, the trailblazer of countries that transitioned during the Arab Spring. Zine El Albidine Ben Ali's predecessor, Habib Bourguiba, was famous for appointing all state administrators from among loyalists of the authoritarian party, Neo-Dustur. To ensure that none of them became strong enough to dethrone him, he frequently reshuffled persons at the top. The result of this was a bureaucracy with a very poor skill set. Ben Ali, in contrast, professionalized his governing apparatus and enforcement agencies. In sharp juxtaposition to Ba'athist states in the region, where positions were awarded according to partisan status, Ben Ali developed a cadre of professional bureaucrats.[11]

To sustain his dictatorship, Ben Ali also relied for support on his police forces. This was necessary because, according to Safwan Masri, the army had "neither the power or political will" to quell the protests against the regime (Masri 2017). According to numerous accounts, in the critical moment of the protests, Rachid Ammar (chief of staff of the armed forces) outright refused orders to fire on protesters (Henry 2007). Later during the transition, it was the army that would provide cover for the protesters, while security forces under command of the interior minister fired on protesters.

Political alignments of authoritarian enforcement agencies also have consequences for how new democracies should conduct TJ if their goal is to stabilize democracy. Following the Tunisian transition, the security forces were thoroughly purged by the new democratic minister of interior, Farhat Rajhi.[12] Meanwhile, the army was largely left intact; their loyalties were clearly with the new democratic government. However, the issue of the police is more complex. As later events showed, Tunisia became the leader in the Middle East in terrorist attacks and supplying fighters to Syria (Macdonald & Waggoner 2018). Arguably, this happened because of Tunisia's weakened internal security forces after the firing of Ben Ali's enforcement apparatus.

---

[11] This should in no way distract from Ali's authoritarian methods.
[12] According to a March 7, 2011 decree issued by the Interior Ministry, the secret police and security apparatus were abolished "to bolster freedoms and civil rights" and to eradicate "outdated institutions that are vestiges of the regime."

This book will show why banning known agents of the *ancien régime* may, under certain conditions, damage democratic quality. A purge of open collaborators removes agents whose expertise may be of use in the new democratic state. Although such agents may use this expertise to advance their own goals, if they are not purged and these goals are transparent to the new democrats, there may exist ways of harnessing this expertise in the service of the new regime.

Tunisia's case stands in sharp contrasts with that of Bolivia where the military was actively involved in propping up authoritarian governments from 1964 until 1982. After the transition, the past was dealt with very mildly. Following a general amnesty for political prisoners, the only mechanism for acknowledging the past was a short-lived truth and reconciliation commission.[13] After two years, and one year before the expiration of its mandate, the commission was disbanded. It took more than a decade before criminal sentences against one of the military dictators and over forty of his collaborators were handed down. The absence of TJ until then could be attributed to the strength of the military at the time of transition, but it is not uncommon for reckoning with the past to take place even when the military is strong (Greece being a leading example here). Moreover, the strength of the Bolivian military, which would have shielded them from TJ, does not explain why purges did not extend to other sectors of the Bolivian state.

A more plausible explanation for the absence of purges in Bolivia is that even though the collaborators of the military dictatorship were not ideologically aligned with the new democratic forces that took over power in Bolivia, they were the only ones who knew how to operate the state. In other words, they were kept in place because dismissing them would result in loss of valuable expertise.

In sum, while there are normative reasons and clear pressures from public opinion to hold accountable those who in the past engaged in human rights abuses, such punishment may not be feasible and at times, may even be counterproductive. New democracies may need the expertise of bureaucrats and cynical agents of the past regime, and may even be forced to keep in office a disliked loyalist of the *ancien régime* if his loyalty comes with much needed expertise. As I argue in this book, the pressing project for new democracies is to learn to harness usable skills of agents of the *ancien régime* when their political alignments do not make them a liability.

---

[13] The National Commission for the Investigation of Forced Disappearances was established by Presidential decree within just days of the transition on October 28, 1982.

At the same time, the universe of former dictatorships abounds in cases where agents of the state held their appointments, thanks to nepotistic ties to the ruler. With nothing to offer but their loyalty, these known collaborators of the state can be easily dispensed with as they have no expertise to offer. In fact, keeping them employed risks the reemergence of authoritarian networks in the new state. The presence of these networks manifests itself in the concentration of political and economic influence, and it permeates new democracies, for instance, in the form of oligarchical networks in Eastern Europe. Such oligarchical cliques are made up of none other than members of the communist nomenklatura who were well positioned to capture the wealth of the privatized state (Grzymala-Busse 2007).

In this book, I depart from the normative and backward-looking approach to TJ according to which the rationales for engaging in or forgoing these policies are retribution or reconciliation. Instead, I pursue a forward-looking argument. First, I argue that making public the secret information that former autocrats could use to influence policy-making in the new democracy should improve the quality of representation. By formally reconstructing the blackmail mechanism that transparency mechanisms undercut, I uncover circumstances under which politicians deliver their mandate and avoid pressure from former authoritarian elites. This allows me to answer the key question: Are states that engage in uncovering secret collaborators of the former authoritarian regime better off than states that do nothing? Second, I look at the effects of firing staff from agencies of the former authoritarian state and of disbanding state agencies. I point to the fact that such purges are not universally beneficial to new democracies. Some new states need the expertise of *ancien régime* agents. Some may take advantage of the fact that preferences of the state agents are not misaligned with those of the new democrats because they were never really loyal to the outgoing dictator.

The remainder of this introduction is organized as follows. Section 1.2 organizes the concepts that will be used in this book. Sectons 1.3 and 1.4 describe the book's contributions to social science, including the Global Transitional Justice Dataset. Section 1.5 offers a road map of the book.

1.2 CONCEPTS AND MECHANISMS OF TRANSITIONAL JUSTICE

The mechanisms of dealing with the past that were described earlier fall into the broad category of TJ, which refers to ways in which new democracies reckon with their former authoritarian past. According to Kaminski et al. (2006), TJ refers to the "formal and informal procedures implemented by a group or institution of accepted legitimacy around the time of transition out of an oppressive or violent social order, for rendering justice to perpetrators, and their collaborators, as well as victims." (p. 295). The first association that many readers may have with TJ is the criminal trials of those, who in the name of an authoritarian ideology, committed atrocities. Indeed, the event that founded the very discipline of TJ was the trial of Nazi perpetrators in Nuremberg (Teitel 2003). This association is strengthened by the outstanding efforts of scholars to document trials and amnesties of perpetrators of human rights violations around the world and to organize them in easily accessible datasets.[14]

In this book, my focus is not on trials but on personnel TJ – that is, non-criminal forms of TJ. For democracy to even have a chance to consolidate, and for peace to have a possibility of taking hold, those responsible for human rights violations must at minimum be removed from office. Trials go further. They actually hold those responsible accountable for what they did in the past. Personnel TJ – lustration, truth commissions, and purges – can be interpreted as a first step in the direction of accountability. Before trials can take place, the leadership of the former regime must first be removed from positions of power.

This book will look closely at two kinds of mechanisms: purges and transparency regimes. The key difference between the two is whether new information is uncovered in the process.

I will call purging the act of banning from office a *known* offender. Purges come in two forms. First, a purge can be *thorough*, whereby every member of an organization created by the former authoritarian regime – the security apparatus, the military, the police, or the department of justice for example – is fired. Sometimes the entire agency is disbanded. The East German secret police, popularly referred to as the "Stasi," was purged in this way following German Unification in 1990. No former Stasi officer retained his or her position. Instead, domestic surveillance operations were taken over by West Germany's *Bundesamt fur Verfassungsschutz*, the Federal Office for the Protection of the Constitution (Vilasi 2015).

Instead of disbanding an entire authoritarian agency, one can also limit a purge to the leadership of that institution or organization. I will refer

---

[14] See for instance Mallinder (2008); Olsen et al. (2010) and most notably Sikkink and Walling (2007); Dancy and Wiebelhaus-Brahm (2018), and the ongoing efforts of the Transitional Justice Research Collaborative (TJRC): Dancy and Montal (2017).

to this type of purge as a *leadership purge*. Typically, these policies are termed "decommunization" (Holmes 1994), "denazification" (Capoccia 2015), or "de-Ba'athification" (David 2006). In 2003, de-Ba'athification prevented 185 members of Saddam Hussein's party from running for the legislature (David 2006). An example of a decommunization bill is the Albanian legislature's creation of a commission to reassess law licenses issued by the state's former communist government. The law had the potential to apply to all persons licensed by the state as lawyers. Initially, the special commission revoked the licenses of forty-seven lawyers.[15] Among the disqualifying conditions were membership in top committees of Albania's Labor Party (the authoritarian communist party) and having graduated from the Faculty of Law at the state's postgraduate school for training communist cadres.[16]

Among what I call transparency regimes, the first mechanism investigated in this book is *lustration*, which vets candidates for public office for ties to the former authoritarian secret police. An example of a lustration law is Poland's April 1997 bill, which required all candidates running for office to declare in advance of the elections whether they had spied on their fellow citizens for *Bezpieka*, the secret police under the communist regime. Former spies who owned up to their collaboration were allowed to run for office, but the information on their collaboration was revealed to voters at the time they cast their ballots. Negative declarations were forwarded to the Lustration Bureau of the Institute of National Remembrance (IPN), which attempted to reconcile them with evidence from Bezpieka's archives, also housed at the IPN. Failure to confirm the declaration would result in a lustration trial. Such a trial could produce a formal declaration that the politician was a collaborator, and the politician in question could end up being banned from running for public office for up to ten years (Nalepa 2010*b*).

The United States' Congress passed a similar provision to the Polish statute after the end of the civil war. The law required that persons who wished to carry out "certain occupations" (including the practice of law) subscribe to an oath that they had never "offered aid to the rebellion." Subsequently, in 1866 in a case called *Ex Parte Garland*, the supreme court struck down the provisions dealing specifically with the disbarring

---

[15] These licenses were subsequently returned after the Constitutional Court struck down key provisions of the law.

[16] See amendment to law Nr. 7541 from December 18, 1991, "On advocacy in the Republic of Albania."

of former members of the Confederate government from practicing as attorneys.[17]

A second type of mechanism that I classify as transparency regimes is truth commissions. These are bodies appointed by the government of a newly democratic state or of a state that has recently recovered from civil strife to disclose the nature of atrocities committed during wartime or under a dictatorship. Truth commissions share many characteristics with lustration. First, both deal with truth revelation. To the extent that truth commissions reveal embarrassing information with the potential of ruining a politician's career, truth commissions and lustration have a similar effect on the quality of representation.

Consider, as an example, the El Salvadoran truth commission, which between July 13, 1992 and March 15, 1993 investigated serious acts of violence occurring since 1980. Victims filed 22,000 complaints with the commission. Sixty percent of these complaints concerned extrajudicial killings, 25 percent involved disappearances, and 20 percent pertained to torture (many complaints alleged more than one form of violence). State agents were found responsible for as much as 85 percent of the violence. The commission attributed "only" 5 percent of the responsibility to the rebel group Farabundo Marti National Liberation Front (FMLN), the leftist paramilitary organization. The report then went on to name specific individuals responsible for the abuses and recommended the disqualification of any culpable military men and civil servants from public employment.

Although some truth commissions stop short of explicitly banning from office perpetrators that have been found guilty of human rights violations, shaming alone can have a powerful effect. If the public condemnation of such acts is strong enough, the mere revelation of the wrongdoers' names can effectively destroy their political careers. Relatedly, revealing the truth about the authorship of human rights abuses prevents the blackmail of perpetrators holding public office at the hands of those in possession of incriminating evidence. A well-functioning truth commission deprives anyone in possession of information about "skeletons in a politician's closet" of the ability to extract concessions in exchange for keeping the embarrassing – or worse, incriminating – information secret. Hence, truth commissions share with lustration laws the prevention of blackmail and enhance democratic representation that way.

[17] See 71 U.S. (4 Wall.) 277 (1867).

TABLE 1.1. *Transitional justice mechanisms discussed in this book*

Reach into the population	Nature of collaboration	
	Secret	Open
Leaders	Lustration	Leadership purges
Leaders and rank and file alike	Truth commissions	Thorough purges

Truth commissions are also similar in format to lustration because they are government-appointed institutions and so carry with them more legitimacy and credibility than do grassroots or NGO-inspired processes of gathering data about past human rights abuses.

In light of all of the aforementioned similarities, I refer to truth commissions and lustration jointly as transparency mechanisms. The capacity of lustrations and truth commissions to add transparency stands in sharp contrast with purges – thorough or leadership-restricted – as the latter deal with overt collaboration and membership in authoritarian and criminal political organizations. Together, these four TJ mechanisms, portrayed in Table 1.1, constitute the institutions for reckoning with the authoritarian past and civil war legacies that I focus on in this book.

The columns of Table 1.1 underscore why it is important to distinguish between the vetting of open and secret members and collaborators of the *ancien régime*. The mechanisms through which transparency and purges affect the quality of democracy in the long term are not the same. In a nutshell, politicians who have in the past been *clandestine* collaborators of the authoritarian regime or authored atrocities secretly can be blackmailed by those who have credible access to information on these "skeletons in the closet." Needless to say, if the public still cares about what happened in the past, the revelation of such skeletons could end a politician's career. In return for their silence, individuals in possession of this evidence can demand rents or policy concessions. Regardless of the currency in which the ransom is paid out by the blackmailed politician, the quality of democracy suffers.

In contrast, purges deal with known collaborators. Getting rid of members who ran the agencies of the former authoritarian regime is like ruling without bureaucrats; here one can think of administrative purges as the reverse of a delegation problem. If a new politician comes into office and carries out a thorough purge, he is forced to implement policy in inherently uncertain conditions: without the expertise of people who used to run the agencies of the *ancien régime*, he cannot know how policy implementation will be affected by states of the world unknown to him.

Conversely, a decision to forgo a purge can be thought of as the equivalent of delegation to an agent who is equipped with expertise and thus able to adjust policies to the state of the world.

The "reach into the population" dimension (the rows of Table 1.1) is no less important, particularly when it comes to the temporal impact of TJ mechanisms. Thorough purges, in contrast to leadership purges, apply a blanket rule to workers of the former authoritarian state. Because of this collective responsibility, the reach into the population of thorough purges is greater as some workers of state agencies are fired even though they personally bear no responsibility for the regime's transgressions. Leadership purges only extend to those rank and file members of the state who participated in the regime's transgressions, however these are defined. Thorough purges typically appear early in the transition. Leadership purges, however, can stretch out long after the transition.

A comparison of lustrations and truth commissions reveals variation along these same dimensions. There is no place a perpetrator of humans rights violations can hide from a truth commission with a sufficiently far-reaching mandate. Not being in the spotlight of public office does not keep one's name from being mentioned during a hearing or as part of a report. In contrast, the operation of lustrations is limited to elites. Even though who is considered an elite and who is not can vary from one lustration law to the next, those who want to avoid having their skeletons in the closet exposed may simply forgo running or holding the positions to which lustration extends. In practice, this could mean that lustration works slower than truth commissions. However, this depends also on what the recommendations of truth commissions are and how well they are implemented (Zvobgo 2019*a*,*b*).

1.3 THE CONTRIBUTIONS

The discussion above underscores the role TJ mechanisms play in determining who is selected into political office. Lustration disincentivizes former collaborators from running for office. Purges are more explicit, because the fire those with direct (leadership) or indirect (thorough) links to the *ancien régime*. Despite this, neither the literature on candidate selection nor the literature on political economy of bureaucracies has paid attention to authoritarian legacies.[18] This book will bring legacies of the *ancien régime* to the forefront of understanding democratic stability.

---

[18] Indeed, when political economists talk about purges, they restrict their attention to authoritarian purges (Jiang & Yang 2016; Montagnes & Wolton 2019).

The literature on democratization, save for a few exceptions that deal mostly with party systems (Grzymala-Busse 2002; Pop-Eleches 2007; Pop-Eleches & Tucker 2011; Riedl 2014), has also failed to appreciate just how important authoritarian legacies are. Authoritarian regimes and their democratic successor states are, for the most part, studied by separate groups of scholars.

On the other hand, scholars are consumed by the debate between retribution and reconciliation (Encarnacion 2014). The first contribution of this book is to stress the role of authoritarian legacies in new democracies, and particularly the importance of these legacies in regulating who works for the new state. This also breaks with existing research on TJ, which has focused on the normative imperatives of dealing with crimes committed in the past. Because of this normative framing, TJ literature has not been able to appreciate that dealing with transgressions that have not even been made public may be more important than reckoning with known perpetrators of the *ancien régime*. The forward-looking orientation of this book fills that lacuna and brings to light just how threatening secret legacies of authoritarian rule are to the new democratic state. Thus, by explaining how TJ regulates selection into office, I also contribute to the literature on democratic backsliding.

Second, this book explains how TJ affects how politicians behave in office conditional on being elected, appointed, retained. This question belongs squarely in the comparative democratization literature. In the last twenty-five years, scholars of comparative democratization have shifted their focus from studying democratic transitions to studying the quality of democracy. This phenomenon is associated with the proliferation of hybrid regimes – that is – regimes that hover between autocracy and democracy (Levitsky & Way 2010). Hybrid regimes are states that employ democratic procedures, such as elections (Gandhi & Lust-Okar 2009), constitutions (Ginsburg & Simpser 2013), and legislatures (Jensen et al. 2014; Wright 2008), but are in fact ruled by closet autocrats (Chiopris et al. 2022). One of the central aspects of democratic quality is the question of programmatic representation. The contribution that my book offers to this literature zeroes in on the linkages between citizens and political parties. When politicians are blackmailed by those who threaten to release skeletons in their closet, they depart from the programmatic commitments they made to their voters.[19]

---

[19] I define programmatic representation as running on platforms that are communicated to voters, being elected to office because of those platforms, and finally implementing the platforms upon being elected.

The nature of these linkages has a critical impact on democratic stability (Pop-Eleches 2010; Tavits 2005). Scholars have noted that parties in newer democracies rely on a number of strategies to build linkages with citizens; these strategies range from offering programmatic party platforms to relying on charismatic candidates or clientelism (Kitschelt & Wilkinson 2007). Mainwaring (1999) argues that under-institutionalized and fragmented party systems with volatile electorates are low-hanging fruit for populist political elites who wish to engage in clientelistic practices. The establishment of programmatic parties is hindered not only by a lack of adequate institutions, but also by the poor quality of political elites. The inexperienced politicians that characterize young democracies are simply more credible when promising private goods than when they promise policy. Establishing clientelistic ties is easier than competing for votes on the basis of programs (Keefer 2007). Political elites might also hold a monopoly on goods or services that the electorate wants to access, which also hinders democratic quality by, for example, reducing the competitiveness of elections (Medina & Stokes 2007). Yet, scholarship devoted to the nature of party–voter linkages and to the quality of representation has largely left out of consideration authoritarian legacies and TJ: It is not clear why there are neither theories nor tests of how dealing with former authoritarian elites and their secret legacies affects the ability of politicians to represent voters. My book fills this gap by showing that blackmail with secret files hurts representation unequivocally.

My third contribution is to the literature on delegation. Notice that the dilemma facing a new politician is familiar to students of delegation or principal–agent models. The agent – in this case, the ex-authoritarian bureaucrat – may have preferences that are so divergent from those of the principal (the new democratic politician) that he uses his expertise to implement the policy he himself prefers. On balance, this policy outcome may be worse for the principal than his own implementation, even when it is lacking in expertise. There is a familiar trade-off between the expertise the *ancien régime* bureaucrat can offer and the extent to which loyalty to the previous regime renders his services a liability. The specific TJ context that makes this dilemma particularly interesting is that both of these features – expertise and preference divergence – have roots in the preceding regime. I will investigate how the mode in which the authoritarian state appoints bureaucrats influences the former state agent's expertise and alignment with the new democratic principal. The final factor I will model is uncertainty, which is one of the key features of regime transitions. Some transitions are more uncertain than others. For instance, in the context of postcommunist transitions, not only political regimes but also economic systems underwent an overhaul. In light of this, the delegation problem in the context of post-authoritarian purges offers a unique opportunity to apply an old, if not somewhat stale, literature to a completely different area of social science.

1.4 A NOVEL APPROACH TO COLLECTING TRANSITIONAL JUSTICE DATA

Though not a theoretical contribution, a non negligible by-product of my research is the construction of a new transitional justice dataset. In order to test the implications of my theory, the Transitional Justice and Democratic Stability Lab that I direct has constructed the Global Transitional Justice Dataset comprising of a time series cross-section of TJ events in all post-authoritarian and post-conflict states since the end of World War II. Despite a growing number of empirical studies examining the broad impact of TJ on democratic stability and peace (Olsen et al. 2010; Thoms et al. 2010; Van der Merwe et al. 2009), there is a knowledge gap pertaining to the impact of purges and transparency regimes on the long-term quality of democratic representation. I devote an entire chapter (Chapter 4) to explaining how my own dataset fills this lacuna.

In a nutshell, the greatest problem with existing datasets is that they reduce sometimes complex progressions of a TJ proposal through the legislative process to a single data point. The danger of this oversimplification is illustrated in Figure 1.3, which presents data on TJ mechanisms as a time series of *positive* and *negative* events for six countries that I will use as archetypal cases throughout the book: Bolivia, Poland, Tunisia, South Korea, South Africa, and Spain.

To allow for better understanding of the figure, I clarify what positive and negative events are using the example of lustration. I define a positive event as the submission of a lustration proposal to the floor of the legislature, the passage of such legislation, the upholding of such legislation as constitutional by a supreme court, or the overturning of a presidential veto against such legislation. I define a negative lustration event, in contrast, as the voting down, vetoing, or striking down by the constitutional court of lustration provisions. Similarly, expanding the set of persons targeted by lustration or broadening the set of "offenses" (where "offense" is defined as secret police collaboration) to include more past or present positions constitutes a positive lustration event, whereas attempts to narrow the set of targets or "offenses" are negative lustration

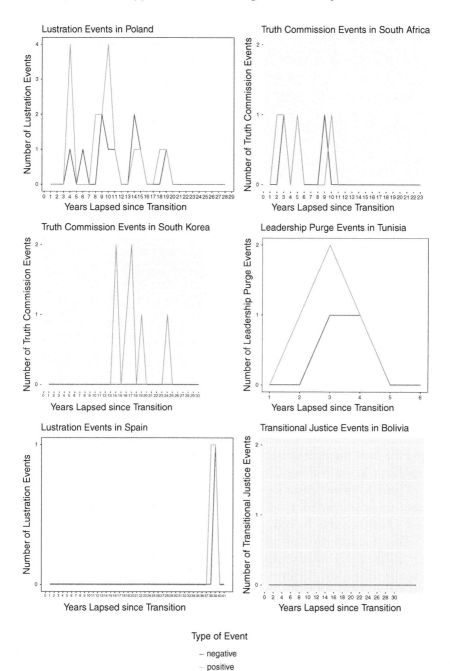

FIGURE 1.3. Severity of transitional justice mechanisms in archetypal country cases of the book

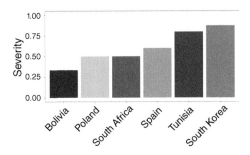

FIGURE 1.4. Truth commissions in archetypal countries

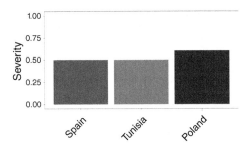

FIGURE 1.5. Lustrations in archetypal countries

events. Positive and negative events in truth commissions, thorough purges, and leadership purges are defined similarly. I will argue that ambiguities in the extant empirical research stem from data collection strategies that are not sensitive to the temporal dimensions of TJ: when and for how long personnel TJ has been implemented. My data brings scholars a key step closer to understanding the impacts of personnel TJ.

Figure 1.3 shows data for lustration in Poland and Spain, truth commissions in South Africa and South Korea, Leadership Purges in Tunisia, and TJ in general in Bolivia.

These figures also disaggregate TJ events over time. Figures 1.4 through 1.7 use the progression of positive and negative events over time to create a summary statistic (TJ severity) for each of the four mechanisms using the Global Transitional Justice Dataset interactive tool. I show the severity[20] of the four personnel TJ mechanisms in the six countries that I will use at various stages of this book to illustrate my argument (countries with zero severity have been omitted from each figure).

---

[20] "Severity" is defined as the ratio of positive transitional justice events of a certain type to the total number of events. The full justification for this measure is provided in Chapter 4.

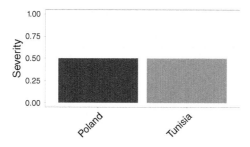

FIGURE 1.6. Thorough purges in archetypal countries

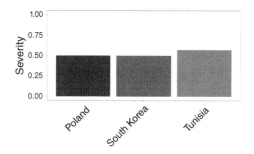

FIGURE 1.7. Leadership purges in archetypal countries

The figure 1.6 two panels illustrate the severity of lustration and truth commissions; the figure 1.7 two illustrate the severity of purges. Countries with no events of a certain type are omitted. We see that Tunisia had the highest severity of truth commissions, although it did engage in all four transitional justice mechanisms, including lustration. In fact, the severity of lustration in Tunisia was almost as high as in Poland. Poland, as Tunisia, had all four types of transitional justice events; however, among transparency regimes, it engaged in lustrations instead of truth commissions. Further, it invested slightly less in leadership purges than Tunisia did (Figures 1.4 through 1.7).[21]

Interestingly, South Africa, most famous for its Truth and Reconciliation Commission (TRC) established after the negotiated transition to democracy in 1994, has only experienced truth commission events, and

---

[21] As a side note, Tunisia's leadership purge score is somewhat deflated by the fact that many of its leadership purges took place before its first elections (and so do not qualify as transitional justice, using the selection criteria discussed in Chapter 4). The Global Transitional Justice Dataset, for instance, does not include the removal of "30 top police officers removed by the Ghannouchi administration" on February 2, 2011 (Preysing 2016).

the severity of those events is only at 0.5 (on a scale from 0 to 1), a stark contrast with, for instance, Tunisia, at 0.8. This is consistent with the reconciliation orientation of the South African TRC whereby, through a confession, perpetrators were granted amnesty from criminal prosecutions.

Notable here is also Spain, which *despite* the "Pact of Forgetting," embraced transparency regimes in the form of both lustrations and truth commissions. Yet, as Figure 1.3 indicates, this happened relatively recently. The case with the lowest scores on any of the TJ mechanisms studied in this book is Bolivia. Indeed, this dearth of TJ is the rationale behind including this case as a more detailed illustration of the phenomena in question. The only transitional justice mechanisms used there were truth commissions, and these events only reached a level of severity equal to slightly over 0.25.

The theoretical argument of this book is that TJ measures that focus on information revelation are very different from the ones that are designed to purge people. Data from the Global Transitional Justice Dataset can also be used to empirically justify this difference. Figure 1.8 shows the disaggregation of TJ into purges – that is, dealing with known forms of collaboration with the *ancien régime* or engagement in human rights violations – and lustration and truth commissions – that is, uncovering formerly secret forms of collaboration and human rights violations. The left panel of Figure 1.8 plots the total number of positive TJ events net of negative events as a function of time lapsed since the transition (left/upper panel) and as a function of the year in which the transition took place (left/lower panel). Here, all transitional justice events have been pooled together, and there appears to be no relationship between TJ and two variables that ought to be good predictors of TJ: time lapsed since transition and year of transition (Barahona de Brito et al. 2001; Elster 2004; Huntington 1993).

However, once we disaggregate the TJ mechanisms into purges (thorough and leadership), lustration, and truth commissions, a clear pattern emerges. Consider first the lower right panel of Figure 1.8, illustrating positive TJ events net of negative events for the four mechanisms as a function of transition year. Lustration prevails in countries that transitioned around 1990, which tend to be the Eastern European ones (Albania, Bulgaria, East Germany, Estonia, Hungary, Latvia, Poland, Slovakia, and Slovenia), as previous scholarship has speculated.[22] There

---

[22] See De Greiff and Mayer-Rieckh (2007); Ellis (1996); Closa Montero (2010); Letki (2002); Stan (2013); Stan and Nedelsky (2015). Note, however, that there are also

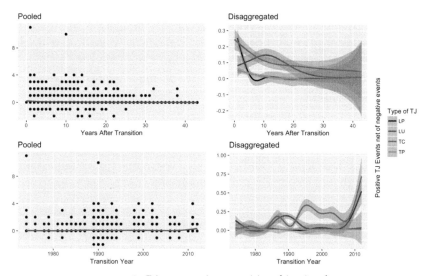

FIGURE 1.8. Disaggregating transitional justice data

is also an uptick in truth commissions around the beginning of the third wave of democratization, but in contrast to lustration events, truth commission events trend upward again in countries with mid-1990s transitions as well as in countries transitioning around 2010.[23] This is consistent with the scholarship on truth commissions: Truth commissions abound in South America (in Paraguay, Ecuador, and Peru) and Africa (in Kenya, South Africa, and Liberia); they can also be found in Indonesia and East Germany. (United States Institute of Peace 2011*b,a,h,e*; Gibson 2006; United States Institute of Peace 2011*f,c,d*).

The story with purges is quite different. First, the occurrence of thorough purges is flat across the range of transition years in my dataset. If they do occur, they appear in the immediate aftermath of a transition (notice the slight uptick on the left end of the upper right panel of Figure 1.8). Leadership purges, on the other hand, seemed to be more popular in the beginning of the third wave transitions (in Latin American countries that transitioned in the seventies and eighties) and their popularity seems to be increasing again after 2005. As in the case of thorough purges, they are concentrated in the early post-transition years.

The insight from the upper panel of Figure 1.8 is that the timing of lustration clearly differs from the timing of purges. While purges – both

---

instances of lustration in other countries. A deeper look into my data reveals that these other countries include Argentina, Spain, and Guatemala.

[23] These include the Arab Spring countries, Tunisia and Egypt, as well as several countries in South and Southeast Asia.

thorough and leadership – take place in the immediate aftermath of transitions to democracy, lustrations peak about ten years following the transition. Truth commissions are implemented soon after the transition or conflict termination but continue to be implemented longer than purges or lustration.

In sum, patterns of purge activity stand in contrast to patterns of lustration and truth commission activity. Similar inferences can be drawn from the GIS-coded version of my data in the form of world maps illustrating severity (and also volatility and urgency) of lustration, truth commissions, and thorough and leadership purges in appendix G.[24]

1.5 ROAD MAP

This book is organized as follows. Chapter 2 presents a formal model that focuses on how lustration can prevent blackmail, arguing that transparency regimes, such as lustrations and truth commissions, have a positive effect on the long-term quality of democratic representation. I capture the blackmail potential of "skeletons in the closet," understood here as evidence of collaboration. If left in the hands of former agents of the *ancien régime*, these "skeletons" can undermine democratic representation. The model uncovers the extent to which implementing transparency regimes can mitigate this danger. Transparency regimes accomplish this by making bluffing more difficult by lowering the a priori belief that embarrassing secrets may still be in the hands of the blackmailers. A more normative implication of this model is that transparency regimes do not always work the way advocates of forward-looking arguments for TJ would want them to. In some equilibria, blackmail with secret police files occurs even without evidence. Yet, an identity result presented in this chapter shows that no matter what the equilibrium, departure from perfect representation always declines with the severity of the transparency regime. This model serves as a baseline relative to which we can now evaluate the consequences of dealing with open collaborators via purges.

Chapter 3 presents a formal model of purges to clarify why the effects of purges on the long-term quality of democracy are quite different from the effects of lustration. To capture the dynamic of administrative purges, I make use of an old workhorse of models of bureaucracy: the delegation model. In order to compare the effect of lustration with that of purges,

---

[24] They are also available at an interactive website: https://tinyurl.com/ybmcj7hf.

the model's results are stated in terms of the same outcome variable as in the model of lustration blackmail: the quality of democratic representation. The model builds on the literature on delegation in American Politics but crucially shows that purging more is not always better for representation. New democracies face trade-offs between using the *ancien régime*'s agents' expertise to reduce noise around policy implementation and facing the possibility that these agents have preferences misaligned with new democratic leaders.

The models presented in Chapters 2 and 3 share a dependent variable – the quality of representation. At the same time, important differences exist between them: The model of lustration deals with secret collaborators and informers who were often not members of the formal authoritarian state (indeed, as the case of Lech Wałęsa indicates, they were frequently dissidents *fighting the authoritarian state*). The consequence of "doing nothing" about secret collaborators is running the risk of electing representatives that will be held hostage by what they did in the past; the model of purges, in contrast, considers known members of the former authoritarian state. Here, the challenge is that of staffing post-authoritarian bureaucracies and law enforcement with competent, yet not disloyal agents. In some instances "doing nothing" is the optimal choice for democratic stability.

The introduction to Part II of the book summarizes the empirical implications of my theory and discusses the empirical strategy for testing it.

Chapter 4 is devoted to a discussion of the data that operationalizes independent variables of this book: the Global Transitional Justice Dataset. Since no existing datasets differentiate between open and closed forms of collaboration, my data collection first separates transparency regimes (truth commissions and lustration) from purges (thorough and leadership-only). In addition, however, I code TJ data as a time series of events. This strategy permits for the use research designs that allow to causally identify the effects of TJ. It also allows me to develop original measures of personnel TJ characteristics: severity, which is used throughout the book, as well as urgency and volatility. Using these measures, I show other differences between the Global Transitional Justice Database and other existing TJ data collection efforts.

In Chapter 5 the blackmail model is tested with a hierarchical model where the units of analysis are political parties nested within post-authoritarian states. This is an appropriate strategy because lustration is an elite-centered transparency regime with most of the affected elites concentrated in political parties. Truth commissions are dispersed in their reach, but act faster than lustration. This characteristic allows me to use a design that accounts for change over time. Hence, to examine the effects of truth commissions, in Chapter 6, I use a difference-in-difference design. Identifying the causal relationship between personnel TJ and quality of democracy is crucial because it is highly plausible that the same characteristics that lead a country to embark on a TJ program may be the ones that down the line allow it to enjoy a high quality of democratic representation. Models using this design consistently identify a causal relationship between truth commissions and democratic quality.

Moving on to testing my theory of purges, recall that one of its key findings is that not all states can embark on purges because at times, the loss in expertise is too great to conduct a purge even when the ideological distance between the bureaucracy of the *ancien régime* and the new succeeding democrats is large. In light of this, some countries simply cannot afford to implement purges at all. This calls for a statistical modeling approach that accounts for some authoritarian regimes (those with low institutionalization) selecting into purges, while others refrain from purge activity. This is the subject of Chapter 7.

Chapter 8 does not test any additional theories, but introduces one new dependent variable: de facto survival of authoritarian elites in parties, the state, and business. This is also a variable constructed in the Transitional Justice and Democratic Stability Lab. This chapter examines how the four personnel transitional justice mechanisms shape actual elite survival. Also, in this "taking stock" chapter of sorts, I consider all mechanisms together. Yet such a "horse race" analysis should be interpreted with caution as it does not speak to the underlying conditions and authoritarian legacies that shape possibilities for transitional justice. This book argues that because each mechanism deals with a different class of *ancien régime* collaborators these mechanisms are not really substitutes. Purges can never perform the function of lustration and truth commissions and vice versa. Nevertheless, this chapter empirically corroborates an important difference among transparency regimes. Namely, the effect of truth commissions on democratization becomes apparent sooner, but fizzles out over time as truth commissions' operation continues. Lustration, on the other hand, seems to require surpassing a certain threshold of intensity before positive effects on the quality of democracy come to fruition.

Chapter 9 draws conclusions and discusses the normative limitations of transparency mechanisms. Increasing the ability of politicians to represent by revealing everyone's skeletons in the closet comes at the cost of exposing the raw and unfettered personal relationships for what they are.

While they learn whether their politicians can be trusted, citizens of new democracies also find out who among their friends, family, and coworkers spied on them. At the same time, open collaborators, such as the cynical Franz's of the former law enforcement apparatus, are allowed to stay on and continue their careers. The democracy-enhancing use of TJ appears normatively disturbing. Yet transparency regimes are far from being "ritual sacrifices." They regulate who becomes a politician and how politicians behave in office. Truth commissions make polities less corrupt while lustrations are better at dissociating political power from economic power and allow politicians to represent voters more faithfully. The effect of purges is more complex as even the feasibility of purges depends heavily on the institutionalization of the previous authoritarian regime, but refraining from purges is often democracy-enhancing.

The overall conclusion is to categorically discredit the virtues of the so-called Spanish Model of transitional justice. Letting sleeping dogs lie, particularly when it comes to yet-to-be-revealed crimes perpetrated by former autocrats, is exactly the wrong way to go about dealing with the past.

PART I

TRANSPARENCY AND PURGES

2

Blackmail and Transparency

In Chapter 1, I argued that democracies do not emerge in a vacuum and that legacies of former authoritarian states permeate the new polity in the form of unsettled scores of human rights abuses, staff of former security agencies, and archives of the former secret police that list who worked as a collaborator of the authoritarian security apparatus. This chapter is devoted to studying how transparency regimes – the disclosure of the identities of collaborators, spies, and saboteurs – influence how well those who are elected to office represent their electorate. In sum, this chapter will explain why lustrations and truth commissions improve the quality of representation in nascent and more mature democracies that have experienced authoritarian rule.

Transparency regimes – the revelation of who, among persons holding public office, collaborated with the secret police to the detriment of the anti-authoritarian opposition – have been called "ritual sacrifices" (Cepl 1992). Even Huntington (1993) maintains that sometimes "amnesty ... is necessary to establish a new democracy on a solid basis." Born out of this understanding is the use of the term "retroactive justice" as synonymous with transitional justice (TJ) (Rev 2005).

The key contribution of this chapter is to show that transparency regimes (lustration and truth commissions), by making public secrets that former autocrats or their agents could use in blackmail, improve the quality of representation. I will show that by revealing acts of secret collaboration with the authoritarian regime, these procedures prevent former authoritarian elites from extorting policy concessions from former collaborators who have become elected politicians but have "skeletons in their closet." Implementing transparency regimes such as lustration laws should help politicians become responsive to their constituencies.

Even though the game I present in this chapter has three types of equilibria, I show that lustration regimes always enhance representation. In addition, the quality of democratic representation depends on lustration's severity, the extent to which dissidents-turned-politicians suffer if their skeletons come out, and the extent to which independent media are able to check bluffs from agents who blackmail politicians with "fake" skeletons.

Although the formal model and the commentary that follows use the terminology of lustration laws, the same model can be used to explain the operation of truth commissions: fundamentally, both procedures perform the same function, revealing past human rights violations that have thus far been kept secret. In Chapters 5 and 6, I will demonstrate that the theory provided in this chapter does indeed underpin the operation of truth commissions and lustrations alike.

That is why this chapter can be treated as a theory of how truth commissions enhance the quality of democracy. But since alongside lustration and truth commissions, also purges are all linked to the objective of barring former authoritarian elites from policy influence, why are they not theorized in the same chapter? As I explained in Chapter 1, lustration bars former elites from policy influence by vetting candidates for public office for *secret* ties to the former authoritarian secret police. It accomplishes this by opening archives of the former regime's secret authoritarian apparatus to uncover who, among persons running for public and political office, had worked as an informer or spy prior to the democratic transition. The proven collaborators are then explicitly banned from holding office or information about their collaboration is released to the voters, who can then decide whether to still cast their votes on thus-compromised politicians. Truth commissions can only indirectly ban former members and collaborators from office, but as long as the voting public or nominating agencies react negatively to truth revelations about the past, they can prevent former authoritarian elites and their agents of repression from serving the new state. Purges, however, operate differently: They prevent *open* agents of the *ancien régime* from exploiting their expertise in a way that would sabotage the policy goals of the state's new leaders. The removal of known collaborators is accomplished by a different mechanism than the uncovering of secret collaborators of the *ancien régime*. That is why purges are analyzed in a separate chapter (Chapter 3).

Lustration provides voters with key information that is necessary to hold representatives accountable: Who, in the past, was or was not a secret collaborator of the *ancien régime*? Although this information does not concern the behavior of the politician in the preceding electoral term, but rather in the previous authoritarian regime, it is just as important for determining if the voters can trust the politician in question to represent them once in office.

2.2 HISTORICAL AND CONTEMPORARY RESEARCH ON LUSTRATION

Lustration is neither a new nor even a modern procedure used by democracies. The Athenian constitution made room for an institution similar to lustration. *Dokimasia*, translated best into English as "scrutiny," applied to anybody who had been appointed to public office, whether by election or by lot. It involved a judiciary proceeding where orators offered arguments on why a candidate may not be fit for office. Dokimasia became very popular following the coup d'état of 404–403 BC, when uncovering secret ties to the Thirty Tyrants (Todd et al. 2007) became a tool of evaluating whether a citizen had the moral character required to hold public office. Collaboration with the Thirty Tyrants, if demonstrated, was considered disqualifying because it indicated a lack of loyalty to the constitution.[1]

In the twenty-first century, skeletons in politicians' closets became known under the term "kompromat." Generally, kompromat (in Russian, meaning compromising materials) refers to either embarrassing information or evidence of a person's illegal activity that, if revealed, could damage that person's career or open them to prosecution.

With a few exceptions, which include Yarhi-Milo (2013) and Felli and Hortala-Vallve (2015), the use of secrets and blackmail to affect policy has not received much scrutiny from political scientists. Yet, these concepts are eminently relevant to current events: In 2017, kompromat made front-page news as it was used to describe Russia's attempts to intervene in the US elections. As Keith Darden points out, this kind of data was routinely collected by Soviet secret services and was used to control people through

---

[1] According to Todd et al. (2007), while dokimasia was routinely conducted outside the 403–380 BC period, it was only contested in the two decades that followed the coup.

blackmail by threatening the compromised with the release of damaging information to the public – or worse, to prosecutors (Darden 2001). Such embarrassing or damaging information, even if collected by authoritarian security forces, may be put to use long after the authoritarian regime itself has expired.

Mechanisms for dealing with former secret collaborators of the *ancien régime* have largely eluded scholarly work. One reason for this gap in analysis is that, beyond anecdotes, we do not know how often security forces rely on secret collaborators. The second is that we cannot directly observe to what extent former authoritarian elites extract concessions from their past collaborators. Successful acts of blackmail are hidden from the eyes of a casual observer. However, if succumbing to such pressures prevents democratically elected politicians from representing voters, one may wonder whether former authoritarian regimes suffer from a deficit of representation and accountability when they fail to make their authoritarian legacies public.

Transparency regimes, such as lustration and truth commissions, can reduce the unfair informational advantage that members of the authoritarian regime hold long after their rule is over. The Polish lustration law, a classic example of lustration introduced already in Chapter 1, does this by requiring all persons holding or running for public office to declare in advance whether they had collaborated with the secret authoritarian police prior to the transition. Information from declarations admitting collaboration is part of the ballot, and voters decide whether to cast their vote for a former collaborator. Negative declarations are sent to a special division of the Institute for National Remembrance, where they are verified against information assembled in the archives of the former secret political police. Proven collaborators who lied on their declarations are banned from running for office for ten years. Although this is the most cited example of lustration (Kaminski & Nalepa 2006; Letki 2002; Nalepa 2010*a*, 2012*b*; Szczerbiak 2002; Williams et al. 2005), it is hardly typical because it allows two types of collaborators to escape direct sanctions: (1) the collaborator who admits he worked as a secret collaborator[2] and (2) the collaborator who failed to own up to his past but was not uncovered. A more typical lustration law carries with it an explicit sanction for anyone who is proven to have worked for the secret police as an informer (as in Hungary) or who fails to provide evidence of his innocence (as in the Czech Republic).

---

[2] See Nalepa (2008) for an argument of why a positive declaration can, under some circumstances, be treated as a sanction.

The South African Truth and Reconciliation Commission, a classic example of a truth commission, also enhanced transparency, reducing the advantage of former members of the Apartheid regime (Gibson 2006; Hayner 2001). The commission was formed in 1995 to investigate crimes committed against the South African people during the Apartheid regime (1960–1994). Its mandate extended to human rights violations committed by both the state and various liberation movements.[3] The commission's mandate provided it with the ability to offer amnesty to those who fully participated in the process and truthfully confessed the full extent of their crimes. It released a five-volume final report to then president Nelson Mandela in 1998. The report detailed the abuses committed by the Apartheid-era National Party government, the state-opposition-turned-ruling-party African National Congress (ANC), and other "leading political figures on both sides of the anti-apartheid struggle" (Keesing's Record of World Events 1998). Yet, just like the Polish lustration law, the South African Truth Commission is hardly typical. Most truth commissions have a narrower mandate, certainly not allowing those who confess their crimes to enjoy amnesty from criminal responsibility. Many truth commissions are not allowed to complete their full mandate, because they run out of financial resources, political backing, or both (Zvobgo 2019a).

Regardless of small differences within truth commissions, within lustrations, and between lustrations and truth commissions, all such TJ mechanisms increase transparency.

By revealing information about past abuses committed by anyone, and not just by politicians, truth commissions also prevent the blackmail of decision-makers – be they in politics or in other positions – with embarrassing information about former human rights violations. Both lustrations and truth commissions influence the quality of representation. First, they determine who can successfully run for or hold public office. Second, a transparency regime shapes how politicians behave once in office: If implemented, lustrations and truth commissions prevent former authoritarian elites from influencing policy in new democratic polities. Where transparency is lacking, blackmailers can pressure politicians into making policy concessions by threatening to reveal compromising information that could jeopardize their careers. If the blackmail is effective, politicians lose their ability to faithfully represent voters.

---

[3] Specifically, it was established via the Promotion of National Unity and Reconciliation Act, passed by the South African parliament in July 1995 (Waldmeir 1997).

Before I introduce the formal model and the main intuition behind it, it is worth explaining that my arguments in support of transparency regimes differ quite significantly from those made in the rest of the literature on TJ. This literature, on the one hand, rarely distinguishes between purges and lustration. On the other hand, it treats lustrations and truth commissions as completely different mechanisms. Arguments in support of truth commissions range from recognizing victims' need to "reconcile" with the past to accentuating victims' rights to know the identity of those who harmed them. Arguments for lustration, in the meantime, range from pointing out that victims of spying have the right to know who informed the authorities of their activities (Stan 2012) to emphasizing the importance of preventing former spies and their leading officers from playing key roles in public service (David 2011; Nedelsky 2013; Stan et al. 2009). The common argument made in favor of both lustrations and purges is the normative and backward-looking one: that former spies, their leading officers, and members of the former regime should be prevented from playing key roles in public service (Nedelsky 2013). Such arguments assume that the question of whether the truth about transgressions by the former authoritarian elites and their collaborators should be unearthed has a definite answer. In fact, as I argue in this book, this question is complex and far from settled.

The relevant formal models I draw on are not theories of TJ per se (the literature on the political economy of TJ is very sparse), but theories of how autocrats form repressive apparatuses and discipline their agents of repression (Hübert & Little 2021; Montagnes & Wolton 2019; Tyson 2018). The autocrat's dilemma is highlighted by (Powell 2014, p. 2): "a weak military can leave them vulnerable to ... civil war, while a strong military ... a coup d'état." Paine (forthcoming) has recently argued that the same reasoning can be applied to internal security forces. Authoritarian leaders have two choices:

1. They can maintain weak or fragmented security forces, thus guarding against a coup d'état but risking resistance from below.
2. They can invest in strong state security at the risk of empowering a strong competitor.

In the first scenario, the autocrat does not really face a discipline problem, though the enforcement apparatus is very weak. In the second, he decides that the threat from below and demand for competent agents of repression are worth the risk of empowering a potential competitor. In a related paper, Dragu and Lupu (2018) use a coordination game with incomplete information to show that paradoxically, repression is most likely to hinge on expectations and become a coordination game when authoritarian leaders need it most (when dissent against them is at its highest).

Although in these first instances of theorizing, the time horizon was limited to the authoritarian regime, in more recent work by Tyson (2018), it has been extended beyond the authoritarian regime, allowing for the possibility of TJ. Tyson models the interaction between a leader and his repressive apparatus in circumstances where the stability of the authoritarian regime is uncertain. The autocrat in these circumstances must compensate his agents of repression to offset the risk they bear of being punished with TJ, should the regime collapse. At the same time, although Tyson's model uses the prospect of TJ to model repressive agents' incentives, his theory assumes that the identity of these agents is known. My model, in contrast, assumes that voters do not know if politicians they are about to elect to office had collaborated with the authoritarian regime and that this information can be exploited by blackmailers.

In another recent publication, Hübert and Little (2021) model the collection of embarrassing information by authoritarian principals as a way of disciplining agents of repression. The authors propose a cheap talk game to account for the possibility of kompromat being leaked. The empirical interpretation of this model, however, is entirely contained within the authoritarian period. My model departs from Hübert and Little (2021) in that it focuses on the consequences rather than the origins of kompromat. The blackmailer in my model cannot generate kompromat, but he can use it to force compromised politicians into making concessions.

Another model with similarities to mine is that by Nalepa and Sonin (2022). There, voters also form beliefs about the probability that they are represented by a compromised politician, but in addition, voters are uncertain about the ideology of the potentially compromised politician.[4] An important distinction between my model and that of Nalepa and Sonin (2022) is that I allow the blackmailer to bluff with the threat of revealing skeletons even if no such skeletons exist. This is only possible if the politician himself does not know whether he collaborated with the secret police. How might this be possible?

---

[4] More specifically, they argue that first, there must be compromised and uncompromised politicians. Second, there must be uncertainty about the uncompromised politician's true policy preferences. Otherwise, any deviation from the uncompromised politician's ideal policy would expose the elected politician as compromised.

In Communist Europe, secret police officers had numerous incentives to recruit members of the opposition as collaborators even when they were not fully aware of the fact that they were being recruited. Officers with more informers were paid more, were promoted faster, and certainly had no incentives to tell their informers that they were being recruited by the secret police. For this reason, I assume that any opposition politician may have had kompromat produced against him or her. This possibility allows blackmailers to bluff, making the signaling model in this chapter nontrivial. Henceforth, when I use the term "collaborator," I will be referring to politicians with kompromat or skeletons in the closet and not necessarily to conscious collaborators.

The next section reconstructs how lustration and truth commissions can undercut the blackmail mechanism laid out above with a game theoretic model of incomplete information. The game directly models how lustration laws limit blackmail by members of the former security apparatus and, consequently, allow politicians to more faithfully represent policy preferences of the electorate.

A key strength of the model is that all distortions from perfect representation are due to the potential for blackmail. This potential exists because of secret authoritarian legacies affecting specific new elites. Critically, this is the only friction to political accountability that produces the theoretical result. Hence, the game theoretic model captures only pathologies in representation that could be addressed by transparency regimes.

2.3 THE FORMAL MODEL

Can transparency regimes such as lustration improve the quality of representation by eliminating the effectiveness of blackmail with dark authoritarian secrets? My model of incomplete information reconstructs the mechanism through which blackmail interferes with politicians' ability to faithfully represent the policy preferences of the electorate. Solving the model allows us to examine the extent to which transparency in the form of lustration or truth commissions can reduce the vulnerability of politicians to their former leading officers.

To be sure, what I propose is not a model of the decision to adopt a transparency regime.[5] Rather, it assumes that lustration, at some level of

---

[5] For such models, see Nalepa and Sonin (2022).

severity (which can be zero), has already been implemented and examines the effects this has on politicians' behavior.

2.3.1 Setup

My model features two players. The first is a politician elected to public office following a transition to democracy. With probability $\sigma \in (0, 1)$, this politician is compromised as a former secret police collaborator, that is, there exists evidence of his collaboration. With probability $1 - \sigma$ the politician is not compromised, that is, there is no evidence of his collaboration. The politician knows the probability with which he is compromised but not whether kompromat against him actually exists.

The second player in the game is his former leading officer, who can threaten to reveal embarrassing information about former collaboration unless the politician implements policies favored by the officer. The officer knows if he is in possession of kompromat, so he knows the true realization of σ.

Voters are not explicit players in my game, yet they feature prominently in the model in the following way: The quality of representation suffers when the politician is vulnerable to extortion by the agent and implements the policy preferred by his former secret police officer instead of the policy preferred by voters. I assume that unless they are blackmailed, politicians implement the policy preferences of their voters regardless of whether they were collaborators in the past. In making this assumption, I remain ambivalent about the reasons for which people actually conceded to collaboration with the secret police and admit that those reasons might have nothing to do with whether they are able to be honest politicians or not.[6] One caveat about making the assumption that when not blackmailed, politicians implement voters' preferences is that I do not claim that politicians universally follow voter preferences. I am, however, trying to use this assumption to isolate the effect of lustration on curbing blackmail with secret police files.

The key tension in my model comes from the fact that while the officer knows whether he possesses the evidence he may threaten to release, the former collaborator-turned-politician does not.

---

[6] As explained earlier, persons may agree to collaborate under duress, out of fear for the life and health of a loved one.

The severity of lustration enters the model as the extent to which kompromat against a politician who collaborated with the secret police has been exposed. This stringency or severity of lustration is represented by η: With probability $1-\eta$, lustration does not reveal enough kompromat to affect the politician in question, and effective kompromat is still in the leading officer's possession. But with probability η, lustration is sufficiently far reaching to have revealed that the politician was a collaborator, so the the evidence the blackmailer would use is ineffective. The level of lustration severity is known to the politician but not its specific realization. That is, the politician knows how likely it is that files against him, if they exist, have evaded the lustration procedure but not whether his specific file remains in the hands of the blackmailer.

Restating this in terms of the motivating example from Chapter 1, if harsh lustration had been implemented in Poland before Wałęsa served as president, Czesław Kiszczak, the secret police chief, would not have been able to use the files against Wałęsa. It is not that some government agency would have confiscated those files (although holding on to secret police files is currently criminalized by the lustration law), but Kiszczak could not have threatened to reveal anything new relative to what lustration would have disclosed already.

Therefore, the probability that operational evidence of the politician's collaboration (kompromat) remains in the possession of the officer is a function of two probabilities: the severity of lustration, η, and the probability that the politician was in fact a collaborator, σ. To summarize,

$\sigma \in (0, 1)$: Pr(politician is former collaborator)
$(1 - \sigma)$: Pr(politician is not former collaborator)
$\eta \in (0, 1)$: Pr(compromising files exposed by lustration law)
$(1 - \eta)$: Pr(compromising files not exposed by lustration law)

In order to simplify notation and especially the exposition of the game tree, it is useful to summarize the combinations of these utilities introducing the parameter $\pi \in (0, 1)$, defined as follows.

$\pi \equiv (1 - \sigma) + \sigma\eta$. This implies that $(1 - \pi) = \sigma(1 - \eta)$. In other words, π represents the joint probability that actionable kompromat is not in possession of the officer. π is an increasing function of lustration severity and decreasing function of the prevalence of collaborators among the political elite.

Equipped with this additional notation, we are now ready to discuss the sequence of play and sketch the game tree.

2.3.2 Sequence of Play

The game starts with a move of Nature, which determines with probability $1 - \pi \in (0, 1)$ that the officer has evidence against the politician and with probability π that he does not. Recall $1 - \pi$ is the combined probability that the politician is a collaborator and that evidence of collaboration survived lustration and remains in the hands of the secret police officer. Holding the proportion of former collaborators among the political elite constant, a higher π in this model represents a more severe form of lustration: The more severe lustration is, the *less* likely it is that unearthed evidence of collaboration indeed remains in the hands of the officer. The Politician, P, knows the value of π (as he knows the value of η and σ) but not its specific realization. In the second stage of the game, the Officer, O, decides whether to make a policy demand of the Politician. I represent this decision by one of two actions in $\{D, -D\}$.

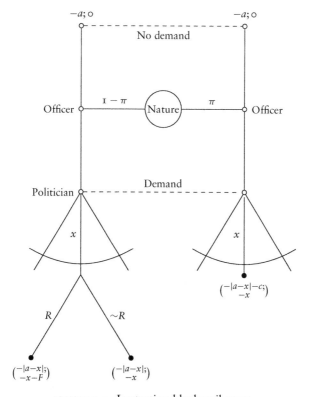

FIGURE 2.1. Lustration blackmail game

If no demand is made, the game ends, and the Politician implements the policy corresponding to his ideal point (Figure 2.1).

For simplicity, I assume that the Politician's ideal point is given by $p = 0$, and the Officer's ideal point is represented by $a > 0$. Thus, a captures the ideological distance between the Politician and the Officer. P observes whether a demand has been made, but not whether evidence against him exists (the realization of π). In the third stage, P decides whether to make a policy concession in response to the Officer's demand, and how big this concession should be. I model this concession as proposing a policy $x \in [0, a]$. If unearthed evidence against the Politician does not exist, the game ends and the Officer pays the cost of bluffing, c with $0 < c < a.$[7] The bluffing cost, c, captures the cost of obtaining and disclosing some plausible information about the Politician's past. This is costlier for the Officer in a world of independent media, where such disclosures are verified by journalists and, if false, exposed.[8]

If the Officer has kompromat against the politician, he decides whether to reveal it (R or $\sim R$). The revelation is interpreted as the Officer exercising his threat of revealing the Politician's skeletons in the closet. In the event that evidence is revealed, the Politician pays the cost of having skeletons in his closet exposed, F (which stands for the fact that as a result of the exposure, he could be fired).

Due to the asymmetric way in which information is distributed in models such as the one above, they are called models of asymmetric information. In addition, I assume that the informed party – the Officer – moves first and places a policy demand on the Politician, who then has a chance to respond to this policy demand. Because the Politician may learn something about the Officer's type from his action, this is a model with "updating," also referred to as a dynamic model of incomplete information. The informed party, moving first, is referred to as the "sender of the signal," while the uninformed party, moving second, is referred to as the "receiver of the signal." For this reason, models such as these are frequently referred to as "signaling models." These models have specific categories of equilibria, called "separating," "pooling," and "semi-separating" (or "hybrid").

---

[7] The second restriction is purely technical and merely simplifies equilibrium calculation.

[8] I assume that the media itself, although playing an important role, cannot on their own serve as a substitute for lustration. Media, regardless how free, do not have the same credibility that a government run lustration process has. When a secret police archive is open, it collects in one place all or most secret police files, which can be used to triangulate information from any specific file. A single media story, on the other hand, is typically limited to a single file.

In the first category, each type of informed party chooses a different action (in this sense, the types "separate"). In the second type of equilibrium, both types "pool" on the same action. Finally, in the third category, at least one of the types uses a mixed strategy, meaning that he sometimes pools with the other type and sometimes separates from the other type.[9]

The strategies, beliefs, and preferences are formally defined in Appendix A, where the game is also solved for equilibrium, but the timeline of the game can be summarized as follows:

1. Nature determines whether the politician running for office is a collaborator (with probability σ) or a non-collaborator (with probability $1 - \sigma$).
2. Also exogenously determined is the severity of lustration, that is, the transparency mechanism responsible for unearthing compromising information about the politician. With probability η, evidence of collaboration has been exposed, rendering blackmail ineffective; with probability $1 - \eta$, it has not.
3. The Officer observes the moves of Nature and decides whether or not to make a policy demand $(D, \sim D)$.
4. The Politician, who does not observe the moves of Nature but observes the action of the Officer, updates his beliefs; if a demand is made, he makes a counteroffer in the form of a policy concession: x.
5. The Officer decides whether to release the kompromat $(R, \sim R)$.
6. The game ends, and payoffs are distributed to both players.

The payoffs are a function of the distance between the players' respective ideal points and implemented policy as well as the two types of costs: (1) the cost to the Politician of being fired as a result of skeletons revealed in his closet, F; and (2) the cost of bluffing incurred by the Officer if he makes an empty threat, c. Critically, there is no additional cost (or benefit) to the Officer from releasing kompromat.

2.4 EQUILIBRIA

The model is solved completely in the formal appendix, where I make two additional assumptions to ensure that the equilibria characterized are unique:

---

[9] This explanation of signaling models assumes discrete types, although signaling models also allow continuous types.

Policy outcome

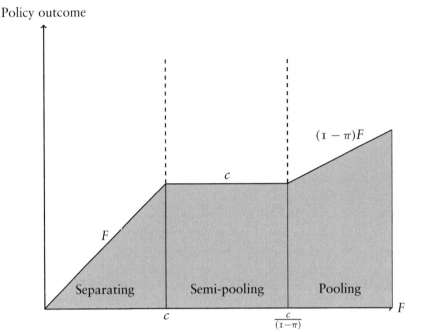

FIGURE 2.2. Policy outcomes in the lustration blackmail game

Assumptions

1. The Officer does not use weakly dominated strategies.
2. The Officer rejects all but the highest counteroffer the politician is willing to make.

Here, I offer some intuitions about how the three types of equilibria come about. This is summarized in Figure 2.2 as a function of F, the cost to the Politician of having skeletons exposed. On the vertical axis is the policy outcome. Recall that since the Politician's (and voters') ideal policy outcome is 0, the greater the value on the vertical axis, the worse is the quality of democratic representation.

Pure Separating Equilibrium
The intuition behind the *pure separating equilibrium* is fairly simple: All Officers equipped with evidence of kompromat against the Politician choose one strategy, and all Officers not equipped with such evidence choose the other strategy. Upon observing the action of the

Officer, the Politician can with certainty predict whether he has skeletons in his closet or not. Defining this equilibrium amounts to finding a counteroffer sufficient to keep the Officer from switching strategies away from this equilibrium, but that are also tolerable for the Politician.

Key for this equilibrium to be sensible is that we avoid the pathological separation where the Officer without evidence makes a demand, while the Officer with evidence of skeletons in the closet refrains from making one. Fortunately, this equilibrium is easily eliminated because for the Officer to not make a demand when he has evidence against the Politician would be to play a weakly dominated strategy, which is ruled out by Assumption 1.

Note that P cannot make a counterproposal x unless O has made a demand. Thus, the worst O can do when making a demand is $-a$, which would be his payoff if P's counterproposal were $x = 0$; that is, if P made no concession at all. Without making any demand, O is guaranteed to receive $-a$ and no more. This leaves only one possible form of separating equilibrium: The Officer with no evidence does not demand concessions, the Officer with kompromat makes a demand; the Politician makes a counteroffer, and that counteroffer is large enough to stave off the Officer's revealing of kompromat. The requirement for this to be a Bayesian equilibrium is that the Politician, upon seeing a demand, is certain that he is dealing with an Officer equipped with kompromat; if he sees no demand, he knows with certainty that no such evidence exists.

A second intuition behind this equilibrium, as seen from Figure 2.3, is that because the Officer can expect a concession only $1 - \pi$ of the time, the concession itself has to be quite large – equal to F.

Finally, for this pure separating equilibrium to exist, the cost of having skeletons revealed (F) relative to the bluffing cost (c) must be high enough. In this pure separating equilibrium, blackmail is effective with probability $1 - \pi$. The flip side of this result is that lustration severity, represented by π, is directly proportional to the quality of democratic representation. Moreover, the quality of democratic representation is inversely proportional to the cost of having skeletons in the closet exposed. Paradoxically, the more voters care that the politician they are about to elect to office is not a former collaborator, the greater must be the concession made by a politician who used to be a collaborator.

Pure Pooling Equilibrium

I now turn to a discussion of the *pooling* equilibrium. In many respects, it is the polar opposite of the separating equilibrium. Here, Officers with

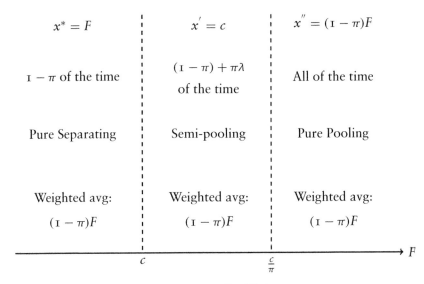

FIGURE 2.3. Equilibria

and without evidence choose the same action, implying that the Politician cannot update his prior beliefs to posterior beliefs by conditioning on the Officer's action. In presenting the intuition for separating equilibria above, I explained that the Officer will always place a demand when evidence is present. Thus, the only possibility for a pooling equilibrium in this game is one where both types of Officer – with and without evidence – make demands.

In this equilibrium, the Officer always places a demand, and the Politician always offers the same counterproposal. As illustrated in Figure 2.3, this counterproposal is $x' = (1 - \pi)F$. This value is clearly lower than in the case of the separating equilibrium. The intuition for why this is the case is as follows.

For such an equilibrium to hold, the dissident has to prefer having his proposal accepted to having skeletons in his closet revealed. However, because only a fraction of the threats to reveal skeletons in the closet can actually materialize, the greatest policy concession the Politician will make, given the Politician's beliefs and the Officer's optimal rejection region, is necessarily lower.

At the same time, this equilibrium exists only when the cost F of having skeletons revealed is quite high relative to the cost of bluffing c, and the probability that skeletons exist is lower or, conversely, when the lustration law is more severe. Note that $1 - \pi$ in the denominator corresponds to the availability of skeletons, and a smaller value makes the entire expression $\frac{c}{1-\pi}$ greater, leaving less "room" for the pooling equilibrium. Since lustration severity is captured by π, the reverse is true for lustration: Higher lustration leaves more "room" for pooling. If this seems counterintuitive, the following further explains the reasoning: When lustration is severe, even if all officers make demands, the chances that a demand is backed by a credible threat of skeletons being revealed is actually low. As a result, the corresponding counteroffer can be correspondingly low as well. The only factor making the counteroffer higher, of course, is the cost of having skeletons revealed. The key here is that the severity of lustration can mitigate against a high cost of having skeletons revealed. To translate this back to empirical implications in transitioning democracies: When new democracies are deeply concerned about former collaborators remaining in office, more severe lustration laws make the policy concession the Politician must make to the blackmailer smaller, increasing the quality of representation.

Semi-pooling Equilibrium

Finally, I turn my attention to the effectiveness of blackmail with secret police files under the *semi-pooling* equilibrium.

In this equilibrium, the Officer plays a mixed strategy. This means that for at least one of the signals, he uses a lottery over his actions: with probability λ he chooses to make a demand, and with probability $1 - \lambda$, he refrains. Technically, the Officer could also play this kind of mixed strategy for both signals. However, I have already established above that not making a demand is weakly dominated when the Officer has access to skeletons and excluded by Assumption 1. I will only be looking for mixing in the eventuality that the Officer has no skeletons.

Intuitively, this equilibrium will occur in the parameter space between the pooling and separating equilibria – that is, for moderate costs of having skeletons revealed and for moderate lustration severity.

In this equilibrium, the officer always makes a demand when evidence is present and, with probability $\lambda_{x*} = \frac{(1-\pi)(F-c)}{\pi c}$, when evidence does not exist. The beliefs supporting such a semi-pooling equilibrium are calculated using Bayes' rule and require the Politician to take into account that if he is seeing a demand, it might be coming from an Officer without information on skeletons in the closet; the probability of this, however, is lower than in the pooling equilibrium. In light of this, more demanding Officers will have kompromat to punish Politicians with if Politicians do not satisfy demands than in the pooling equilibrium. Consequently, the demand has to be correspondingly lower. In Appendix A, I calculate this equilibrium demand to be $x' = c$. The parameter λ, meanwhile, the probability that an officer without kompromat makes a demand is inversely related to the severity of lustration. This is intuitive: Severe lustrations ought to make bluffing less common.[10]

It should now be apparent why the assumptions described in Section 2.4 above are necessary. Without making both assumptions, there is an additional pooling equilibrium in which the Officer never places a demand; if a demand is made, the Politician (regardless of beliefs) offers nothing; and the Officer does not reveal kompromat (the latter is possible because the Officer is indifferent between revealing kompromat and not revealing it). The Officer is also, in this equilibrium, indifferent between making a demand and not making one. Moreover both of these play critical roles. The first assumption without the second would admit equilibria where the Politician offers less than the maximum he would be willing to offer and the Officer accepts. The second assumption without the first allows one to construct an equilibrium where the actions are similar (no demands or offers are made as kompromat is not being revealed), but is supported by off-equilibrium path beliefs according to which any Officer making a demand is unlikely to have kompromat. Assumption 2 is also responsible for why the three different equilibrium counterproposals result in the same formula for the expected quality of democratic representation, which I explain Section 2.4.1.

2.4.1 Quality of Representation under the Three Equilibrium Types

How does the quality of democratic representation relate to the effectiveness of blackmail under the separating, pure pooling, and semi-separating equilibria? I noted in the beginning of Section 2.4 that the size

---

[10] Note that although the parameter π captures the severity of lustration (η) and scarcity of collaborators (σ) jointly, I only focus on the implications of lustration, and the prevalence of collaborators is neither something easy to observe, or something that can be manipulated following the transition to democracy. It is simply an attribute of the former authoritarian regime that makes my model more realistic. At the same time, in the model of Nalepa and Sonin (2022), this parameter is modeled independently of whether or not lustration is implemented. In their model, however, lustration does not appear as a continuous parameter.

of the counteroffer is largest in the separating equilibrium and smallest in the pooling equilibrium. At the same time, demands are much less frequent in the separating equilibrium than in the pooling or semi-pooling equilibria.

Before discussing an extension of my analysis to truth commissions, I also derive an identity result, characterizing the Perfect Bayesian Equilibrium (PBE) outcome. Consider Figure 2.3.

Recall that my model assumes that absent pressure from the Officer, the Politician would carry out the policies desired by the voters, which correspond to his ideal point. Ultimately, what I am most interested in across all equilibria is the extent to which the Politician can withstand pressures from the Officer to abandon his ideal point, o. Because this ideal point corresponds to the platform he was elected on by voters, I argue that this ability to stick with his ideal point corresponds to the quality of representation. In addition to the values of x^*, x'', and x', which correspond to the counteroffers proposed by the Politician (in the separating, pooling, and semi-separating equilibria, respectively), I present the average levels of misrepresentation. Recall that I interpret the quality of representation as resistance to the Officer's blackmail. Conversely, misrepresentation is interpreted as the departures from o, the Politician's ideal point.

In order to derive the expected level of misrepresentation, I weigh the PBE outcome in each equilibrium by the frequency of its occurrence. In the case of the pure separating equilibrium, this is simply $(1 - \pi(F)) + (\pi)o$, as the Officer only proposes $x^* = F$ when evidence exists, which is $1 - \pi$ of the time. The remaining π of the time, he reverts to o. In the case of the pure pooling equilibrium, the average policy is implemented at $1 * ((1 - \pi)F)$, as the Officer always places a demand and the Politician always responds with $x'' = (1 - \pi)F$. In the case of the semi-separating equilibrium, the calculation of the policy implemented is somewhat more complex because the officer always places a demand when evidence exists, which occurs $1 - \pi$ of the time, and λ^* of the time when evidence does not exist. Hence, the total frequency of placing a demand is given by $(1 - \pi) + \pi \frac{(1-\pi)(F-c)}{\pi c}$. The Politician responds to this demand with x', bringing the expected policy outcome to $(c)((1-\pi) + \pi \frac{(1-\pi)(F-c)}{\pi c}) + \pi(1 - \frac{(1-\pi)(F-c)}{\pi c})o$, which, as in the previous two cases, reduces to $(1 - \pi)F$.

These expected policy outcomes are described in Proposition 2.1, which follows directly from my derivation above. I summarize this analysis in a proposition that also forms the basis for the main hypothesis tested in Chapter 5, which is that lustration severity increases the quality of representation:

Proposition 2.1. *The PBE outcome, interpreted as the expected level of misrepresentation, is given by the same formula across all three equilibria:* $(1 - \pi)F$.

Under all three equilibria, average misrepresentation decreases with lustration severity, which is represented by π. In addition, note that under the semi-separating equilibrium, and especially under the pooling equilibrium, TJ does not entirely prevent blackmail. Under the pure separating equilibrium, bluffing never occurs, and the amount of misrepresentation tracks the amount of evidence left in the Officer's possession (so it is directly responsive to the severity of lustration). This equilibrium becomes easier to achieve as the costs of bluffing increase because for higher values of c, it is easier for F to be low enough to satisfy the $c > F$ constraint.

In the semi-separating equilibrium, the Officer always makes a demand when evidence exists and with probability λ^* when evidence does not exist. The key feature of the semi-separating equilibrium is that when it is played, the Officer extracts policy concessions, with probability λ^*, undermining representation, even when evidence does not exist. Misrepresentation does not exactly track lustration, but in $1 - \lambda^*$ of the cases, when evidence has been swept by the lustration process, bluffing does not take place. This equilibrium occurs when the cost of revealing skeletons, F, is moderate.

In the pooling equilibrium, bluffing occurs every time evidence does not exist regardless of how much evidence TJ has left in the hands of former officers. From the normative point of view, the separating and the semi-pooling equilibria are better than the pooling equilibrium: Under this equilibrium, the severity of lustration has no bearing on the frequency of blackmail. Nevertheless, the magnitude of concessions is not as large as in the other two equilibria. This pooling equilibrium occurs when having skeletons in the closet revealed by the former secret police is very damaging to the Politician's career (when F is high).

Consequently, a higher c makes the constraints on F easier to satisfy. Thus, it makes the separating equilibrium more likely vis à vis the semi-pooling equilibrium or the semi-pooling equilibrium more likely vis à vis the pure pooling equilibrium. As a result, raising the costs of bluffing, c, allows the transparency mechanism to eliminate incentives to misrepresent voters' preferences.

A key implication that follows from Proposition 2.1 is that departures from perfect representation are constant for all values of a. This means that the effectiveness of blackmail does not depend on how far apart the ideal points of the Officer and the Politician are. This is somewhat surprising as intuitively, one might expect the ideological proximity of ideal points to matter. Indeed, this specific result – the irrelevance of distance between ideal points – is not robust to changes in the functional form of the players' preferences: With quadratic preferences, the effect of distance is negative on quality of representation; this is consistent with the empirical results presented in Chapter 5.[11] Yet, out of concern for simplicity and because distance is not my main variable of interest, I keep the expression $(1 - \pi)F$ as a succinct summary of my expectations. Critically, however, the result about the effect of lustration severity on total misrepresentation is preserved by the change in functional form of the utilities.

Returning again to assumptions described in Section 2.4, Assumption 2 also helps understand why, in expectation, the quality of representation in each equlibrium is expressed by the same formula, $(1 - \pi)F$. This is simply the *ex ante* damage that the Officer can inflict on the Politician. In light of this, the average policy deviation can never exceed $(1 - \pi)F$; if it did, the Politician would improve his payoff by choosing an action that would incentivize the Officer to release kompromat.

Relatedly, it is not surprising that if the Officer extracts as much concession as possible, that concession will equal the expected damage he can inflict on the politician. The ultimate effect of lustration is that it reduces how much the Officer can threaten the Politician and as a result, the Politician caters to his preferences less.

2.4.2 Discussion

The most important finding from the model I have solved is that the more stringent the lustration law, the better the quality of democratic representation. I show that this holds regardless of the class of equilibrium I identify. Since what I propose in this chapter is a signaling model, the three types of equilibria are separating, semi-separating, and pooling.

---

[11] In Ang and Nalepa (2019), we examine whether these results are not being driven by modeling assumptions, and specifically by the functional form of the utility functions. There, we solve the model for quadratic as opposed to "tent" preferences. Although my result on the effect of costs of revealing skeletons on the separating equilibrium is robust to this change in assumptions, my result on the effect of preference divergence is not. After changing the functional form to quadratic, the distance is shown to have a negative effect on total misrepresentation.

The conventional wisdom on how lustration operates matches the intuition of the separating equilibrium: Lustration separates compromised politicians from uncompromised ones. The former are immune to blackmail, while the latter succumb to it. Because in a separating equilibrium, lustration *separates* the two types of politicians, it would seem that only this type of equilibrium serves the normative goal of transparency. Yet, I show that under the two other equilibria – semi-pooling, which partially separates the two types, and pooling, which does not separate at all – increasing the severity of lustration universally increases the quality of representation. This is somewhat surprising, as under both of these additional equilibria, blackmail – and the accompanying extraction of policy concessions by the blackmailing agent – occurs even with lustration policies in place. For this reason, separating equilibria are particularly attractive, and it is worthwhile knowing the circumstances under which they arise. The second finding from the analysis of the model is thus that the chances of a separating equilibrium decrease as the preferences of the newly elected politician and the former secret police agent diverge, but the quality of democratic representation is not affected by this distance.

Since separating equilibria most closely reflect how conventional wisdom understands lustrations to work, it may seem worrisome that these other equilibria exist at all. After all, in the pooling equilibrium, lustration does nothing to modify voters' beliefs regarding the past collaboration of the politician they are about to reelect. Semi-separating equilibria only provide partial information. Because of this, it is vital to stress that regardless of whether blackmail with information about skeletons in the closet actually occurs (that is, regardless of the type of equilibrium), the severity of lustration always improves the quality of democratic representation. Moreover, this result is theoretically robust to assumptions about the functional form of players' preferences.

My model is not impervious to criticism, however. First, the assumption that a politician does not know that he is a collaborator may strike some readers as unrealistic. How could the collaborator himself be unaware of his involvement? Sadly, the realities of collaborator recruitment in robust authoritarian regimes, such as the ones in Eastern Europe, show that such occurrences were common. Secret police officers were encouraged and rewarded to recruit collaborators broadly and worked under cover. It was common for students and laborers involved in dissident movements to share information with strangers who later turned out to be secret police officers. Officers, in turn, registered even casual conversations as recruitment events, as they sought to maximize the recruitment numbers and not intelligence. As for intelligence itself, even the most benign information could be used to recruit additional collaborators. Minute details of the contents of a university lecture detailed by a student marginally involved in the dissident movement, for example, could be put to use to recruit key student activists. All the secret police had to do was overwhelm the potential recruit with information of their lives that they already had in their possession. The target of recruitment would feel helpless and succumb to the recruitment effort. This technique worked in part because the first "collaborator" rarely thought he or she was doing anything wrong. After all, who does not like to share the details of a riveting lecture they just attended? Years later, following the transition, this has led to tragic discoveries when, after the opening of secret police archives, many Eastern Europeans learned that they had provided the police with information. In Poland, the scale of such undercover recruitment efforts led the Constitutional Court to include a special exemption to the lustration law for "unconscious collaborators." This allowed targets of lustration proceedings to argue that they had been unaware that they were the subject of recruitment efforts. Poland's first President, Lech Wałęsa, described in the introduction to this book may have been such an "unconscious collaborator" and in recent years convincing evidence supporting such collaboration was discovered by historians (Chodakiewicz 2009).[12]

Another illustration of the ambiguity with the category of collaboration comes from the film by Florian von Donnersmarck, *The Lives of Others*. In this fictional story about a Stasi officer spying on a high-profile theater director, during the bugging of the director's home with eves-dropping devices, the Stasi officer realizes that his team's activity was noticed by the director's neighbor. He knocks on her door and threatens that if she even says a word about the spy operation to the theater director, her daughter will lose her spot at university. Next, as he turns to leave, he says "Make sure to send Frau Meineke a gift in appreciation of her collaboration." Alongside the gift would be a receipt that Frau Meineke would sign, providing the Stasi, as well as future blackmailers, with evidence of her collaboration.

The second problem that concerns the model is that the action of the Officer in the last stage is not unique in equilibrium. The blackmailing secret police officer is just as well-off releasing the kompromat as he is

---

[12] More specifically, according to Chodakiewicz (2009), Wałęsa later admitted that he had spoken with security agents prior to becoming Solidarity leader but categorically refused any kind of collaboration, and IPN provided evidence corroborating the latter claim.

keeping it to himself. Nalepa and Sonin (2022), in fact, show that any general model of kompromat with a unique equilibrium in which kompromat works must have at least four cross-cutting types that allow the voter's uncertainty to translate into a blackmailer's leverage over politicians. First, there must exist compromised and uncompromised politicians. Second, there must be uncertainty about the uncompromised politicians' true policy preferences. Otherwise, any deviation from the uncompromised politician's ideal policy would expose the elected leader as compromised, and the transparency regime would simply ban ex-collaborators from running for office. In a transparency regime, moderate politicians would be elected to office and the politician with the ideal point closest to the median would be elected. Without transparency, Nalepa and Sonin (2022)'s model shows that a potential blackmailer can exploit the fear of electing a compromised politician (whose policy position is preferred by the median voter to the policy position of an uncompromised challenger). The blackmailer induces these moderate politicians to move policy away from the median voter. The voter, in turn, anticipates this to be the case and votes instead for the challenger with more distant policy positions but whose collaborator status is not under question.[13]

The upshot of this analysis is that a lack of transparency always translates into policy that is farther from the median voter than it would be under a transparency regime. Hence, the consequences for the quality of democratic representation are exactly the same as in the model I presented here.

Extension to Truth Commissions

The formal model of lustration can be adapted to accommodate truth commissions. The game tree would look the same, with slight differences in the identities of the actors. Instead of a Politician taking an action, some other elite member would play this role. Similarly, the person exercising blackmail does not need to be a secret police officer; anyone privy to information about human rights abuses committed by former elites and interested in leveraging that information to extract concessions from elite members can play this role. These concessions may take the form of

---

[13] In the Nalepa and Sonin (2022) model, this kind of politician corresponds to the successor autocratic party – that is, the party whose members could have been known members of the former regime, but not secret collaborators.

rents or privileged access to resources the elite member controls. Truth commissions, by revealing information about past abuses, work in the same way as lustration does to prevent this information from being used.

2.5 CONCLUSION

This chapter has reconstructed the role of transparency regimes in determining how faithfully politicians represent voters once in office. Regardless of their retroactive value, lustration and truth commissions enhance the quality of democracy by making blackmail with secret police files or other skeletons in the closet impossible. The model clearly shows that blackmail is still possible even after lustration and truth commissions have been implemented, at least in some circumstances. Such blackmail with secret authoritarian legacies takes place when voters place a very high premium on having elites that are clean of suspicions of collaboration and when the costs of bluffing are low. Chapter 5 will develop this intuition further, but media independence is the easiest empirical interpretation of the costs of bluffing. Bluffs by secret officers who do not actually have evidence of collaboration can be uncovered more easily in contexts where independent journalism is well developed.

Even though lustration does not eliminate blackmail completely, the effect of lustration severity on the quality of democratic representation is positive. The quality of representation is monotonically increasing in transparency because the concessions the Politician must make in the pooling and semi-separating equilibria are smaller than those under the separating equilibrium.

The three types of equilibria are presented in Figures 2.2 and 2.3 as a function of F, the cost to the Politician of having his skeletons revealed. The set of conditions for the pooling equilibria is distinct from the set of conditions defining the separating and semi-ing equilibria, with the critical element being the magnitude of F relative to c, the cost of bluffing, and π, the probability that evidence against the Politician has been made transparent by a lustration or truth commission.

I have shown that for very low costs of revealing skeletons in the closet, there exists a separating equilibrium in which the Officer only makes a demand if evidence exists, and the Politician makes a counteroffer $x^* = F$. Second, if the costs of revealing skeletons are very high relative to the costs of bluffing, there exists a pooling equilibrium in which the Officer always makes a demand irrespective of whether evidence exists, and the Politician makes a counteroffer $x'' = (1 - \pi)F$. Third, for moderate costs of revealing skeletons in the closet, there exists a semi-pooling equilibrium where the Officer sometimes bluffs (i.e., makes a demand even when he has no evidence), and the Politician responds with a counteroffer $x' = c$. In all equilibria, the counteroffer is made and accepted.

The main contribution of this model is that it develops a robust result about the effect of lustration severity on the quality of democratic representation: Increasing lustration severity always increases the quality of representation. This chapter also identifies conditions under which former secret police officers extract policy concessions from politicians even after lustration has been implemented. I identify (pooling and semi-separating) equilibria under which lustration is compatible with bluffing. Under these equilibria, lustration does not prevent departures from perfect representation. These empirical implications are developed further and illustrated in Chapter 5.

3

Purging the Authoritarian State

In Chapter 2, I presented the first of two theoretical arguments against the "Spanish Model" of transitional justice (TJ). Although the Spanish Model, or "doing nothing," when applied to lustration policies – policies that deal with secret collaborators – may not produce immediate negative consequences for democratic stability, it strengthens the power of authoritarian networks. In this chapter, I ask whether the same can be said for purges – TJ mechanisms that deal with known collaborators.

Anecdotal evidence suggests that purges may actually hurt a nascent democracy. As an example, consider Iraq's policy aimed at purging new democratic institutions of former Ba'athists. According to sources cited by Roman David (2006), de-Ba'athification prevented 185 members of Saddam Hussein's party, mostly Sunnis, from running in legislative elections in 2003. Despite its promise to promote societal reconciliation, this policy only ignited ethnic tensions. Jon Elster (2004) describes France's policy of *épuration*, banning former Vichy collaborators from holding office following World War II, as having very similar effects.

In other contexts, purges may be a welcome TJ mechanism. Consider as an illustration, the purge of the Tunisian Gendarmerie, Ben Ali's political police, which by some counts numbered 150,000 workers (or one security officer per eighty Tunisians). In contrast to the military, which was quick to start disobeying Ben Ali in the midst of the protests, the Gendarmerie remained extremely loyal to the dictator. As early as February of 2011 (less than one month following the self-immolation of Mohamed Bouazizi), thirty top police officers were removed from their posts by the interim prime minister Mohammed Ghannouchi.[1] A top military officer was appointed to head the national security service, and career military officers were named as new police chiefs for seven key regions in the country. Following this leadership purge, in March of 2011, the entire secret police agency was disbanded. Yet, as Bouguerra (2014) points out, the "intelligence service in Tunisia was divided into two agencies ... the Directorate General of Special Services (SS), which worked on general intelligence information, and the Directorate General of Technical Services, which provided the same information but through technical instruments such as phone tapping or Internet control. The Directorate of State Security (DSE) coordinated the SS and ST." (p. 2). The suspension of the DSE effectively dissolved the political police and was welcomed by ordinary Tunisians. However, many experts cautioned that it would disrupt the smooth functioning of the entire intelligence system that filtered information and provided analysis. Beyond the halting of intelligence gathering, suspending the political police also entailed closing down smaller units within the General Directive for Public Safety; these included traffic police, public safety police, crowd control police, and others. All servicemen employed by these agencies were replaced by new, dramatically under-trained staff.

Taken together, these introductory remarks bring into stark relief that purges – that is, the removal of *known* members of the *ancien régime* and their organizations – are complex processes and call for analysis separate from transparency regimes.

This chapter employs the tools of formal theory to explore the relationship between purges and the quality of democracy. First, it will show that not all nascent democracies can afford to embark on wide-scale purges. This is because any new democratic politician who is considering purges is presented with a fundamental trade-off between loyalty and expertise. This trade-off is not unique to post-authoritarian democracies.

The loyalty–competence trade-off was noticed originally in a paper by Egorov and Sonin (2011), who explain why rulers, but in particular dictators, have to balance their desirability for loyal agents on the one hand and for skilled ones on the other ("the very competence of the vizier

---

[1] Similarly, the party of Ben Ali, the Constitutional Democratic Rally (*Rassemblement constitutionnel démocratique*, RCD), did little more than to prop up Ben Ali's rule and had no independent role in state administration. Consequently, its disbanding had few bad consequences for democratization, and indeed made room for the creation of new parties disconnected from the previous authoritarian regime.

makes him more prone to treason" (Egorov and Sonin 2011, p. 904). Unsurprisingly strong rulers will hence resolve the dilemma differently than weak rulers. The former will choose competence over loyalty, as they do not feel threatened by competent agents; the latter will invest in loyal agents, as competent agents pose a threat.

This idea can be generalized to the strategies of organizing security and repressive apparatuses by authoritarian rulers. Paine (forthcoming) in work discussed in Chapter 2, considers the tradeoff between appointing a professional (hence equipped with expertise) army and a personal (hence loyal but relatively less skilled) militia. He argues that autocrats will appoint professional rather than personalist militaries when they are more concerned about large revolutionary threats from below than about external threats. The reason is that neither kind of security force can survive a revolution from below: A postrevolutionary state must start with a blank slate, and such turnovers result in everyone being fired from the military. In light of this, professional militaries, their higher expertise notwithstanding, are not more effective at fighting revolutionary threats than personal militias. They have better expertise but no incentive to use it. In contrast, in the case of external threats, professional militaries can count on leniency. Indeed, in some instances, they even collaborate with external challengers to the autocrat. In light of this, they put less effort into averting external threats. Consequently, the autocrat who fears such threats is better off investing in a personal militia.

In a related paper, Alexander Debs (2016), although he does not talk specifically about the incentives of leaders and their rank and file, adds nuance to this point of view by drawing attention to regime type. Specifically, uniformed personnel from former military regimes fare better under new democratic rulers than under nondemocratic rulers because their skills are not threatening under the new democracy (democracies select rulers based on citizenship support and not brute force). Debs uses this insight to predict that transitions from military rule to democracy should appear more swiftly than from other dictatorships. I use this insight to argue that skills of those working to sustain the former authoritarian regime need not be useful in the new democratic regime. This, in turn, affects the incentives to purge.

In work that uses social networks, Josef Woldense (2018) points out that rulers can alleviate the trade-off between loyalty and competence by shuffling employees laterally from one geographic region to another. This way, agents never become so entrenched and powerful as to pose a threat to the ruler but continue to amass experience on the job. In short, he calls into question the incompatibility of having skilled and yet nonthreatening employees.[2] Yet not posing a threat does not immediately imply loyalty. What if the agent just does not find it worthwhile to put in effort?

In a recent paper addressing this dilemma, Alexei Zakharov (2016) considers an interaction between a dictator and individual subordinates where the dictator can choose the specific level of loyalty (and correspondingly lack of competence) he needs from his subordinates. A controversial prediction from his model is that unskilled agents invest in loyalty because they are aware that their limited skill set renders them unemployable by future rulers. But skilled agents, knowing that they can find lucrative employment under any regime, have an incentive to shirk.

Implicit in this and Paine's account, however, is that loyalty to the autocrat on the one hand and professionalization on the other cannot go hand in hand: A loyal military cannot be professional; whenever there is a conflict between fulfilling the autocrat's wishes and making the correct decision, the loyal military will ignore what their professional training tells them to do. Consider, however, as a counter example the military in Park Chung Hee's postcoup South Korea, where according to Joo-Hong Kim, Park, taking advantage of the Korean War of 1950–1953, "had transformed a rag-tag army, consisting of former colonial officers and independence fighters of all ideological stripes split into innumerable factions, into a a professionalized military with the potential to lead the country into modernity" (Kim 2011, p. 169). By the time Park launched his coup, Kim adds, "the armed forces had become the most cohesive and modernized institution in South Korea." And yet, despite this professionalization, Park succeeded in transforming it into a loyal partner. The military enforced five of his installments of martial law and three garrison decrees during Park's eighteen-year rule. The professionalization of the army was in no way hampered by Park's politicization of the armed forces and its expansion into nonmilitary arenas. The South Korean case motivates my modeling decision to allow for loyalty (represented as preference divergence) to be combined with professionalization (represented as expertise) to various degrees.

Another departure from Paine, Zakharov, Egorov and Sonin, and Woldense, however, is that I am interested less in the incentives of the former autocrat and more in the incentives of the democrats who succeed him. In the democratic context, the trade-off between loyalty and expertise becomes nuanced by the fact that agents with expertise

---

[2] For a similar argument in the context of Putin's Russia, see Olimpieva (2021).

and weaker loyalty to the outgoing, authoritarian regime may be more loyal to the new democratic regime. Hence, in some circumstances, the loyalty–competence trade-off can be averted. Moreover, since the new democrats inherit a state staff potentially loyal to the autocrat, their decision is better framed as one not about whom to appoint but about whom to purge from the authoritarian state apparatus.

This brings into stark relief the distinction between my understanding of purges and that of the broader TJ literature. The TJ literature treats administrative purges (such as decommunization, de-Ba'athification, and denazification) and lustration as the same type of mechanism for dealing with the past (Binningsbø et al. 2012a; Elster 2004; Pinto 2008). In this book, I concede that all of these institutions are forms of personnel TJ in that they aim at eliminating members and collaborators of the previous authoritarian regime from the democratic state's apparatus. However, I also draw a sharp distinction between dealing with secret collaboration (through lustration) and known collaboration (through purges). This restriction of the term purges to open forms of collaboration is at odds with some of the literature, so I clarify the my usage in a special section devoted to terminology.

3.1.1 Terminology

Most scholars pool all categories of personnel TJ – collaboration with known and unknown collaborators – under one heading. For instance, Olsen, Payne, and Reiter write that lustration events are often referred to in terms of the group that is banned from public office, as in "denazification," "decommunization," and "de-Ba'athification." These authors use the term "lustration" to refer to "official state policies to purge individuals from positions they currently hold or to ban them from holding specific positions in the future" (Olsen et al. 2010, p. 38). This use of the term "lustration" is at odds with the definition used in this book, which applies the term to refer to clandestine collaboration with the *ancien régime*.

The authors of the widely recognized Post-Conflict Justice (PCJ) Dataset (Binningsbø et al. 2012a) have also pooled personnel TJ events into one category. These researchers, however, refer to all personnel forms of TJ using the term "purges," which describes "the acts of removing politicians, armed forces members, judiciary or other members of society for their (alleged) collaboration with or participation in a conflict and limiting their influence accordingly" (Binningsbø et al. 2012a, p. 736). In part because their data collection effort is limited to societies recovering from conflict and only covers the first five post-conflict years, these authors only locate fifteen post-conflict episodes that are followed by purges thus defined. One of the contributions of my Global Transitional Justice Database, described in Chapter 4, is to offer a time series of personnel TJ events that begins with a country's transition to democracy, does not end after some fixed period, and spans the entire democratic period. Later in this chapter, I offer examples of purges from the de la Rúa administration in Argentina, which long postdate the immediate aftermath of a transition.[3]

Finally, while some authors, including Roman David (2011) and Cynthia Horne (2017a), disaggregate personnel TJ mechanisms, they do so in a different way than I do in this book. David defines lustration as a "special public employment law that stipulates the conditions for the access of persons who worked for or collaborated with the political or repressive apparatus of socialist regimes to certain public positions in new democracies." At the same time, he limits the application of this term to Eastern Europe. He justifies this decision with the fact that prior to 1990, lustration was not used to describe TJ procedures (David 2011, p. 67). While it is true that the term "lustration" has rarely been used to describe disqualification for public employment of secret and clandestine collaborators of a former regime, such procedures have been implemented both before 1990 and beyond Eastern Europe, as illustrated by the Athenian example of dokimasia in Chapter 2.

Cynthia Horne, meanwhile, tries to "back out" the concept of lustration from ways in which policymakers have used it. Taking a disaggregating approach, she presents an overlapping categorization of personnel TJ events that includes vetting, lustration, and purges. She limits the use of the term "purge" to describing blanket bans extending collectively to members of certain organizations linked to the *ancien régime*. In contrast, a lustration procedure considers each case individually. She stipulates lustration to be part of a broader category of "vetting," which can ban from holding office members of the *ancien régime* based on criteria other than participation in or collaboration with the former authoritarian regime.

Both David's and Horne's approaches limit the scope of lustration to Eastern Europe. Critically, neither David nor Horne distinguish between procedures based on revealing new information about secret

---

3 While Argentina is not one of the archetypical cases used in this book, I choose it over Spain for this illustration because Spain's efforts were so delayed that no one remained to be purged.

collaboration (which I call "transparency regimes" and which include both lustrations and truth commissions) and bans that rely on open membership in *ancien régime* organizations (which I call "purges").

The rest of this chapter is organized as follows: In Section 3.3, I present some illustrative examples of purges in the "thorough," "leadership," and "perfunctory" categories.

Section 3.4 develops a formal theoretic framework to explain the concept of purges – that is, TJ procedures that limit the presence in office of *known* collaborators. Recall that known collaborators are members of the *ancien régime* who served it in an official capacity as party members, bureaucrats, or uniformed personnel but not as secret informers. I develop the theory in three stages.

The first (baseline) model contrasts the trade-off between uncertainty and loyalty. It models the decision to purge as the reverse of a delegation problem (Callander 2008; Epstein & O'Halloran 1999). Building on the intuition that firing staff members of a security or enforcement agency comes at the cost of losing potentially valuable expertise, this baseline model implies that democratic representation is not always boosted by thorough purges. The second model analyzes whether adding discretionary limits to the principals' toolkit will help control the agent. Originally introduced to the delegation and agency literature by comparativists (Huber & Shipan 2002), discretionary limits restrict the agents' range of actions *ex ante*, allowing the principal to better control the agent. Finally, the third model relaxes the assumption of perfect expertise on the part of the agent. Section 3.5 provides illustrative examples using the book's archetypal cases. Section 3.6 provides the conclusion.

3.2 ILLUSTRATIVE EXAMPLES OF PURGES

There are three types of purges: thorough, leadership, and perfunctory. A thorough purge denotes the disbanding of an entire segment of the *ancien régime* institution without discriminating between leaders (those issuing orders) and rank and file (those following orders). The dissolution of communist secret police agencies in postcommunist Europe exemplifies thorough purges. The purging of the East German Stasi (Ministerium fur Staatssicherheit) is now legendary and described by multiple historians and political scientists (Childs & Popplewell 2016; Koehler 1999; Miller 1998). Initially, following Erich Mielke's resignation, the East German Council of Ministers renamed the Stasi to the "Office for National

Security." However, less than two months later, the new prime minister of the German Democratic Republic (GDR), Hans Modrow, ordered its dissolution. The Ministry of Internal Affairs inherited the buildings and facilities of the former Stasi, but none of the employees were rehired.[4] The ministry took over some of the tasks performed by the Stasi (notably the ones that did not involve spying on the opposition). This thorough purge came at a cost, however. Numerous journalistic accounts document the gainful employment of former Stasi officers in the business holdings of Martin Schlaff, an Austrian businessman; in the 1980s, Schlaff had made a small fortune by supplying senior Stasi officers with products that were precluded from trade under "CoCom," the embargo imposed on the Soviet bloc by the West (Tillack n.d.; Borchert 2006).

Of course, thorough purges need not be limited to the secret intelligence and police apparatuses. A Human Rights Watch report describes a purge of the judiciary in Panama:

> from top to bottom, judges who held posts under Noriega resigned or were purged and have been replaced by new ones, almost all of whom lack prior judicial experience: all nine of the Supreme Court judges resigned and were replaced; the newly-constituted Supreme Court then dismissed or had to replace 13 out of the 19 judges of the *Tribunales Superiores*, the intermediate appellate courts; and approximately two-thirds of the 48 trial-level circuit judges, were, in turn, removed or replaced by the newly appointed appellate judges. (1991)

According to the *New York Times*, the Argentinian president de la Rúa purged the intelligence apparatus of over 1,500 agents responsible for involvement in the so-called dirty war only two months after taking office (Krauss 2000). Purged agents were either dismissed or forced into retirement. Instead of releasing the list of names of those purged, entire sections of the agency were let go, suggesting that no discrimination was made between those giving or following orders or based on the level of involvement. According to the report, this "housecleaning … mean[t] nearly a 50% reduction in military intelligence personnel, and officials

---

4 Childs and Popplewell (2016) report that most of the Stasi employees had to turn to some other means of earning their living. However, a significant number did find reemployment in the policy or private security world. In Saxony, it was reported that more than 500 ex-Stasi operatives had been taken over by the police. This includes 161 former full time Ministry for State Security employees and 262 unofficial collaborators. In addition, 370 ex-members of the DDR criminal police were in employment in 1994. (p. 195)

said they would leave nonmilitary intelligence work to civilian agencies"
(Krauss 2000, Section A, p. 6).

The story from Poland, involving the disbanding of the begrudged
Służba Bezpieczeństwa (SB), is less well known but gives a useful illustration of the complexities surrounding thorough purges.

As of July 1989, the SB employed 24,107 officers. After an ordinance of
the Minister of Internal Affairs was implemented, this number dropped
to 6,681. Entire departments making up the SB – specifically II, III, IV,
V, and VI—were liquidated.[5] These reforms, however, did not constitute
a formal purge. According to Leskiewicz (2016), the 1989 Roundtable
Agreement put Czesław Kiszczak (the former SB chief mentioned also in
Chapter 2) in charge of the Department of Internal Affairs. As minister,
he was left responsible for reorganizing the SB. Taking advantage of this
privilege, he reassigned the most compromised employees from the dissolved departments into the Citizens' Militia units (the Citizens' Militia,
Milicja Obywatelska, was the former communist state's police force).[6]
It was not until two members of the former opposition proposed legislation creating completely new police and security agencies, that the
prospect of actual purges in Poland's security apparatus became a reality.
As a result of the bill, any new operations, including those on existing
cases under SB investigation, were terminated. Officers conducting espionage, counterespionage, and investigations into economic crimes had to
stop working immediately. Only anti-terrorist activities and a few general
service departments such as the bureau for deciphering, the communica-
tions bureau, the passport division, and the population registry division
were permitted to continue.[7]

The leadership of what remained of SB hoped to be awarded positions
in the new Office for State Protection, *Urzad Ochrony Panstwa* (UOP),
even though the activities of the UOP, which included combating interna-

---

[5] These departments were responsible for counterintelligence, combating anti-state activities, infiltration of religious organizations, protection of the state economy, and protection
of the state agriculture, respectively.

[6] The minister made use of two regulations, "Ordinance number 890 MSW of January 22,
1990 changing the ordinance about the status of MO and SB" and "Ordinance number
075/89 of August 24, 1989 on the liquidation and reconstruction of some organizational
units of the Ministry of Internal Affairs."

[7] The very fact that these departments had been subsumed under the secret police in the
communist state only indicates how extensive the reach of the secret police had been
under communism in Poland.

tional terrorism, white collar crime, and espionage, were quite different from those that had been the focus of the SB. Despite these preferences for continued employment, the bill passed in the legislature in early 1990. A critical part of the act addressed the fate of former SB employees. Not only were the 6,681 remaining original SB staff to be let go, but the purge extended to all officers who were employed by the SB as of late July 1989. As a result, the purge included staff that Kiszczak had intended to shield through transfers to the Citizens' Militia. The Citizens' Militia was disbanded, and a new police force was created in its place.

Implementing the new legislation was complicated by the fact that Kiszczak was still at the helm of the Department of Internal Affairs. In June 1990, Prime Minister Tadeusz Mazowiecki indicated to him that "there cannot be peace" while he remained minister. The following day, Kiszczak resigned, and his deputy, former oppositionist Krzysztof Kozlowski, took over. Later in his memoirs, Kiszczak expressed deep regret "that he was not in a position to protect the staff that had worked under him for so many years especially since despite an agreement at the *Roundtable Talks* and the peaceful transition of power that ensued, calls for revenge and accountability intensified" (Beres & Skoczylas 1991).

With Kiszczak ousted, Kozlowski was finally in a position to purge the leadership of the organization. This purge started with the dismissal of the second vice-minister, 5 generals, and 16 department directors as well as their immediate deputies, totaling 202 staff members. Once the leadership had been purged, he was able to implement the newly passed legislation, which called for the firing of all employees of the SB and their rehiring only after they had been vetted by stringent verification committees that had been provided for by the new legislation. Verification was coordinated by a Central Verification Commission (Centralna Komisja Weryfikacyjna), chaired by Kozlowski himself. The central commission oversaw the work of forty-nine regional verification commissions. The regional commissions were made up of the UOP regional chief, the regional police chief, a police trade union representative, and persons who "had earned the trust of the local community and boasted high moral authority." In practice, the additional verification commission members included two members of parliament, one senator, a regional "Solidarity" trade union activist, and a few persons nominated by the UOP chief, however their membership varried from 8 member (in Ciechanowskie) to 23 (in Poznanskie).

Former members of the SB (as of August 23, 1989, that is, the date prior to Kiszczak's reshuffle) were allowed to apply to be vetted for a position in the UOP as long as they were under fifty-five. In the application, the candidate had to explain how his or her services would be of use to the new democratic regime. Only candidates cleared of any suspicion were admitted to service in the new UOP and police force. Verification committees were featured in Wladyslaw Pasikowski's 1992 film "Psy." The film, quoted in the beginning of this book, opens with the chair of the verification committee reading out loud the file of the main protagonist, Franz Mauer. Since the warnings and sanctions in his file far outnumbered the honorable mentions, the chair asks if Mauer feels obligated to "faithfully serve the new Polish Republic." Franz replies, "I do, to the very end, be it mine of hers." And he is allowed to be rehired.

According to Slawomir Dudek, of all SB employees as of mid-1989, only 14,500 – that is, 60 percent – applied to be vetted. Initially, only 8,681 convinced the verification commissions of their credentials, but a further 4,500 appealed the regional verification committee decisions; among those, 1,800 had their initial decisions reversed. This brought the total number of former employees positively vetted to be rehired by the UOP to 10,439 and the number of those who failed to 3,595. As one of Kozlowski's deputies pointed out, successfully passing verification merely made a candidate eligible for reemployment. It is not clear exactly how many of the over 10,000 were ultimately rehired, but the newly created UOP only had about five thousand vacancies. (Dudek & Gryz 2003).

The reason this Polish example qualifies as a thorough purge is that the entire structure of the SB was dismantled, with all of its employees collectively fired. All officers old enough to have participated in the repression of the sixties were forced into retirement. Other SB staff were only permitted to reapply for employment in the new agencies after being screened by a verification commission that separately considered their individual cases.

A leadership purge, in contrast to a thorough purge, is limited to the top echelon of the hierarchy of the enforcement apparatus: It discriminates between the leadership of the organization and the rank and file. A good illustration of a leadership purge is the Bulgarian *Panev*

Law, passed on December 9, 1992 by the Bulgarian National Assembly.[8] Among its many provisions, the law prohibited from holding positions in "Executive Bodies of Scientific Organizations and the Higher Certifying Commission" people who had taught at the Communist Academy for Social Sciences and Social Management and those who had taught History of Communist Parties, Leninist or Marxist Philosophy, Political Economy, or Scientific Communism. All persons covered by the law had to provide written statements regarding their prior employment and party activities. A refusal to provide such a statement was regarded as an admission of guilt. According to its author, Georgi Panev, the underlying idea behind the purge "was to bar persons of the higher totalitarian scientific structures and former collaborators of the former state security from academic and faculty councils and from the supreme academic awards commission, awarding scientific degrees and other academic qualifications." As this ban did not extend to all academicians, but rather only to those who had trained the communist state's upper leadership, this ban can be considered a leadership purge. Most academic staff who had worked under the previous regime retained their jobs.

Finally, a perfunctory purge is a vetting process that only extends to the rank and file or to the lowest echelons of the hierarchy of the enforcement apparatus. Such purges may occur while the authoritarian regime is still in office, in which case they are a preemptive move by the outgoing authoritarian regime. Such preemption shields the regime from more severe TJ at the hands of the incoming democratic regime (Kaminski & Nalepa 2014).[9]

A perfunctory purge can also be instituted by an incoming democratic government when it cannot conduct a leadership purge because its hands are tied by a peace agreement with the outgoing military autocrats (Nalepa 2010b). Under such circumstances, forgoing purges altogether is not feasible because of third-party or international pressures. Such a purge occurred in Nicaragua. Nicaragua's autocracy ended in 1979, when the former Nicaraguan president, Anastasio Somoza Debayle, was defeated by the Sandinista National Liberation Front (FSLN or the "Sandinistas").

---

[8] The full name of the bill was "Law for Temporary Introduction of Additional Requirements for Members of Executive Bodies of the Scientific Organizations and the Higher Certifying Commission."

[9] Technically, preemptive perfunctory purges do not satisfy the definition of TJ; for this reason, they are omitted from the Global Transitional Justice Dataset.

The new government had to manage a civil war that broke out as the Central Intelligence Agency (CIA)-backed Contras staged terrorist attacks over the course of the next eight years (Hoekstra 2021). Fighting finally came to a close when Violeta Chamorro emerged victorious in the 1990 elections.

Although the United States preferred her to the Sandinistas, they still pressured her to reform the security forces.[10] These pressures notwithstanding, Chamorro decided to forgo a purge of military commanders and only purge troops, reducing their number from 80,000 to only 20,000. Notably, while Chamorro had long been a Sandinista critic, she retained General Ortega, the former president and FSLN leader, most likely in order to preserve peace. Three months later, when she did fire a long-time Sandinista Chief commander to make good on her promise to lead a "government of national reconciliation," she replaced him with another Sandinista (Otis 1992).

A second perfunctory purge example comes from El Salvador. Like Nicaragua, El Salvador had experienced a party-based authoritarian government, classified by some a party-military (Geddes et al. 2014), followed by a civil war that left 75,000 people dead. The first competitive elections free from political violence were held in 1994, though the peace agreements were signed earlier, in February of 1992 (Archive 1992). On January 4, 1993, despite pressure from the UN to carry out a leadership purge in the military, President Cristiani, to demonstrate "good faith over the peace accords ...Keesing's Record of World Events announced reductions in the armed forces from 63,000 to 31,500 troops." However, the top echelon of the leadership remained mostly intact (1993).

3.3 THE MODEL

The lustration and truth commissions model presented in Chapter 2 showed how transparency regimes enhance democratic representation by preventing blackmail of current politicians by former authoritarian elites. Lustration, I argued, exposes potentially embarrassing informa-

---

[10] At one point, the US Congress threatened to withhold the release of 100 million dollars to Nicaragua unless some personnel changes took place. This pressure was in part due to charges that US funds had been funneled to Sandinista groups; this withholding of aid may also be interpreted as pressure to purge.

tion about collaboration with the authoritarian regime's enforcement apparatus, making it impossible for former authoritarian elites to extort policies in exchange for keeping skeletons in politicians' closets hidden. A crucial theoretical prediction of Chapter 2 is that democratic representation improves in direct proportion to the amount of lustration implemented.

This chapter is devoted to modeling purges. The models I present here yield predictions for the effect of purge severity on democratic representation that differ starkly from the predictions I make about the effect of lustration. While the quality of political representation increases monotonically with the severity of lustration, the severity of purges may be associated with worse effects for democratic representation. Moreover, the very feasibility of implementing purges depends on conditions present in the authoritarian regime itself: Following a purge, new democratic leaders must replace the fired agents with new staff who share the leaders' preferences but lack the skills necessary to implement policy. How costly this decision is depends on: (1) the uncertainty at the time of the transition; (2) how closely the new leaders preferences are aligned with the authoritarian agent; and (3) the expertise of the former authoritarian agent.

Consider the general dilemma: Following a transition to democracy, an incoming government inherits a state apparatus that is staffed by employees of the former authoritarian regime. These employees possess expertise that the incoming government lacks. Yet, these bureaucrats or uniformed members of the enforcement apparatus may well have residual loyalties to the *ancien régime*.[11] Thus, their preferences diverge from those of the incoming democratic government. In light of this, they may use the expertise they possess from their service in the *ancien régime* to sabotage the policy program of the new democratic government. Given the risks posed by these bureaucrats, the incoming government faces the choice to purge the state administration – fire all personnel employed by

---

[11] Note that in this section, I assume that generically, persons working under the predemocratic regime depart from the Weberian ideal type of a bureaucrat in that they do not automatically acquire the preferences of the "ruler" or establish what Weber refers to as a "community of interests" (Weber 1968). On the contrary, since working for an ideologically tainted authoritarian regime requires at least some ideological commitments on the part of the administrative staff, those loyalties are difficult to shed immediately.

the former autocrats – or to retain most of the state employees and only focus on the leadership.

Three features characterize an ideal bureaucracy. First, bureaucrats ought to have more expertise than rulers or lawmakers themselves. One way in which states ensure that this happens is by mandating entry exams and requiring that minimum qualifications be satisfied before a person can become a civil servant (Simon et al. 1950; Wilson 2019). Second, bureaucrats are supposed to share a "commonality of interests with the rulers" (Weber 1968) to ensure that the policy they try to implement closely or exactly matches the ruler's ideal outcome. To the extent that a gap exists between the preferences of rulers and their bureaucrats, a "principal–agent" problem arises. Third, bureaucrats should not shirk their responsibilities. In other words, when not monitored, they should work exactly and with the same intensity as when they are monitored (Brehm & Gates 1999). Shirking is the only feature of the three listed previously that is not accounted for in the models I present.

It is easy to see why a bureaucracy in the aftermath of a democratic transition may fall short of these three ideals. Bluntly put, the inherited bureaucracy may be incompetent and disloyal to the new regime. First, the state of the *ancien régime* may have been staffed via patronage networks and hence lack the expertise necessary to implement policy. Indeed, authoritarian regimes are often brought down by poor policy outcomes and subpar economic performance (Gasiorowski 1995).[12] Second, employees of the previous authoritarian regime's state apparatus frequently have loyalties to the outgoing regime: Working in the authoritarian state was a moral choice made only by those who, in one way or another, accepted the authoritarian ideology and the lack of competitive democratic elections that would hold their political bosses accountable. Third, regardless of his or her ideological leanings, the autocrat's departure can be associated with "orphaned bureaucracies" (Ang 2019), which obviously contributes to the preference gap between the new democratic politicians and state apparatus staff members inherited from the previous

---

[12] However, Remmer (1990) shows how economic vulnerability is the consequence rather than the cause of democratization.

regime. "Orphaned" bureaucrats are also likely to be shirkers, though, as remarked above, I will not be modeling this feature.[13]

On the other hand, the bureaucrats of the *ancien régime* may be equipped in expertise that translates well into the conditions of the new democratic polity. In the words of Anna Grzymala-Busse (2002), they may have usable skills that new democratic politicians desperately need.

My framing of the purge problem as a principal–agent dilemma draws on models of delegation from the institutions literature in American and comparative politics (Bendor & Meirowitz 2004; Callander 2008; Epstein & O'Halloran 1999; Huber & Shipan 2002). The classical analysis of delegation was offered according to Bendor and Meirowitz (2004), by Alexander Hamilton, who defended transferring control from less-informed officials to more-informed agents in anticipation of the fact that because the latter are better informed, they will make better choices.[14]

Delegation models assume a single *principal* who can either act on his own or delegate authority over policy to another actor, referred to as the *agent*. The principal in the delegation literature is typically a legislature, and the agent is typically a bureaucrat who, equipped with expertise, can implement policy better suited to accommodate states of the world that are unfamiliar to the legislature. However, delegating policy authority to the bureaucrat comes at a risk, as he may use his expertise to move the ultimate policy outcome away from the legislature's ideal point; this is especially likely if the preferences of the legislature and the bureaucrat are misaligned. The delegation literature refers to this phenomenon as *bureaucratic drift* (Gehlbach 2013).

Building on this framing, I treat a purge as analogous to a refusal to delegate to possibly unfaithful agents. In doing so, I assume that the new democratic regime lacks expertise to implement policy as efficiently as employees of the *ancien régime*. Thus, even though the democratic successors know the policy outcomes they want, and I assume that this

---

[13] For a comprehensive treatment of bureaucracies that accounts for shirking and sabotage, see Brehm and Gates (1999).

[14] According to this traditional interpretation, expressed by Hamilton in Federalist No. 23, choosing optimal policies is state contingent. Since principals are oblivious to the true nature of the state, they are best served by delegating to agents who know the real state of the world.

policy corresponds to voter preferences, they cannot anticipate the policy distortions that arise at the time of implementation.

In Section 3.3.1, I illustrate the application of the delegation model to problem of purges using Gehlbach (2013)'s the standard presentation of the problem. I use the first two models from Chapter 5 of his *Formal Models of Domestic Politics*. In the first of the two models, the new democratic politician considers two options: to purge or not to purge. In the second model, which is an interpretation of Huber and Shipan (2002), the politician is able to set discretion limits for the old regime's administrative staff if he refrains from a purge. After adapting these two classical delegation models to the purge-specific context, I present a third (original) model, where I relax the assumption of perfect expertise on the part of the agent. Note that in this last model, I allow for the dissociation between loyalty (interpreted as preference alignment with the new democratic rulers) and expertise.

3.3.1 The Decision to Purge as a Simple Delegation Model

I begin with considering a one-dimensional policy space sketched out in Figure 3.1. The model features a Politician, P, with ideal point o, and a former enforcement Agency Officer, A, with ideal point $x_A \epsilon(\text{o}, 1)$. In the first stage, the Politician determines whether to conduct a purge. This action corresponds to the decision to delegate in the classic principal–agent framework. Conducting a purge is equivalent to *not delegating* power to the agent of the former authoritarian regime. Instead, the Politician can appoint a loyal antiauthoritarian dissident to implement policy. This loyal agent has no adequate expertise (though he shares preferences with the appointing politician), hence will implement policy with as much error as the Politician would himself. This loyalist, although an actor in the narrative is not a player in the series of games presented here. Alternatively, in an action corresponding to *delegation* from the classic model, the new democratic politician may choose to retain the staff of the authoritarian agency (this action is labeled as ∼ *Purge*). Following the Politician's decision, Nature determines the policy shock to be applied following the choice of policy. This shock corresponds to the inherent uncertainty under which policy decisions are being made in the transition aftermath. I represent this shock as $\omega \epsilon \{\varepsilon, -\varepsilon\}$. To keep things tractable,

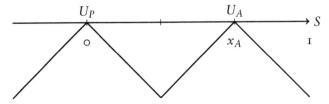

FIGURE 3.1. Issue space (S) and players' preferences

there are just two possible shocks: one negative and one positive. I will assume that either policy shock is equally likely: that is, $Pr(\omega = \varepsilon) = Pr(\omega = -\varepsilon) = \frac{1}{2}$. This policy shock is observed by the Agency Officer, but not by the Politician. In the third and terminal stage of the game, the Politician's loyalist (in the event of a purge) or the Agency Officer (in the event of refraining from a purge) chooses the policy.[15]

The preferences of the players are determined by the distance between their ideal points and the policy that is the final outcome of the game. This final outcome, x, is the joint product of the policy choice in the second stage and Nature's determination of the policy shock, according to the expression $x = p + \omega$. The strategies and preferences are defined formally in Appendix B, but the game tree in Figure 3.2 summarizes the players, strategies, and the timing of play. Recall that since the loyalist of the Politician shares identical policy preferences with the Politician and hence will have exactly the same best response as the Politician, I can model this as a game between just two players: the Politician and The Agency Officer.

Since this is a game of complete, albeit imperfect, information, the solution concept is Subgame Perfect Nash Equilibrium. The game tree representing the baseline model is presented as follows.

This game can be solved by backward induction. I first consider the right-hand side of the game tree. Note that since the Agency Officer observes ω, he can implement policy to "perfectly absorb" the exogenous

---

[15] As an extension of the model one could consider a case where the replacement officer appointed following a purge shares the Politician's preferences to a greater extent than the original Agency Officer from the authoritarian period, but their preferences do not overlap exactly. This extension would make purges somewhat less frequent but the general comparative statics of the model still hold.

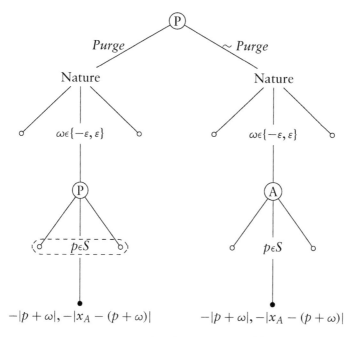

FIGURE 3.2. Baseline purges model

policy shock and bring the final outcome to his ideal point. That is, when the shock is positive, he chooses $p^* = x_a - \varepsilon$ and when it is negative, he chooses policy $p^* = x_A + \varepsilon$. In light of this, the politician's expected outcome from a leadership purge is $-x_A$.

Consider now the left-hand side of the game tree in Figure 3.2. Since the Politician cannot observe the policy shock, his best response, given the symmetry of ω, is $p = 0$. Note that actually any $p \epsilon [-\varepsilon, \varepsilon]$ is a best response; however, $p = 0$ is robust to changing the utility functions from "tent" to quadratic.[16] As a result, the expected utility to the Politician from purging is given by $-\varepsilon$.

In the left panel of Figure 3.3, I compare the realized policy outcome (in light grey) under the no purge scenario with the realized policy under the purge scenario (in black) as a function of the magnitude of the shock, ε.

The green line in the upper quadrant corresponds to the realized outcomes following a purge when the policy shock is positive (hence the increasing slope), while the light grey line in the lower quadrant corresponds to the negative policy shock scenario (hence the decreasing slope).

[16] Bendor and Meirowitz (2004) show that changing the players' preferences in this way does not change the end result of the analysis otherwise.

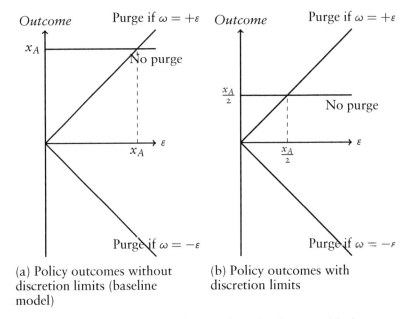

(a) Policy outcomes without discretion limits (baseline model)

(b) Policy outcomes with discretion limits

FIGURE 3.3. Policy outcomes in baseline and discretion limits model of purges

Both lines have nonzero slopes because when the Politician purges the former state apparatus of members of the *ancien régime*, the price he pays is proportional to the degree of uncertainty. Recall that the Politician is trying to minimize the distance between this realized policy and his ideal point, which is at o and so corresponds simply to the x-axis. The extent to which the final outcome departs from the Politician's ideal point increases, intuitively, with the size of the shock.

The outcome under the purge scenario, represented by the black line in Figure 3.3, corresponds to the realized outcome without a purge. This outcome does not depend on the value of ε. The two lines cross at the point where $\varepsilon = x_A$, implying that for values where ε is below x_A, the Politician is better off purging the administrative apparatus, but for $\varepsilon > x_A$, retaining the authoritarian administrative apparatus produces a policy closer to the Politician's ideal point.

Backward induction leads us immediately to the solution to this baseline model: The Politician will purge if $\varepsilon < x_A$ and refrain from doing so if $x_A \leq \varepsilon$. In other words, the Politician will refrain from conducting a purge when the uncertainty associated with the policy shock is greater than the preference divergence between the Politician and the Agency Officer. This result is merely an application of Bendor and Meirowitz (2004) to purges.

While the parameter x_A is easy to interpret as the divergence in preferences between the new democratic Politician and the Agent of the former authoritarian regime, the interpretation of ε is perhaps somewhat less intuitive. It is best thought of as a measure of uncertainty following democratic transitions Transitions that are more abrupt and lead to considerable economic, social, and political unpredictability can be interpreted as high ε environments, while smooth protracted transitions, offering more predictability, can be interpreted as low ε circumstances. Alternatively, one may think of ε as the ability of the new democracies to appoint and train new administrative staff. Along these lines, one could imagine a scenario where ε decreases over time, as newly trained and skilled bureaucratic staff becomes available.

3.3.2 Discretion Limits

The next model I consider not only allows the Politician to decide between purging and refraining to do so, but also allows him to set "discretion limits" if he chooses the latter. Discretion limits are interpreted as lower and upper bounds on where the Agency Officer may implement policy p. This allows the Politician to draw on the agent's expertise while also retaining some degree of control. Empirically, these can be directives on how a specific policy is to be implemented, what the chain of reporting and monitoring policy outcomes is supposed to be, or how far policy changes can reach. In their path-breaking book, Huber and Shipan (2002) operationalize discretionary limits with the number of words contained in each bill from a given jurisdiction. This operationalization relies on the assumption that less discretion implies more words.

It is important to note that whether discretionary limits can be imposed at all depends on the institutionalization of the new democratic regime, which in turn depends on the institutionalization of the *ancien régime*, a topic I model explicitly in Section 3.3.3.

Circumstances where discretion limits may be useful when a standard delegation model fails are easy to imagine. Consider any case where the preference divergence between the new democratic politician and outgoing administrative staff of the former regime is considerable, but where the staffers' expertise is so valuable that purging them could pose a dangerous threat to the new democracy. As an example, consider the decisions facing the postapartheid regime in South Africa. The preference of the outgoing apartheid regime and the ANC-led government clearly diverged. At the same time, with over thirty years of tenure, the South

African regime had trained and skilled bureaucrats who were no doubt better at implementing policies than any new workers would be. All these bureaucrats were white. Yet the African National Congress (ANC) refrained from purging them and instead attempted to set clear discretion limits to compel these agents not to exploit their knowledge to the new regime's disadvantage.

Had such tools of control been unavailable, the ANC government would have had to purge apartheid-era bureaucrats. Fears of such purges were reinforced by memories of Rhodesia, now Zimbabwe, and the "white flight" that followed purges and expropriations carried out there. (Southall 2020). Instead, the ANC proposed a gradual phasing out of old apartheid-era civil servants by implementing affirmative action programs with target dates for achieving certain quotas in representation of non-white ethnic groups (Naff & Capers 2014).

The first goal of solving this model is to see whether discretionary limits, when present, change the relationship between uncertainty (represented by ε) and preference divergence (represented by x_A) that was identified in the baseline model.

In this model, I retain all assumptions about players and preferences from the baseline. Hence, the Politician has an ideal point at 0, and the Agency Officer has an ideal point at x_A.

The strategy set of the Politician is modified to reflect that he sets the discretion limit when he forgoes a purge. However, given the preferences of the Politician and Agency Officer (at 0 and x_A, respectively), it is clear that there is no need for the Politician to set a lower bound for the discretion limits: The Agency Officer would never want to implement policy to the left of the Politician's ideal point. Since A's ideal point is to the right of that of P, he always prefers a realized policy at the Politician's ideal point to a policy at any point to the left of this ideal point. Thus, the left bound on the discretionary limits need not be set at all, and the action corresponding to the discretion limit can be represented by just one parameter, $r \in \Re^+$.

A direct consequence of imposing discretion limits is that the Agency Officer no longer has perfect shock absorption. In the model, this is represented by setting the discretion limit so that $r < x_A + \omega$. With this setting, the Agent can never achieve his ideal point, so the Politician may refrain from purging him without fearing that the policy will swing too far.

The game tree of this version of the model is provided in Figure B.1.

The reasoning behind finding the optimal discretion limit, r, can be summarized as follows: First, note that if P conducts a purge, the optimal policy is, as before, $p = 0$, with an expected payoff of $-\varepsilon$. If the Politician chooses to forgo a purge, he has to set the discretion limit, r, to maximize his utility. The solution to this version of the model is provided in Appendix B.2. Here, I focus on examining focal discretion limits such as $r = \varepsilon$. For this specific discretion limit, the Politician's expected utility is $-\frac{x_A}{2}$, as shown in the appendix.

To see that the discretion limit $r = \varepsilon$ is the unique best choice, consider two possibilities: (1) that r is set higher than ε, and (2) that it is set lower than ε.

If the discretion limit is set higher, to some $r = \varepsilon + \delta$, A would have to set policy to $min\{\varepsilon + \delta, x_A + \varepsilon\}$ for $\omega = -\varepsilon$ and to $min\{\varepsilon + \delta, x_A - \varepsilon\}$ for $\omega = \varepsilon$. This would result in P's expected utility $-\frac{x_A + \delta}{2}$. If, on the other hand, the discretion limit is set lower, to some $r = \varepsilon - \delta$, A would propose $p = min\{\varepsilon - \delta, x_A + \varepsilon\}$ for $\omega = -\varepsilon$ and $p = min\{\varepsilon - \delta, x_A - \varepsilon\}$ for $\omega = \varepsilon$, leading to P's expected utility $-\frac{\delta}{2} - \frac{x_A}{2}$.

Since in both cases, P's utility is lower than in the instance where $r = \varepsilon$, I conclude that the Politician's optimal discretion limit is $r = \varepsilon$. P's expected utility with this discretion limit leads to the conclusion that P will forgo a purge as long as $x_A < 2\varepsilon$. This result can be contrasted with the baseline model. It is clear that when the Politician can set discretion limits, he will stop short of a purge even if the administrative apparatus inherited from the *ancien régime* diverges in its preferences from those of the Politician twice as much as in the baseline model (where discretion limits were not available).

The rationale behind P's choice is captured in Figure 3.3, where the light grey line corresponds to the expected outcome from Purge and the black line to the expected outcome from no Purge. As soon as ε exceeds $\frac{x_A}{2}$, no Purge generates higher utility for the Politician. To see this, note that given the Politician's ideal point at zero and the fact that the utility function is the negative absolute value of the distance between the ideal point and the policy outcome, we only need to focus on comparing the upper light grey line to the black line. The left panel of Figure 3.3 allows for a direct comparison of the model with discretion limits to the model without. In the panel on the right, the light grey and black lines intersect for lower outcomes than in the panel on the left. It is clear that discretion limits allow politicians to refrain from purges in a wider spectrum of situations – including even those that are not characterized by much uncertainty – than when implementation of discretion limits is not feasible.

3.3.3 Modeling the Value of Expertise

The purge models presented in Sections 3.3.1 and 3.3.3 both assume that the Agency Officer of the *ancien régime* has complete and perfect expertise in the sense that he can always (in the model from section 3.3.2, when given the sufficient discretion) move the outcome exactly to his ideal point. In this section, I relax this assumption and instead allow the expertise of the agent to vary. This reflects the fact that not all autocrats institutionalize their regimes and offer their agents the opportunity to become skilled professionals whether at state administration or law enforcement. Such institutionalization includes creating tenure in the state administration, offering clear paths of advancement within the ranks of law enforcement organizations, and attracting the most talented and skilled professionals by offering attractive wages, job security, or both.

In order to formalize the expertise that the Agency Officer has to offer, I will relax the assumption that the Agency Officer gets to perfectly observe the exogenous shock. Note that in some circumstances in the model with discretionary limits, A does not get to implement the policy that would completely absorb the distortion stemming from the move of Nature. Now, I will assume that instead of observing the direction of the exogenous shock perfectly, the Agency Officer receives a signal of the shock; this signal can be of high or low quality. When the signal reflects the true nature of the policy shock, the Agency Officer is better able to absorb the shock and bring policy toward his ideal point; when it does not, he cannot absorb the shock as well. This is an intuitive way of modeling expertise: Bureaucrats with poor expertise are often thought of as bad when it comes to "reading signals" from their area of specialization.

Where do employees of the *ancien régime*'s state apparatus acquire expertise? In other words, what determines whether they have better or worse capacity for shock absorption? A natural interpretation would be the level of institutionalization of the previous authoritarian regime. As Rauch and Evans (2000) point out, regimes, including authoritarian ones, vary considerably in the extent to which their bureaucracies rely on meritocratic recruitment and internal promotion instead of on nepotistic appointments and the promotion of agents for loyalty as opposed to skills.

Herein lies the main departure of my model from existing models that extend the traditional approach described in Section 3.3, such as those of Huber and McCarty (2004) and Bendor and Meirowitz (2004). Huber and McCarty (2004) allow for agents to have imperfect expertise, but model it as additional noise, μ, that accompanies the policy implementation by the agent. As the magnitude of this noise goes to zero (representing an agency better skilled at policy implementation), the condition for delegation reduces to the one from the baseline model. Correspondingly, as μ increases, any benefits from delegation become outweighed by the uncertain performance of the agent. Translating these insights to the case of purges would mean that even though no purge has taken place, the agent of the *ancien régime* can still make mistakes in his implementation of policy, and his capacity to overcome these mistakes is reflected in μ. The question then becomes: When does the new democratic politician retain a low-capacity agent of the *ancien régime*? The answer boils down to the severity of the trade-off between the divergence in preferences between the new and old regime and the capacity of the former bureaucrats in the new regime.

An alternative approach to modeling bureaucratic capacity or expertise is to introduce uncertainty to the way that the signal about the exogenous shock is transmitted. This is the approach of Bendor and Meirowitz (2004), who assume that with a certain probability, π, the Agency Officer receives a perfectly informative signal of the value of the random shock, ω, and with probability $1 - \pi$ the agency receives a perfectly uninformative signal, adding nothing at all to what the principal already knew. After solving this model, the authors find that the original trade-off between preference divergence is directly proportional to the informativeness of the signal; that is:

$$\pi \varepsilon^2 > x_A^2 \qquad (3.1)$$

Next, Bendor and Meirowitz (2004) go on to model π as an endogenous choice of the agent. In a democratic context, this is a very sensible extension, as it is indeed up to the bureaucrats themselves to determine whether or not to acquire expertise. *Extending this to the context of post-authoritarian purges, where all the expertise was either acquired in the past or not at all is problematic however* Another sensible alteration is to change the signaling technology to reflect the fact that expertise can vary on a continuum and need not be symmetric with regard to detecting positive or negative signals.

Building on Bendor and Meirowitz's contributions to modeling signals as noisy, the new institutionalization parameter that I introduce here will allow me to account for the fact that the expertise of the agent is highest (that is, the probability of a correct signal is much higher than the probability of an incorrect signal) when the preceding authoritarian regime was highly institutionalized, and lowest when the preceding authoritarian regime was poorly institutionalized.

Specifically, define $Pr(s = i | \omega = j)$ as the probability that A receives a signal i when the policy shock is j, $\forall i, j \epsilon \{-\varepsilon, \varepsilon\}$.

Consequently,

$Pr(\varepsilon | \varepsilon)$ is the probability that the signal the officer receives is high when the policy shock is indeed positive (correct signal).

$Pr(-\varepsilon | \varepsilon)$ is the probability that the signal the officer receives is low when the policy shock is positive (incorrect signal).

$Pr(-\varepsilon | -\varepsilon)$ is the probability that the signal the officer receives is low when the policy shock is indeed negative (correct signal).

$Pr(\varepsilon | -\varepsilon)$ is the probability that the signal the officer receives is high when the policy shock is negative (incorrect signal).

Next, I assume that $\forall i, j \epsilon \{\varepsilon, -\varepsilon\}$:

1. $Pr(i|j) \epsilon (0, 1)$.
2. $Pr(i|i) + Pr(j|i)) = 1$.
3. $Pr(i|i) > Pr(j|i)$.

These three conditions formalize intuitive expectations. Condition 1 states that there is no perfectly correct or perfectly incorrect signal. Condition 2 states that given a policy shock, either a low or high signal must be issued. Condition 3 states that the signals are not perverse. That is, the probability of an incorrect signal for a given policy shock is never higher than the probability of a correct signal.

The probabilities defined are next used to introduce the institutionalization parameter, s as follows:

$$s = \frac{Pr(-\varepsilon | \varepsilon)}{Pr(\varepsilon | \varepsilon)} = \frac{Pr(\varepsilon | -\varepsilon)}{Pr(-\varepsilon | -\varepsilon)} \tag{3.2}$$

Therefore, $s = 0$ when A never receives an incorrect signal (perfectly informative), and $s = 1$ when the likelihood of a correct and incorrect signal is equal (no information). I bind s between 0 and 1 so that the signal is always imperfectly informative.

The parameter $s \epsilon (0, 1)$, where 1 represents the least possible expertise and 0 represents the highest possible expertise, represents the institutionalization of the *ancien régime*. The parameter s is related to the precision with which the Agency Officer can read the signal that the policy shock was ε and not $-\varepsilon$ so that the probability of a correct signal is greater than $\frac{1}{2}$.

After observing s, the Politician decides whether to implement a purge. In the event of a purge, he is forced to implement policy by himself without knowing if the policy shock will be positive or negative. As in the two previous models, he implements his ideal point, o. As a result, his expected utility from a purge is $-\varepsilon$. On the other hand, if P decides to forgo a purge, then the Agency Officer gets to observe an informative signal about the quality of the shock. As explained earlier, the informativeness of this signal is determined by the institutionalization parameter, s, as follows: $P(\varepsilon)$ represents a signal that the policy shock is high, and $P(-\varepsilon)$ represents a signal that the policy shock is low. After observing the signal, but not the shock, the officer decides which policy to adopt. Since his decision is contingent on the kind of signal he received, two actions are needed to define his strategy. p represents his action when the signal is high (that is, the policy shock, ω, is equal to ε), while q represents his action when the signal is low (that is, the policy shock, ω, is equal to $-\varepsilon$).

Preferences could be Euclidean. However, for ease of solving maximization problems, I switch the players to quadratic preferences; that is, the Agent's payoff is given by:

$$U_A(s;p,q) = \begin{cases} -(x_A - (p+\omega))^2 & \text{if signal is } \varepsilon \\ -(x_A - (q+\omega))^2 & \text{if signal is } -\varepsilon. \end{cases}$$

The Politician's payoff is defined analogously but for a corresponding ideal point of o:

$$U_P(s;p,q) = -(p+\omega)^2.$$

The strategy sets of both the Politician and Agency Officer are defined in Appendix B.3, but they can also be easily gleaned from inspecting the game tree in Figure 3.4.

Note that in keeping with convention, moves of Nature take place in the beginning of the game; the sequence of the game has the Politician moving directly after Nature's determination of the shock, ω. The game tree is accurate – note that all four nodes at which the Politician moves are in the same four-element information set. The Agency Officer knows s but does not know the realization of ω.

Although this is a game of imperfect information,[17] there is no updating of beliefs of players based on actions of other players. Thus, the solution concept is Subgame Perfect Equilibrium. As before, the game can be

---

[17] The Politician determines whether to purge in conditions of uncertainty.

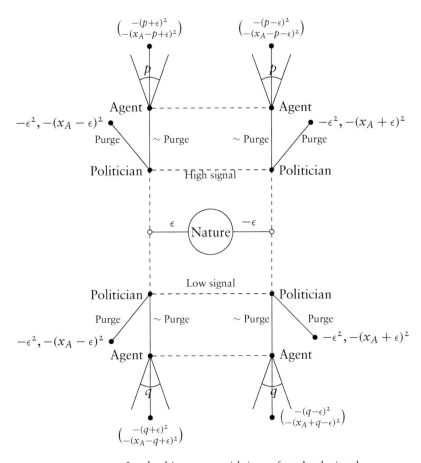

FIGURE 3.4. Leadership purges with imperfect shock signals

solved by backward induction. In the appendix, I first calculate the optimal strategy of the Agency Officer as a function of s, x_A, and ϵ, and then show the circumstances under which the Politician prefers implementing a purge over refraining from one. The optimal policy choices p^* and q^* are given by:

$$p^* = x_A - \frac{\epsilon(1-s)}{1+s}, q^* = x_A + \frac{\epsilon(1-s)}{1+s}. \quad (3.3)$$

Table 3.1 shows the Agent's best responses in terms of p^* and q^* if the Politician refrains from a purge for four hypothetical values of s. Recall that in the event of a purge, the policy outcome will always be $-\varepsilon$ when the realization of ω is low and ε when the realization of ω is high.

TABLE 3.1. *Equilibrium policy outcome as a function of s*

Institutionalization	$BR_A(s) = p^*$	q^*	Outcome when $\omega = \varepsilon$	Outcome when $\omega = -\varepsilon$
$s = 0$	$x_A - \varepsilon$	$x_A + \varepsilon$	$\frac{x_A - \varepsilon}{2}$	$\frac{x_A + \varepsilon}{2}$
$s = \frac{1}{4}$	$x_A - \frac{3}{5}\varepsilon$	$x_A + \frac{3}{5}\varepsilon$	$x_A - \frac{4}{5}\varepsilon$	$x_A + \frac{4}{5}\varepsilon$
$s = \frac{1}{2}$	$x_A - \frac{1}{3}\varepsilon$	$x_A + \frac{1}{3}\varepsilon$	$x_A - \frac{8}{9}\varepsilon$	$x_A + \frac{8}{9}\varepsilon$
$s = \frac{3}{4}$	$x_A - \frac{1}{7}\varepsilon$	$x_A + \frac{1}{7}\varepsilon$	$x_A - \frac{48}{49}\varepsilon$	$x_A + \frac{48}{49}\varepsilon$

Building on the formulas used to produce this table, the Politician's utilities from deciding to purge or not can be calculated and compared. Notice that given the Politician's ideal point is o, the utility from refraining from a purge can be calculated as:

$$EU_P(\sim P, \omega = \varepsilon) = -\left(x_A - \frac{\varepsilon(1-s)}{1+s} + \varepsilon\right)^2 \frac{1}{s+1}$$
$$- \left(x_A + \frac{\varepsilon(1-s)}{(1+s)} + \varepsilon\right)^2 \frac{s}{s+1}, \quad (3.4)$$

when the shock is positive, and

$$EU_P(\sim P, \omega = -\varepsilon) = -\left(x_A - \frac{\varepsilon(1-s)}{1+s} - \varepsilon\right)^2 \frac{s}{s+1}$$
$$- \left(x_A + \frac{\varepsilon(1-s)}{(1+s)} - \varepsilon\right)^2 \frac{1}{s+1}, \quad (3.5)$$

when the shock is negative. Because the shock is negative half of the time and positive half of the time, the Politician will prefer to refrain from a purge when:

$$\frac{EU_P(L; p^*, q^*; \omega = \varepsilon)}{2} + \frac{EU_P(L; p^*, q^*; \omega = -\varepsilon)}{2} > -\varepsilon^2, \quad (3.6)$$

or

$$\left(x_A - \frac{\varepsilon(1-s)}{1+s} + \varepsilon\right)^2 \frac{1}{s+1} - \left(x_A + \frac{\varepsilon(1-s)}{(1+s)} + \varepsilon\right)^2 \frac{s}{s+1}$$
$$+ \left(x_A - \frac{\varepsilon(1-s)}{1+s} - \varepsilon\right)^2 \frac{s}{s+1} - \left(x_A + \frac{\varepsilon(1-s)}{(1+s)} - \varepsilon\right)^2 \frac{1}{s+1} < 2\varepsilon^2$$
$$(3.7)$$

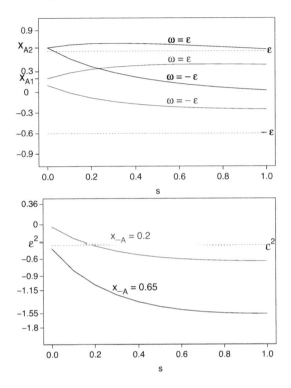

FIGURE 3.5. Policy outcomes (top) and payoffs to the Politician (bottom), resulting from purges and non-purges

The decision of when it is beneficial to refrain from purges is presented graphically as a function of s in Figure 3.5. Figure 3.5 illustrates the expected policy outcome (top panel) as well as the Politician's utility outcome (bottom panel) as a function of s.

Consider first the top side panel. The "whiskers" shaped lines originate at two different values of the parameter x_A: $x_{A1} = .2$ and $x_{A2} = .65$, which correspond to Agency Officers gime with very distant (x_{A2}) and very proximate (x_{A1}) preferences to the politician. Since I set $\varepsilon = .6$, x_{A1} has been chosen so the preference divergence is lower than the exogenous policy shock, while x_{A2} has been chosen so the preference divergence is higher than the policy shock.

The top line for each case reflects the policy outcome, following a purge in the event that the shock is positive; the bottom line reflects the policy outcome following a negative shock. The dashed gray lines represent the policy outcomes associated with no purge (recall that the optimal strategy of the Politician's loyalist agent when he forgoes a purge is to implement policy at his ideal point). We see that in the case of divergent preferences, the policy associated with forgoing a purge is better for the Politician only if the shock is positive (see the top set of "whiskers"). When preferences are aligned more closely, a purge is worse for the politician regardless of the direction of the shock. Using these two cases and simply looking at the policy outcomes does not suggest that the optimal decision of the politician depends on s.

Recall, however, that the Politician does not observe the shock direction. For this reason, to illustrate the Politician's optimal decision, I turn to the bottom panel of Figure 3.5, which compares the utility associated with both actions for the exact same values of the Agency Officer's ideal point, $x_{A1} = .2$ and $x_{A2} = .65$. The payoff from purging is represented by the grey dashed line at $\varepsilon^2 = .36$. The picture that emerged from this analysis is more nuanced. First, for divergent preferences, a purge is always associated with higher utility. This is clear from the fact that the grey dashed line is always above the bottom line (corresponding to $x_A = .65$). For the case of proximate preferences ($x_A = .2$), however, the action associated with the higher payoff depends on the insitutionalization parameter, s: For low levels of s, corresponding to high levels of institutionalization, the Politician is better off refraining from a purge and harnessing to his advantage the skills of the *ancien régime*'s administrative apparatus. Yet, as the level of institutionalization decreases, the benefit from forgoing a purge declines and at some intermediary level of s, the Politician is better off purging the *ancien régime*. The exact level of institutionalization at which a purge is more beneficial than retaining members of the former regime is the intersection of the top line and the dashed line. This is the point that solves:

$$x_A = \frac{\varepsilon(1-s)^2}{(1+s)^2}, \tag{3.8}$$

or equivalently:

$$s = \frac{\varepsilon^{\frac{1}{2}} - x_A^{\frac{1}{2}}}{x_A^{\frac{1}{2}} + \varepsilon^{\frac{1}{2}}}. \tag{3.9}$$

Intuitively, for low levels of professionalization, the benefits of retaining the previous regime's employees – even those with preferences that are proximate to those of the new democratic politician – are outweighed by a purge. With little expertise to offer, workers of the *ancien régime* cannot count on keeping their employment.

3.4 DISCUSSION AND COMPARATIVE STATICS

The solution to the model with imperfect expertise implies that when the shock is positive (a factor that the Politician cannot anticipate ex ante) and when s is lower (corresponding to a highly institutionalized prior regime), refraining from a purge is better than purging. Yet, when the shock is positive but s is higher (corresponding to low institutionalization of the prior regime), purging may be better. It is also clear from the top line in the bottom panel of Figure 3.5 that decreasing the magnitude of the shock, ε, moves the point where the dashed line (corresponding to expected payoff under purge) and the solid line (corresponding to the expected payoff under no purge) cross to the left, requiring more institutionalization before forgoing a purge is better. If uncertainty over the shock is lowered, making policy decisions without any expertise at all should be cheaper.

Recall that the empirical interpretation of s is that the expertise of the agent is highest (the probability of a correct signal is much higher than the probability of an incorrect signal) when the preceding authoritarian regime was highly institutionalized and lowest when the preceding authoritarian regime was poorly institutionalized. This allows me to formulate expectations about the causes of purges on the one hand and their consequences on the other.

First, I expect that following highly institutionalized authoritarian regimes, politicians should refrain from purges. This is because the substantial expertise of agents of the former regime is likely to help them choose policies that absorb the kinds of exogenous shocks that plague regime transitions. Forgoing any type of purge altogether should improve the quality of democratic outcomes relative to those in countries that undertake purges when institutionalization is high.

On the other hand, following poorly institutionalized environments, forgoing purges is detrimental to the quality of democracy. Agents with low expertise are just as bad at correcting for policy shocks as the new politicians themselves, but instead try to reach their own successor-authoritarian ideal point. Hence, a purge should bring about a better quality of democracy than doing nothing at all.

In a nutshell, the effects of both kinds of purges depend heavily on the degree to which the previous authoritarian regime was institutionalized. This is because institutionalization translates into higher levels of expertise among former agents of authoritarian agencies. Purging bureaucrats and officers equipped with skills that can be used for managing the new democratic regime (Hicken & Martínez Kuhonta 2011) will likely sabotage policies of the new democracy and weaken the quality of representation.

In contrast, a poorly institutionalized authoritarian regime is staffed with agents whose level of expertise is too low to warrant trading off their potential to skew policy outcomes for precision of implementation; increased purging in formerly under-institutionalized regimes should lead to improving the quality of democracy. These effects ought to be more prominent in the case of thorough purges than in that of leadership purges because in the former, entire agencies are being disbanded.

These empirical implications will be illustrated with data from the Global Transitional Justice Dataset in Chapter 7. The remainder of this chapter is devoted to several case study illustrations of this argument using the archetypal countries of this book.

3.5 ILLUSTRATIVE EXAMPLES

The subject of Chapter 3 has been dealing with known or open collaborators. Since purges are the reverse of a delegation problem, I showed that under most circumstances, the severity of purges does not have a monotonic effect on the quality of representation. In fact, whether purges work at all depends on three factors. The first is how distant the preferences of the former authoritarian elites are from the preferences of new democratic politicians (preference divergence). The second critical factor is the magnitude of the exogenous shock that the new democratic politician faces when implementing policy. To some extent, every post-transition environment is riddled with uncertainties, so we may be tempted to ignore this parameter and assume that ε is always large. However, I will distinguish between polities where these conditions are more acute because the transition took the form of a revolution (such as Tunisia) and those where the transition was negotiated over many months or years (such as Poland or South Africa). I argue that in the latter, the shock is smaller.

TABLE 3.2. *Model's predictions of whether a purge is expected following the transition as a function of uncertainty (ε), preference divergence (x_A), and institutionalization (s)*

Institutionalized			~ Institutionalized		
Uncertainty	$x_A \to \circ$	$x_A \gg \circ$	Uncertainty	$x_A \to \circ$	$x_A \gg \circ$
ε high	~ Purge	Possibly purge	ε high	Either	Definitely purge
ε low	~ Purge	Probably purge	ε low	Possibly purge	Purge

Finally, the third determinant of when politicians delegate is institutionalization of the former authoritarian regime's enforcement and bureaucratic apparatus.

The predictions from this chapter on whether purges are feasible are summarized in Table 3.2.

Several caveats are in order here. First, these are clearly not normative predictions, but rather predictions of what a new democratic politician motivated by bringing policy as close to his ideal point as possible would do. For instance, newly elected democratic politicians in South Africa or other post-authoritarian countries may feel compelled to address normative pressures from the public and fire apartheid-era officers even if their replacements do not have a fraction of their expertise. After all, the essence of purges is that they deal with *known* members and collaborators of the *ancien régime*. Hence, it is to be expected that purges for normative reasons and in response to pressure from public opinion will be implemented in contexts diverging from these predictions.

Second, some of the parameters modifying our expectations regarding purges are harder to measure than others. Proximity of preferences between the outgoing regime's administration and the new democratic politicians is hard to approximate for at least two reasons. First, these ideal points cannot be recovered from expert surveys or roll call votes because they are nested within authoritarian regimes that have ended. Second, even in contemporary democratic regimes, political scientists lack routines for placing bureaucrats on policy dimensions. Assessing uncertainty, or the magnitude of the shock, is similarly difficult.[18] The length

---

[18] A final statistical consideration, as I explain in Chapter 7, is that this divergence between outgoing autocrats and incoming democrats is not easily measured over time;

TABLE 3.3. *Predictions of whether a purge is expected following the transition as a function of uncertainty (ε), preference divergence (x_A), and professionalization, (s): application to archetypal cases*

Institutionalized			$\sim$ Institutionalized		
Uncertainty	$x_A \to \circ$	$x_A \gg \circ$	Uncertainty	$x_A \to \circ$	$x_A \gg \circ$
ε high	S. Korea (other military)	S. Korea (Hanahoe)	ε high	Tunisia (military)	Tunisia (secret police)
ε low	Poland	S. Africa	ε low	Spain	Bolivia

and abruptness of the democratic transition can offer some approximation, but such evaluations can at most be conducted for a handful of cases. It is much easier to use existing data to evaluate the level of professionalization or institutionalization of the *ancien régime*, as I will elaborate on in Chapter 7. One can also use knowledge of specific country cases to populate Table 3.2 with illustrative examples. Below, in Table 3.3, I do so for the archetypal cases discussed in this book as follows:

The distribution of the cases across the uncertainty dimension matches the length of their transitions. The level of institutionalization for this handful of cases is based on my reading of secondary sources. Following these sources, in the first two cases, I split dealing with the enforcement apparatus into dealing with the army and the police forces.

Tunisia

According to Masri (2017) and Perkins (2014), the Tunisian military refused to carry out Ben Ali's orders in defense of the regime. In addition, the military had been historically weak. Masri calls Tunisia an "Arab anomaly" in part due to the fact that labor unions in the country had traditionally been strong, while the military had been chronically under-institutionalized. Hence, the Tunisian military can plausibly be assigned to the cell with aligned preferences ($x_A \to \circ$) and very low professionalization. Yet, even within Tunisian enforcement agencies, there are differences in institutionalization. The secret police resembled a praetorian guard and was, in contrast to the military, very loyal to Ben Ali, though equally lacking in expertise when it comes to effective quelling of the opposition. At the same time, the transition in Tunisia was

consequently, controlling for these conditions can only be done within random effects models. In the fixed effects framework, country effects include any potential constant characteristics of different units.

so rapid that it seems justified to evaluate the level of uncertainty to be high. As I described in Chapter 1 and demonstrated in Figure 1.3, Tunisia was indeed a country with a high intensity of purge activity even though it has only been a democracy for six years in the GTJD.

South Korea

Another country where disaggregating agencies of the *ancien régime* seems justified for the purpose of our analysis is South Korea. Chung Hee Park, during his eighteen-year rule, created two parallel career tracks within the military, with separate but credible rules of advancement and promotion. The first were the armed forces, whose main goal was deterring North Korea. The second arm included the security forces who, in the words of Joo-Hong Kim, "traded honor and prestige for power" (Baik 2011, p.171). The latter branch's promotion path was slower, but its members were argued to have more influence on domestic politics and acted as Park's personal militia in addition to providing him with much needed security. Park would ultimately authorize all promotions himself.

Following the transition, Korea's TJ focused on truth commissions, as illustrated in Figure 1.3. However, March 8, 1993 saw the beginning of a thorough purge of the so-called, Hanahoe group (the "Group of one"), an unofficial private group of military officers whose members were graduates of the eleventh class of the Korean Military Academy of 1955. The Hanahoe had maintained great influence in the security branch of Park's military, as Park himself was a graduate of that class. Had the organization been left intact, it would have remained a bulwark of authoritarian influence. Key members of Hanahoe were forced into retirement, but in addition to this, in January of 1994, the National Assembly revised the laws on major intelligence agencies, forcing the Agency for National Security Planning (the equivalent of South Korea's CIA) and the Military Security Command to limit political influence. This was accomplished by placing both the military and the security apparatus under congressional oversight (Sang-Hun 2015). The thorough purge of the Hanahoe group is consistent with the predictions from Table 3.2.

South Africa

South Africa's state administration was professionalized but was also restricted under the apartheid to Afrikaners, resulting in a high degree of preference divergence between the enforcement agents and bureaucrats of the apartheid regime and the ANC democratic government. Despite this misalignment of preferences, uncertainty associated with the transition was quite low due to the protracted nature of the transition to democracy. More than five years prior to the signing of the transition pact, the leadership of the apartheid regime had come to the realization that "brute force could keep the Afrikaner in power until the next century, but it was not worth the cost in economic development"(Waldmeir 1997, p.53). With the Cold War's end, the international community's attention turned to sanctioning states violating human rights regardless of whether they claimed to be protecting the world from communism, as the apartheid frequently did (Price 1991). Yet taken together, Figure 3.5 and Table 3.3 implies that South Africa should have conducted purges. At the same time, wide-scale purges were complicated by school boycotts, which had become one of the main forms of protest against the apartheid regime. Consequently, the ANC did not have a well-trained bureaucratic elite ready to replace that of the apartheid regime. Indeed, there were no purges at all in the aftermath of the transition in South Africa. Instead, the country invested all of its resources in an extensive transparency regime. The unfolding of events leading to the creation and functioning of the Truth and Reconciliation Commission (including its hearings and final report) are illustrated in Figure 1.3 in Chapter 1. I discuss this mechanism in greater detail in Chapter 6.

Poland

Much has been already said in this chapter about Poland. The gradual transition means that the ε representing uncertainty was low. Preference divergence between the communist agents of enforcement and bureaucrats and the incoming democrats (former dissidents) was also low: Only several months before the democratic transition, the democratic dissidents had negotiated terms of the democratic turnover with members of the communist authorities, who included the military and secret police chiefs (hence, $x_A \to 0$). Given the sheer degree of centralization of the communist regimes, especially the highly professionalized and centralized military and law enforcement apparatus, Poland should be placed in the lower left cell of the left-hand side of table 3.3. According to predictions from Table 3.2, given these parameter values, Poland should have refrained from purging. In fact, it went down a path of purging half way (see Figure 1.3 from Chapter 1, where both the level of thorough and leadership purges is at 5). The instance of secret police purging described in the introduction to this chapter was probably the most severe of all purges that were conducted in this country, with many of the former agents permitted to continue in their positions. This outcome is partially consistent with our expectations summarized in Table 3.2. In light of the fact that only nine years before the transition to democracy, the repressive apparatus implemented a Martial Law regime, the preferences of the enforcement apparatus and new democratic rulers could be interpreted as quite divergent, which could explain the imperfect match.

Spain

Spain presents a complicated case because, as described in Chapter 1, the Pact of Forgetting blocked the possibility for TJ. It is also complicated by the nature of the Franco dictatorship itself, which offered some members of the state administration vast autonomy.[19] At the same time, however, Payne writes that almost up to his death, Franco personally met with members of his cabinet and prided himself on "not trusting anyone." This attitude of *trusting but controlling*[20] is clearly illustrated in a comment of Salgado Arawjo (who was also a member of Franco's inner circle): "Surely, His Excellency does not want to have ministers with independent personalities who could create difficulties" (Payne 2011, p. 399). It would similarly be tempting to refer to Spain's military as professionalized by virtue of the fact that Franco himself was a military general. Nevertheless, beginning with his victory over Republicans in the civil war and throughout World War II and its aftermath, the military's budget steadily declined (the percentage of the budget devoted to the military decreased between 1940 and 1945 from 41 percent to 34 percent). According to Payne, this led to the marginalization of, at first, the junta and later, the broader military. According to Payne (2011), "during the first phase of the regime before 1945, military personnel would hold 45.9 percent of the ministerial appointments and 36.8 percent of all government positions" (p. 236). By 1974, the percentage of the military in the top state administration was down to 15.8 percent.

---

[19] According to Payne (2011, p. 398), "cabinet ministers and principal subordinates were almost always given great latitude in running their departments" and backs this with a quote from one of his former ministers, Lequerica, "being a cabinet minister is the only serious thing you can be in Spain. To be a minister of Franco is to be a little king."

[20] A maxim attributed to Lenin.

In light of these considerations, I classify Spain under Franco as an under-institutionalized authoritarian regime. This classification is in line with the criteria put forward by recent research on authoritarian institutionalization from Anne Meng (2020). Meng uses as one criterion of institutionalization whether the regime managed to outlive its founding leader. Despite Franco's best efforts to nominate a successor who could lead Spain under Franco's constitution beyond his death, the generalissimo failed at this task, as King Juan Carlos initiated transition negotiations promptly following Franco's death.

Bolivia

Finally, I consider the low TJ case of Bolivia. Bolivia had an abrupt transition, as the dictator wielding the longest period of dictatorship, Rene Barientos, died while in office. However the transitions between successive regimes showed remarkable continuity (Malloy & Gamarra 1988). Hence, I determine the uncertainty at the time of transition to be low. The military (US-funded, similarly to the South Korean military) lagged behind it in military success. Its only claim to fame was the assassination of Ché Guevara, the Cuban secret police chief and revolutionary. Moreover, what kept Barientos in power was a pact between the peasant movement and military against the urban trade unions, suggesting that the military would not be able to survive on its own. After considering all these factors, the Bolivian case is classified as one of low institutionalization. As Figure 1.3 indicates, there were practically no purges in Bolivia – or for that matter any kind of TJ – following the transition to democracy. This too is consistent with the predictions from Table 3.2.

3.6 CONCLUSION

This chapter has discussed purges as a personnel TJ mechanism that functions differently from lustration and produces different effects for the quality of democratic representation. Building on existing models of delegation, I developed a nuanced theory of purges that showed that the very feasibility of purges in the aftermath of a transition to democracy depends on the uncertainty associated with policy implementation, the loyalty of former agents to the *ancien régime*, and the past regime's institutionalization. The empirical implications of this model led to several hypotheses about the relationship between purges and the quality of democratic representation. Specifically, the effects of purges depend heavily on the degree to which the previous authoritarian regime was institutionalized, which has implications for the expertise that former authoritarian agents can offer the new democratic politicians. To the extent that this expertise is usable in the new democratic context (Grzymala-Busse 2002), purging these agents will come at a cost to the new democracy and negatively affect indicators of democratic quality. In contrast, under-institutionalized authoritarian regimes lack experts. Purging their bureaucracies and law enforcement apparatuses should lead to improving the quality of democracy.

Although the models presented here make an argument against purges that relies on the information deficit created by the departure of agents of the state, one can easily construct other reasons for which carrying out purges is risky for a new democracy. One reason is suggested by the illustrative case from Section 3.2, which describes how former Stasi officers found permanent employment in Martin Schlaff's holdings and engaged in money laundering and tax evasion operations across Europe. The film *Psy* by Wladyslaw Pasikowski, which provided the opening quote for this book, illustrates an even more gruesome dynamic from Poland: some of the fired SB officers joined organized crime groups, where their former bosses had already established themselves in leadership positions and engaged in trafficking weapons, drugs, and humans. This effect of thorough purges – forcing rank-and-file law enforcement agents to seek employment with their former bosses – is akin to the dynamic described by Ben Lessing in an article devoted to the unintended consequences of mass incarceration (Lessing 2017). According to Lessing's argument, the inevitability or close inevitability of being confronted with the gang's leader in prison makes rank and file gang members more likely to obey the orders of prison gangs when they are still on "the outside." The parallel argument for the case of purges would run as follows: depriving rank and file secret police officers of legal employment in the enforcement apparatus of the new democratic state forces them to seek employment with their former leading officers outside of the state's official agencies. Consequently, a thorough purge pushes former secret police officers with usable skills into organized crime led by former leaders of the secret political police.

The Tunisian example offers further illustrations of this phenomenon. According to Bouguerra (2014), purges of the Tunisian political police foreshadowed fears of international terrorism. Would the agency and its brand new staff be capable of robust counterterrorism and counter-extremism measures? Already in October 2014, the Harriri Center for the Middle East of the Atlantic Council feared that "the weakened state of the Tunisian government following the revolution, combined with the general amnesty decree and political polarization between secularists and Islamists, allowed for a resurgence of jihadist groups." The thousands of casualties that have since resulted from terrorist attacks (Masri 2017) and the vastly successful ISIS recruitment campaign carried out on Tunisian soil, illustrate the unintended consequences purges can have on crime.

CONCLUSION TO PART I

The main argument presented in this book thus far can be summarized in two points:

First, revealing the truth about collaboration, and the associated bans on holding public office imposed on secret collaborators, can have a different effect than punishing former elites and perpetrators of human rights whose collaboration in the old regime is known. In a world without lustration, *unknown* collaborators of the authoritarian regime (or perpetrators who committed atrocities on its behalf in secret) can be blackmailed with "skeletons in the closet". As long as the public still pays attention to what happened in the past, the revelation of such skeletons can terminate political careers. In return for their silence, individuals in possession of credible evidence of skeletons in the closet can demand rents or policy concessions. The possibility of such blackmail reduces the quality of democracy. In light of this dynamic, I expect transparency regimes to enhance the quality of democracy more consistently than purges – that is, personnel TJ procedures that sanction known forms of collaboration.

Second, the mechanism behind the vetting of *known* collaborators – which I define as purges – is different. Purges reveal no new information. In fact, purging state institutions of elites who maintained the former authoritarian regime, when this purging reaches a sufficient depth, can be conceptualized as the reverse of a delegation problem. If a newly elected politician takes office and vets the administrative apparatus so thoroughly that he removes all bureaucrats with policy expertise, he has to delegate implementing policy in the inherently uncertain conditions of a post-transition environment to untrained amateurs. Without the expertise of the people who ran the agencies under the *ancien régime*, he cannot know how policy implementation will be affected by unknown states of the world. Thus, purges, and especially thorough purges, whereby entire agencies of the *ancien régime* are disbanded, are the equivalent of refusing to delegate to an informed agent. Forgoing purges, on the other hand, can be thought of as the equivalent of delegation to an agent who is equipped with expertise and so able to adjust policies to the state of the world. Due to this uninformed post-transition bureaucracy that results from thorough purges, I expect increases in thorough purges to decrease the quality of democracy more than increases in leadership purges, which remove only the chief autocrats or perpetrators of human rights violations.

At this point, an attentive reader may be asking herself the following question: Instead of two separate exercises – one in lustration and one in purges *why can we not consider a unified model of lustration and purges?* Since these two procedures are not substitutes, the main takeaway thus far from my book in not that in the aftermath of transition to democracy, lustration ought to be chosen over purges. These two processes – lustrations, that is, mechanisms dealing with former secret collaborators and purges, that is mechanisms dealing with open supporters of the *ancien régime* – are different in nature and apply to different situations. In the case of lustration, blackmail is possible, implying the presence of a blackmailer; in the case of purges, blackmail is not possible because there is no secret information to blackmail with.

In the aftermath of transition from authoritarianism, new democratic rulers are presented with both types of collaborators – open and closed – even if some regimes have more of one than the other.[21] Hence, they do not really have a choice of which mechanism to use and in some circumstances will benefit from both; in others only from lustration.

Moreover, lustration is not really a choice available to politicians to the same extent across different countries for two reasons. The first, is highlighted in a related paper by Nalepa and Sonin (2022). In it, the authors suggest a compelling reason why incumbents refrain from implementing transparency regimes *even when they themselves have no skeletons in the closet.* Incumbents may have incentives to suppress transparency, reducing the quality of representation in new democracies, because they are more likely to win elections when their challengers can be blackmailed with kompromat concerning the latter's past collaboration.[22]

---

[21] One could imagine that regimes with more centralized and powerful secret police apparatuses would have more secret than open collaborators, for example.

[22] The authors focus on modeling the strategic interaction between a median voter, an incumbent, a (potentially compromised) challenger, and an agent of the *ancien régime's* security apparatus. Just as in the model from Chapter 2, the member of the *ancien régime's* security apparatus has private information about whether a member of the opposition and challenger to the incumbent has done something embarrassing, such as collaborated with the security police prior to the transition. In addition to not knowing

Critically, and consistently with the model from Chapter 2, transparency regimes in Nalepa and Sonin (2022)'s model also improve the quality of representation by eliminating concessions that compromised politicians make toward the blackmailer. Similarly to the theory presented in Chapter 2, Nalepa and Sonin assume that the surfacing of kompromat instantly destroys the career prospects of the compromised politician. They also assume that the incumbent in power has no skeletons in her own closet. In doing so, they derive their findings for the case where transparency, on the surface, *should benefit the incumbent most.* Yet, they identify a wide range of circumstances where lustration is not implemented. Strategic considerations that have more to do with electoral politics than TJ per se are hence the first obstacle to implementing lustration. This obstacle is specific to the clandestine nature of collaboration that is to be addressed with TJ. The second obstacle is associated with the very sources that have to be consulted to determine who was and who was not a secret collaborator of the *ancien régime.*

To illustrate this argument, consider the set of post-communist countries. In East Germany lustration was clearly an option, as the archives of the STASI were left almost intact. The transition was abrupt leaving little time for former officers to leave. In Poland, where the transition process was more protracted, and files had managed to make their way out of archives and into the hands of potential blackmailers, clawing them back was challenging, yet doable. But then there were countries such as Georgia or Lithuania, where, following the breakup of the Soviet Union, the KGB moved all of its files to Moscow. The challenge of implementing lustration rested there not so much on politicians themselves, as on the good will of those who controlled archive access. To a considerable degree, the success of lustration depends on how much evidence can be feasibly disclosed. Organizing material left over by secret police apparatuses into easily accessible archives can be time consuming; the establishment of a truth commission that will engage victims willing to share testimonies requires buy-in from victims and perpetrators alike.

The upshot of this analysis is that the availability of lustration depends on two factors beyond the control of democratic politicians embarking on TJ: first, it depends on whether the conditions identified by Nalepa and Sonin are satisfied (that is, on whether an uncompromised incumbent is in office and on whether he is moderate enough relative to the opposition

if the politician they are voting for is compromised, however, voters also are uncertain about the ideological position of the opposition challenger.

challenger); second, it depends on the extent to which the authoritarian regime relied on secret information; how many secret collaborators it had; and what is the state post-transition of the archives.

This stands in sharp contrast to purges, where the possibility of firing someone is always there; although, as I show in my model, it may not be the equilibrium choice. Therefore, to some extent, the underlying political interaction is different.

I believe that this difference in circumstances under which lustration and purges are introduced justifies analyzing them with distinct models (albeit, models that share the outcome variable: the quality of democratic representation).

NORMATIVE IMPLICATIONS

In light of this, I propose to interpret the two models as an argument for why there is an important difference between lustration and purges. Lustration with its "more is better" feature invites new democratic politicians to disclose as much as possible and feasible, the content of former secret police archives. Yet a crucial theoretical result of Chapter 3 in particular, is that while democratic representation improves in direct proportion to the amount of lustration implemented, it does not improve in proportion to the intensity of purges. Purges, although they may seem to placate a backward-looking public, can have dire consequences down the line. Especially if those who staffed the *ancien régime*'s administrative apparatus are experts with preferences that are not excessively misaligned with preferences of leaders of the new democratic regime, purging them may come at great cost to the new democracy. Hence when it comes to purges, new democratic leaders, sometimes, quite often in fact, will have to "pull their transitional justice punches."

The theory presented in Chapter 2 could be interpreted as the "forward-looking" argument (in contrast to the "backward-looking" or retroactive argument) in support of transparency regimes: By revealing information about former secret collaborators of the authoritarian regime, lustration prevents former authoritarian elites from extracting policy concessions from elected politicians. Absent lustration, former agents of the secret police could blackmail collaborators who have assumed political office and threaten to reveal skeletons in their closets in the event of refusal to implement desired politicies. Hence, implementing lustration laws should allow all politicians to become responsive to their constituencies. No such forward-looking argument universally holds for purges.

This is a considerably more nuanced and careful argument, addressing the question of whether TJ helps or hurts democracy than offered by the broader literature on TJ in the last few decades. Most normative scholars, largely informed by several anecdotal cases have remained skeptical that TJ can help successful democratization without jeopardizing the rule of law. Others have advocated for the so-called Spanish Model of TJ (Elster 1998, 2005 and Rosenfeld 1997). These authors used Spain's reserved way of dealing with former authoritarian collaborators (sealing off the archives of Franco's secret police) to build their case that "doing nothing" is the best approach for new democracies to deal with past authoritarian regimes (Elster 2004). Citing misuses of de-Ba'athification, scholars have complained that all personnel forms of TJ fail to promote societal reconciliation (David 2006). Among historical examples, they have cited France's policy of épuration, banning former Vichy collaborators from holding office after WWII as having very similar effects (Elster 2004).

Most of these theories castigating personnel forms of TJ, however, have focused on the immediate aftermath of the transition. In the first part of the book, I posit the theoretical possibility that the Spanish model of "doing nothing" may not produce immediate negative consequences, but over time may strengthen the power of authoritarian networks and particularly the networks involving secret legacies of the authoritarian regime. Damaging information collected by the former authoritarian secret police for the benefit of authoritarian elites may turn elected politicians into clients of agents who threaten to reveal their skeletons in the closet.

Lending credence to these normative theories, note, however, that the model of transparency regimes presented in Chapter 2 does corroborate some of their findings. For instance, I find that pooling equilibria occur more frequently when the cost to the politician of having his skeletons in the closet exposed is high. Empirically, this might happen in the immediate aftermath of the transition from authoritarianism, when the salience of who was and was not a collaborator with the *ancien régime* is at its highest. This may imply that lustration implemented shortly after the transition works less well than when lustration is implemented later after the transition. Thus, if these scholars comparing lustration to "witch hunts" and "ritual sacrifices" are using the early experiences with transparency regimes as their empirical evidence,[23] it is entirely possible that they are picking up on the bluffing-rich pooling equilibria.

---

[23] None of this early work is based on systematic data collection.

The theory also implies that when a country is capable of scrutinizing false information about skeletons in the closet (for example, by having a free media or a comprehensive and effective right to information law), blackmail occurs only in instances where evidence of collaboration actually exists. In other words, TJ works as intended only when damaging information can be objectively verified. The logic driving this finding is as follows: former collaborators-turned-politicians cannot know with certainty if files against them survived the transition, so former agents can bluff politicians into thinking such evidence exists if this bluff cannot be easily challenged. Hence, if such information cannot be properly scrutinized, former agents will be able to extort (via bluffing) policy concessions from politicians even when they do not actually have skeletons to reveal.

In equilibria that allow for bluffing (in pooling and semi-pooling equilibria), blackmail is effective despite lustration. I contrast such equilibria with the separating equilibrium, where blackmail is only effective insofar as lustration procedures leave evidence behind. However, even if lustration does not perform as normative theorists would like it to – that is, in the pooling and semi-pooling equilibria – the formal model predicts that the bluffing former secret police officer will adjust his demand down.

Demonstrating that lustrations have the predicted effects is the subject of the second part of this book. Yet even given the aforementioned caveats, the severity of transparency regimes has a positive and monotonic effect on the quality of representation. I thus expect truth commissions and lustration to outperform purges and "doing nothing."

To a large extent, however, the normative literature by chastising lustration and recommending purges, which seem to be what the public supports more, has gotten it backward. It is not lustrations, but purges that should be used with caution. The second part of the book will demonstrate this empirically.

PART II

IMPLICATIONS FOR DEMOCRATIC STABILITY

INTRODUCTION TO PART II

In the first part of this book, I developed an argument for using transparency regimes, such as lustrations and truth commissions, by new democracies dealing with legacies of their authoritarian past. Transparency regimes prevent those with access to kompromat from extracting policy and other concessions from politicians with skeletons in the closet. I also argued that the results of administrative purges are more ambiguous. In contrast to the vetting of secret collaborators, I analyzed purges in the framework of a delegation model. Purging members who ran agencies of the former authoritarian regime is akin to purging bureaucrats; thus, administrative purges are the reverse of a delegation problem. If a new politician executes an effective and thorough purge, ridding the agency of all civil servants and law enforcement agents working for with the *ancien régime,* he or she must implement policy in inherently uncertain conditions. Without the expertise of prior administrators who ran the agencies, the new politician is hamstrung evaluating and implementing policy. On the other hand, forgoing purges is analogous to delegating to an agent with subject-matter expertise and thus the ability to implement the new politician's post-authoritarian policies.

The second part of the book is devoted to empirical illustrations and tests of this theoretical argument.

I will open it in Chapter 4 with a discussion of the original dataset that I have constructed with the help of my team from the Transitional Justice and Democratic Stability Lab. Here I not only explain in detail how the dataset was created but also compare it to its predecessors and use the archetypal cases of the book to illustrate its properties. This Global Transitional Justice Database is the source of the main independent variables of interest: lustration, truth commissions, and two categories of purges. Chapters 5, 6, and 7 are each devoted to one of these three mechanisms. In the end, Chapter 8 analyzes the effects of all four mechanisms on the quality of democracy.

In all chapters 5, 6, and 7, I conceptualize the outcome variable of interest – quality of democratic representation – as the politician's ability to get his ideal point implemented. I assume that this ideal point corresponds to the preferences of the voters. Of course, this assumption does not require agreeing with the dubious claim that elected representatives always represent voters' interests. Instead, I seek to uncover the distortion to representation that originates specifically in not dealing with legacies of the *ancien régime*, be these legacies secret (as in the case of lustration and truth commisssions) or open (as in the case of purges).

In order to measure quality of democracy, Chapters 5 and 6 will introduce and motivate three different dependent variables: programmatic representation, political corruption, and power distributed by socioeconomic status (which is a measure of association between political power and economic wealth). Why do we need three different variables? Largely because some research designs work better with some variables than others, but also because the different personnel TJ mechanisms affect different parts of the population (lustration, for instance, deals with politicians, purges with former bureaucrats and agents of repression, and truth commissions with everyone).

Truth commissions have a similar effect to lustration but, with the exception of a general comparison of mechanisms at the most macro level, are analyzed in a separate chapter of the book.[1] The reason for this is that although they are transparency regimes (as lustration), truth commissions have a naturally broader reach: They are capable of revealing the skeletons of anyone in society, and not only politicians. As a result, I expect to be able to detect the effects of truth commissions after shorter periods of time than lustrations. This suggests that while a hierarchical modeling frameworka hierarchical modeling framework is suitable for analyzing the effects of lustrations, which take longer to disseminate, a design that takes time seriously, such as a difference-in-differences approach is more appropriate for studying the effects of truth commissions.

Such a design allows us to "borrow the trajectory of the untreated" (with truth commissions) countries to construct, for each country that experienced truth commission events, a counterfactual of what the quality

---

[1] Hence, Chapter 5 referred to above, on the programmatic representation of parties, uses only lustration severity among the TJ independent variables.

of its democracy would have been had the truth commission events not taken place. Truth commissions constitute the universe of cases in Chapter 6.

As mentioned earlier, if purges are to be avoided, the institutions of the former authoritarian state must have been developed enough to allow elites to gain expertise that is valued in the new democracy. Hence Chapter 7 will additionally call for a way to measure institutionalization of the preceding authoritarian regime. I will use a newly constructed measure, developed by Hanson and Sigman (2022), who create a Bayesian latent variable out of coercive, extractive, and administrative indicators of state capacity.

The availability of this measure and its precision are vital for the purpose of testing the model from Chapter 3 because as Table 3.2 indicates, whether a new democratic polity should purge or not is contingent on the professionalization of its administrative apparatus. We must first, therefore, account for former authoritarian regimes *selecting* into purges before we can test the model's predictions regarding the quality of democracy brought about by purges.

The final substantive chapter of this part of the book is devoted to a joint analysis of all the personnel TJ mechanisms in the book and their effect on survival of authoritarian networks. It contrasts the de jure measure used in the previous chapters with a de facto measure that explores the presence of the former authoritarian elite in several sectors: the state, political parties, and business.

4

Measuring Transitional Justice

The first generation of empirically oriented transitional justice (TJ) research concentrated on explaining patterns and trajectories of the implementation of specific TJ measures (Lundy & McGovern 2008; Mallinder 2008; Pettai & Pettai 2014; Stan et al. 2009). More recently, to understand the impact of TJ on the quality of democracy, scholars have begun to investigate TJ as an independent variable (Sikkink 2011; Sikkink & Walling 2007). Noteworthy because of their coverage of lustration policies are contributions by Horne (2017b) and Olsen et al. (2010). Horne examines the relationship between the nature of TJ mechanisms and trust, suggesting that revealing the notoriety with which citizens were spying on one another may decrease interpersonal trust in countries with a large network of covert collaborators. At the same time, her research indicates that a wide and compulsory lustration procedure may result in substantial bureaucratic turnover, thereby increasing political trust in governmental institutions. Horne's research was among the first to disaggregate trust in this manner; much of the previous literature assumed that TJ was essential for trust building. Yet, although she provides a rich description of lustration trajectories for as many as twelve countries, they are all in postcommunist Europe.[1] Moreover, Horne extends the

---

[1] Most contributions to the lustration literature suggest that this transitional policy is limited to postcommunist Europe (Closa Montero 2010; De Greiff & Mayer-Rieckh 2007; Ellis 1996; Letki 2002; Stan 2013; Stan & Nedelsky 2015). This is, however, an artifact of restricting the search for personnel TJ to the term "lustration" and its derivatives, when in fact, vetting the state apparatus for secret and open members and collaborators of the former authoritarian regime is called by different names in different parts of the world – these names range from "vetting" and "purging" and "housecleaning" to specific terms such as "denazification," "decommunization," and "de-Ba'athification."

use of the term "lustration" to post-authoritarian purges that is, the removal from office of collaborators whose nature of collaboration is well known. This is in jarring contrast with the etymology of the word "lustrate," which comes from Latin and refers to shedding light and making something transparent.[2] As I show later, in Chapter 7, her finding of negative effects for the application of what she calls "lustration laws" to institutions of the state is consistent with my findings on the ambiguous effects of purges.

Data collection efforts that expand beyond postcommunist Europe have also been undertaken. One example is Olsen et al. (2010). These authors, however, reduce an entire process of implementing lustration to the one year when it was implemented.

As mentioned previously, I discuss the operationalization of the dependent variables that emerged from the models in Chapters 2 and 3 in the specific chapters devoted to testing the dynamics laid out in those chapters: in Chapters 5 and 6 for transparency regimes and in Chapter 7 for purges.

This chapter is devoted to measuring TJ. I first lay out a data collection strategy that both takes time seriously and disaggregates TJ to an unprecedented level. It introduces my Global Transitional Justice Dataset (GTJD).[3] This dataset is the first to disaggregate TJ events in three novel ways. First, it breaks down TJ events into a time series that spans the years between the date of a country's democratization and 2016. Second, it disaggregates TJ mechanisms into those, such as purges, that deal with open forms of collaboration and human rights violations, and those, such as lustration and truth commissions, that deal with secret forms of collaboration and human rights violations. It complements existing datasets on events related to TJ by focusing not only on post-conflict societies (as the Post-Conflict Justice [PCJ] dataset does), or post-authoritarian societies (as the Transitional Justice Database [TJDB] does), but rather on both. Third, the TJ events themselves, the building blocks of my measures, are divided into positive and negative events, which for any given country can be visualized as a time series.

---

[2] See Webster's II New Riverside Dictionary: lustrate [Lat. lustrare, lustrat] to purify, make bright.

[3] This chapter draws on joint work with Genevieve Bates and Ipek Cinar published in *Perspectives on Politics* as "Accountability by Numbers: A new GTJD (1946–2016)." In adapting it to this book I have made changes to the original text and any mistakes caused by these modifications are my sole responsibility.

Extant quantitative studies of the effects of TJ have not found a strong significant effect of personnel TJ (i.e, purges and lustrations) on the quality of democracy. This non-finding is puzzling as one would expect personnel TJ to particularly stand out as critically important for the objective of limiting the influence of former elites because it deals with authoritarian elites most directly.

This chapter demonstrates that the ambiguities in these earlier findings stem from data collection strategies that (1) are not sensitive to the temporal dimension of TJ and that (2) do not account for whether the type of collaboration with the former authoritarian regime was secret or open.

I demonstrate the advantages of my disaggregation strategy by using these data to construct the main measures of TJ intensity used in this book: severity measures. The granular structure of the data allows researchers to construct additional measures, depending on their theoretical questions of interest. I provide two examples of such additional measures: urgency and volatility. Severity, however, along with its various modifications – to better fit the statistical models I employ – is the main workhorse measure of this book. I will also compare and contrast my measure of TJ severity with the ones proposed by the authors of PCJ (Binningsbø et al. 2012*a*) and TJDB (Olsen et al. 2010).

4.1 WHY DO WE NEED A NEW TRANSITIONAL JUSTICE DATASET?

Data on personnel TJ mechanisms is notoriously hard to collect, in no small part because, as mentioned earlier, researchers refer to these mechanisms using general terms ranging from "vetting" and "purging" to "house-cleaning," or specific terms such as "denazification," "decommunization," or "de-Ba'athification." This may explain why many researchers and most databases pool all personnel TJ events under one heading of "purges" or "lustration." Researchers who have contributed theoretical accounts of TJ such as Jon Elster (2004) as well as scholars who have developed datasets of personnel TJ treat lustration and administrative purges (such as decommunization, de-Ba'athification, and denazification) as the same type of mechanism for dealing with the past. According to PCJ, "purges" are any "acts of removing politicians, members of the armed forces, judiciary (...) for their (alleged) collaboration with or participation in a conflict and limiting their influence accordingly" (p. 736). Yet the PCJ only locates fifteen such events.

Olsen, Payne, and Reiter similarly pool personnel TJ mechanisms into one category, calling it "lustration." They define lustration as "the mechanism that occurs when the state enacts official policies denying employment in public positions to individuals because of their former political acts or identity" (Olsen, Payne Reiter 2010a, p. 38). Using this definition, these authors were only able to record fifty-four instances of lustration. Later in this chapter, Table 4.1 will demonstrate that I find many more lustration events than the Olsen et al. team was able to. The vast discrepancy is attributed to the fact that these authors (as well as the PCJ) code the presence or absence of lustration with a dummy variable while I differentiate across time between distinct lustration events, both positive and negative. Second, the Olsen et al. team's collection was biased to only look for lustrations in Eastern Europe. This caused them to miss numerous lustration events (whether one uses Olsen et al.'s definition or mine) outside of postcommunist Europe.

In a recent book, Cynthia Horne (2017a) underscores a failure to distinguish between lustration and purges. She defines the former as "a form of vetting – the set of parliamentary laws that restrict members and collaborators of former repressive regimes from holding a range of public offices, state management positions, or other jobs with strong public influence (such as in the media or academia) after the collapse of an authoritarian regime"(Horne 2017a). "Purges," meanwhile, extend collectively to members of organizations linked to the *ancien régime*. Thus, whereas "lustration" denotes a procedure that considers each case individually, purges presume collective responsibility. Horne notes further that lustration is part of a more general category of "vetting," which she defines as any ban on holding office; vetting does not have to be limited to members of or collaborators with the *ancien régime*. Aligning with the criticism laid out by Horne, I believe that the negligible effects of personnel TJ mechanisms on the quality of democracy identified by Olsen et al. (2010) and Binningsbø et al. (2012a) may have at their roots the failure to separate purges from lustration.[4]

Roman David (2011) takes a similar disaggregating approach, but, like Horne, limits the scope of lustration to Eastern Europe because "prior to 1990, this term was not used to describe transitional justice proce-

---

[4] Olsen et al. (2010) also include truth commissions in regressions as explanatory variables, but even these are marginally significant for only one type of outcome variable: variously constructed terror scales.

dures" (David 2011, p. 67).[5] While it is true that the term "lustration" was rarely used outside of Eastern Europe to describe the disqualification for public employment of secret and clandestine collaborators with the former regime, my data reveal that such procedures were implemented both before 1990 and beyond Eastern Europe. Consider as an example the Portuguese decree from March 22, 1975, which stipulated that any member of the armed forces who was found to be "incompetent" or not prepared to make a declaration of loyalty to the Movimento das Forças Armadas (Armed Forces Movement) could be placed on reserve. Under the same decree, all military members involved in the coup attempt of March 11 of that year were expelled from the forces, and their property was confiscated (Pinto 2001).[6]

The failure to distinguish purges from lustration is one problem with existing data. Another is the difficulty that scholars face when trying to pinpoint when exactly a mechanism of a certain type was implemented. This has led many researchers to aggregate all TJ activity of a certain type into a single variable that signifies the presence or absence of that TJ mechanism in a given country. Noteworthy in their attempt to surmount these problems are efforts by the TJDB team (Olsen, Paine, & Reiter) and the Transitional Justice Research Collaborative (TJRC).[7] Both record the year in which a TJ mechanism of a given type was implemented, allowing a country to have multiple events. While these datasets offer a considerable improvement over previous TJ datasets, they still condense much of the process and assume away the possibility of reversals (Bakiner 2016).

Furthermore, particularly in the case of personnel TJ, it is difficult to exactly pinpoint a decisive moment when these mechanisms are implemented. Instead, legislation is frequently first proposed, then amended, and eventually passed. Following this, it is sometimes struck down by a constitutional court or presidential veto only to be reintroduced on the legislative floor again. Moreover, with the passage of time, the scope of

---

[5] David defines lustration as a "special public employment law that stipulates the conditions for the access of persons who worked for or collaborated with the political or repressive apparatus of socialist regimes to certain public positions in new democracies. (2011, p. 67)"

[6] Chapter 8 provides two case studies of countries high on the lustration severity scale that are outside of Eastern Europe: Brazil and Paraguay.

[7] The TJDB includes data on five transitional justice mechanisms including amnesties, trials, truth commissions, lustrations, and reparations. The TJRC covers amnesties, trials (including domestic, foreign, international, and civil), vetting, truth commissions, reparations, and customary justice.

TJ mechanisms can be expanded or curtailed, or the legislation can be completely revoked. Data projects trying to identify a specific year in which a procedure was finally implemented reduce TJ to a "one-shot event." Ignoring the temporal nature of these processes assumes away their nonlinearity. My method of documenting the entire process of personnel TJ as it unfolds over time requires fewer judgment calls and is able to account for regressive changes in personnel TJ implementation. Furthermore, a by-product of the panel structure of my data is that it allows scholars to employ research designs that are not available to them with just cross-sectional structures. At the same time, all research designs suitable for cross-sectional formats can be used as well: One can do with disaggregated data anything that is possible with aggregated data, but not the other way around.

In sum, existing transitional justice datasets either pool complex events, leading to the collapsing of TJ into a simple dummy variable, or fail to disaggregate personnel transitional justice into mechanisms that deal with secret and open collaborators.

In Chapters 1 and 2, of this book, I argued that although lustration and purges are forms of personnel transitional justice in that they aim to eliminate from the state apparatus members and collaborators of the previous authoritarian regime, lustrations actually have more in common with truth commissions because they uncover information that was kept secret before the transition. Further, the effect of lustration severity on democratic representation is very different from the effect of purge severity on democratic representation. While the quality of political representation increases monotonically with lustration severity, this is not necessarily the case with purges. Moreover, purges are not feasible in all new democratic polities to the same extent.

Recall the key difference between lustration – dealing with unknown collaborators – and purges, that is, dealing with known members and collaborators of the former *ancien régime*: Politicians who in the past were clandestine collaborators or committed atrocities in secret can be blackmailed with threats to reveal such information to the public by those with credible access to information on such skeletons in the closet. Needless to say, if the public still pays attention to what happened in the past, the revelation of such skeletons could end a politician's career. In return for their silence, individuals in possession of credible evidence of skeletons in the closet can demand rents or policy concessions. Regardless of the currency in which the ransom is paid out by the blackmailed politician, the quality of democracy suffers.

As I explained in Chapter 3, the mechanism behind purges is different: since getting rid of members who ran the agencies of former authoritarian regime is similar to firing bureaucrats of a government agency, one can think of administrative purges as the reverse of a delegation problem. If a newly elected politician takes office and carries out a thorough purge, he is forced to implement policy in conditions with which he is unfamiliar. Without the expertise of people who used to run the agencies under the *ancien régime*, he cannot know how policy implementation will be affected by states of the world unknown to him. Conversely, a decision to forgo a purge can be thought of as the equivalent of delegation to an agent who is equipped with expertise and thus able to adjust policies to the state of the world.

The main insight from my adaptation of the delegation model in Chapter 3 is that the agent – in this case, the staff member of the authoritarian agency – may have preferences that are so misaligned with those of the principal (the new democratic politician) that he will use his expertise to implement policy he himself prefers. On balance, this policy outcome may be worse for the principal than his own implementation, riddled with lack of expertise as it is.

These two intuitions suggest that purges and lustrations are very different mechanisms, associated with very different consequences for the ability of politicians to represent the interests of their voters. In light of this, these two categories of personnel TJ ought to be disaggregated. The remainder of this chapter describes the dataset that accomplishes this task and demonstrates other intuitive uses of this dataset.

4.2 TAKING TIME SERIOUSLY: TRANSITIONAL JUSTICE AS A TIME SERIES

Mechanisms for righting wrongs committed by former ruling elites, and commentary on these wrongs, date back to the ancient Athenian democracy and its attempts to deal with crimes committed by the Thirty Tyrants (Todd 2000). For obvious reasons, my dataset cannot cover a time span stretching back to the fifth century BC. Adhering instead to conventions in the conflict literature (Binningsbø et al. 2012a; Olsen et al. 2010; Sikkink & Walling 2007), my research team and I document the occurrence of these mechanisms in all countries that experienced civil war or transitioned to democracy between 1946 and 2016. Globally, there are eighty-three such states.

My country selection criteria build on the existing Autocratic Breakdown and Regime Transitions (GWF) dataset (Geddes et al. 2014) and the PCJ database (Binningsbø et al. 2012a). I select countries that, as indicated by the GWF dataset, transitioned from a military, personalist, or party-based authoritarian regime in the post-1946 period. I include countries that are no longer democratic, but that experienced a democratic spell after 1946.[8] My dataset also encompasses countries with multiple indicators of regime type, such as Burundi, which transitioned in 1993 from a military-personalist regime, or Indonesia, which transitioned from a party-personalist-military regime. I exclude all countries that are currently authoritarian and have remained authoritarian for most of the post-1946 era as by my definition, these countries are unable to implement TJ.

As far as democracies having experienced civil conflict are concerned, I begin by following exactly the same criteria as the PCJ database; that is, I include all armed conflict episodes that have ended in the 1946–2016 time period. While the PCJ database has a conflict-episode structure, I aggregate the conflict episodes identified in the PCJ dataset to the country level and remove all long-term authoritarian regimes that never became democracies in order to remain consistent with the rest of my data.

If a country dissolved into a collection of smaller countries as a result of successful secession efforts, as Czechoslovakia and Yugoslavia did, I include any applicable TJ events from the original country as the TJ events for the most relevant successor country – that is, the one that actually inherited the TJ institutions. All additional countries are coded as having transitioned at the date of independence. For example, I code the Czech Republic as the successor country following the 1993 dissolution of Czechoslovakia. The Czech Republic thus inherited the post-1989 TJ events attributed to Czechoslovakia. Slovakia is then coded as having transitioned in 1993. Serbia is coded as the successor country to Yugoslavia, while Slovenia, Bosnia and Herzegovina, Croatia, Macedonia, Kosovo, and Montenegro are all coded as having transitioned at their respective dates of independence.

---

[8] Examples of such countries include Russia, Egypt, and Thailand.

Finally, I include information on countries and conflict periods that led to TJ but that had been excluded from previous datasets.[9] I chose explicitly to include small countries because such countries are immune neither to periods of authoritarian rule nor to periods of conflict, and as seen in the cases of East Timor or Kosovo, can implement all forms of personnel TJ.

4.2.1 Dataset Construction Technology

To create my dataset, the TJ and Democratic Stability Lab started with two major electronic databases: Keesings' Record of World Events and the Lexis Nexis Academic Universe.

We searched them for information found in Keesings and Lexis Nexis about events related to purges, lustration, and truth commissions in all relevant countries, beginning from the date of the transition to democracy, the start of the post-conflict period, or both (in the case of conflicts which occurred in democracies), and ending in either 2016 or the year in which the country reverted to authoritarianism.

There are, of course, serious limitations to relying on electronic databases alone. For one, they are biased toward large countries and countries with authoritarian regimes and conflicts that are better penetrated by the global network of human rights oriented NGOs and journalists. For this reason, I supplemented my database searches with numerous secondary sources, ranging from historical accounts in monographs and chapters in edited volumes to articles.[10]

Based on these searches, the team and I created a chronology document for each country. The chronology includes relevant information about the preceding authoritarian regime (or regimes) and transition, conflict and post-conflict period, or both. Next, we provide records of each TJ event in chronological order, noting the date, a brief identification of the event, the relevant state and non-state actors, a more detailed description of the event, and the source where the information was obtained. In order for a personnel TJ event to be relevant, it must include an actor in his or her governing capacity enabling (in a positive event) or disabling (in a negative event) the pursuit of personnel TJ.

[9] Examples include Cyprus, which is excluded from GWF based on size, and Kenya, which is excluded from PCJ despite its postelection violence in 2007–2008. This postelection violence in Kenya produced numerous domestic TJ events, including a truth commission.
[10] A bibliography of these secondary sources is provided on the Global Transitional Justice Database website: tjdemstabilitylab.com

To be more specific, I define a positive TJ event as the submission of a TJ proposal to the floor of the legislature, the passage of such legislation, the upholding of such legislation as constitutional by a supreme court, or the overturning of a presidential veto against such legislation. In the case of truth commissions, the publication of the commission's report(s) and the extension of the commission's mandate are also considered to be positive TJ events. I define a negative TJ event, in contrast, as the voting down, vetoing, or striking down by the constitutional court of a TJ proposal or law. Expanding the set of persons targeted by TJ or broadening the set of "offenses" (where "offense" is defined in light of the TJ procedure in question) to include more past or present positions constitutes a positive TJ event, whereas attempts to narrow the set of targets or "offenses" are coded as negative TJ events.

The guiding principle in determining if an event is negative or positive is whether it advances the TJ process forward or backward. Consider Onur Bakiner's (2016) observation that some truth commissions were disbanded before they could finish their work (examples provided by Bakiner include Indonesia, Turkey, Mexico, and Nepal). The temporal organization of the data, which accounts for progressive as well as regressive events, allows me to account for such setbacks in the work of truth commissions.

After each event's category was determined (purge, lustration, or truth commission), it was coded as positive or negative. Events that were not relevant for the dataset were labeled as such, with an explanation of why they were excluded.

The number of positive and negative TJ events was then aggregated to create an annual panel, with countries as the cross section and time since transition as the temporal dimension. A panel assembled in this way allows for the creation of many different measures of TJ. In addition, the raw chronologies themselves allow researchers to experiment with different systems of disaggregation.[11]

---

[11] For instance, among the events included in the chronologies are ones that could not be classified as purges, lustration, or truth commissions. These were labeled "nonevents" and include trials, amnesties, apologies, and victim compensation. Other researchers may want to create their own categories out of these events, an undertaking made possible by our organization of the chronologies. Moreover, the technique of labeling events as positive or negative could be fruitfully applied to criminal trials. The initiation of an investigation, along with an indictment, could be the first positive event in a trial proceeding. Reducing the number of counts on which a defendant is charged would be a negative event, as would acquittal or the commuting of a sentence.

A time series of positive and negative TJ events can also produce trends for individual countries, such as the ones presented in Figure 4.1 for lustration.

Recall that these trends should not be interpreted as periods when personnel TJ was implemented, though they correlate with those periods. Instead, the dark line represents the number of events in a given year since the transition advancing the lustration process, while the light line represents the number of events delaying lustration.

These trends can be thought of as building blocks out of which scholars can construct measures pertaining to various aspects of personnel TJ. In Section 4.2.2, I offer examples of such measures and illustrate how they may be used to portray the TJ profiles of the countries making up the archetypal cases of this book (Figures 4.7 to 4.10).

4.2.2 Creating Measures of Transitional Justice

Measures are never constructed in complete abstraction from research questions (Coppedge 2012; Goertz 2006).[12] My dataset collection and this specific book are motivated by the question of how dealing with former authoritarian elites impacts the quality of democracy. However, "dealing with former authoritarian elites" could mean dealing with them harshly or mildly or not at all; dealing with them immediately or later after the transition; or being consistent in pursuing a certain type of personnel TJ process.

In order to capture these three aspects of dealing with former authoritarian elites and their collaborators, I develop three measures that use my yearly positive and negative personnel TJ events as building blocks: (1) severity, (2) urgency and delay, and (3) volatility. I introduce each in turn as follows.

Severity

Among those evaluating personnel TJ, there is a high demand for an instrument to capture its intensity. Such a measure would place the severity of a personnel TJ procedure somewhere between the two extremes of

---

[12] Measures created in this section were developed for an article with Genevieve Bates and Ipek Cinar, "Accountability by Numbers: that appeared in *Perspectives on Politics*, Volume 18, Issue 1, March 2020, pp. 161–184.

Years since transition

—— Positive events   —— Negative events

FIGURE 4.1. Positive and negative lustration events in seventy-five post-authoritarian countries (excluding post-conflict only countries) from regime transition to 2016

minimal and severe. One way to approach this is by taking the accumulation of relative changes in the law since the transition as follows:

$$S = \frac{\sum_t (P^t)}{\sum_t (P^t + N^t) + 1},$$

where t is the subscript over time, N^t is the number of negative events in a country in period t, and P^t is the number of positive events in period t. This measure is simply the total number of positive events over the total number of events. In a country with no personnel TJ, S will obviously take on 0; the "+1" in the denominator ensures that the measure is well defined. The more positive events a country has among its total events, the closer its score is to 1.

A possible criticism one could mount with regard to this measure is that it treats positive and negative events asymmetrically. I believe this inherent asymmetry in how positive and negative events enter the severity measure corresponds to a lopsidedness between the two types of events. Recall that positive events are TJ events that move the transitional justice process institutionally forward, and negative events are events that reverse it. First, negative events without earlier positive events are extremely rare in the dataset (in the case of lustration, to take one example it only happens in Slovakia, which neglected to adopt the lustrations that were implemented in Czechoslovakia before the "velvet divorce"); typically, negative events require at least a few positive events first. Second, assume even that a law is adopted and then immediately revoked. This implies that some period of time must have lapsed between the two events. But during that time, the passage of the law would already start having effects. In the case of purges, some members of the former state could have been let go and found employment elsewhere. In the case of transparency regimes, some steps may have been taken to remove kompromat from the hands of agents of the former authoritarian state. This situation is not the same as the situation with no events whatsoever. Hence, this feature of the measure is actually a desirable one.

Consider as an illustration (Figure 4.2), the application of the severity measure to thorough purges.

Even though existing datasets treat all purges as equal and the same, my measure demonstrates a fair degree of variation. With the caveat that only countries scoring a measure greater than zero are included, Figure 4.2 ranks thorough purges from least severe (Comoros) to most severe (Latvia). In Latvia, post-transition governments initiated a series of purges that banned anyone who had been active in the Soviet Communist Party or its affiliate organizations from running for office. These bans were upheld despite numerous court challenges throughout the 1990s and 2000s (Stan et al. 2009). This differs starkly from Comoros, where a weak purging of the military was initiated after its 2006 transition to democracy. Several years later, the purge in Comoros was undone, and the "militia" loyal to the previous regime were reintegrated into the military (UN Integrated Regional Information Networks (Nairobi) 2011).

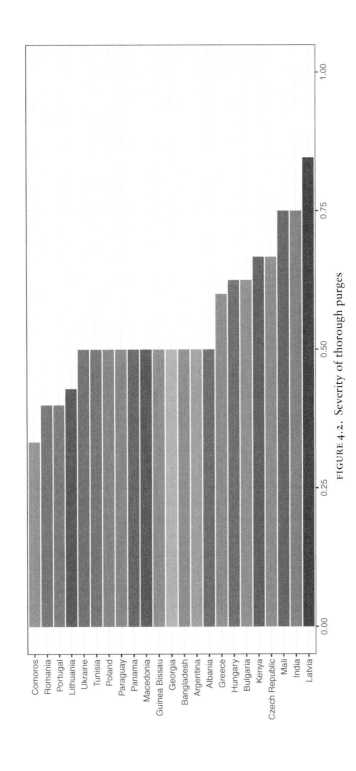

FIGURE 4.2. Severity of thorough purges

In Section 4.1, I justified the need for a new transitional justice dataset by pointing out the shortcomings of existing datasets. Recall that these other datasets – TJDB and TJRC – are not organized as panels, but instead just tally up what they consider to be implementations of each mechanism. In addition, they do not distinguish between personnel TJ that uncovers secret collaborators (lustration) and holds open collaborators accountable (purges). Despite this pooling on two dimensions relative to the GTJD, it is worth comparing how these datasets evaluate TJ in different former authoritarian and post-conflict states relative to the GTJD according to this new severity measure. Table 4.1 spanning the next two pages compares my lustration severity measure to "lustration" from TJDB and "vetting" from the TJDB.

To take one example from the top of the table, consider Albania and Argentina. While the event counts implied by TJDB and TJRC equate lustration in Albania and Argentina – with two events for TJDB, and two and three vetting events, respectively, for TJRC – my measure of severity shows a clear distinction between the two countries: Lustration in Argentina was significantly more severe (.83) than in Albania (.55). Albania, in fact, has much more in common with Bulgaria (.59), which has three lustration events according to TJDB. As shown in Table 4.1, the nature of my disaggregated data allows for a much more nuanced understanding of the severity of personnel TJ.

Other Illustrative Measures: Urgency and Volatility

While severity is probably the TJ measure most needed by the research designs I employ in this book, TJ scholars around the globe have long called for a measure to capture how long a country waits for a TJ event. The most intuitive approach would be to record with an indicator variable the year of the first positive event of a given type. This minimalist measure offers much flexibility, as it can be used as a treatment variable in a host of statistical models, but is quite constraining. With respect to measuring lustration, it equates, for instance, Russia, which had never moved beyond a single lustration proposal that was promptly defeated in the Duma (the Russian legislature) and Paraguay and Brazil, which are two outliers in their lustration severity, as highlighted in Chapter 8. The next most straightforward measure would be to count the number of years lapsed before the first positive transitional justice event as a proportion of years lapsed since the transition itself. Herein, however, lies the problem with the censored nature of my data. Should a country that transitioned five years ago and implemented lustration in its fourth year

TABLE 4.1. *Comparison with other transitional justice databases*

Countries	TJDB (Lustration)	TJRC (Vetting)	Severity (Lustration)
Albania	2	2	0.545
Argentina	2	3	0.80
Bangladesh	0	0	0.50
Benin	0	0	0
Bolivia	0	0	0
Bosnia	3	5	0.667
Brazil	0	0	0.80
Bulgaria	2	4	0.588
Burundi	0	0	0
Cape Verde	.	0	0
Chile	0	0	0.667
Colombia	0	0	0.50
Comoros	.	0	0.50
Croatia	0	0	0
Cyprus	.	0	0
Czech Republic	2	2	0.81
Dominican Republic	1	1	0.50
East Timor	0	0	0
Ecuador	0	0	0
Egypt	0	0	0.50
El Salvador	0	0	0
Estonia	0	1	0.762
Georgia	0	1	0.556
Germany	1	2	0.80
Ghana	0	0	0
Greece	2	5	0.842
Grenada	.	0	0
Guatemala	0	0	0.75
Guinea Bissau	1	0	0.60
Guyana	.	0	0
Haiti	0	0	0
Honduras	0	0	0
Hungary	1	2	0.684
India	0	0	0.75
Indonesia	0	0	0
Kenya	0	1	0.667
Kosovo	.	0	0
Latvia	.	1	0.778
Lebanon	0	0	0
Lesotho	0	0	0
Liberia	0	2	0
Lithuania	1	4	0.75

TABLE 4.1. (*Continued*)

Countries	TJDB (Lustration)	TJRC (Vetting)	Severity (Lustration)
Macedonia	o	1	0.636
Madagascar	o	o	o
Malawi	o	o	o
Mali	o	o	0.833
Mexico	o	o	0.667
Moldova	o	o	0.50
Mongolia	.	o	o
Montenegro	.	o	o
Nepal	o	2	0.50
Nicaragua	o	o	0.50
Niger	o	o	o
Nigeria	1	1	0.50
Northern Ireland	.	o	0.50
Pakistan	o	o	0.50
Palestine	.	o	o
Panama	o	o	0.667
Paraguay	1	1	0.833
Peru	o	o	0.50
Philippines	o	1	o
Poland	1	2	0.625
Portugal	1	2	0.706
Romania	o	2	0.692
Russia	o	o	0.30
São Tomé and Príncipe	o	o	o
Senegal	o	o	o
Serbia	o	1	0.833
Sierra Leone	o	o	o
Slovakia	.	1	0.714
Slovenia	.	1	0.429
South Africa	o	o	o
South Korea	o	o	0.50
Spain	1	o	0.50
Sri Lanka	o	o	o
Sudan	1	o	o
Taiwan	.	o	o
Thailand	o	o	o
Tunisia	o	o	0.667
Turkey	1	1	o
Ukraine	.	o	0.692
Venezuela	o	o	o
Zambia	o	o	0.50

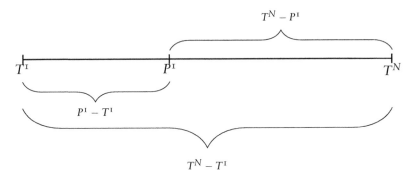

FIGURE 4.3. Urgency measure

of democracy be equivalent to a country that transitioned twenty years ago and implemented lustration only four years ago? The naive measure of delay proposed above would give both a score of .8. Yet, the latter country seems to be more of a latecomer to the lustration process than the former.

Importantly, it is hard to vet elites for collaboration with the authoritarian regime in the immediate aftermath of transition. In contrast to purges, lustration may rely on uncovering and organizing files of the secret political police, an activity that, depending on the level of organization of these files, may take years to complete. Similar delays caused by the very nature of unearthing evidence plague truth commissions. In order to account for such startup costs, I propose to measure urgency/delay for each country with:

$$U = \frac{T^N - P^1}{(T^N - T^1)(P^1 - T^1)},$$

where T^N is 2016 or the last year of the democratic spell before the country's reversal to authoritarian rule,[13] (T^N need not be 2016, as illustrated in the case of Thailand, which experienced a military coup in 2014.) P^1 is the first year following the country's transition that featured a positive personnel TJ event, and T^1 is the first year following the country's transition.[14] To understand how this measure works, consider Figure 4.3.

In the numerator, $T^N - P^1$ corresponds to how soon the first positive TJ event occurs. The larger its value, the more urgent is the implementation

---

[13] I clarify that in all three measures, superscripts do not represent exponents but time indices.

[14] In countries like Thailand, T^1 will be subtracted from the year of the authoritarian reversal rather than from 2016.

of personnel TJ. The denominator contains two expressions: (1) the length of the democratic spell, $T^N - T^1$, which is used to account for the fact that countries with longer democratic spells have more opportunities to engage in TJ, and (2) $(P^1 - T^1)$, a weight capturing the number of years lapsed before the first positive TJ event. Both of these expressions lower the value of the urgency measure.

U assumes the value of zero when a country has no positive TJ events. Given that urgency and delay are a function of time, a country that has not yet implemented a particular type of TJ cannot possibly have a nonzero value for the measure. The measure will approach the value of 1 when P^1 approaches T^1 – that is, when the first positive event occurs very soon after the transition. Because T^1, T^N, and P^1 can only take positive integer values and $T^1 < P^1$, the measure will never actually assume 1. The measure is also well defined (the denominator cannot be zero).[15] For a substantive illustration of the urgency measure, Figure 4.4 presents its values for the GTJD universe of truth commission events.

This exercise captures the tremendous simplification that occurs when scholars try to capture the implementation of TJ with a dummy variable. Clearly, the extremely delayed transparency regime in Spain cannot be treated as equivalent to the urgently implemented transparency regime in Greece. While Spain transitioned to democracy in 1976, it did not begin a TJ process until nearly forty years later, when a proposal to declassify military reports from the Franco era was made in the legislature in 2013 (Congreso de los Diputados, Comisión de Cultura 2013). Greece, however, embarked on TJ almost immediately after its July 1974 transition, removing the leadership of the armed forces, police, and banking and public sector by mid-August of that same year (Alivizatos & Diamandouros 1997; Keesing's Record of World Events 1974).

Finally, TJ scholars may be interested in *volatility of TJ*, a measure that would capture the stability of TJ. Note that I cannot use variance for this purpose, because the events are of two types – positive and negative. I can, however, take advantage of the two types of events and focus on the magnitude of policy swings regarding a given TJ mechanism in a given country. Policy swings can be interpreted as dramatic shifts from positive to negative events or vice versa. As a result, volatility would only be defined for countries that have experienced both positive and negative events. One could measure volatility simply with the number of years

---

[15] I code the data beginning with the first year after the transition, which is consistent with the fact that the first positive event has to take place *after* the transition.

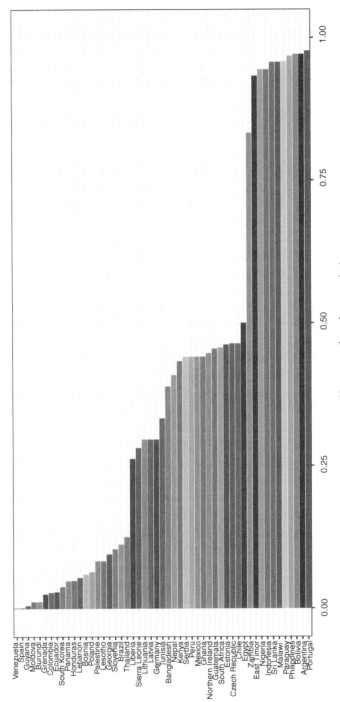

FIGURE 4.4. Urgency of truth commissions

separating the year with the maximum number of positive events and the year with the maximum number of negative events. Such a measure, however, would fail to account for the fact that a country can experience both positive and negative events over the course of the same year. Thus, in order to capture this net value of positive and negative events, I propose:

$$V = \frac{max_t\{P^t - N^t\} - min_t\{P^t - N^t\}}{(|median_t\{T^{max}\} - median_T\{T^{min}\}|) * max_c\{max_t\{P^t - N^t\} - min_t\{P^t - N^t\}\} + 1}.$$

The value of $(P^t - N^t)$ is highest in the year in which a country records the maximum number of positive events net of negative events and is at its lowest when a country records the maximum number of negative TJ events net of positive events. Thus, $max_t\{P^t - N^t\}$ is the maximum of net events, and $min_t\{P^t - N^t\}$ is the minimum of net events. The difference between these two expressions, which constitutes the numerator in the measure, captures the policy swing in personnel TJ that is referred to above.

The denominator of this measure is made up of two parts. The first, subtracting $median_T\{T^{min}\}$ from $median_T\{T^{max}\}$, accounts for the number of years the country in question took to experience such a policy swing. Volatility should increase when there are fewer such years. At the same time, because the maximum and minimum net values could be associated with more than a single year in a country's post-transition history, I take the median year of all maximum net values and the median year of all minimum net values. Since it does not matter whether the uptick in positive events precedes or succeeds the uptick in negative events, I take the absolute value of the difference between the two medians. The second expression in the denominator is a weight ensuring that the measure does not exceed 1. The denominator represents the largest possible swing across all countries in my data (hence the subscript "c" in the maximum expression: $max_c\{max_t\{P^t - N^t\} - min_t\{P^t - N^t\}\}$.

The operation of this seemingly complex measure is conveniently illustrated in Figure 4.5. To make the figure more transparent, I refrain from including multiple years with the maximum and minimum scores of $(P^t - N^t)$, which are labeled at T^{max} and T^{min}, respectively, in the figure.

P takes the value of zero when a country does not experience any policy swing in TJ and approaches 1 when a country exhibits a significant policy swing in a relatively brief time period. Note that the limitation of a measure that can only be applied to countries that exhibited both positive and negative personnel TJ events implies that whether volatility

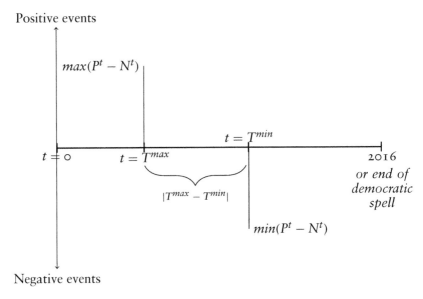

FIGURE 4.5. Volatility measure

is defined for a given country at all will vary from one TJ mechanism to another. Volatility in TJ of a given type is not defined for countries that did not implement transitional justice of that type or for countries that experienced only positive or only negative events. Such countries have no policy swings. This explains why Figure 4.6, illustrating the application of volatility to the case of truth commissions, has fewer countries than the figures illustrating severity and urgency. Figure 4.6 illustrates the operation of this measure using lustration as an example.

Volatility, by far the most complex of the three measures presented here, exposes the potentially greatest flaw of TJ coding procedures relying on dummy variables that only capture whether a country has experienced TJ, regardless of whether the datasets are structured as panels or cross sections. First, consider cases such as Ukraine, Spain, and Albania, where volatility is very low. These three countries' volatility values correspond to situations where TJ was implemented once and for all; thus, the coding is not affected by the time at which data were collected. Contrast this with highly volatile countries such as Lithuania, Romania, and Estonia, where TJ was implemented only to be revoked shortly after. In such countries, the coding of the presence or absence of the TJ mechanism is highly dependent on the moment in time when data collection took place.

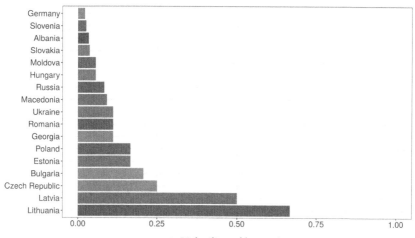

FIGURE 4.6. Volatility of lustration

Below, I use urgency and volatility to explore the archetypal cases of this book against all other countries in the Global Transitional Justice Database for which the measure is defined.

Low Lustration Urgency: Poland and Tunisia

The first figure looks at lustration policies in Poland and Tunisia with regard to severity on the horizontal axis and urgency on the vertical axis.

Poland and Tunisia share many characteristics. They were both first to transition in their respective waves of democratization and are both ethnically homogeneous, which are two important "control" variables one might want to take into account in assessing the effect of TJ on quality of democracy.

As far as lustration is concerned both countries delayed the implementation of lustration. Recall that according to the logic presented in Chapter 2, lustration delayed is lustration implemented when voters care less about who served as a secret collaborator, which makes bluffing more difficult. Consequently, such delayed lustration works closer to the normative ideal by avoiding the blackmailing of innocent politicians. This in turn should boost the effect of lustration severity, which was not low to begin with (.5 in Tunisia and .67 in Poland). Both countries were fast democratizers. Within the fourth wave, Tunisia was essentially the only MENA country that ten years on remained democratic (Nugent 2020), although not without problems (Chromiak 2019; Chromiak & Salman 2016), especially recently.

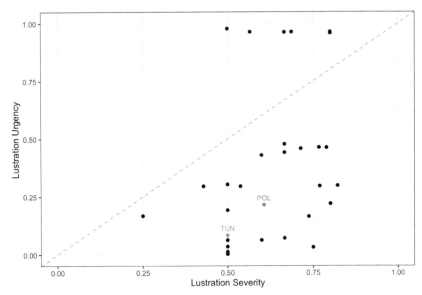

FIGURE 4.7. Lustration urgency and severity: Poland and Tunisia relative to other GTJD countries with both scores above 0

Poland continued to be the success story of democratization in Eastern Europe until the 2015 victory of Law and Justice (PiS). At that point, the country has been steadily declining according to indicators of democracy, including scores used in Chapters 6–8 of this book. Scholars have argued that one of the pretexts of this backsliding, which first manifested itself in limiting judiciary independence, has been the exclusion of judiciary from lustration (Chiopris et al. 2022; Nalepa 2020). There is some truth in the excuse PiS used for judiciary reforms, as indeed, every time Poland attempted to extend lustration to the judiciary, the laws were struck down by the Constitutional Tribunal. This has been picked up by my measure of lustration volatility (omitted from the Figure 4.7) that puts Poland at .167, the fourth highest volatility in my entire universe of cases. Thus, it is possible that the high volatility dampened the otherwise beneficial effects of low urgency and high severity of transparency regimes in Poland.

Low Truth Commission Urgency: Spain
The next figure considers an instance of extremely low urgency, this time in the case of truth commissions. Spain, as described in detail in Chapter 1 was a late-comer to TJ. When the Pact of Forgiveness was finally broken,

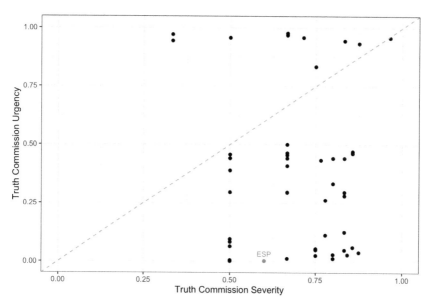

FIGURE 4.8. Truth commission urgency and severity: Spain relative to other GTJD countries with both scores above 0

almost three decades had past since Franco's death. Also, as explained in Chapter 1, Spain's democratization effort advanced despite forgoing TJ efforts. The Figure 4.8 suggests that despite the delay, Spain did catch up to other countries, in the GTJD.

On December 26, 2007, the Spanish Cortes passed the Law of Historical Memory,[16] which in and of itself was not yet a truth commission, though became very significant in the Spanish TJ trajectory. It was the first time a proposal mentioned efforts to make moral reparations to the victims of Civil War and the Dictatorship. Despite not lustrating or setting up a truth commission per se, the parliamentary debates surrounding the law proposed numerous transparency-oriented amendments. They were not passed in the final version of the law save for one critical aspect, which was later picked up in succeeding legislation.

The law included: general recognition of victims and a provision for further reparations to them, a declaration of illegitimacy of civil war/dictatorship persecutions and trials, a commitment of the govern-

---

[16] The law was titled "Law 52/2007, of 26 December 2007, ensuring the recognition of, expansion of rights of, and establishment of measures in favor of those who suffered persecution or violence during the civil war and dictatorship."

ment to take part in the search for mass graves, and the removal of Francoist symbols from public spaces. Key in this first Memory law was the recuperation and protection and eventual making public of documentation of the civil war. The law not only guaranteed access to such archives but also authorized the government to acquire and collect further documentation pertaining to repression during the civil war.

This law set off an avalanche of TJ legislation in the Cortes including proposals to modify the 1977 Amnesty Law, declassifying Franco era military documents on a wide variety of repressions (proposed in December 2011, unsuccessfully put to a vote in January 2012, and eventually passed in October 2013), resolutions to urge the judicial investigation of Francoist crimes (February 2012) and proposals of creating a truth commission in various forms. Although none of the attempts at creating a truth commission with very wide prerogatives succeeded, the overwhelming amount of research, exhumations, and declassification that was poured into these various efforts, did bring transparency back to Spain. The revelations led not only to the removal from their positions of persons responsible for crimes committed in secret, but even to some prosecutions, such as the criminal trial of a doctor responsible for stealing a newborn from an imprisoned political dissident. The ongoing events in Spain collectively suggest that, as a policy choice, "thick lines" and postulates to "let sleeping dogs lie" cannot work for long (Kovras 2013).

High Truth Commission Urgency with High Volatility: Bolivia and South Africa

Next, I compare and contrast against other cases in the dataset, Bolivia and South Africa, which are two countries with truth commissions characterized by relatively high volatility and high urgency (Bolivia) and moderate urgency (South Africa).

Bolivia, a former military dictatorship led by Garcia Meza, a general with ties to the drug trade, boasts a TJ chronology that is very sparse on personnel mechanisms. It has, for instance, no lustration nor either thorough or leadership purges and hardly any criminal trial activity. At the same time, early on in the autumn of 1982, the newly installed civilian government led by Hernan Siles Zuazo issued a decree, creating a National Commission of Inquiry into Forced Disappearances. Yet merely a year and a half later, and a year short before fulfilling its mandate, the commission was disbanded. It had not even had a chance to publish an interim report. No other commission of inquiry was ever appointed.

This early positive event followed by an early negative event is what contributed to the high volatility (note that there are only four countries with higher volatility than Bolivia) and high urgency of Bolivia's score in truth commissions.

South Africa's democratic transition took place via a peaceful pact. Less than three months following the first competitive elections that paved the way to democracy, the justice minister announced the creation of the truth commission. The Truth and Reconciliation Commission (TRC) set the standard for such commissions around the world, and its very name has become synonymous with the phrase "successful truth commission."

At the same time, legislation extending and modifying its various provisions was far from uncontroversial, contributing to moderately high volatility.

Among the controversies was that although the TRC was created to "investigate gross human rights violations that were perpetrated during the period of the Apartheid regime from 1960 to 1994, including abductions, killings, torture," its mandate also covered violations committed by liberation movements. The commission was also empowered to grant amnesty to perpetrators who confessed their crimes truthfully and completely to the commission.

This last prerogative was appealed by families of murdered dissidents to the constitutional court, but to no avail. The court ruled that "reconciliation should be placed above revenge" and that the commission would continue to grant amnesties to those who voluntarily confessed and could prove that their crimes had been politically motivated.

Over time, the commission was also granted powers to search and seize property as well as to subpoena witnesses. The commission began holding hearings in 1996, but its work was extended in 1998.

South Africa's truth commission trajectory was not as urgent as Bolivia's, but just as volatile. Various powers of the commission raised controversy, but the accumulation of events amounted to a much more severe outcome (.5 in South Africa in contrast to Bolivia's .33).

Purge Severity and Urgency South Korea

In this section, I look into the severity and urgency of leadership purges using the last archetypal case of this book – South Korea. Recall from our discussion in the conclusion to Part I of the book that South Korea was a former military dictatorship or rather a succession of two military regimes. The most disciplined unit designed for sustaining the dictatorship was the so-called Hanahoe group made up of officers from the same

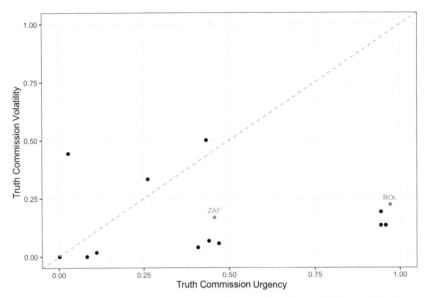

FIGURE 4.9. Truth commission urgency and volatility: South Africa and Bolivia relative to other GTJD countries with scores above 0

class of the military academy as Chun Doo-hwan who seized power in 1979 and became the leader succeeding the Fourth Republic. This group, whose name meant "an association of one for all and all for one" was purged by the democratic President Kim Young-sam. Korea's dictatorship was a highly institutionalized dictatorship. According to the measure of state capacity described in detail in Chapter 7 for the decade preceding the democratic transition it scored between 1.127 and 1.473, which is in the top decile of all authoritarian regimes in the GTJD. As reflected in Figure 4.9, the purge events in Korea were swift, but not extensive. The reason is because the purges extended only to the Hanahoe membership, which was the group exhibiting the highest loyalty to the former dictator and consequently, most likely to sabotage the new democratic government. Other units of the military apparatus were largely spared and no thorough purges were conducted in South Korea. This is broadly consistent with the predictions of the model about causes of purges from Chapter 3, where the two factors moderating the desire to purge are institutionalization of the *ancien régime* on the one hand, but also proximity in preferences between agents of that regime and the new democratic politician. While the first was high in South Korea, the latter was so great that purges extending to the Hanahoe were actually beneficial (Table 3.3).

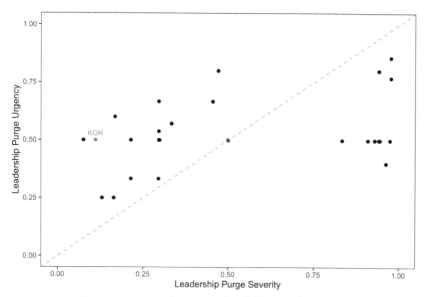

FIGURE 4.10. Purge urgency and severity: South Korea relative to other GTJD countries with scores above 0

4.3 CONCLUSION

This chapter introduced readers to the GTJD, the source of the key independent variables used to address how authoritarian legacies influence the type of TJ that can be used by new political leaders to improve democratic quality. Where authoritarian legacies abound in secret collaborators and where most of the authoritarian repression was carried out in secret, lustrations and truth commissions are called for. Where collaboration with the regime was more open than secret, the only viable mechanism to pursue with regard to personnel is purges. Yet, new democracies may not be in a position to carry out purges if doing so would result in losing valuable expertise.

This theory of TJ called for the creation of an original dataset along with measures of TJ, and so this chapter introduced the GTJD. This dataset is innovative in a number of ways. First, it records TJ as events unfolding over time following the year of transition. This allows me to account for instances of delayed TJ. It also allows me to design innovative ways of measuring aspects of TJ such as volatility and, critical to this book, severity. I encourage scholars to use my TJ events data as building blocks for constructing new measures motivated by their specific theoretical interests.

A second innovation of my dataset is that it parses out similar yet distinct ways of dealing with personnel of the former authoritarian regime – namely, purges and lustration. Whereas purges remove from office elites whose actions under the former authoritarian regime were known or perpetrators who committed crimes that are common knowledge, lustration and truth commissions reveal information that was kept secret. I argue that due to this, lustrations have more in common with truth commissions than they do with purges.

5

Lustration and Programmatic Representation

In Chapter 4, I explained the data collection strategy that I adopted to answer the theoretical question posed in the first part of the book: How does transitional justice (TJ) impact democratic life in a country recovering from authoritarian rule? My strategy for measuring the independent variable in this study involves disaggregating TJ into transparency regimes (lustration and truth commissions) on the one hand and purges (of the thorough and leadership variety) on the other. Following this coding, I proposed a flexible way of measuring the intensity of TJ that takes the ratio of positive TJ events to negative events. This measure, which I termed "severity," can be adjusted to provide values that vary over time. In this chapter,[1] I use severity to examine the effect of transitional justice on democratic quality. First, I focus on lustration; Chapter 6 examines the effects of truth commissions, and Chapter 7 is devoted to purges. In Chapter 8, I summarize the effects of all three TJ mechanisms on the quality of democracy measured as Power distributed by Socioeconomic Status.

5.1 HOW DOES LUSTRATION AFFECT POLITICIANS' RESPONSIVENESS?

I begin with an examination of the implications of the model from Chapter 2, which I used to make predictions about the quality of

---

[1] The statistical analysis presented in this chapter relies on coauthored work with Milena Ang, which appeared as "Can transitional justice improve the quality of representation in new democracies?" in *World Politics*, Volume 71, no. 4 (2019): 631–666.

representation in response to lustration – that is, legislation dealing with secret forms of collaboration.

The model in Chapter 2 represents the dynamic between individual politicians and officers of former authoritarian regimes. The main implication of the model is that lustration prevents blackmail, curbing departures from policies that would be desirable for the electorate. Put differently, I argue that in a perfectly representative democracy, the politician's ideal point would correspond to policies that the voters would like to see implemented.

Since the outcome of interest is the distance between the politician's ideal point and the final policy that is implemented, the model predicts individual departures from such perfect representation. Obtaining the necessary evidence to document these departures would require careful analysis of the preferences of individual politicians and former authoritarian elites.

In an era where political parties have become ubiquitous and closely control the expression of individual legislators, such data is impossible to obtain for all countries in out dataset. Hence, instead I opt to test the model's implication using a combination of party-level data on ideological positions and quality of representation, and country-level data of lustration policies. I operationalize quality of representation with programmaticness. I elaborate on this concept in Section 5.2.

5.2 PROGRAMMATICNESS

In order to operationalize the parameter that characterizes equilibrium predictions from Chapter 2, we need a measure of the degree to which politicians are able to implement the policies they prefer for purely ideological reasons; that is, the degree to which participants, free from pressures of patronage and blackmail can implement policies voters desire. Indeed, this conceptualization is very close to what is considered in the comparative politics literature as programmatic representation or simply programmaticness (Carroll & Nalepa 2014, 2020; Kitschelt & Freeze 2010), defined by the following three characteristics:

1. Parties run on policy platforms;
2. Voters are aware of these platforms and elect parties on the basis of these platforms;
3. Parties aspire to implement these platforms upon election.

Programmaticness is ideal for measuring my outcome of interest because the measure captures both the cohesion within a party, and the salience of policies that such parties represent. Programmaticness is also ideally suited for bridging the gap between individuals in my model and parties. The justification for this runs as follows: The ideological cohesion of a party relies on its members sharing the same ideological platform and supporting policies that advance this platform. Salience ensures that this is a relevant platform for the voters.

Notice how legacies of authoritarian rule interfere with programmatic representation: Should one of the party members be blackmailed into making policy concessions to a former agent, the departure from the shared platform would decrease party cohesion. Hence, I believe that we can rely on data aggregated at the party level to pick up irregularities in individual behavior. Notably, the blackmail of politicians by members of the previous authoritarian regime, if successful in extracting concessions from the politicians, constrains their ability to faithfully represent voters. To the extent that programmatic representation involves delivering policies that represent broad wishes of the electorate, the theory from Chapter 2 makes predictions about how transparency regimes enable such representation by eliminating the possibility of using compromising information to extract policy concessions.

In light of this discussion, in order to measure quality of representation as programmaticness, I propose to use a modification of the measure constructed by Herbert Kitschelt and his coauthors from the Democracy and Accountability Linkages Project (DALP) (Kitschelt & Freeze 2010; Kitschelt & Singer 2018).

The original measure made by the creators of DALP was constructed from a large-scale survey of experts in 88 different countries answering questions about the cohesion, salience, and polarization of 506 parties. I restricted this dataset of partisan programmaticness to countries that transitioned from party-based authoritarian rule after 1946. This resulted in over 300 parties in 61 countries, as not all countries from the Global Transitional Justice Dataset are represented in DALP.

In DALP, programmaticness is conceptualized as a combination of three party characteristics: (1) the salience of party platforms; (2) parties' cohesion around these platforms; and (3) the polarization of parties in the party system. Kitschelt et al. constructed an index based on responses to questions tapping into each of these components. While salience and cohesion are very desirable properties in a measure, polarization poses a problem, in light of the conceptual proximity of polarization and the distance between the ideal points of the former authoritarian elites

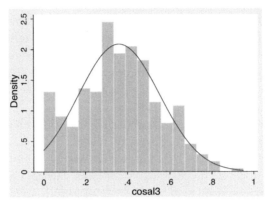

FIGURE 5.1. Histogram of measure of party cohesion and salience, based on
DALP, by taking polarization questions out of the cosalpo3 measure

and new democratic elites in my model.[2] By controlling for distance,
as I intend to, I would be placing a variable responsible for distance
between parties both on the left-hand side – as a component of the
dependent variable – and on the right-hand side of the regression. Using
it this way would produce biased parameter estimates. To remedy this
problem, I created a new measure that leaves out questions pertaining
to polarization.[3] It is a score between o and 1 that comprises just the
cohesion and salience dimensions of the original variable. The graph in
Figure 5.1 shows the histogram of this measure using the 315 parties for
which this measure was created (Figure 5.1).

The added value of DALP is that it offers a party-based measure;
this yields multiple measures per country – as many as there are parties
that were evaluated by experts in each country, allowing me to better
approximate the model's predictions. Hence, this measure will be used
in a hierarchical modeling setup. In contrast, the next variables I propose offer multiple measures per country because they are measured
over time.

Although programmaticness is associated in the literature with high-
quality democratic representation, it has not been used in the past in

---

[2] I am grateful to Anna Grzymala-Busse for highlighting this problem with using the original
programmaticness measure.
[3] This measure was prepared with the valuable assistance of Milena Ang and with the raw
data provided by Herbert Kitschelt. The details of this construction have been relegated
to Appendix 8.1.

conjuction with data on TJ. In contrast, scholars who have constructed global transitional justice datasets that span TJ implementation over time have used as dependent variables trust in governmental institutions (Horne & Levi 2004), peace (Binningsbø et al. 2012*a*), and regime stability (Olsen et al. 2010). They have not found that lustration matters for these outcomes (Binningsbø et al. 2012*a*; Olsen et al. 2010; Thoms et al. 2010; Van der Merwe et al. 2009). The reason for this could be linked to the different and highly aggregated definition of lustration (recall that it includes both purges and lustration). However, the null findings could also be attributable to outcome variables that are only superficially connected to the quality of democratic representation.

Having summarized the empirical implications of the model from Chapter 2 and the operationalization of programmaticness, in Section 5.3, I list the specific hypotheses, which I will be testing with a hierarchical model.

5.3 HYPOTHESES

The model's main implication is that the probability that information from secret police files has been exposed by lustration (parameter π in the model) raises the quality of representation because it prevents blackmail of politicians with these secret files. This can be stated as the following hypothesis:

Main hypothesis: All else kept constant, the quality of representation will increase as the *severity* of lustration increases.

Lustration is operationalized with the severity measure developed in Chapter 4:

$$S = \frac{\sum_t (P^t)}{\sum_t (P^t + N^t) + 1}.$$

This is, to be clear, the version of the lustration measure that aggregates all lustration events into one value, seemingly discarding the information of how lustration unfolds over time and failing to leverage the time series aspect of the data. The reason I make this choice is dictated by the fact that lustration is a slow-moving process. For one, the collection of secret police files into a common archive is a lengthy and often protracted procedure. Once all files are in place, one may have to wait long for lustration to take full effect. In 2017, according to one of my interlocutors, Poland's lustration division chairman, Radoslaw Peterman, the backlog of lustration cases in the country's Institute of National Remembrance had reached 370,000 cases, which in Radoslaw Peterman's view, would take decades to process.[4] As I explain in the following, the hierarchical modeling framework allows me to integrate variables that vary over time and within larger units of analysis with those that do not.

Recall that the model yielded several additional implications that justify the inclusion of additional variables as controls in the statistical model presented.

An important parameter to control for in testing the model from Chapter 2 is the distance between the blackmailer and the new democratic politician. Despite the fact that in democratic polities, politicians can occupy many different positions in the policy space, my unit of analysis is a party within a country. As explained in Section 5.2, I justify this by practicality and the fact that in an era of high party discipline, it is hard to disentangle politicians' preferences from their parties. At the same time, this modeling selection allows me to account for the fact that democratic parties' ideal points are different from one another, and some are closer to the blackmailer than others. *This is another reason for the multilevel (or hierarchical) modeling analysis – that is, one that breaks down variation in the quality of parties within countries into two parts: the between country level and the within country level (as parties that vary within the same country share the same sources of variation).*

An important second empirical implication of the model is that quality of representation decreases as the cost of having compromising information revealed increases (parameter F in the model of Chapter 2). This means that as voters and, consequently, politicians become more concerned with having skeletons in their closet revealed, blackmailers with access to secret police files can distort policy more. In order to operationalize this concern over exposed skeletons in the closet, I make use of the fact that in democracies recovering from authoritarian rule, the salience of who was and who was not a collaborator diminishes over time. This claim finds support in the literature on historical memory and is also corroborated by the fact that in a young democracy, more voters will have experienced (and will remember) life under autocracy (Pop-Eleches 2007, Pop-Eleches & Tucker 2011, 2012) than in a seasoned democracy (Bernhard & Kubik 2014; Cohen 1995; De Brito et al. 2001; Stan 2006;

---

4 Radoslaw Peterman, personal communication, Warsaw Poland, June 2015.

Wilde 1999). Hence, I operationalize the cost F as the years lapsed since the transition.[5] This leads to my second hypothesis:

Additional hypothesis: All other things held constant; as the time lapsed since the transition to democracy increases, the quality of representation will increase.

This operationalization is somewhat coarse because the cost of revealing collaboration is not only a function of how voters react to allegations of collaboration but also of other institutional features. For example, it could be that revelations about collaboration are costlier in electoral systems with the personal vote (such as Single Member Districts or Open List Proportional Representation) than in systems where voters cannot directly specify which candidate gets elected into office (Carey & Shugart 1995; Cheibub & Nalepa 2020). Alternatively, voters may be more interested in elections in some countries than in others; this would imply that revelations are mediated by an overall interest in electoral participation or turnout. The advantage of the measure I settled for – based on the assumption that the political cost of exposed skeletons in a politician's closet should be higher, on average, in recently transitioned countries than in countries that transitioned a long time ago — is its simplicity, allowing me to avoid difficult judgment calls.

The third implication of my theory is that the ideological distance between Politicians and Officers does not impact the quality of democracy. However, as mentioned earlier, this finding is not robust to changing the functional form of players' utility functions to quadratic (see Ang & Nalepa 2019, for an alternative specification of the blackmail model). Particularly in light of this, it is important to control for distance between players' ideal points in the regressions. Similarly to the case of the dependent variable, programmaticness, my operationalization of distance relies on the DALP dataset at the level of party within country. Specifically, I take advantage of the fact that DALP reports average ideological placements of political parties in countries from my sample. Since some of these parties are successor authoritarian parties, I use their placement to proxy for the ideological placement of blackmailing officers. Next, for each non-successor party p in country k, I define *party distance* as the absolute

---

[5] Consistently with the GTJD, the date of transition is taken from the Authoritarian Regimes Database (Geddes et al. 2014), which my research assistants and I have updated through 2018.

difference in left–right placement between party p and the country's successor authoritarian party.

The disaggregation of programmaticness into party scores is permissible under the HLM framework, but also substantively justified. It is hard not to agree that parties even within the same country will vary *in how well they can represent voters and* this representation depends critically on the kinds of ties that parties maintain with their voters. The juxtaposition of programmatic ties and clientelistic ties with voters in particular has received a lot of attention in comparative politics (Auerbach & Thachil 2018; Kitschelt 1999; Kitschelt & Wilkinson 2007; Stokes et al. 2013).

Some countries in my sample do not have a successor party to the authoritarian regime. For these countries, I replaced the missing distance with the average distance between successor and non-successor parties across all remaining countries, and I included an indicator variable to account for these cases.[6]

Finally, I attempt to control also for the cost of bluffing, c. Importantly, in the model from Chapter 2, the cost of bluffing does not appear in the predicted misrepresentation. However, an increase in the costs of bluffing to the Officer increases the chances of a non-separating equilibrium, an equilibrium where TJ does not work as "it should" (in the sense that even with lustration, bluffing takes place). Thus, in addition to the quality of representation, the cost of bluffing affects whether politicians are bluffed or blackmailed with actual evidence.

I propose to operationalize the cost of bluffing affects with the Press Freedom Index as reported by Reporters Without Borders. To avoid confusion, I linearly transformed this variable to make lower rankings correspond to lower press freedom. The reasoning behind this operationalization is as follows: When an officer of the authoritarian regime tries to bluff a politician into thinking that he is in possession of evidence against the politician, such a bluff can be easily exposed in an environment with free media. Put differently, claims regarding collaboration between a politician and the former secret police will likely be reported, and if the press is free, claims will be investigated and eventually denounced if they are found to be false. A wide literature discusses the thoroughness of journalists in revealing evidence of former secret police conduct (Chapman 2009; Laplante & Phenicie 2009; Pinto 2010). Although the scrutiny offered by

---

[6] See Appendix C for a replication of my analysis limited to the subsample of countries for which I do have information on the successor party.

journalists is not perfect, the higher the degree of media independence, the more likely it is that an Officer's bluff will be called.

5.4 THE STATISTICAL MODEL

Taking together these empirical implications leads to the following linear specification:[7]

$$programmaticness_{p,k}$$
$$= \beta_k + \beta_d * party\ distance_{p,k} + \beta_s * severity_k$$
$$+ \beta_n * years\ since\ transition_k + \beta_c * press\ freedom_k$$
$$+ \beta_X \sum X_k + e_{p,k} + e_k. \tag{5.1}$$

where programmaticness is operationalized as *cosal3* for party p in country k.[8] In addition to the main variables of interest described earlier, the model incorporates a series of country-level control variables ($\sum X_k$), as well as a series of country-specific intercepts (β_k).

As implied by the previous equation, the outcome of interest (*programmaticness*) and one regressor (*party distance*) are party-level attributes, while the remaining variables are measured at the country-level. To account for this structure, I use a hierarchical linear modeling (HLM) framework. Given that parties are nested within countries, estimating this model using ordinary least squares regression (OLS) would risk biased and inefficient results because characteristics of parties within the same country are not independent of one another. Traditional solutions to working with data of this kind (such as fixed effects or clustered standard errors) cannot be applied here because some countries only have one party that is not an authoritarian successor.

HLM is a compromise between assuming all parties are independent from each other and assuming that all variation across parties can be explained by their country. A multilevel approach models variation in the dependent variable as a function of party-level and country-level characteristics. To estimate the specific model described earlier in equation (5.1), I use a series of country-level coefficients (β_j) that share an underlying

---

[7] See Appendix C for a derivation of this specification.
[8] The details on how this measure was derived from DALP data are provided in Appendix 9.5.1.

distribution with a global mean (μ_{β_j}) and standard deviation (σ_{β_j}).[9] This equation is the best way of modeling the outcome of interest, given the data available.

Raudenbusch and Brisk (2002) describe HLM as one of the most flexible statistical frameworks in that it accommodates both time variant and invariant independent variables as well as permits data to have a nested structure. They point out that, theoretically, there is nothing inconsistent in allowing an intercept to be affected in the same way over time by one feature but in ways varying over time by other features. In political science, HLM models have been presented as random effects models and are perceived as inferior to the more conservative, fixed effects models. But using a fixed effect model here would require employing the time-variant measures of lustration. I argued previously that this is not substantively justified because the effects of lustration take time to influence the quality of democracy, more so than other transparency mechansims and purges, especially. However, to make up for what some readers might consider a deficiency, in the case of remaining mechanisms, I use designs that take full advantage of the time-variant nature of the data.

Before presenting and discussing the results, I address one possible concern: If countries where lustration was successfully implemented also have parties that are better at representing voters, I risk overestimating the relationship between lustration severity and quality of representation. Such overestimation, however, would have been captured by the country-level intercepts. Put differently, if countries that implemented lustration were also those with more programmatic parties, this regularity would be captured by the country-specific estimates.

The results of the estimations are shown in Table 5.1. For ease of interpretation, all variables have been linearly transformed to range between 0 and 1. All models presented here include country-level intercepts (estimations for β_j) and an indicator variable controlling for missing successor parties, both of which are omitted from the table for space considerations. The table reports the average change in *programmaticness* by a non-successor party associated with an increase by one unit in the covariate of interest.

---

[9] Assuming that all parties are independent of one another would require estimating a fully pooled model with one global intercept. Assuming total dependency on country characteristics would mean a traditional fixed effects approach that would estimate one intercept per country (minus a base category). The advantage of the multilevel model is that when there is very little observed variation at the country-level, the coefficient can be estimated to be close to the mean, μ_{β_j}.

TABLE 5.1. *Programmaticness and severity of lustration*

	Model 1	Model 2	Model 3	Model 4
Lustration severity	0.278***	0.255***	0.208***	0.209***
	(0.062)	(0.064)	(0.069)	(0.070)
Distance	−0.107***	−0.109***	−0.111***	−0.111***
	(0.034)	(0.034)	(0.034)	(0.034)
Years since transition		0.150	0.108	0.113
		(0.103)	(0.107)	(0.115)
Freedom of the press			0.370*	0.369*
			(0.215)	(0.217)
Opposition status				0.005
				(0.038)
Constant	0.278***	0.217***	−0.039	−0.044
	(0.036)	(0.055)	(0.158)	(0.163)
Country intercepts	Y	Y	Y	Y
Missing successor	Y	Y	Y	Y
Observations	313	313	307	307
Log likelihood	184.327	184.036	179.721	177.384
Akaike inf. crit.	−356.654	−354.073	−343.442	−336.768
Bayesian inf. crit.	−334.177	−327.849	−313.627	−303.226

Note: $^*p < 0.1$; $^{**}p < 0.05$; $^{***}p < 0.01$

The resulting estimations are generally consistent with the implications of the theoretical model from Chapter 2. Most importantly and consistently with the main hypothesis, they show that higher scores of lustration *severity* are associated, on average, with more programmatic parties. The effect is statistically significant at the 0.05 percent confidence level, and robust to the inclusion of country-specific intercepts and other relevant covariates. In addition, its average effect is substantial: The difference in programmaticness between a country that did not attempt any lustration at all (with a *severity* score of 0) and a country with the highest lustration *severity* (with a *severity* score of 0.82) is 0.17 points, according to the point estimate of Model 3. Since the variable *quality of representation* ranges from 0 to 1, this average effect accounts for one-fifth of the possible range of my outcome of interest.

Note that the number of parties used in the regression models may seem to be low relative to all parties for which DALP data exist. What accounts for the lower than 535 number of parties in the remaining models is a combination of the fact that post-conflict countries are not included in the dataset and that each country "loses" the successor party, for whom distance is not calculated. In addition to this, data on press freedom from the Journalists without Borders were not available for a couple of countries, hence the difference in the number of observations.

The relationship between lustration severity and quality of democracy interpreted as programmaticness can be shown in yet another way. Figure 5.2 presents the relationship between *programmaticness* and *lustration severity* by plotting the *severity* score (horizontal axis) against the average country effects estimated in a model predicting programmaticness with only *party distance* and a series of country-specific intercepts that capture average country-programmaticness. Figure 5.2 suggests a positive relationship between these two variables. Furthermore, this pattern seems to be much clearer for the observations that fall in the right half of the panel, that is, the countries that implemented more severe lustration policies. This variation supports my decision to measure TJ continuously rather than as a dichotomous variable.

Second, the evidence shows that the severity of TJ, and specifically of lustration policies, is positively related to the quality of representation. This result is promising insofar as it suggests that lustration policies produce, on average, greater programmaticness.

Since the theoretical model from Chapter 2 also shows that the proper functioning of lustration policies is affected by other factors, such as a free press to prevent bluffing, I turn now to discussing the tests of my additional hypotheses.

First, I find a negative and statistically significant effect of the ideological distance between each party and its successor (*party distance*). This finding is intuitive, though inconsistent with the model's predictions – where distance was predicted not to have an effect at all. However, as I pointed out earlier, the irrelevance of distance between the blackmailer and the politician from the model in Chapter 2 is not robust to specifying the utility functions of the players' as quadratic (Ang & Nalepa 2019). A hypothesis consistent with empirical implications from the model with quadratic preferences is that as the distance between each party and the successor party increases, the programmaticness should decrease. This result is not only what happens empirically, but the empirical finding is robust, as I show in Section 5.5.

We can also see that the results are not driven by preexisting dynamics between the opposition and authoritarian parties (for instance, parties that existed during authoritarianism could share characteristics that make

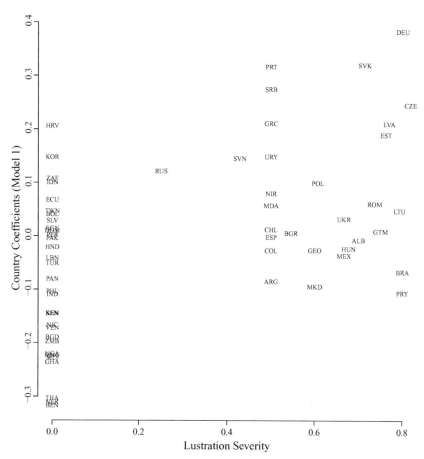

FIGURE 5.2. Severity of lustration and average quality of democracy: intercept by country

their members more likely to be blackmailed). I control for this possible confounder using a measure of how active the opposition was in representative state institutions during the authoritarian era. Cheibub et al. (2010) report data on the standing of the opposition in authoritarian legislatures.[10] I turned their variable *opposition status* into an indicator that takes the value of 1 if there were multiple parties represented in the legislature and 0 otherwise.[11] As can be seen from Model 4 in Table 5.1, the inclusion of this variable does not change my results.

[10] Specifically, Cheibub et al. (2010) record whether the authoritarian regime had no legislature, a single-party legislature, or a multiparty legislature.
[11] Even though the original variable assumes a third value (no legislature), my sample contains only two former authoritarian regimes without legislatures.

Models 3 and 4 include the variable *years since transition*, which I use as a proxy for the cost of having skeletons revealed (F). In the additional hypothesis described previously in this chapter, I anticipated that over time, as voters become desensitized to authoritarian legacies, politicians pay lower costs for being exposed as collaborators of the former authoritarian regime. As a result, they become more resistant to blackmail, and the quality of representation increases. According to Table 2, the coefficient associated with *years since transition* is not statistically significant, either in Model 2, 3, or 4. I conclude from this that counting years since the transition took place is a poor proxy for the costs of having skeletons in the closet revealed. At the same time, even if coarse as a measure, it is useful to point out how robust the severity coefficient is to including this variable as a control.

The last two models of Table 5.1 include *press freedom*, the variable operationalizing parameter c, the cost of bluffing. I find that the variable is positively related to programmaticness, although this association is only positive at the 90 percent level. I also find that it does not change the estimated effects of the rest of the theoretically relevant regressors, which I take as evidence supporting my main hypotheses.[12]

The models reported here are static, meaning that they take a snapshot of a country and thus cannot produce evidence of changing quality of representation over time. Nevertheless, they have many redeeming features. First, DALP extends to over eighty democracies and exhibits almost perfect overlap with the set of countries included in the Global Transitional Justice Dataset. Competing datasets, such as the Chapel Hill Expert Survey or the Manifesto Project, would not allow me to measure quality of representation for even half of the countries in the Global Transitional Justice Dataset. Yet, to ensure that the results presented in this chapter are not an artifact of the static nature of the statistical model, in Chapter 8, I present a model that uses all the distinct TJ mechanisms to predict another dependent variable that operationalized quality of democracy, but is measured over time. As I show in that chapter, lustration appears as the strongest predictor of high democratic quality.[13]

---

[12] Interestingly, the constant term is no longer statistically significant when *press freedom* is included. I interpret this as a type of omitted variable bias: in Models 1 and 2, the average effect of a free press and time since transition is encapsulated by this constant.

[13] Quality of democracy is measured there with the VDem variable, Power distributed by Socioeconomic Status, which captures the extent to which political wealth is associated with economic wealth.

5.5 DISCUSSION AND ROBUSTNESS CHECKS

Given how critical political scientists are regarding the ability of HLM models to identify causality, I subject my statistical model to a number of robustness checks. The most technical of these, such as replicating the results with only countries that have successor parties (so forgoing the imputation), have been relegated to Appendix C, but many of the substantively intuitive ones are included here. I begin with selections into treatment, and proceed through testing for reverse causality and alternative specifications of the policy distance variable.

Selection into Treatment

I first consider the possibility that more economically developed countries have both more positive lustration events and a more programmatic parties. To test for this possibility, I regress *lustration severity* in country k on *gdp per capita* at the time of its transition (*tyear*), on the years lapsed since the transition (*years since transition*), and on the competitiveness of the inaugural elections measured as the *margin* of victory. I additionally include a dummy indicating whether country k held such inaugural elections at all. This model takes the form:

$$severity_k = b_0 + b_1 * log(gdp \ per \ capita_{k,tyear})$$
$$+ \ b_2 * years \ since \ transition_k$$
$$+ \ b_4 * margin_{k,eyear} + b_5 * miss\_ele_k + e_k.$$

I use it to estimate *predicted lustration severity*. Next, I allow this variable to stand in for lustration severity in each of the models estimated in Table 5.1. The key to this probe is that *predicted severity* captures only economic and political determinants of lustration severity. Table 5.2 indicates that my main finding is robust to this probe.

Including GDP per Capita

Information on economic development can be used in yet another way to stress test my results. Economic development and state capacity are factors that could explain both lustration severity and the quality of representation. To correct for this potential source of endogeneity in my models, I control for logged GDP per capita. The results are provided in Table 5.3.

TABLE 5.2. *Robustness check: using predicted lustration severity in regression of programmaticness*

	Model 1	Model 2	Model 3	Model 4
Party distance	−0.106***	−0.106***	−0.107***	−0.096***
	(0.034)	(0.034)	(0.034)	(0.034)
Predicted severity	0.587***	0.579***	0.518***	0.375***
	(0.104)	(0.119)	(0.118)	(0.112)
Years since transition		0.016	−0.034	0.096
		(0.109)	(0.107)	(0.108)
Press freedom			0.420**	0.357*
			(0.191)	(0.200)
Opposition status				−0.007
				(0.037)
Constant	0.171***	0.166***	−0.121	−0.046
	(0.032)	(0.046)	(0.055)	(0.141)
Country intercepts	Y	Y	Y	Y
Observations	307	307	307	307
Log likelihood	184.076	182.781	184.387	180.693
Akaike inf. crit.	−356.151	−351.562	−352.774	−345.387
Bayesian inf. crit.	−333.790	−325.474	−322.959	−315.572

Note: $*p < 0.1$; $**p < 0.05$; $***p < 0.01$

Using Only pre-2008 Country Years to Test Reverse Causality
Another robustness check involves discarding all post-2008 observations and calculating the measure of lustration severity using only pre-2008 data as this is when DALP data was collected. This robustness test checks for the possibility that instead of lustration contributing to programmaticness, it is the other way around: Programmaticness causes lustration. The results reported in Table 5.4 are robust to this probe also.

Conditions of the Opposition
The final robustness check I consider responds to the inadequacy of measuring the ideological distance between the Politician and the blackmailing Officer with the difference in policy positions of a successor and a non-successor party. What if the policy position of the successor party is a poor approximation of the location of the blackmailer? After all, this

TABLE 5.3. *Robustness check: replication controlling for economic development using GDP per capita*

	Model 1	Model 2	Model 3	Model 4
Lustration severity	0.161**	0.126*	0.082	0.082
	(0.065)	(0.066)	(0.068)	(0.069)
Party distance	−0.109***	−0.111***	−0.111***	−0.111***
	(0.034)	(0.034)	(0.034)	(0.034)
log(gdp per capita)	0.104***	0.109***	0.108***	0.108***
	(0.027)	(0.027)	(0.026)	(0.026)
Years since transition		0.187**	0.139	0.142
		(0.094)	(0.095)	(0.102)
Press freedom			0.366*	0.366*
			(0.190)	(0.192)
Opposition status				0.002
				(0.035)
Constant	−0.569**	−0.680***	−0.928***	−0.930***
	(0.224)	(0.226)	(0.255)	(0.259)
Country intercepts	Y	Y	Y	Y
Missing successor	Y	Y	Y	Y
Observations	307	307	307	307
Log likelihood	183.092	183.601	184.680	182.243
Akaike inf. crit.	−352.184	−351.202	−351.360	−344.485
Bayesian inf. crit.	−326.096	−321.387	−317.818	−307.217

Note: $*p < 0.1$; $**p < 0.05$; $***p < 0.01$

blackmailer worked for the pre-transition authoritarian party and a lot may have changed in their policy preferences since that time. How vast that change is depends in part on the status of the anti-authoritarian opposition at the time of transition. Absent controls for the relationship between the pre-transition opposition and the government, the empirical finding regarding *party distance* may be biased. One way to account for this relationship is to use the successor vote share in the inaugural democratic election following the democratic transition. A second alternative is to use the margin of victory in that inaugural election. Table 5.5 reports results from this robustness check, indicating that my results are robust to this probe also.

TABLE 5.4. *Robustness check: replication using restricted lustration severity sample to 2008*

	Model 2	Model 3	Model 4	Model 5
Lustration severity (pre-2008)	0.261***	0.258***	0.188***	0.190***
	(0.066)	(0.066)	(0.070)	(0.071)
Party distance	−0.102***	−0.104***	−0.105***	−0.105***
	(0.035)	(0.035)	(0.035)	(0.036)
Years since transition		0.003	0.002	0.003
		(0.002)	(0.002)	(0.003)
Press freedom			0.573**	0.570**
			(0.226)	(0.228)
Opposition status				0.007
				(0.038)
Constant	0.309***	0.265***	−0.164	−0.169
	(0.038)	(0.054)	(0.173)	(0.176)
Country intercepts	Y	Y	Y	Y
Missing successor	Y	Y	Y	Y
Observations	294	294	288	288
Log likelihood	170.425	166.017	163.998	161.663
Akaike inf. crit.	−328.849	−318.035	−311.996	−305.326
Bayesian inf. crit.	−306.748	−292.250	−282.692	−272.359

Note: $^*p < 0.1$; $^{**}p < 0.05$; $^{***}p < 0.01$

5.6 CONCLUSION

In this chapter, I investigated how lustration, understood as the policies that reveal information about prior collaboration with secret authoritarian elites, influences programmatic representation of political parties. The evidence presented here corroborates the theoretical predictions from the formal model from Chapter 2, according to which officers of the former authoritarian regime use secret police files to blackmail new democratic elites. The mechanism presented in Chapter 2 outlined how evidence of past collaboration can be used to force democratic elites to implement policies that are amenable to former authoritarian elites instead of voters. Based on the theory I developed, I predicted that former authoritarian elites' ability to shape policy is greater when TJ is legislated less frequently, and that these elites' influence decreases with how much voters care about authoritarian skeletons in their politicians' closets. I also made predictions

TABLE 5.5. *Robustness check: replication using successor party voteshare and margin of victory*

	Model 1	Model 2	Model 3	Model 4	Model 5
Lustration severity	0.278***	0.255***	0.208***	0.215***	0.206***
	(0.062)	(0.064)	(0.069)	(0.068)	(0.069)
Party distance	−0.107***	−0.109***	−0.111***	−0.115***	−0.111***
	(0.034)	(0.034)	(0.034)	(0.034)	(0.034)
Years since transition		0.150	0.108	0.093	0.104
		(0.103)	(0.107)	(0.105)	(0.108)
Press freedom			0.370*	0.348	0.367*
			(0.215)	(0.212)	(0.216)
Successor vote share				−0.003*	
				(0.002)	
Margin of victory					0.001
					(0.002)
Constant	0.278***	0.217***	−0.039	0.046	−0.050
	(0.036)	(0.055)	(0.158)	(0.163)	(0.160)
Country intercepts	Y	Y	Y	Y	Y
Missing successor	Y	Y	Y	Y	Y
Observations	313	313	307	307	307
Log likelihood	184.036	179.721	175.681	174.469	
Akaike inf. crit.	−356.654	−354.073	−343.442	−333.362	−330.939
Bayesian inf. crit.	−334.177	−327.849	−313.627	−299.820	−297.397

Note: $^*p < 0.1$; $^{**}p < 0.05$; $^{***}p < 0.01$

about the effects of the ideological distance between former autocrats and former dissidents: as this distance increases, so does the ability of former autocrats to extract concessions via blackmail.

Data to test these predictions came from the Global Transitional Justice Dataset, originally constructed for this purpose, and from the Democratic Accountability and Linkages Project.

Scholars of democracy and democratization rely overwhelmingly on expert surveys for measures of the quality of democracy. This is understandable as many of the concepts they strive to measure are inherently unobservable. The measure used in this chapter focused on the programmaticness of political parties and is based on surveys where country experts are asked to rate the quality of representation of specific post-transition parties. This measure allowed me to most directly examine the impact of lustration on programmaticness, that is, the extent to which parties deliver policies desired by the electorate; by extension, this allows for a direct examination of the mechanisms behind the role of these procedures in preventing blackmail with information about past collaboration, which may impede programmaticness. Since the quality of representation and the policy positions of parties are measured at the party level, this measure is ideally suited for operationalizing parameters from the Chapter 2, where both representation quality and policy positions are critical.

Recall from Chapter 2 that the frequency of the separating equilibria depends on the proximity between the position of the new democratic politician and that of the former authoritarian elite. Although a measure of the spatial location of a party does not map on to my theory as well as a measure of the ideal point of a specific politician would, it is better than cruder measures at the country level.

The findings of this chapter by and large corroborate my theoretical predictions, especially confirming the prediction about the effects of lustration severity on programmatic representation. Lustration decreases the amount of potentially embarrassing information that remains hidden and can be used for blackmail and so prevents blackmail of current politicians by former authoritarian elites.

Yet, lustration does not always prevent blackmail: I also find that holding all else constant, a lack of press freedom can sabotage transparency efforts. Allegations of collaboration need to be investigated and verified; in a liberal democracy, this task is often performed by a free press. In the absence of independent media, blackmail can occur through bluffing: that is, threatening to accuse current politicians of having ties with the former authoritarian regime even when no actual evidence exists.

This chapter concludes the contribution of this book to analyzing the effects of transparency on party programmaticness.

6

Truth Commissions and the Quality of Democracy

In Chapter 5, I tested the implications of the model from Chapter 2 for how well politicians represent voters when in office. I focused there only on the effect of lustration on political parties' ability to deliver policy platforms to voters. This was sensible in light of the fact that lustration targets politicians whose past may sabotage their ability to engage in programmatic exchanges with voters. The measure of programmatic representation I used came from the Democratic Accountability and Linkages Project and concentrated on party organizations as vehicles through which representation is delivered.

Of course, the cost of using this measure is that it was taken only at one point in time and therefore does not allow me to exploit fully the power of GTJD time series.

To remedy this, in the Chapters 7–9, I use two categories of measures that have been collected over time. Both come from the Varieties of Democracy Project (Coppedge et al. 2018). The first is the Political Corruption Index, which is composed of variables based on several questions pertaining to corruption in different branches and at different levels of government. I will use both the general index, which provides measures for all countries and post-transition years in the Global Transitional Justice Dataset (GTJD), as well as the components of this index.[1]

The second V-Dem measure, also collected as a time series, is Political Power distributed by Socioeconomic Status. The advantage of this mea-

---

[1] Although there are some components that empirically match the concepts I want to match much more closely, they suffer from missing values for some country-years. For this reason, I predominantly will be using the general Political Corruption Index.

sure is that it is very unlikely to be endogenous to the same factors that are responsible for the onset of transitional justice (TJ) implementation. At the same time, it seems to tap very well into the observable characteristics of authoritarian elite reproduction by capturing the failure to dissociate political power from economic dominance.

Together with programmaticness from Chapter 5, this brings the total number of ways of operationalizing quality of democracy to three. The employment of three different measures allows me to create a variety of research designs for testing predictions of the models from the first part of the book. Whereas Chapter 5 used hierarchical modeling for analyzing nested data with a specific party in a country as the unit of analysis, here I use dif-in-dif and synthetic matching to analyze the entire GTJD panel.

6.1 THE TRANSPARENCY ENHANCING FUNCTION OF TRUTH COMMISSIONS

This chapter is devoted to the second type of transparency regime discussed in this book – truth commissions. My understanding of truth commissions builds on Hayner (1994): They are state-sanctioned "bodies set up to investigate a past history of human rights abuses in a particular country, which can include violations by the military or other government forces or armed opposition forces" (p. 14).[2] In a departure from recent scholarship by Onur Bakiner (2016), I do not exclude commissions of inquiry that examine human rights violations committed in more specific events than an entire period of authoritarian rule or civil war.[3]

The most famous example of a truth commission is the South African Truth and Reconciliation Commission (TRC), which is described also Chapter 4 (Gibson 2006; Hayner 2001). Established via the Promotion of National Unity and Reconciliation Act, in July 1995 (Gibson 2006), it could investigate human rights violations committed by the state and various liberation movements, and it had the prerogative to offer amnesty to those who fully participated in the process and truthfully recounted their crimes, thus incentivizing perpetrators to come forward to share their story. In 1998, after touring the country for a couple of years, con-

---

[2] Hayner elaborates that truth commissions should (1) not focus on ongoing human rights abuses as a human rights ombudsman might; (2) examine a pattern of human rights abuses over time rather than a specific event; (3) be temporary; and (4) have an official sanction from the state to carry out its operations (Hayner 1994, p. 14).

[3] Hence, I include parliamentary human rights commissions or commissions of inquiry investigating only specific and limited in time incidents.

ducting hearings that were nationally broadcast on public radio, and collecting testimonies, the Commission released a five-volume final report. The report detailed the abuses committed by the apartheid-era National Party government the African National Congress (ANC) – the opposition-turned-ruling party – and other "leading political figures on both sides of the anti-apartheid struggle." (Keesing's Record of World Events 1998, p. 42536).

Truth commissions are much broader in scope than lustration and can affect any member of society (Zvobgo 2019b). They are also much broader in their mandate. Kelly Zvobgo (2019b)'s Varieties of Truth Commissions project sheds light on just how much diversity exists in the functions performed by truth commissions. With varying mandates, truth commissions can name individual perpetrators,[4] provide amnesty for participation,[5] and even provide direct reparations to victims.[6] Many, if not all, truth commissions make specific policy recommendations geared toward ensuring that such abuses do not occur in the future (Dancy & Thoms 2022).[7] Some even go on to recommend prosecution against certain perpetrators, as occurred with the Truth and Reconciliation Commission of Sierra Leone (Zvobgo 2019a,b).

At the same time, the TRC exemplifies well why truth commissions belong squarely in the category of transparency mechanisms. Although the commission held hearings for a number of known offenders, many of their crimes implicated unknown perpetrators, and in many instances the abuses that were revealed had not been previously disclosed. By making the history of abuses transparent, the TRC prevented agents with insider knowledge of who committed what crimes and where from blackmailing the perpetrators by threatening to reveal to the public what they had done. Absent the transparency produced by the commission, threats to denounce perpetrators of egregious and violent acts unless they gave in to the economic or policy demands of blackmailers may have derailed political representation in South Africa. In this sense, truth commissions

---

[4] as the Commission on the Truth for El Salvador did.

[5] as the South African Truth and Reconciliation Commission did.

[6] as has been suggested by the mandate of Kenya's Truth, Justice, and Reconciliation Commission.

[7] Dancy and Thoms (2022) point out that although truth commissions contribute to more democratic behaviors, they are, however, less likely to bring about institutional change and are not associated with higher levels of judicial independence or more checks and balances on the executive.

remove *kompromat* or "skeletons in the closet" from the domain of political representation, decreasing the corruptibility of the new polity.

Both truth commissions and commissions of inquiry increase transparency when they are established. Moreover, in the years that a truth commission is particularly active, its transparency effects should be especially prominent. Finally, the longer a truth commission is in operation, the higher the likelihood that information about individual perpetrators may eventually come to light.[8] Since transparency pertaining to individual perpetrators is the mechanism that my theory focuses on, I will build on these three aspects of truth commissions in developing my measures in Section 6.3.

So how do truth commissions improve the quality of the newly inaugurated democratic regime following a transition to democracy? I argue that they accomplish this through two related mechanisms.

The first, is much like lustration: *unknown* or *secret* collaborators of former regimes might want to take part in the new regime. Absent transparency mechanisms, they are susceptible to blackmail with the threat of revealing their 'skeletons in the closet, that is, revealing that they participated in atrocious acts. These threats, especially when they come from persons with credible access to such evidence, can distort policy and representational outcomes. The threat of revealing skeletons holds sway over former elites, because the public likely cares about not being represented by past abusers. Thus, revealing such skeletons could chastise a public official, and end his or her career. In return for not denouncing them, blackmailers can demand rents or policy concessions, either of which corrupts the new democracy. Unearthing secret collaborations prevents the blackmail of former secret agents of repression who should find themselves in positions of power.

In Chapter 2, I investigated this blackmail mechanism with a formal model showing that lack of transparency can distort representation even when only "innocent" candidates are running for office. The mere presence of secret authoritarian legacies enables blackmailers to pressure candidates into running on a nonrepresentative platform (i.e., a platform that diverges from the general voting population). The mere possibility of a collaborator of the previous regime running for office can tarnish the reputation of other candidates, leading to the reelection

---

[8] Even if a commission does not identify perpetrators by name, it is reasonable to believe that the passage of time and ongoing truth commission activities can encourage those who are more likely to know individuals by name, rank, and/or affiliation to step forward.

of extreme incumbents. Transitional justice (TJ) procedures that reveal past atrocities, such as truth commissions, benefit voters regardless of the voters' preferences for normative TJ. In other words, the beneficial effects of TJ, in particular the effects of revealing skeletons in the closet, take hold regardless of – and sometimes despite – the public's demand for retribution.

There is also a second mechanism through which uncovering secret collaborators improves democratic quality: by upending existing authoritarian networks that linger on even after the transition to democracy. Former secret collaborators, if undisclosed, can be manipulated by former authoritarian elites. Consider again the South African example, where even prior to the transition, the ANC would hold so-called People's Courts against suspected apartheid collaborators. Those found guilty would be subjected to the excruciating torture of having a burning tire placed over their head (Price 1991). This example illustrates the stigma associated with the suspicion of being a collaborator. Even if, following the transition, collaborators were not subjected to the horrific "doughnut death" as the burning tire sentence was called (Price 1991), they would arguably go to far lengths to avoid being revealed. But the TRCs act of publishing names of those working for the apartheid also disarmed the power of authoritarian networks that may well have survived the transition to democracy otherwise.

Without a transparency mechanism in place, former authoritarian elites can threaten to expose secrets to extract policy concessions. Voters are kept in the dark about whose interests politicians are really representing. By disclosing secret authoritarian legacies, truth commissions fulfill democratic goals by informing voters about candidates and allowing them to choose "honest" politicians. Politicians who have been named and shamed as collaborators by truth commissions can continue to try to represent voters, but such politicians will be more transparent to voters as their actions in office are less likely to be driven by the interests of blackmailers threatening to reveal skeletons in their closet. Truth commissions also undermine authoritarian networks and render them obsolete.[9]

---

[9] Of course, truth commissions can also enable the punishment of former perpetrators of abuses by, for example, creating a file that can be used in a criminal justice trial. But since my argument focuses on the effect of uncovering the truth, the sanction itself is neither necessary nor sufficient for the mechanism that I have highlighted here.

An important difference setting truth commissions apart from lustration, however, is their sweeping breadth. While lustrations only target politicians and persons in higher echelons of public office, truth commissions can affect anyone.

The South African TRC illustrates the unparalleled reach of truth commissions into society. The TRC was formed in 1995 to investigate crimes committed against the South African people during the apartheid regime (1960–1994), covering human rights violations committed by both the state and various liberation movements. The commission was allowed to offer amnesty to those who fully participated in the process and truthfully confessed the full extent of their crimes. Its work exposed abuses committed by the apartheid-era National Party government, the African National Congress (ANC) – the state opposition-turned-ruling party – and other "leading political figures on both sides of the anti-apartheid struggle" (Keesing's Record of World Events 1998). Even before releasing its report, the proceedings of the TRC were widely publicized. The commission traveled around the country and its hearings were broadcast by radio and television. For this reason, it is justified to expect the transparency effects of truth commissions to be available more immediately than in the case of lustration.

In sum, truth commissions remove opportunities for blackmail – which may threaten the quality of democratic representation – and provide voters with information necessary for removing "dishonest" officials who were plausibly connected to former authoritarian elites. Importantly, these effects are brought about by the transparency aspect of the TJ mechanism, an effect that I argue is theoretically and empirically distinct from the criminal punishment of former members and collaborators of the authoritarian regime who abused human rights publicly. Therefore, truth commissions will improve the quality of democracy in two directly observable ways. First, by revealing abuses committed by secret agents of repression, truth commissions will undercut the blackmail mechanism described above and will reduce political corruption. Second, by revealing the compromising information to voters about the true characters of persons who may potentially continue occupying public office, truth commissions will reduce the power of authoritarian networks.

Among TJ mechanisms, truth commissions are probably the least controversial, at least at a conceptual level (i.e., before any reports have been issued) because they do not have direct punitive consequences and, at least promise to result in reconciliation. An implication of this reputation, however, is that the same factors that allow for truth commission implementation may also be responsible for altering the quality of democracy. This is one of the classic endogeneity problems plaguing political science.[10] As a result, identifying the effects of truth commissions on the quality of democracy is notoriously difficult.

In this chapter, I use a difference in difference (dif-in-dif) design to identify the causal effects of truth commissions. Such designs allow researchers using observational data to build plausible counterfactual scenarios by using the trajectory of the untreated observations to predict where the treated would be had they not received treatment. In the context of truth commissions, this means exploiting the trends in the quality of democracy in countries without truth commissions to predict the counterfactual trajectory of quality of democracy in countries with truth commissions. The structure of the GTJD is ideally suited for this research design. A dif-in-dif approach unleashes the full potential that a panel of disaggregated TJ events has to offer.

Previewing the results, I find that truth commissions decrease political corruption and decrease the power of former authoritarian elites as predicted by Political Power distributed by Socioeconomic Status. The latter effects are particularly credible because I find strong evidence satisfying the parallel trends assumption. Moreover, this effect of truth commissions persists even after accounting for lustration activity. Taken together, these models can serve as corroborative evidence that transparency regimes in the form of truth commissions enhance the quality of democratic representation.

The remainder of this chapter is organized as follows. In Section 6.2 and 6.3, I review how TJ scholars have dealt with endogeneity concerns and what this implies for research designs. Section 6.4 introduces my dependent variables. It is followed by a discussion of the dif-in-dif strategy applied to the problem at hand and includes a discussion of the parallel trends assumption in section 6.5. Sections 6.6 and 6.7 introduce the statistical model and estimations. In Section 6.8, I interpret the results with a special focus on how the effect of truth commission events compares to that of lustration events. The conclusion summarizes and draws normative implications.

---

[10] One could conceivably leverage the same criticism against my findings in Chapter 5 by arguing that the same factors that promote lustration could make experts more likely to perceive parties as running on identifiable and salient platforms. To alleviate these concerns, see Appendix C, which provides evidence against this kind of spuriousness. See, in particular, the model of "selection into lustration" in Table 5.4. Moreover, lustration is not nearly as popular with advocates of democratization as truth commissions are.

6.2 DEALING WITH THE ENDOGENEITY
OF TRANSITIONAL JUSTICE

Previous scholarship on the effects of TJ institutions in transitional and post-conflict settings has used several techniques to address endogeneity concerns. In their work on the relationship between post-conflict justice processes and civil war recurrence, Loyle and Appel (2017) take an instrumental variable approach, using the presence of TJ institutions in the region as an instrument. Assuming that neighbors with and without such institutions are assigned to post-conflict countries at random and assuming that TJ institutions easily diffuse throughout their regions, these authors find that truth commissions, reparations, amnesties, and comprehensive trials – which they call "motivation post-conflict justice" – decrease the likelihood of conflict recurrence. As an additional robustness check to identify the determinants of post-conflict justice implementation, these authors also employ a strategy of matching on observables. The results are consistent with their instrumental variable analysis .

Prorok (2017) also uses an instrumental variable approach, identifying three plausible instruments to estimate the causal effects of International Criminal Court (ICC) investigations on conflict duration in civil wars. Using as instruments a state's affinity with the permanent five members of the UN Security Council, a state's affinity with its neighbors, and the number of neighboring states that have ratified the Rome Statute, Prorok finds that ICC involvement in a conflict setting significantly reduces the probability of conflict termination when government and rebel groups have committed similar levels of atrocities. The court's counterproductive impact decreases as the number of atrocities committed by one party to a conflict increases relative to that committed by other parties.

Loyle and Appel (2017) and Prorok (2017) have made important contributions to understanding the causal effects of national and international-level TJ processes on conflict termination, an important prerequisite to having a robust democracy. Their research, however, stops short of telling us how these mechanisms affect the long-term quality of democracy. Balcells et al. (2022) investigate the long-term effect of memorialization efforts, such as the erection of museums devoted to victims of authoritarian repression, on political behavior. Concentrating on Chile, whose regime ended in 1984, Balcells and her coauthors focus on detecting effects even among generations not directly affected by the Pinochet regime. Their identification strategy is to use a field experiment with subjects randomly assigned to visit a museum devoted to victims of military rule in Chile or an art museum, which – as it is unrelated to politics – serves as the control group. The authors find the treatment to have a significant effect, compared to the control condition, on evaluations of the former regime and on political behavior. However, follow-up surveys with the panel revealed the relatively short-lived nature of the effects. In almost no instances did the effects last longer than six months.

While Balcells et al. make use of one experiment, field experiments are not feasible for the assessment of the effects of personnel TJ measures, such as lustrations and truth commissions. A potential solution to this is to rely on natural experiments as Capoccia and Pop-Eleches (2020) do in their study, investigating the effect of TJ on the robustness of democratic institutions. These authors make use of a natural experiment – the division of Allied-occupied Germany into four zones – to estimate the effects of TJ policies on democratic consolidation in post-WWII Germany. Treating assignment to different denazification policies (trials and punishment) in each of the four occupation zones as exogenous, they estimate the effects of TJ policies on Germans' readiness to uphold democratic values. The dependent variable is measured with survey data from 1957. Their key dependent variable probes public support for a one-party political system. Capoccia and Pop-Eleches (2020) ultimately find that the scope and severity of TJ implementation has a profound effect on attitudes toward democratization. This fascinating and innovative work is, however, unable to address questions about the broader effect that TJ mechanisms may have for countries other than post- World War II Germany. This analysis also tells us little about the effects of lustration (as defined in this book) and truth commissions because while lustrations were in fact administered in Allied-occupied Germany in the immediate post-WWII time period, Capoccia and Pop-Eleches (2020) consider this mechanism jointly with purges.[11]

6.3 RESEARCH DESIGN: EXPLOITING TIME AND INTENSITY OF TRUTH COMMISSIONS

My research builds on these initial approaches, recognizing that understanding the effects of lustration, purges, and truth commissions requires

---

[11] An expansion of the Global Transitional Justice Dataset to include all former autocracies that transitioned to democracy before 1946 reveals a definite lustration event in the French Zone in October 1945.

isolating the effect of these TJ mechanisms from factors that contributed to the implementation of TJ in the first place, as the latter might be highly correlated with the quality of democracy indicators.

The panel structure of the Global Transitional Justice Dataset allows me to extract these effects over time using a slight modification of the measure of transitional justice severity developed in Chapter 4. There, to measure the intensity of various TJ mechanisms, I constructed a measure of severity that is static over time. This measure is defined as the total number of positive TJ events that occurred in country i over the total number of events $+1$ (1 is added to the denominator to avoid dividing by zero).

In all my regressions in this chapter, I use lags of these measures, as any plausible model of the effect of TJ on the quality of democracy should allow for some lapse of time between the occurrence of TJ and the outcome, which in my case is the quality of democracy variable.

In order to capture the effects of truth commissions over time, however, and to allow for more effective interpretation of the dif-in-dif coefficients, a measure that updates annually is needed. I begin by using a "minimalist" measure,

$$TJ_{i,t}^1 = \begin{cases} 1 & \text{if } \sum_1^{t-1} P_{it} > 0, \\ 0 & \text{otherwise} \end{cases} \qquad (6.1)$$

where P_{it} represents the number of positive truth commission events in country i in year $t - 1$. This measure corresponds to the transparency inducing effect of having any positive events at all, no matter how isolated. It codes the year with the first positive truth commission event as 1 and continues to code as 1 every subsequent year, regardless of the ensuing trajectory. Theoretically, this measure suggests that although a single positive truth commission event typically implies more events to follow, even this small and isolated event would result in more transparency than no positive events at all. An additional virtue of this measure is its simplicity. I use it in all regressions below as a first model.

My second measure is more sensitive to the volume of transparency produced by each year's truth commission events and corresponds to the idea that more transparency is better for democracy than less transparency. The measure counts net events in country i in year $t - 1$:

$$TJ_{i,t}^2 = \begin{cases} 1 & \text{if } P_{it-1} - N_{it-1} > 0, \\ 0 & \text{otherwise} \end{cases} \qquad (6.2)$$

where N_{it-1} represents the number of negative truth commission events in country i in year $t - 1$.

My third measure acknowledges the added effect of an accumulation of transparency events from the past. A truth commission issuing a report will have a greater impact if in the preceding years, its powers were expanded or its mandate extended. The measure counts the cumulative net events in year $t - 1$ (measured as the total negative events in year t subtracted from the total positive events in year $t - 1$):

$$TJ^3_{i,t} = \begin{cases} 1 & \text{if } \sum_1^{t-1} P_{it} - \sum_1^{t-1} N_{it} > 0. \\ 0 & \text{otherwise} \end{cases} \qquad (6.3)$$

All three measures correspond to the transparency-inducing aspects of truth commissions discussed earlier. In one sense, these measures resemble the previous severity measures discussed in Chapter 4 in that they continuously capture the intensity of TJ; however, in contrast to the static measures described in Chapter 4, they make use of the unfolding of TJ over time and leverage the time series aspect of the Global Transitional Justice Dataset.

Figure 6.1 illustrates how this last measure is applied to transparency regimes – that is, lustrations and truth commissions – in the Global Transitional Justice Dataset. Countries are stacked on the vertical dimension, while the horizontal dimension represents years since the transition. Dark cells illustrate years in which the cumulative net TJ events were positive ($\sum_1^{t-1} P_{it} - \sum_1^{t-1} N_{it} > 0$), and light cells illustrate years in which the cumulative net TJ events were negative or equal to zero ($\sum_1^{t-1} P_{it} - \sum_1^{t-1} N_{it} \leq 0$). White cells represent data that has not yet been revealed because the country in the corresponding row has not been democratic long enough.[12]

A quick comparison of the top and bottom panels of Figure 6.1 suggests that although lustration is more widespread than the literature on Eastern Europe suggests, it is not as widespread as truth commissions are. There also seems to be a substitution effect between the two mechanisms: where lustration is more prevalent, truth commissions are more rare, and vice versa.

All the measures presented previously are dichotomous variations of the severity measure. This is because indicator variables are easier to interpret in a dif-in-dif framework. However, in Chapter 7, devoted to testing the theory of purges, I use a fixed effects framework, which unleashes the full potential of the GTJD with a panel of continuous measures without reducing them to indicators.

---

[12] Since the countries in the dataset are transitioning to democracy at different times, the panel is unbalanced.

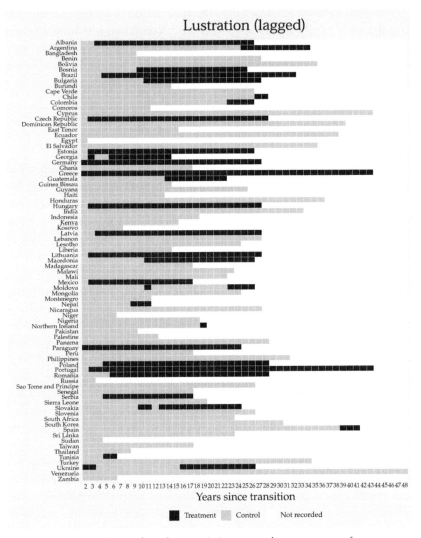

FIGURE 6.1. Lustration and truth commissions at a glance, measure from Eq. (6.3)

Note: Dark cells represent years in which net cumulative truth revelation procedures were positive; light cells represent years in which net cumulative truth revelation procedures were negative; white cells represent censored data.

FIGURE 6.1. (*Continued*)

6.4 INTRODUCING THE DEPENDENT VARIABLES

The dependent variables I use in this chapter come from V-Dem , the Varieties of Democracy Project. V-Dem is a dataset spanning 221 countries and 116 years for most polities.[13] The dataset was created by country

---

[13] Some polities did not survive as independent states for the entire covered period. For a detailed list and explanation of country unit selection, see Coppedge et al. (2017).

experts (approximately five independent experts per country) who subjectively coded a host of regime characteristics that are not directly observable over time. V-Dem is exceptional among expert surveys in that it corrects for how differences of opinion or mistakes cause experts to diverge in their evaluations. Traditionally, datasets report expert-coded data with means and standard deviations, ignoring the fact that expert reliability and the way in which experts apply an ordinal scale to ratings may vary systematically. V-Dem, in contrast, uses Item Response Theory to model and adjust for differences in how experts apply scales (Pemstein et al. 2015). To allow for scaling the independent coding by country experts, V-Dem scholars also encouraged experts to "bridge code" a second or third country and, more recently, also asked them to complete anchoring vignettes. While experts have less expertise in evaluating these second and third countries than they do at evaluating their first countries, this effort allowed V-Dem methodologists to compare the use of the ordinal scales across coders and correct for systematic differences.

In total, V-Dem researchers reached approximately three thousand country experts. To arrive at five indices of democracy – electoral, liberal, participatory, deliberative, and egalitarian – they asked the country experts hundreds of questions. However, each of the indices uses some variable to which TJ is potentially endogenous. Thus, in lieu of using any of the five V-Dem indices, I use specific expert evaluations that tap into quality of democracy directly. Among V-Dem variables that stand out as particularly useful for this purpose are Political Power distributed by Socioeconomic Status (*v2pepwrses*) and the Political Corruption Index (*v2xcorr*), which I discuss in turn in the following section.

Power Distributed by Socioeconomic Status

The first dependent variable I use in this chapter taps directly into the ability of authoritarian elites to survive the transition and for their networks to flourish. To understand its suitability, it is useful to consider why the power of former authoritarian elites may extend beyond the life span of an authoritarian regime. Autocrats may be well positioned to capture state resources at the time of democratic transition, which they can then use to entrench themselves in power (Albertus & Menaldo 2014; Brun & Diamond 2014; Haggard & Kaufman 2016).

The outgoing autocrats' access to resources can be cut off if they or their successors are voted out of office, following the transition to democracy. Many autocrats, however, amass their fortunes in secret. For an illustration, one need to look no further than the blockbuster documentary created by Russian dissident, Alexei Navalny, "Putin's Palace" (The Economist 2021). Uncovering kleptocracy alone is not sufficient, however. If there is a delay between the disclosure and the removal of the kleptocrats from office, they have sufficient time to stash away their fortunes. Further cases from around the world demonstrate that even if the kleptocrats are removed from office, these removals may only be temporary (Kitschelt 1999). Grzymala-Busse (2002), for instance, attributes the revival of successor authoritarian parties to the organizational advantage authoritarian parties hold over parties that are newcomers to the party system. This organizational advantage allows them to make better use of state resources when they eventually do find themselves in government. TJ could be the last resort to curb the privileged position of members or parties of the former autocrats, their collaborators, or their enforcement apparatuses (David 2011; Escriba-Folch & Wright 2015; Stan et al. 2009; Vinjamuri & Snyder 2004).

In light of this argument, truth commissions may plausibly be interpreted as mechanisms preventing former authoritarian elites from holding on to such economic resources. Therefore, a variable measuring the association between economic wealth and political power is an ideal candidate for operationalizing the strength of authoritarian networks. In addition, given the temporal nature of my data, an ideally suited dependent variable also measures this association over time. Fortunately, the V-Dem expert survey contains such a measure.

Called "Power distributed by Socioeconomic Status" (*v2pepwrses* or PdSES), the variable is based on the following question posed to V-Dem experts: "is political power distributed according to socio-economic position?" (Coppedge et al. 2017).[14] In his clarification note, John Gerring elaborates that the measure was designed to gauge the extent to which economic inequalities translate into political power (Coppedge et al. 2017b). Other scholars of nondemocratic regimes have noted

---

[14] Answers to the question were distributed along a five-point scale. The possible answers included (0)"Wealthy people enjoy a virtual monopoly on political power. Average and poorer people have almost no influence"; (1)"Wealthy people enjoy a dominant hold on political power. People of average income have little say. Poorer people have essentially no influence"; (2)"Wealthy people have a very strong hold on political power. People of average or poorer income have some degree of influence but only on issues that matter less for wealthy people"; (3)"Wealthy people have more political power than others. But people of average income have almost as much influence and poor people also have a significant degree of political power"; and (4)"Wealthy people have no more political power than those whose economic status is average or poor. Political power is more or less equally distributed across economic groups" (Coppedge et al. 2017b).

that the ability of economic elites to lock in political power is one of the markers of high capacity authoritarian states. In the case of some nondemocracies, the link between political and economic power can be fully institutionalized. For instance, Florian Hollenbach (2019), in his article on elite interests and public spending in nineteenth century Prussia, explains how in the empire's cities, after ranking the male population from the richest to the poorest, the share contributing a third of the tax revenue had the same voting power as the share contributing the second third of the revenue and as the share of the male population contributing the bottom third of the tax revenue, even though, obviously, these groups were numerically unequal.

Power distributed by Socioeconomic Status is also a particularly reasonable measure of quality of democracy for our purposes because while it measures an important aspect of democracy, it is unlikely to be correlated with rule of law, which could also affect the implementation of TJ. If the goal of TJ is to undermine the privileged position of authoritarian elites, this score should increase with the severity of the TJ mechanism in question. I have transformed the original variable to range between 0 and 1 and made higher values indicate higher quality of democracy (and hence lower levels of association between political and socioeconomic power).

Political Corruption Index

To measure the leverage that former agents of the *ancien régime* with access to kompromat hold over politicians with skeletons in the closet, I turn to V-Dem's index of political corruption. This index is created out of six different questions regarding corruption in three different branches of government – the legislature, the judiciary, and the executive.[15] Its advantages are that within the executive, it treats bribery and embezzlement separately and that it distinguishes between corruption taking place in high levels of government ("grand corruption") and lower in the public sector ("petty corruption"). The index takes on values between 0 and 1.[16]

While the Political Corruption Index does not get directly at the extent to which politicians are influenced by blackmail with secret

---

[15] For example, the question about executive corruption is "How routinely do members of the executive, or their agents grant favors in exchange for bribes, kickbacks, or other material inducements, and how often do they steal, embezzle, or misappropriate public funds or other state resources for personal or family use?"

[16] Specifically, it is made up of questions coded as variables $v2x_pubcorr$, $v2x_execorr$, $v2lgcrrpt$, $v2jucorrdc$, $v2excrptps$, and $v2exthftps$ (Coppedge et al. 2018).

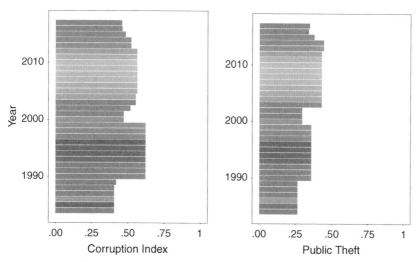

FIGURE 6.2. Political corruption index and one of its components: public theft Argentina (1984–2016)

police files, it does measure how much they succumb to pressures that impede their ability to deliver on voters' wishes once in office. Figure 6.2 shows the averages in political corruption (left) and public theft (right) for all countries in the GTJD over the entire period they were democratic. Both here and in all uses of the Political Corruption Index in this book, I have transformed it so that lower values (closer to 0) represent less corruption, and higher values (closer to 1) represent more corruption. This choice was dictated by making it directly comparable to other measures of quality of democracy used in this book.

When interpreting Figure 6.1, there does not appear to be much variation across countries. This appearance is caused by the fact that most of the variation comes from the within-country trends, as illustrated in Figure 6.3. This figure presents, for all countries in the GTJD, trend lines for both of my dependent variable measures – Political Corruption and Political Power distributed by Socioeconomic Status. The Argentinian case is in bold to allow the reader to focus on one case that offers especially rich variation. The figure shows considerable variation both across and within countries, which is a key advantage of the V-Dem

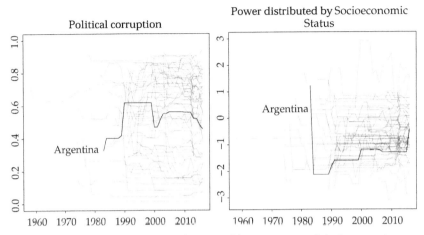

FIGURE 6.3. Trend lines for dependent variable measures: political corruption and Political Power distributed by Socioeconomic Status

dataset over other datasets offering indicators for quality of democracy, such as Polity IV.[17]

6.5 THE IDENTIFICATION STRATEGY AND PARALLEL TRENDS

The classic explanation of the dif-in-dif method relies on comparisons of time trends in countries that have been treated with the independent variable of interest – in my case, truth commissions – and those that have not received treatment. As long as the "treated" and "control" countries have been matched to ensure that their pretreatment trends on the dependent variable are similar enough (satisfying the parallel trends assumption), such a comparison is warranted. The case without the treatment serves as a counterfactual to the case with the treatment. Given appropriate data, this method can be generalized to panel data and incorporated into a regression framework. The data requirements, however, are quite stringent, as they require both the dependent and independent variables to vary across countries and over time.

The first of the V-Dem dependent variables operationalizing quality of democracy I use here is the Political Corruption Index (*v2xcorr*). In order to use the dif-in-dif framework, I must assume that absent treatment,

[17] This figure was created with the help of Milena Ang.

Countries treated in or before year 2   Countries treated in or before year 5

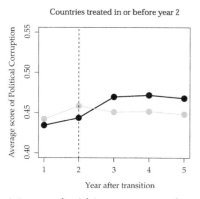 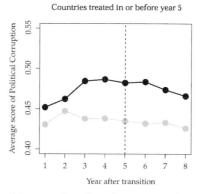

(a) treated within two years of transition

(b) treated within five years of transition

FIGURE 6.4. Parallel trends for Political Corruption Index, treatment: truth commissions as positive net cumulative events (within two and five years)

political corruption trends would develop according to a similar pattern in treated countries as in countries that were never treated with TJ.

The first couple of graphs in Figure 6.4 compare the average values of the Political Corruption Index in countries that never received treatment (in light grey) with average values of the Political Corruption Index in countries that received treatment within the first two (left) or first five (right) years following their democratic transition. Figure 6.5 compares the average values of the index in the untreated countries with those treated within the first ten years following the transition. The treatment year is marked with a dashed vertical line and "treated by a truth commission" is interpreted as taking the value of 1 in the cumulative net events measure described in Eq. (6.3).

The first apparent observation here is that countries treated with truth commissions, regardless of when the treatment took place, have almost always, on average, less political corruption than countries not treated with truth commissions do. The only exception here is among countries treated within the first two years of transition to democracy (left panel of Figure 6.4.) as there, following treatment, countries that were treated experience a decline in the trend – recall that in our transformation, higher levels mean less corrupt, or more democratic.

Another thing to observe is that countries that adopted "late" truth commissions (within five or ten years), score higher on the political corruption measure than countries that were not treated. This corroborates the intuition for engaging this research design in the first place: a pooled analysis across time and space would find a correlation between truth

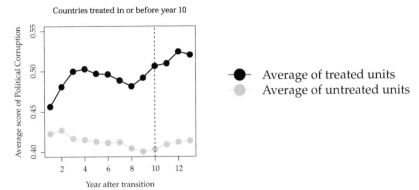

FIGURE 6.5   Parallel trends for Political Corruption Index, treatment: truth commissions as positive net cumulative events (within 10 years)

commission events and political corruption, but it would be spurious.[18] Second, the gap between the treated and untreated widens as we extend the period of time during which the treatment is allowed to occur. More concretely, the gap between untreated countries and those treated by year 2 is .015, but about .05 by year 5 and .1 by year 10. The trends are mostly parallel prior to the treatment, which is marked with a vertical dashed line.

It is worth pointing out that in these parallel trends figures, the control group is constant and always made up of countries that were "never treated," but the group of treated countries changes in each figure. In the first (left of Figure 6.4), it is smallest as it contains only countries treated within the first two years of transition, while in Figure 6.5, it is largest and contains all countries that were treated within the first 10 years.[19]

A final point to keep in mind while interpreting these figures is that many factors (economic wealth key among them) in addition to TJ affect political corruption trends. In fact, these other factors are responsible for a majority of the variation in political corruption. Since the dif-in-dif design calls for time-varying covariates, many factors – such as historical legacies – are impossible to control for. However, I can control in all regressions for GDP per capita.

[18] In Appendix D, I supply such an OLS regression and indeed show such a significant relationship.
[19] There are alternative ways of designing the control group. For instance, one could set it to be always the compliment to the treatment group.

This means that the parallel trends assumption must only hold conditional on GDP per capita. At the same time, because presenting parallel trends graphs conditional on continuously measured variables is very difficult to do, the graphs of parallel trends presented earlier do not take this variable into account.

Having completed a discussion of the assumptions necessary to conduct dif-in-dif, I now continue to the actual model.

6.6 THE STATISTICAL MODEL

A traditional dif-in-dif framework with just one pretreatment and one posttreatment period would estimate:

$$Y_{i,t} = \mu_i M_I + \lambda T + \gamma D_{i,t} + \beta X_{i,t} + \epsilon_i.$$

where $D_i = 1$ if country i experienced TJ of a given type, and $D_i = 0$ otherwise. M_I is the country dummy and assumes 1 when the TJ event is associated with country i.[20]

In the classic dif-in-dif setup, there are only two periods: $t = 0$ for the pretreatment period and $t = 1$ for the posttreatment period. Consequently, μ_i can be interpreted as the country intercept and λ as the posttreatment intercept. $T = 0$ in the pretreatment period, and $T = 1$ in the posttreatment period. $X_{i,t}$ represents the set of covariates upon which the treatment effect is conditioned. Note that a consequence of the above notation is that $D_{i,t} = M_i * T$.

The panel structure of my data calls for two important adjustments to the model.

First, each country receives the treatment at a different time t (that is, each country has a different year that marks the pre- and posttreatment period). Second, each country appears in the dataset for multiple periods. To correctly specify the dif-in-dif model with multiple time periods, I build on Angrist and Pischke (2008) and Besley and Burgess (2004), and propose to estimate the following model:

$$Y_{i,t} = \mu_i M_i + \lambda_t T_t + \gamma D_{i,t-1} + \beta X_{i,t} + \epsilon_i. \tag{6.4}$$

This is essentially a two-way fixed effect regression where μ_i represents country-specific fixed effects and λ_t represents year-since-transition specific fixed effects. T is the time period dummy and is equal to 0 in every

---

[20] Note that there are one fewer dummies than there are countries.

year lapsed since the transition except for T in row $Y_{i,T}$. Note that in the regression framework, I use $D_{i,t-1}$, the treatment from the year preceding the year in which the dependent variable was recorded. $D_{i,t-1}$ can also be written as $\mu_i * \lambda_{t-1}$; it takes the value of 1 when country i was treated in period $t-1$. $X_{i,t}$ represents the set of covariates conditioning the treatment. Here, I use a single covariate: GDP per capita.

In a paper from 2018, Andrew Goodman-Bacon shows that this general dif-in-dif estimator is a weighted average of all possible two-group and two-period dif-in-dif estimators in the data, with the greatest weights given to treatments that occurred close to the "middle of the panel" (Goodman-Bacon 2018). This is because the weights are directly proportional to the treatment variances.[21]

6.6.1 Results

I begin by estimating the effect of severity of truth commissions on the Political Corruption Index. Recall, that this index has been inverted so that larger values represent not more, but less corruption. Hence positive coefficients on measures of truth commission events mean that they are better for democracy. In the following section, I estimate the effect of truth commissions on Power distributed by Socioeconomic Status. All models presented here control for GDP per capita (logged).

Political Corruption
Table 6.1 presents three models, summarized also in Figure 6.6, each pertaining to one of the three measures of truth commission events.

6.6.2 Discussion

First, it is clear that truth commissions, regardless of how they are measured, have a positive effect on reducing corruption: Relative to countries with no positive events at all, having one positive event decreases corruption by almost 3.5 percentage points. Years following years with more positive events than negative events see an uptick of almost 1.2 percentage points and years following a cumulative number of positive events exceeding negative events see political corruption decreasing by 3 percentage points.

---

[21] In the case at hand, middle of the panel would refer to cases treated after at least three years after the transition compared to those that were never treated.

TABLE 6.1. *Effect of truth commission events on political corruption*

	Minimalist	Net	Net cumulative
Truth commission event	0.0351**	0.0125**	0.0307**
	(0.016)	(0.006)	(0.015)
log(GDPpc)	0.0307	0.0308	0.0309
	(0.040)	(0.040)	(0.040)
Constant	−0.229	−0.190	−0.226
	(0.325)	(0.318)	(0.326)
Observations	1,747	1,747	1,747
R^2	0.960	0.960	0.960

Standard errors in parentheses
Truth commission events are lagged
All models include country and year specific intercepts
$*p < 0.1, **p < 0.05, ***p < 0.01.$

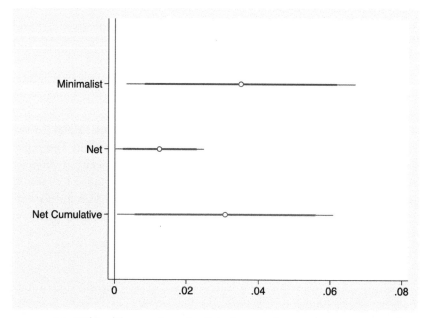

FIGURE 6.6. Dif-in-dif regression of political corruption on three measures of truth commission events with country-clustered SE

Moreover, in interpreting the figure, it is important to note that the thickness of the confidence intervals corresponds to the significance level of the coefficient. The thinnest line, approaching zero, corresponds to significance at the .01 level and the thicker line corresponds to significance at the .05 level. I present the confidence intervals at two different levels of significance to provide as much transparency about the results as possible. A second caveat, important to mention for interpreting the results, is that combining fixed effects at the country level with time fixed effects (as is necessary for dif-in-dif) results in a very conservative test. Relaxing either of these fixed effects, or replacing them with random effects, would produce much more significant results. Yet the goal of this empirical exercise is to be accurate rather than to pursue significance at all costs.

While political corruption is a broad category that ought to tap into the extent to which persons in public office can be blackmailed with the threat of revealing secrets from their authoritarian past, we can replicate this analysis for some of its components, described earlier in Section 1.4 introducing the dependent variables. In the following, I present the results for legislative corruption (*v2xlgcrrpt*), judicial corruption (*v2jucorrdc*), public sector corruption (*v2xpubcorr*), and executive corruption (*v2xexecorr*).[22]

These components can be understood as casting a narrower net and focusing on the acts of bureaucrats and administrators of the state and the extent to which these actors are willing to take bribes.

As can be seen from Figure 6.7, none of these alternative variables, however, produces results that depart significantly from what I uncovered in the case of the general Political Corruption Index.

The next subsection presents results from regressions similar to the ones above, but uses the association between economic status and political power (PdSES) as the dependent variable. The association between economic and political power, as I explain below is intended to capture persisting legacies of the former authoritarian state, as in such authoritarian states, economic and political power are closely associated with one another.

---

[22] Specifically, these subcomponents are operationalized as follows: public sector corruption is constructed out of answers to: "To what extent do public sector employees grant favors in exchange for bribes, kickbacks, or other material inducements, and how often do they steal, embezzle, or misappropriate public funds or other state resources for personal or family use?"; executive corruption codes answers to: "How routinely do members of the executive, or their agents grant favors in exchange for bribes, kickbacks, or other material inducements, and how often do they steal, embezzle, or misappropriate public funds or other state resources for personal or family use?"; judicial corruption is constructed out of answers to: "How often do individuals or businesses make undocumented extra payments or bribes in order to speed up or delay the process or to obtain a favorable judicial decision?" and legislative corruption codes answers to: "Do members of the legislature abuse their position for financial gain?"

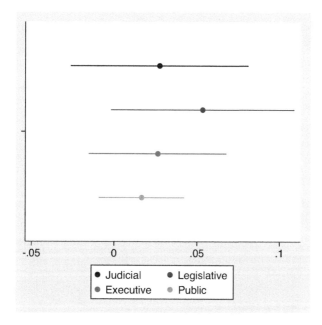

FIGURE 6.7. Coefficients from dif-in-dif regressions of components of Political Corruption Index on truth commission events

Note: All regressions are using country-clustered SE and net cumulative events to measure the intensity of truth commissions

Power Distributed by Socioeconomic Status

The second V-Dem variable I seek to predict with data on truth commissions is "Power distributed by Socioeconomic Status (PdSES)," described in detail in Section 6.4. This variable, recall, measures the ability of former authoritarian elites to resist turnover and continue to accumulate political and economic wealth. It taps into a very different aspect of quality of democracy than corruption, which is why it complements the analysis well. Moreover, as remarked earlier, it is conceptually unrelated to rule of law and concerns for accountability – two concepts so proximate to TJ that it would be problematic to place them on opposite sides of a regression.

I again begin by investigating the parallel trends assumption when using PdSES as the outcome variable. In Figures 6.8 and 6.9, treatment with truth commissions has been operationalized in exactly the same way as in the case of political corruption – with positive net cumulative events, described in Eq. (6.3). As before, I note the expanding universes of cases in the treatment group, as I interpret treatment as encompassing countries

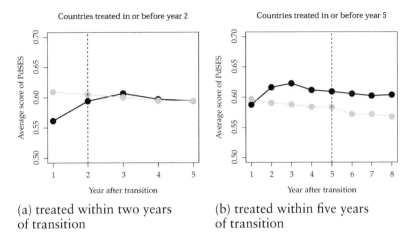

FIGURE 6.8. Parallel trends for Power distributed by Socioeconomic Status, treatment: truth commissions as positive net cumulative events (early to moderate adopters)

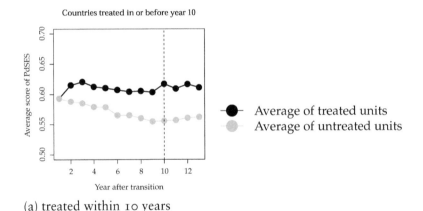

FIGURE 6.9. Parallel trends for Power distributed by Socioeconomic Status, treatment: truth commissions as positive net cumulative events

treated within 2, within 5, and within 10 years of transitioning to democracy. The control group consist in each case of countries never treated with truth commissions.

Comparing the PdSES trends of countries treated with truth commissions to their control groups reveals that for all but very late adopters, the trends before treatment are parallel. In addition, for early adopters (left of

TABLE 6.2. *Effect of truth commission events on PdSES*

	Minimalist	Net	Net cumulative
Truth commission event	0.0314*	0.00794*	0.0296*
	(0.016)	(0.005)	(0.015)
log(GDPpc)	−0.0245	−0.0245	−0.0243
	(0.032)	(0.034)	(0.033)
Constant	0.774***	0.792***	0.775***
	(0.267)	(0.268)	(0.268)
Observations	1,747	1,747	1,747
R^2	0.862	0.859	0.861

Standard errors in parentheses
Truth commission events are lagged
All models include country and year after transition specific intercepts
$^*p < 0.1, ^{**}p < 0.05, ^{***}p < 0.01$

Figure 6.8) there is a very clear uptick in quality of democracy following treatment. In this group, PdSES was actually lower prior to treatment than the control group, but increases following treatment. These trends clearly indicate that a dif-in-dif framework is an appropriate approach to investigating the effect of truth commissions. They also suggest that truth commissions may help eliminate vestiges of authoritarian rule to the extent that these vestiges are captured by PdSES.

Table 6.2 shows the results from the dif-in-dif regressions of PdSES on truth commission events, again using three different measures: minimalist, net events per year, and cumulative net events per year (also in Figure 6.10).

In order to make these results directly comparable with the effects on political corruption, I have transformed this quality of democracy indicator from a 5-point to a 1-point scale. The strongest effects – for the minimalist and cumulative net measures – are associated with changes of 3 percentage points. These models indicate that truth commission events decrease the extent to which political power is coupled with economic power, though less significantly than political corruption.

What is the reason for the weaker results in models where quality of democracy is measured with the concentration of political power among economic elites? One possible reason is that the countries in the GTJD may have very different former authoritarian elites. In some, elites may have controlled the mode of transition to the point of excluding themselves from the reach of transparency mechanisms, such as truth commissions. In others, they may have failed to do so. This conjecture is

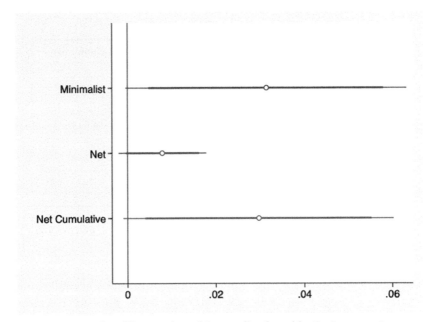

FIGURE 6.10. Dif-in-dif regression of Power distributed by Socioeconomic status on three measures of truth commission events with country-clustered SE

based on theories consistent with the works of Albertus and Menaldo (2018), Haggard and Kaufman (2012) and Ansell and Samuels (2010). Spelling it out, one would expect truth commissions to increase the quality of democracy as economic influence becomes decoupled from political power in states where the operation of truth commissions would not be constrained by constitutions designed by outgoing authoritarian elites.

To test this conjecture, I disaggregated the GTJD into two subsets using Albertus and Menaldo (2018)'s variable "Autocratic Constitution." The advantage of this variable is that it also records the year when the autocratic constitution was amended.[23] The first subset, including countries such as Chile, Peru, and Ukraine before 2004 consists of countries where the outgoing autocrats had a considerable say in designing the constitution. These countries are marked as elite-led in Table 6.3 and Figure 6.11. Other countries – including Argentina, Brazil and Hungary after 2013,

---

[23] There were several instances where I updated the Albertus-Menaldo coding or provided my own. Specifically, Albertus and Menaldo mistakenly lists Czech Republic as authoritarian-controlled, and omits Grenada, Guatemala, Guyana, and South Africa. Moreover these authors code Hungary as authoritarian beyond 2013, even though Victor Orban decisively in that year amended the former authoritarian constitution.

TABLE 6.3. *Effect of truth commission events on PdSES, accounting for outgoing elite control of constitution design*

	Not Authoritarian-led			Authoritarian-led		
	Minimalist	Net	Net cumulative	Minimalist	Net	Net cumulative
Truth commission event	0.0461**	0.0156***	0.0421**	−0.0329	−0.00368	−0.0248
	(0.020)	(0.006)	(0.020)	(0.027)	(0.010)	(0.024)
Log(GDPpc)	−0.0538	−0.0590	−0.0527	0.0855	0.0747	0.0845
	(0.039)	(0.043)	(0.040)	(0.070)	(0.070)	(0.071)
Constant	1.071***	1.136***	1.081***	0.0136	0.108	0.0123
	(0.347)	(0.372)	(0.346)	(0.717)	(0.695)	(0.722)
Observations	1,223	1,223	1,223	524	524	524
R^2	0.918	0.913	0.917	0.759	0.756	0.758

Standard errors in parentheses

Truth commission events are lagged

All models include country and year after transition specific intercepts

$*p < 0.1$, $**p < 0.05$, $***p < 0.01$

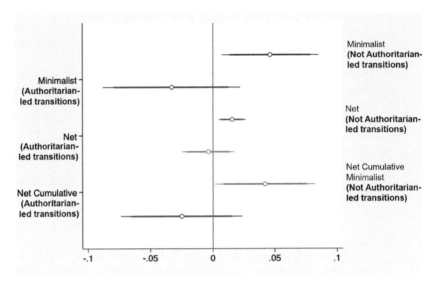

FIGURE 6.11. Dif-in-dif regression of Power distributed by Socioeconomic status on three measures of truth commission events with country-clustered SE. Countries have been subseted into "Authoritarian-led" transitions (confidence intervals on the left) and transitions where Autocrats were removed from the process (confidence intervals on the right)

among others – are new democracies where outgoing authoritarian elites had a very limited influence over the design of the constitution.

Table 6.3 shows the effect of truth commission events measured according to the minimalist, net, and net cumulative measures on PdSES, but separating the effects for democracies where ex-authoritarian elites controlled the constitutional process. It is dramatically clear that the transparency effect is driven largely by democracies where autocrats did not control the constitution-making process. This suggests that upending authoritarian networks left lingering following the democratic transition is easier to achieve through truth commissions when autocrats have been removed from the helm of democracy.

This effect is also clearly visible in Figure 6.11. There, for the Minimalist, Net and Net Cumulative measures of truth commission events, the top confidence interval represents countries with transitions that took place outside of authoritarian control. The bottom confidence intervals represent countries where autocrats controlled the transition and constitution writing process. In the latter, the effects of truth commissions are indistinguishable from zero.

With the above caveat in mind, I conclude that the data analysis carried out in this section within a dif-in-dif framework supports my main expectation that truth commissions are an effective tool for improving the quality of democracy.

6.7 ROBUSTNESS CHECK: SYNTHETIC MATCHING

Before concluding this section, I illustrate my main finding with a synthetic matching estimation[24] performed as a robustness check for the earlier estimations. The logic underlying synthetic matching is to "borrow" information from any number of untreated units to create an artificial ("synthetic") counterfactual that can be compared to the trajectory of a treated unit. In my case, the units making up the synthetic control are countries that have not established a truth commission. These observations are compared on a number of covariates to the treated unit during the pretreatment period to create a series of weights. In my case, the countries are compared to South Korea, after the transition, but before experiencing a positive cumulative net truth commission score. These weights are then assigned to each of the untreated units to create a weighted average of political corruption for the synthetic control. As a result, the synthetic control is a weighted average of the outcome variable that spans both the pre- and posttreatment period. Following this process, one can compare the trajectory of the dependent variable of the treated unit to the synthetic match (Abadie et al. 2015).

In its original presentation, synthetic matching requires a balanced panel and a single treated unit. In addition, since the method estimates the weights based on the pretreatment trajectory, the analyst must collect data on the untreated units from a number of time periods before the treatment occurred. Since for countries that transitioned earlier, we observe more years in the dataset than for countries that transitioned later, the panel is unbalanced. In addition, countries experience multiple and uneven in length units with treatment, as some countries experience truth commission events immediately upon transition whereas others take years to implement them. This results in varying treatment lengths across our set of countries. Despite these obstacles, the data can be processed to conduct a conservative synthetic matching robustness check. Because the synthetic control method is not designed for units that "fall out of treatment" I use the minimalist measure, described in Eq. (6.1).

Among the set of archetypal cases studied in this book, there is only one – South Korea – for which it is possible to construct a synthetic match because both of its truth commission events occurred within four years

---

[24] This robustness check was performed thanks to Milena Ang.

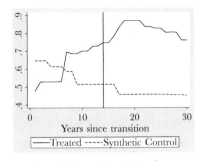

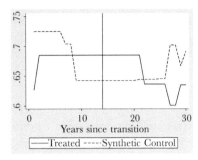

(a) South Korea's political corruption against its synthetic match

(b) South Korea's PdSES against its synthetic match

FIGURE 6.12. Effects of truth commission events in South Korea: synthetic matching

of the democratic transition. In order to be part of the synthetic control, a country must not only be untreated, but must also have experienced as many democratic years as the treated country. In the next step, we use GDP per capita as the matching covariate. Assigning the appropriate weights results in a balanced panel, where we are able to estimate the synthetic matching parameters.

Figure 6.12 compares South Korea with its synthetic control according to political corruption and PdSES, our two outcome variables. In each subfigure, a vertical line marks the year since transition when the South Korea first experienced a positive truth commission event. In the case of political corruption (left panel), we see that in the pretreatment period, South Korea (solid line) is more politically corrupt than its synthetic control (dashed line). However – as I argue in response to the treatment – it outperforms the synthetic control over time.

Performing a similar analysis, but using PdSES as the outcome variable paints a slightly different picture. As the right panel of Figure 6.12 suggests, South Korea experiences a worsening quality of democracy according to PdSES. According to estimation in panel b, South Korea (solid line) exhibits steeper downward trends than countries in the control group (dashed line). Consequently, the synthetic matching results using PdSES partially support our hypotheses. This is consistent with the weaker results for the association between PdSES and truth commission events reported earlier. Truth commissions appear to be effective in reducing political corruption that emerges from lack of transparency about what happened in the past, but less effective at breaking up corrupt networks.

My theory is ambivalent regarding how long it takes for a truth commission to reduce political corruption, but presenting a complete trajectory against its synthetic control in Figure 6.12, suggests a time frame for when this effect of truth commissions might materialize, resulting in divergence between the trajectories of treated and untreated countries. Simply eyeballing the chart, it appears to happen within a couple of years. In Appendix D, I further address the question of time that it takes for a truth commission to have an effect, by replicating the main dif-in-dif regressions for ten alternative lags.

6.8 COMPARISON WITH LUSTRATION

Before reaching the conclusion of this chapter, I consider also models that include both transparency regimes discussed in this book – truth commissions and lustrations – at the same time.

Since both truth commissions and lustrations are transparency regimes, a natural question to ask is what is the extent of substitution or complementarity between the two. According to my severity measure, truth commission events are correlated with lustration events only at .14, which suggests the two function as substitutes. Does this mean that they affect the quality of democracy in the same way? There are reasons to doubt this is the case. First, lustration is focused on the political elite, so its effects should be seen in organizations that concentrate elites, such as political parties. At the same time, the Political Corruption Index may well be picking up on phenomena much more widespread throughout society, matching the transparency effects of truth commissions rather than lustrations. Truth commissions' transparency reach into the population is unlimited and may touch any level of society.

Beginning with the minimalist measure, the models presented in the first three columns of Table 6.4 capture the effects of each transparency regime having at least one positive event.

When interpreting the results of these regressions, It is important to keep in mind that coefficients represent effects relative to different comparison groups.

In Models 1 and 2, the coefficients represent having experienced at least one positive event of a given type (lustration in Model 1 and truth commissions in Model 2). Thus, the comparison group is defined by countries that never had an event of *that* type, though they could have experienced an event of the other type (or of any other type, for that matter).

Model 3, on the other other hand, includes both types of transparency regimes. Hence, the control group includes countries that had neither a truth commission nor a lustration event.

Perhaps surprisingly, in contrast to truth commissions, the minimalist measure of lustrations alone has no significant effect on political corruption. That is, relative to countries that have had no positive lustration events, having a positive lustration event makes no difference in corruption. In countries that had a lustration event, having at least one truth commission event decreases political corruption by almost 5 percent (.031-(−.018)). This suggests that truth commissions decrease political corruption regardless of whether the country has a lustration program as well.

Of course, the minimalist measure used here is very simple – perhaps overly so. What is considered a positive event could be as insignificant as a mere proposal of a bill to the legislature, even when this proposal goes nowhere, as happened with Russia's lustration bill of 1992 (Stan et al. 2009). Moreover, this measure is not able to discriminate between countries that accumulate different numbers of positive events.

In light of this, I supplement these models with the additional measure of net cumulative positive events in Table 6.5. The first model uses just net cumulative lustration events, the second uses just net cumulative truth commissions, the third adds the minimalist and net cumulative measures for just lustration, and the fourth model adds both measures for just truth commissions. Note that based on the previous comment on the changing comparison groups, the interpretation of the net cumulative events coefficients in Models 4 and 5 is that they capture the effect of having more positive than negative events in a country where a positive event of that type has already occurred. Also note that the effects of truth commission events only become stronger in this context (increasing from .025 to .046). Model 5 contains both lustration and truth commission events according to both the minimalist and net cumulative measure. The effect of having a truth commission event occur at all is robust relative to changes in the comparison groups reflected here. Independently of lustrations and the net

TABLE 6.4. *Political Corruption Index and occurrence of transparency regimes*

	Political Corruption Index		
	(1)	(2)	(3)
Lustration occured	−0.012		−0.018*
	(0.008)		(0.008)
Truth commission occured		0.028***	0.031***
		(0.006)	(0.006)
GDP per capita	0.018	0.018	0.020
	(0.011)	(0.011)	(0.011)
Observations	1,740	1,740	1,740
R^2	0.062	0.073	0.076
Adjusted R^2	−0.010	0.001	0.004

Note: $*p < 0.05$; $**p < 0.01$; $***p < 0.001$
Lagged transparency mechanisms (at least one event occurred), country + year fixed effects

accumulation of truth commission events, it reduces political corruption by 5 percent. In sum, having at least one positive truth commission event reduces political corruption regardless of whether lustration events have occurred and whether there are more positive transparency events than negative ones.

These findings are consistent with earlier predictions: I expected truth commissions to improve the quality of democratic representation and, in fact, to improve it more than lustration. Although it is somewhat discouraging to not find similar effects for lustration. Several caveats are worth mentioning here. First, neither of the models considered above allows me to control for previously discussed modifiers of lustration effects. Recall that these modifiers may include free media and varying costs of revealed skeletons. Also, it is plausible that because truth commissions have a non-exclusionary character compared to lustration, they have the ability to reveal more secrets than lustration alone.

In Chapter 8, I try to tackle the problem of measuring TJ effects by collapsing the time series into the most sensitive measure of severity – the one defined in Chapter 4 – and conducting analysis within a hierarchical modeling framework that takes into account the substitution and complementarity of all four TJ mechanisms. These final analyses suggest that in order for lustration to be effective in changing the quality of democracy, it must be carried out consistently beyond a certain threshold of severity (Table 6.5).

TABLE 6.5. *Political Corruption Index and Cumulative Transparency Regimes*

	Political Corruption Index				
	(1)	(2)	(3)	(4)	(5)
Lustration net cum pos.	−0.013* (0.007)		−0.013 (0.011)		−0.014 (0.011)
Truth commission net cum pos.		0.025*** (0.006)		−0.018 (0.022)	−0.016 (0.022)
Lustration occured			−0.001 (0.013)		−0.005 (0.013)
Truth commission occured				0.046* (0.023)	0.046* (0.023)
GDP per capita	0.019 (0.011)	0.018 (0.011)	0.019 (0.011)	0.018 (0.011)	0.021* (0.011)
Observations	1,740	1,740	1,740	1,740	1,740
R^2	0.063	0.071	0.063	0.073	0.077
Adjusted R^2	−0.009	−0.001	−0.010	0.001	0.004

Note: $*p < 0.05$; $**p < 0.01$; $***p < 0.001$
Occurred and Net Cum Positive transparency mechanisms, country + year fixed effects

6.9 CONCLUSION

Recall that among elites who sustained the former authoritarian regime are persons whose involvement in it is known, such as high-ranking officials of authoritarian parties, and those whose identity is unknown, such as secret police informers and people who spied on their friends, family, and coworkers. I have argued that even though truth commissions do not typically reveal information about former spies, they reveal information that would otherwise go undetected and can thus be considered transparency regimes on par with lustration.

In this chapter, I investigated the effects of truth commission events disaggregated across time and space on the quality of democracy in postauthoritarian states. The outcome variables I use to operationalize this concept are two measures from the V-Dem expert survey: the Political Corruption Index and Power distributed by Socioeconomic Status.

Unlike Chapter 5, the structure of the data used here allowed me to probe a causal theory of how transparency regimes affect the quality of representation. My general expectation is that more transparency should lead to better democratic outcomes because revealing the truth about the past misdeeds of elites prevents members of authoritarian or conflict-era networks from extorting policy concessions from elected politicians. Absent truth revelation, former agents of the secret police can blackmail collaborators in political office and threaten to reveal skeletons in their closets when blackmailed politicians refuse to respond to their demands (Ang & Nalepa 2019). I further suggested that truth commissions should be more effective than lustration at improving the quality of democracy because truth commissions cast a wide net in society, providing more opportunities for the past to come to light. Lustration, on the other hand, is often restricted in its reach to public officials and thus faces more obstacles. Its effects may therefore take longer to observed.

Using a dif-in-dif research design, I found that truth commissions significantly decrease political corruption according to all three of the measures I propose. Lustration, a plausible substitute for truth commissions, does not undermine the potential of truth commissions for enhancing democratic quality. Moreover, the effect of having at least one positive truth commission event is robust to reducing political corruption regardless of the accumulation of transparency events. This suggests that beyond the mere creation of a truth commission, each transparency-enhancing step in the TJ process reduces political corruption.

Similar regressions with PdSES as the outcome variable yielded somewhat weaker but positive and statistically significant results, particularly after disaggregating countries in the GTJD into those that experienced authoritarian elite-led transitions and those that did not.

Taken together, in a dif-in-dif setting, there is overwhelming support for truth commissions contributing positively to the quality of democracy, with the mere occurrence of a positive truth commission event increasing PdSES by almost 4 percentage points. However, the occurrence of a positive lustration event decreases PdSES even more (by nearly 5 percent).

How can these relatively weak or even negative results for lustration be reconciled with the HLM results from Chapter 5? There may be several reasons. In the case of the dissonance with the HLM results from Chapter 5, the issue lies in the different dependent variable – programmaticness of political parties as measured by DALP is a very different concept from either political corruption or PdSES as measured by V-Dem.

The opposite effects of lustration and truth commission events in a dif-in-dif framework are somewhat harder to explain because of the same outcome variables, but I note three plausible explanations. The first hinges on how truth commission severity is measured for the dif-in-dif research design versus how lustration severity is measured in the HLM framework. After I discussed at length the benefits of disaggregating TJ events into a time series, most of this information is discarded for the purposes of using dif-in-dif and operationalizing a treatment variable. This is the price paid for addressing the inability to account for trends in the data or the unobserved covariates.

A second possibility is based on my reading of Josh Goodman-Bacon (2018), who demonstrates that a dif-in-dif framework where units are treated at different times is a weighted average of all the comparison groups that can be constructed based on treatment times. The weights are created so that the modal period of treatment gets the highest weight, whereas the rarest treatment periods may even get negative weights. This means that if the severity of lustration must "build up" in order to be effective for decreasing corruption and improving PdSES levels, these effects will be discounted. Instead, the dif-in-dif framework is picking up the first instance when positive events exceed negative events.

Related to the above, a more substantive interpretation of the contrast between the effects of lustration and truth commissions in the diff-in-diff setting hinges on the way that lustration operates. Perhaps, compared to truth commissions, lustration requires a larger mass of positive events relative to negative events. If this is the case, a measure that is more sensitive to such intensity would lead to different outcomes for the two kinds of transparency regimes. As indicated earlier, the diff-in-diff framework compelled me to force a count measure of TJ events into an indicator variable. An alternative specification would use the original severity measure developed in Chapter 4 in an HLM framework, which is exactly what I do in Chapter 8. There, I will explore in detail the mechanisms by which each TJ mechanism operates to increase or decrease the quality of democracy measured by PdSES.

7

Purges and the Quality of Democracy

Chapters 5 and 6 tested select implications of the formal models presented in Chapter 2. In Chapter 5, I examined the effects of lustration on programmatic representation. Next, in Chapter 6, I examined the effects of truth commissions on the quality of democracy; there, instead of using party–voter linkages to measure the quality of democracy, I focused on political corruption and the ability of former authoritarian elites to continue consolidating economic with political power (Power distributed by Socioeconomic Status). These last two variables were intended to capture the breadth of transparency offered by truth commissions. Moreover, analyzing the temporal variation in truth commission events from the Global Transitional Justice Dataset (GTJD), Chapter 6 allowed the reader to appreciate the speed with which truth commissions enhance the quality of democracy. As I will demonstrate in the Chapter 8, this speed is considerably slower for lustration laws. Jointly, these chapters of Part II offer considerable corroboration for the theory that transparency regimes are, in general, democracy enhancing.

7.1 INTRODUCTION

The goal of this chapter is to test the prediction from Chapter 3, which yielded two key insights: (1) that institutionalization of the preceding authoritarian regime moderates the benefits gained from purging and that (2) consequently, it affects the incentives to purge the former authoritarian state. My insights are consistent with other theories in comparative politics. According to Anna Grzymala-Busse (2002), technocrats that had been employed by the previous authoritarian state have skills that make them more valuable than brand new bureaucrats the new democracy might assign in their place. Grzymala-Busse calls these technocratic skills "usable pasts." The implication of the theory of "usable pasts" is that the new democratic regime ought to try to harness the expertise of former authoritarian tenchnocrats to its advantage.[1]

Recall that if the expertise of the agent – modeled there as the quality of the signal – is low, the benefits from a purge may outweigh the loss of expertise to the new democratic regime. This implies that we will need to account for the moderating effect of institutionalization in the way purges influence democratic quality. The strategy of accounting for causes of purges in evaluating the consequences of this personnel TJ mechanism is laid out in detail in Section 7.2. Section 7.3 will offer a way of accounting for institutionalization of the outgoing authoritarian regime. To measure how professional the staff of the outgoing authoritarian regime was, I rely on an index of state capacity. Section 7.4 uses a a simple statistical approach to measuring the impact of purges: After splitting the samples of country years into "high" and "low" capacity, I report the effects of purges in the two groups. As an alternative statistical approach, I create an interaction term between institutionalization and purges, this time using institutionalization of the authoritarian regime preceding the transition by ten years.

7.2 HOW TO MODEL THE DATA GENERATING PROCESS?

I begin with considering the results of a simple ordinal least squares (OLS) regression of the form

$$QDI_{it} = \alpha + Purge_{it}\beta + x_{it}\gamma + c_i + \epsilon_{it}, \qquad (7.1)$$

where QDI_{it} is an indicator of the quality of democracy (in this case political corruption or Power distributed by Socioeconomic Status), c_i is the country-fixed effect, $Purge_{it}$ represents purge severity, x_{it} is a vector of "control" covariates, and ϵ_i is a random disturbance term.

Purges can be measured with the minimalist measure introduced in Chapter 6 (presented again in Eq. (7.2)). Recall that this modification of transitional justice (TJ) severity from Chapter 4 assigns 1 to the first year,

---

[1] However as Mark Deming (2020, p. 32) in his pathbreaking dissertation on Authoritarian Successor Parties (ASP) notes "experience [acquired] in the dictatorship is a mixed bag; elites' usable pasts are almost always offset by the linkage to excesses of the former dictatorship."

experiencing a positive event and continues to assign 1 to all subsequent years in that country. All other country-years are coded as 0:

$$TJ_{i,t}^{1} = \begin{cases} 1 & \text{if } \sum_{1}^{t}(P_{it}) > 0; \\ 0 & \text{if } \sum_{1}^{t}(P_{it}) = 0, \end{cases} \tag{7.2}$$

where P_{it} represents the number of positive purge events in country i in year t.

In order to be able to account for situations where more than one purge is implemented in a single year, I will also use the net purges measure defined earlier in Chapter 6 and expressed below as:

$$TJ_{i,t}^{2} = \sum_{1}^{t} P_{it} - N_{i,t}, \tag{7.3}$$

where $N_{i,t}$ represents the number of negative purge events in country i in year t. Finally, I will also use the third severity measure used in the Chapter 6 assigning 1 to year t if cumulative net events up to that year are positive and 0 otherwise:

$$TJ_{i,t} = \begin{cases} 1 & \text{if } \sum_{1}^{t}(P_{it} - N_{i,t}) > 0; \\ 0 & \text{if } \sum_{1}^{t}(P_{it} - N_{i,t}) \leq 0. \end{cases} \tag{7.4}$$

This measure is summarized in Figure 7.1, which follows the same structure as similar figures in Chapter 6 created for lustration and truth commissions. Leadership and thorough purge severity are presented separately.

The first panel of Figure 7.1 shows the data for leadership purges, and the second panel shows the data for thorough purges. Recall from Chapter 6 that dark cells represent years where net cumulative purge events were positive, and light cells represent years in which they were negative. White cells represent censored data, that is, data from countries with shorter democratic tenures, where we have not yet had the opportunity to observe purge events.

A clear difference between these data and the data on truth commissions is that there are fewer countries with cumulative positive purge events – whether thorough or leadership – than with truth commissions. This is not surprising. Purges are not events that unfold over long periods of time. Rather, they are implemented typically at the onset of transition and if revisited later, it is to scale them back, not intensify them.

Table 7.1 presents estimations based on the simple OLS regression described in Eq. (7.1). I first regress political corruption on purges using

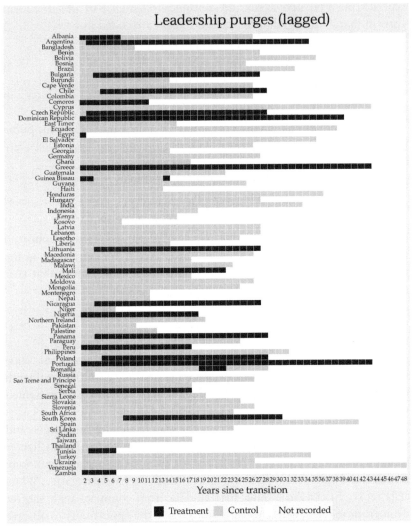

FIGURE 7.1. Leadership and thorough purges according to the net cumulative measure

the minimalist measure. Table 7.2 shows the results from the same model but with Power distributed by Socioeconomic Status as the dependent variable.

Table 7.1 contains three models. Model 3 uses leadership purges as the main independent variable; Model 2 uses thorough purges; and Model 1 uses a general purge category, where thorough and leadership purges

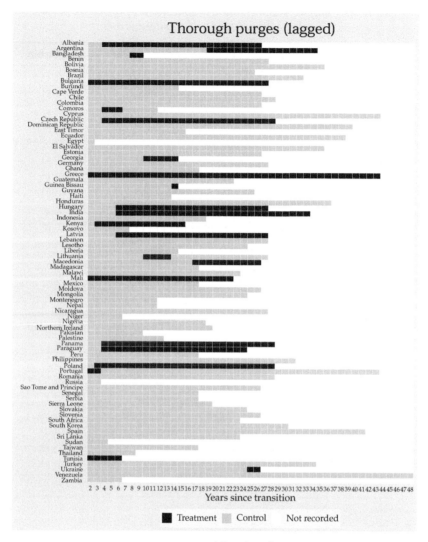

FIGURE 7.1. (*Continued*)

have been pooled together. The upshot of this analysis is that purges are not a significant predictor of political corruption. The coefficients across all types of purges are positive with the effect driven by leadership rather than thorough purges. Table 7.2 shows the same models but with Power distributed by Socioeconomic Status as the indicator of quality of democracy.

TABLE 7.1. *Simple OLS regression of political corruption on purges: fixed effects and clustered standard errors*

	All purges	Thorough	Leadership
Lagged minimalist purges	0.0230	0.0191	0.0433
	(0.77)	(0.70)	(1.25)
log GDP	0.0190	0.0207	0.0174
	(0.45)	(0.47)	(0.42)
Year after transition	−0.000106	−0.000148	−0.0000803
	(−0.06)	(−0.08)	(−0.05)
Constant	−0.992	−1.028	−0.957
	(−0.97)	(−0.98)	(−0.96)
Observations	1,758	1,758	1,758

t statistics in parentheses
*$p < 0.05$, **$p < 0.01$, ***$p < 0.001$

TABLE 7.2. *Simple OLS regression of power distributed by socioeconomic status on purges: fixed effects and clustered standard errors*

	All purges	Thorough	Leadership
Lagged minimalist purges	−0.357***	−0.428***	−0.321**
	(−3.87)	(−3.47)	(−2.64)
log GDP	0.204	0.174	0.209
	(0.85)	(0.73)	(0.83)
Year after transition	−0.00528	−0.00388	−0.00603
	(−0.54)	(−0.40)	(−0.60)
Constant	−4.140	−3.448	−4.278
	(−0.72)	(−0.60)	(−0.71)
Observations	1,758	1,758	1,758

t statistics in parentheses
*$p < 0.05$, **$p < 0.01$, ***$p < 0.001$

The results here are significantly negative: Thorough purges appear to be particularly harmful for the quality of democracy. Not much, however, should be read into these results. Crucially when I replicate the results using the continuous cumulative measure of net purge events, the significance disappears. Consider Table 7.3, which shows the same simple OLS regressions for both quality of democracy indicators: political corruption (left three columns) and concentration of political power and economic wealth (PdSES).

TABLE 7.3. *Simple OLS regression effect of purges on political corruption and PdSES with alternative purge measure*

	Pol. corruption (all purges)	Pol. corruption (thorough)	Pol. corruption (leadership)	PdSES (all purges)	PdSES (thorough)	PdSES (leadership)
Lagged net cumulative purges	0.000 (−0.02)	0.002 (0.14)	−0.00389 (−0.30)	−0.077 (−1.55)	−0.108 (−1.84)	−0.0271 (−0.28)
log GDP	0.0199 (0.46)	0.0198 (0.46)	0.0197 (0.46)	0.190 (0.77)	0.196 (0.80)	0.189 (0.75)
Years after transition	0.000 (−0.02)	0.000 (−0.03)	0.000 (−0.01)	−0.005 (−0.53)	−0.006 (−0.56)	−0.006 (−0.61)
Constant	−1.007 (−0.97)	−1.005 (−0.98)	−0.999 (−0.96)	−3.834 (−0.65)	−4.030 (−0.69)	−3.848 (−0.64)
Observations	1,758	1,758	1,758	1,758	1,758	1,758

t statistics in parentheses
*$p < 0.05$, **$p < 0.01$, ***$p < 0.001$

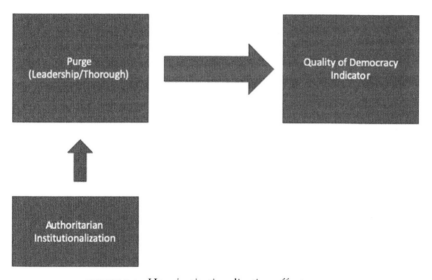

FIGURE 7.2. How institutionalization affects purges

The results become completely insignificant for either purge measure and either indicator of quality of democracy.

Critically, the models used in this table and the two above fail to account for the moderating effect of the previous authoritarian regime's institutionalization discussed in Chapter 3. Figure 7.2 summarizes the argument of how purges, prior institutionalization, and quality of democracy are related to one another.

Failure to account for prior institutionalization produces biased estimates because the correlation between purges (*Purge_{it}* above) and the error term in Eq. (7.1) (ϵ_{it} above) is not 0 if institutionalization indeed influences the decision to purge, as my model from Chapter 3 argues it does. The reason this bias occurs is that if my formal model of purges is correct, regimes without purges are different than regimes with purges because the former may have inherited a more professionalized bureaucratic and enforcement apparatus. In other words, the institutionalization of some authoritarian regimes – such as South Africa's apartheid, South Korea's Park Chung Hee era, and Poland's Communist regime – allowed their successor democratic regimes to avoid wide-scale purges. Because purging a professionalized bureaucracy and/or enforcement apparatus is suboptimal, it is a mistake to think that after accounting for whether or not a purge occurred, the remaining error term is distributed similarly for both kinds of regimes.

Figure 7.2 also draws attention to the fact that with a suitable measure of what it means to inherit a professionalized bureaucracy and enforcement apparatus, we can apply some of the widely available statistical techniques to assess the effects of purges. Section 7.3 proposes such a measure, which is based on evaluating state capacity.

7.3 MEASURING INSTITUTIONALIZATION

Political scientists have, for a long time now, been developing measures of state capacity that could be used for such purposes. The overwhelming problem with these existing measures, however, is that they smuggle in normative evaluations of regime type. Consider the dilemma of evaluating which authoritarian regimes are better at extracting tax revenue. Clearly, some authoritarian regimes are better than others at tax extraction even with weaker coercive apparatuses. Hence, a desirable measure should take into account both coercive and extractive features without downplaying these scores in the case of authoritarian regimes. This is very important for my purposes also because professionalization of state agencies can but need not, go hand in hand with a state's repressive apparatus. Authoritarian regimes have to distribute their coercive capacity across tax extraction and dealing with anti-authoritarian resistance. The more the opposition challenges the state, the more the state must transfer away from extraction and toward repression. Moreover, neither of these aspects touch upon an authoritarian state's ability to administer scarce resources. In an effort to account for all these aspects of state capacity, I take advantage of a new measure of state capacity developed by Hanson and Sigman (2022). These authors decompose state capacity into three dimensions: coercive capacity, extractive capacity, and administrative capacity. They measure each dimension separately using existing indicators and next, apply Bayesian latent variable analysis to recover how many actual dimensions of state capacity there are.

The Hanson–Sigman measure of state capacity (Hanson & Sigman 2022) addresses several conceptual difficulties associated with measuring state capacity. At least two of these are pertinent to this project. First, it is easy to conflate state capacity with regime type. Consequently, authoritarian regimes all too often end up with lower capacity scores than democracies do. Second, the presence of political corruption is often seen as indicative of low-state capacity. Yet, the presence of some corruption need not prevent the state from achieving its goals. For my specific purpose of explaining quality of democracy with regressions that include state capacity, it is critical that the measure of capacity be stripped of regime type characteristics and indicators of political corruption. Hanson and Sigman's measure is ideal for this purpose as it begins by decomposing capacity following Skocpol (1979) into administrative capacity, coercive capacity, and extractive capacity.

Extractive capacity or raising revenue is seen as the most central function of the state (Tilly et al. 1992). Coercive capacity is closely linked to the Weberian concept of states, wielding a monopoly on the use of violence. It is to some extent the most problematic dimension of state capacity, as authoritarian regimes that use more repression may appear to have higher state capacity. Furthermore, it is exactly the repressive agents of the former authoritarian regime who ought to be purged. However, a comparison of the overall capacity scores of former authoritarian military regimes with those of nonmilitary authoritarian (party-based and personalistic) regimes reveals that capacity is not higher for democracies recovering from junta-led governments. The third dimension of capacity–administrative capacity–seems closest to the institutionalization of the former regime. This concept is linked to the Weberian idea of detaching policy execution from lawmaking and vesting the former in a professionalized bureaucracy. High administrative capacity goes hand in hand with a professional civil service whose career advancement is independent of political turnover.

Conceptually, the three dimensions of state capacity seem distinct, but as Hanson and Sigman show, empirically, indicators of all three are explained by the same latent variable because "though distinct conceptually, the three [aspects of capacity] are interrelated in practice" (Hanson and Sigman 2022, p. 14): Generating tax revenue depends both on enforcing property rights (coercive capacity) and counting citizens and how much they owe. Coercive capacity clearly depends on extractive capacity (armies are expensive to support), but also depends indirectly on administrative capacity (states need to know whom to tax, for instance). Finally, a professional bureaucracy is expensive and depends on extractive capacity just as coercive capacity does.

The mean capacity score in the entire Hanson–Sigman dataset is .25 with a standard deviation of .95. For country-years included in the GTJD the mean score is .1647487, and the standard deviation is .6732103.

For my purposes in this chapter, the Hanson–Sigman capacity measure is superior to existing institutionalization measures. One of the oldest measures of authoritarian regime institutionalization is the variable I used to test the blackmail model in Chapter 5, proposed by Gandhi and Prze-worski (2007). This variable, coded as *lparty*, considers the role and position of opposition parties under the authoritarian regime. Consequently, it simultaneously captures the existence of a legislature and the existence of an opposition overt enough to allow itself to be formally included in an authoritarian institution. While this is an excellent measure for evaluating the legislative potential of a regime facing a democratic transition, it tells us little about the quality of other institutions of the state, and most notably, its administrative and enforcement apparatus.

A competing measure to that of Gandhi and Przeworski (2007) was developed by Meng (2020). Based on a formal model of authoritarian regime institutionalization, she shows that institutionalization interpreted as an authoritarian survival strategy will only be pursued by autocrats who feel potentially threatened. The way that these autocrats dissipate threats to stay in power is through credible power-sharing: They formalize the rules of succession and/or nominate independent defense ministers.[2] This model informs the indicators of institutionalization Meng creates. The first is based on the presence of power-sharing appointments in presidential cabinets, and the second is based on the quality of constitutional

---

[2] Meng writes: "institutions bind only when they empower specific elites, therefore providing potential challengers with the ability to hold incumbents accountable." (Meng 2018, p. 32).

rules.[3] Both of these variables serve as indicators of institutionalization because they reflect limits on executive power. Constitutional succession policies formalize the succession order, therefore guaranteeing the continuity of the regime beyond the current incumbent. Term limits place restrictions on the number of terms the incumbent can serve, therefore guarding against personalist forms of rule.

This measure is a great improvement over existing measures of institutionalization, which include not only that of Gandhi and Przeworski (2007) but also efforts to consider a regime institutionalized if an authoritarian party is present. As Meng points out, a majority of autocratic ruling parties are unable to survive past the death or departure of the founding leader, which suggests that these parties are not highly institutionalized or capable of functioning without latching onto a particularly charismatic leader.

Unfortunately, Meng's measure of institutionalization is not available beyond Sub-Saharan Africa, but even if it were available for all countries in the GTJD, it would still not necessarily get us farther than the *lparty* measure, as it, too, focuses on political institutionalization, leaving unaddressed the issues of state capacity that seem more relevant for decisions about purging the state of experts.

7.4 SPLITTING THE SAMPLE BY CAPACITY SCORE

The first way I examine the effect of purges on quality of democracy is by examining the distribution of the capacity variable, to see if we can actually divide the countries in the Global Transitional Justice Dataset into "low"-capacity and "high"-capacity states, using *capacity* = 0 as a cutoff. Figure 7.3 indicates that the variation in purge activity is much greater for the high-capacity states than for low-capacity states. This makes intuitive sense, as high-capacity states may be embarking on purges for reasons other than preserving or removing experts. They may be responding to pressures from public opinion or satisfying candidate entry requirements from international organizations. Bulgaria is an excellent example of this phenomenon. In the ten years leading up to the democratic transition in 1990, the country never had a capacity score lower than 1.074, and my model would probably predict that it should have refrained from

---

[3] Within constitutions, her dataset includes two dummy variables: (1) whether there is a succession policy that specifies who would serve as the interim president in the death or departure of the president and (2) whether there are term limits.

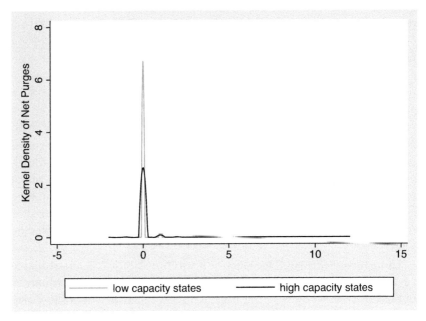

FIGURE 7.3. Kernel density plot of net pooled purges

purges. At the same time, following the demise of the Soviet Union, NATO had requested that all candidate countries purge their military ranks of vestiges of the communist past. In the shadow of the disintegration of the Warsaw Pact, the pressure to join some military alliance or other was mounting. Consequently, Bulgaria embarked on a series of purges of the military and security apparatus.

With this in mind, I conducted fixed effects regressions on low (below 0) and high-capacity (above 0) subsets of the GTJD data using Power distributed by Socioeconomic Status as the dependent variable. The results for leadership purges are presented in Table 7.4 and in Figure 7.4 they are also contrasted with the pooled purges category.[4]

What is apparent from this analysis is that in the low capacity countries, purges do indeed bolster the quality of democracy, as reflected by Power distributed by Socioeconomic Status. In the case of high capacity countries, purges simply do not have a significant effect. This is consistent with my remarks above that there are additional reasons why formerly highly institutionalized countries may want to engage in purges.

---

4 The results for the pooled purges category are presented in Table E.1 of Appendix E.

TABLE 7.4. *Split sample (by capacity) regressions of PdSES on leadership purges: country-fixed effects and country-clustered standard errors*

	Low capacity	High capacity
Lagged net leadership purges	0.220**	−0.00341
	(2.79)	(−0.07)
log GDP	0.225	0.110
	(0.83)	(0.31)
Years after transition	−0.00218	−0.00677
	(−0.16)	(−0.53)
Constant	−4.856	−1.806
	(−0.78)	(−0.21)
Observations	760	998

t statistics in parentheses
$*p < 0.05, **p < 0.01, ***p < 0.001$

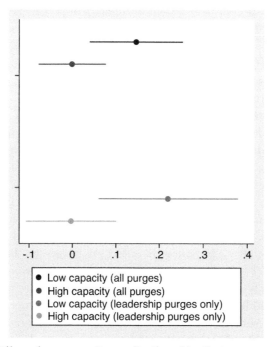

- Low capacity (all purges)
- High capacity (all purges)
- Low capacity (leadership purges only)
- High capacity (leadership purges only)

FIGURE 7.4. Effect of purges on Power distributed by Socioeconomic Status after splitting samples into countries that are low and high capacity at the time of transition

Sometimes, they might be simply responding to public opinion. Moreover, this effect is more pronounced in the case of leadership purges and so this effect has nothing to do with disbanding typical authoritarian agencies such as the security police.

Next, I look at the effects of purges on political corruption. Here, however, instead of splitting the sample into "low"- and "high"-capacity countries, I take advantage of the availability of this measure over time. I created a time-variant measure of authoritarian institutionalization, taking into account that the supply of bureaucrats and authoritarian staff following the transition changes over the course of the post-authoritarian democracy. While in the first year following the transition, persons who were employed ten years before the transition are still likely to be in the workforce and have an impact on the performance of state agencies, ten years after the transition, they will be retiring and purging them should not have an effect. Thus, I created a measure of authoritarian institutionalization assigning to each post-transition year, t, an authoritarian institutionalization measure equal to *capacity* in year $t - 10$. Specifically, the statistical model I use is:

$$QDI_{it} = P_{it}\gamma_1 + P_{it} * Inst_{it-10}\gamma_2 + \mathbf{x}_{it}\beta + \mathbf{c}_i + \epsilon_{it}, \qquad (7.5)$$

where QDI_{it} is political corruption at time t in country i; P_{it} is my measure of purge severity; $Inst_{it-10}$ is the measure of authoritarian institutionalization (with the ten year lag described earlier); $\mathbf{x}_{it}$ is a $1 \times k$ vector of time-varying independent variables that could predict the quality of democracy indicator; and c_i is the country-fixed effect. More specifically, when $Inst_{it-10} < 0$ democracy follows a poorly institutionalized authoritarian regime and while γ_1 provides the effect of purges on political corruption, γ_2 will provide the added effect of purges in poorly institutionalized regimes. I expect this effect to be positive. Conversely, when $Inst_{it-10} > 0$, democracy follows a well-institutionalized authoritarian regime and $\gamma_1 + \gamma_2$ provides the effect of purges on PdSES in such environments. I expect $\gamma_1 + \gamma_2$ to be moderately negative.

In the models with fixed effects, there is no need to code purges with an indicator variable, so in order to unleash the full potential of the GTJD, I run models with net cumulative purges per year. Moreover, as previously the score has been transformed so that higher values represent less corruption and greater quality of democracy.

Table 7.5 presents the results, for three independent variables – leadership purges, thorough purges, and all purges combined. Interestingly, we

TABLE 7.5. *Effect of purges on corruption conditional on capacity*

	Leadership purges	Thorough purges	All purges
Net cumulative purges	0.0565	0.0811	0.0825
	(0.0832)	(0.048)	(0.057)
Authoritarian	0.0572	0.0786*	0.0643
institutionalization	(0.0391752)	(0.035)	(0.04178)
Net cum purge × Inst.	0.003	−0.123*	−0.0348
	(0.086)	(0.055)	(0.07)
log GDP	0.227***	0.209**	0.226***
	(0.0597763)	(0.061)	(0.058)
Year	−0.0105***	−0.009**	−0.0108***
	(0.003)	(0.003)	(0.003)
Constant	14.97**	13.47**	15.56**
	(4.858811)	(4.972)	(5.037)
Observations	600	600	600
σ_u	0.487	0.452	0.486
σ_e	0.060	0.0597	0.0599
ρ (fraction of variance due to u_i)	0.985	0.983	0.985
R^2 within	0.1269	0.1425	0.1372
R^2 between	0.1058	0.1084	0.1066
R^2 overall	0.1375	0.1395	0.1383

t statistics in parentheses
*$p < 0.05$, **$p < 0.01$, ***$p < 0.001$
74 groups, country-fixed effects and country-clustered standard errors in parentheses

see that for leadership purges alone, institutionalization does not appear to moderate their effect on political corruption, nor do leadership purges even have an independent effect on corruption. In the case of thorough purges however, there is an interesting effect, broadly consistent with my expectations. Formerly institutionalized regimes appear to decrease the effect of thorough purges on quality of democracy measured with political corruption: for every additional net cumulative purge event, a standard deviation change on the capacity scale produces slightly more than 8% change in political corruption.[5] At the same time, the direct effect of

---

[5] The time variant state capacity measure has a standard deviation of .66; thus if a unit change in cumulative purges contributes to a .123 decrease in political corruption, a standard deviation change contributes to an .81 change.

former authoritarian institutionalization partly offsets that effect. This is not a particularly surprising effect as we would expect autocracies with higher state capacity to be better at eliminating corruption and for these effects to last some time past the democratic transition.

I also note that between the country-fixed effects and country-clustered standard errors, the assumptions of this model are quite conservative. For instance, without such clustering of standard errors, statistical significance would increase in both purge categories and match my theoretical prediction. That it is only significant in the thorough purge category is likely caused by the fact that thorough purges are much more dramatic and hence the potential loss of expertise is greater. But the reason could also be more complex. Recall that my theoretical model posited that purges may harm democratization efforts if those who are let go had both the necessary expertise and sufficient ideological proximity to the new democratic politicians (ideologically distant experts are likely to sabotage policy implementation for their own ideological gain). In the previous statistical model, I do not control in any way for ideological proximity of agents. Yet it is entirely likely that the kinds of authoritarian agencies that are thoroughly purged following the democratic transition are agencies that invested in ideological recruitment, such as the secret police or censorship office.[6] Hence, the category "thorough purge" may be picking up on purges of staffers ideologically proximate to the former autocrat and distant to the incoming democratic government.

7.4.1 Alternative Measure of Institutionalization

The role of institutionalization of the previous authoritarian regime in moderating the effect of purges can also be demonstrated using an alternative measure of institutionalization, which I already used previously, as a control variable, in Chapter 5 – Gandhi's *lparty* variable. As in Section 7.3, in order to take advantage of the availability of this measure over time, I created a time-variant measure of authoritarian institutionalization assigning to each post-transition year, t, an authoritarian institutionalization measure equal to *lparty* in year $t - 10$. *lparty* itself, as explained in Chapter 5, is a three-category variable, which I have transformed into a dummy. The dichotomous nature of the variable lends itself to easier interpretation when it is part of an interaction term.

---

[6] Communist Poland, for instance, had an agency called the Department of Press and Association Oversight, *Glowny Urzadu Kontroli Prasy, Publikacji i Widowisk*.

TABLE 7.6. *Effect of purges on power distributed by socioeconomic status: fixed effect model with interaction term*

	(1)	(2)	(3)	(4)
Net l.purges, no institutionalization	0.136*** (5.11)		0.105*** (3.77)	
Net l.purges, institutionalized	−0.0556*** (−4.90)		−0.0511*** (−4.45)	
Net t.purges, no institutionalization		0.118 (1.93)		0.0952* (2.01)
Net t.purges, institutionalized		0.0929 (0.71)		0.0762 (0.52)
Net cumulative leadership purges			0.127 (1.54)	
Net cumulative thorough purges				0.0518 (0.54)
Log GDP	−0.101 (−0.41)	−0.103 (−0.41)	0.0478 (0.37)	0.0404 (0.31)
Years after transition	0.00577 (0.63)	0.00588 (0.61)		
Constant	3.024 (0.51)	3.088 (0.51)	−0.603 (−0.19)	−0.353 (−0.11)
Observations	1371	1371	1371	1371
Fixed/random effects	fixed	fixed	fixed	fixed
Clustered std. errors	yes	yes	yes	yes

t statistics in parentheses
*$p < 0.05$, **$p < 0.01$, ***$p < 0.001$
Note: All purge measures are lagged one year, as in the remaining tables in this chapter.

Given this ease of interpretation and in order to unleash the full potential of the GTJD, I run models with net cumulative purges per year as well as net purge events per year.[7]

In Table 7.6, the first model regresses PdSES on net leadership purges, breaking the effects down into formerly non-institutionalized (top row)

---

[7] Recall from Chapter 6 that this last measure is defined as, where $P_{i,t}$ represents country i's positive purge events in year t, and $N_{i,t}$ represents negative events in the same country and the same year.

$$TJ_{i,t} = P_{i,t} - N_{i,t}, \tag{7.6}$$

and institutionalized (second row) cases. The second model applies the same analysis for thorough purges. The third model, as a robustness check, includes both net cumulative leadership purges and net leadership purges; the fourth model offers the same robustness check for thorough purges.

In the case of leadership purges, after the interaction terms are introduced (Model 1) and even after cumulative net purges are controlled for (Model 3), the effect in formerly institutionalized regimes is indeed negative (though moderately so), while in poorly institutionalized regimes, the effect is positive.

Models 2 and 4 look at the effect of thorough purges. Here, I expect both effects – following poorly and well-institutionalized authoritarian regimes – to be stronger. In a poorly institutionalized regime, a thorough purge should be the most effective way to reduce PdSES because if state agents have no expertise to take advantage of, the new democracy is better off dismantling the entire agency and starting from scratch in its state rebuilding effort. On the other hand, a thorough purge implemented following a highly institutionalized state can backfire as the new democracy dispenses with much needed expertise.

The results indicate that across purges, in poorly institutionalized environments, leadership purges increase the quality of democracy. An additional leadership purge event taking place in the preceding year increases the quality of democracy, as reflected by PdSES, by 14 percent when net cumulative leadership purge events are not controlled for and by over 10 percent when those events are controlled for. This is to be expected as with no expertise loss, purges are not costly and can only have an enhancing effect on the quality of democracy. In contrast, an additional leadership purge event taking place in a formerly institutionalized state decreases PdSES by more than 5 percent; this effect is consistent after cumulative leadership purges are controlled for. Following institutionalized authoritarian regimes, leadership purges come at the cost of losing valuable expertise and may consequently diminish democratic quality. In the case of thorough purges, there is also a significant positive effect following poorly institutionalized regimes. An additional thorough purge event in such a state increases the quality of democracy according to this measure by almost 10 percent.

These results are consistent with the earlier findings, save for the fact that the effects of leadership purges are now stronger than the effects of thorough purges, which is probably linked to the fact that this alternative measure of institutionalization is less of a measure of state capacity and more of a measure of power-sharing stability. At the same time, it broadly supports the theory I present in Chapter 3.

7.4.2 Limitations of Fixed-Effect Regressions

In Chapter 3, I showed that an agent of the former authoritarian state who has preferences misaligned with those of the new democratic leaders (the principals) may apply his expertise to sabotage policy. Hence, in my regressions, I should control for preference alignment between the principal and agent. This cannot be controlled for in a way that varies over time, and thus cannot be included in a fixed effect regression as it would be completely collinear with the country- fixed effects. A similar problem occurs with measuring uncertainty, a parameter from my theory of purges responsible for increasing the cost of purging agents of the former regime. In the conclusion to Part I of the book, I argued that the mode of transition – for instance, negotiations as opposed to sudden implosion – can stand in as a proxy for this uncertainty. Where the regime collapse is sudden, the level of uncertainty is greater; where negotiations are long and protracted, uncertainty is kept in check. There are two problems, however, with operationalizing uncertainty so that it can be used in a statistical model. The first is associated with the fact that each country's transition in the GTJD would have to be evaluated independently with the nature of the transition in mind. The second obstacle is technical: uncertainty at the time of transition also would be perfectly correlated with the country fixed effects and so cannot be included in the regression.

To get around these problems, in Appendix E, as a robustness check I conducted a two-stage least squares analysis. Using a selection model is an alternative way of accounting for the fact that states can "select" into purges based on how institutionalized their bureaucrats or enforcement apparatus was prior to the transition. Structurally, such a model is equivalent to an instrumental variable approach. Conducting this analysis requires a convincing discussion of the assumptions involved in such an analysis (the exclusion restriction and that institutionalization affects the endogenous regressor – purges) and the development of reduced form regressions (out of a first-stage and second-stage regression). The results of this analysis are consistent with the findings presented earlier: after accounting for institutionalization of the prior authoritarian regime, leadership, but especially thorough purges reduce the concentration of economic and political power and reduce political

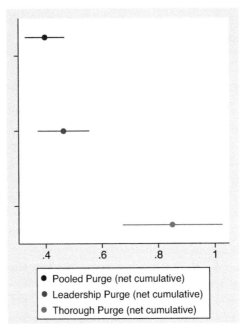

FIGURE 7.5. Effect of pooled, leadership and thorough purges on Power distributed by Socioeconomic Status: two-stage regression

corruption. These results, for Power distributed by Socioeconomic Status, are summarized in Figure 7.5.

7.5 CONCLUSION

This chapter used fixed effects models to test the implications of the second part of my theory about TJ. In Chapter 3, I argued that conducting purges in a post-authoritarian state does not unambiguously promote democratic stability. The effects of purges depend on the expertise of the agents of the former authoritarian state, on how misaligned their preferences are with the policy preferences of the new democratic politicians, and on the uncertainty accompanying the transition. This chapter focused on exploring the moderating effect of the agents' expertise, which is shaped by the training and experience they accumulated under the former authoritarian state. Scholars of authoritarian regimes provide several measures of the capacity of these regimes, allowing for extensive robustness tests of my hypotheses. I explored the effects of purges on two quality of democracy indicators, political corruption and concentration

of political power and economic wealth (Power distributed by Socioeconomic Status), and found particularly strong effects in the case of the
latter. I also disaggregated purge events into those targeting the leadership
of formerly authoritarian agencies and those targeting entire agencies
(thorough purges). Although both kinds of purges improve the quality
of democracy following a low-capacity authoritarian regime, on balance,
leadership purges seem to have a more powerful effect on reducing concentration of power and wealth (measured by PdSES), while thorough
purges seem to have a stronger effect on reducing political corruption.
This makes intuitive sense: if the former authoritarian agency was poorly
run, purging only its leadership may reduce economic influence of the
politically powerful, but does not address the problem of broad corruption. Sometimes creating an entirely new agency may be the only solution.

As a robustness check, I also tested this theory within a two-stage
regression framework. Whether or not this framework is justified depends
on our readiness to accept the exclusion restriction, which is that authoritarian institutionalization affects the quality of democracy only through
purges. For this reason I rest most of the burden of proof on the fixed
effects model and relegate the 2SLS discussion to Appendix E.

8

Taking Stock: Joint Analysis of All Mechanisms

The second part of my book set out to accomplish two tasks: (1) develop a global dataset of lustrations, truth commissions and leadership and thorough purges and (2) use the newly created dataset to examine the impact of all four transitional justice (TJ) mechanisms side by side on three aspects of democratic quality: programmatic representation, political corruption and the association of political powere with economic wealth. The first of the three dependent variables are used in Chapter 5 in a nonfixed effects setting with a fully developed hierarchical model where I exploit the full gamut of the severity scale; the second and third of the three are used in Chapter 6, where in a dif-in-dif framework I examine the effects of truth commissions on corruption and the strength of authoritarian networks. Finally, in Chapter 7, I analyzed the effect of purges on these last two variables.

I argued that lustrations are complex mechanisms that must reach a threshold of intensity before they can bear fruit. This is in sharp contrast to truth commissions, which, as we saw in Chapter 6, even following a small nudge in the positive direction, start improving the quality of democracy.

In this chapter I show that lustrations, once they exceed this threshold, go beyond just removing secret collaborators: They also affect the fates of top authoritarian elites by making it much harder for them to hold key positions in the post-authoritarian state and in political parties. Subsequently, it seems that these elites go into the private business sector. However, purges (and leadership purges in particular) seem to sometimes prevent them from exiting into business.

In the second part of the chapter, in one final argument for using lustration to deal with secret collaborators, I consider again the entire time series dataset, but relax the rigid constraints of fixed effects regressions and as I did in Chapter 5, run a series of hierarchical models using all four mechanisms.

8.1 DE JURE VERSUS DE FACTO TRANSITIONAL JUSTICE

So far, this book has introduced scholars to a two-part theory of how personnel TJ can impact the stability and representativeness of a new democracy. I then proposed a new method for organizing transitional justice data: My Global Transitional Justice Dataset (GTJD) disaggregates transitional justice mechanisms – lustration, truth commissions, and purges – into time series of positive and negative events. After explaining why this kind of disaggregation is needed, I showed how researchers can use the granular data structure to construct measures that can then be used to test a variety of TJ hypotheses. I tested hypotheses on impacts of transparency mechanisms and purges on quality of democracy indicators. I expected lustrations and truth commissions to monotonically increase the quality of democratic representation and remove former authoritarian elites and their collaborators from positions of influence. At the same time, I expected purges to only do so if the prior authoritarian regime was not-institutionalized. Hence, I argued, purges have a non-monotonic effect. In addition, within purges, thorough purges should be more costly to implement following highly institutionalized authoritarian regimes.

Yet, one of the shortcomings of the proposed measures and even of my granular data in the form of TJ chronologies is that neither provides information about whether the TJ process was actually enforced. Focusing on institutional events of passage and on the striking down of TJ provisions gives only a *de jure* picture of the TJ process, which may or may not reflect the *de facto* process. I avoided coding the implementation and effectiveness of TJ for a variety of reasons, the most important of which is that it is too difficult to disentangle from the quality of democracy itself. Instead, I focused efforts on a parallel data collection process that measures the "raw output of the transitional justice process." This output is the presence of former authoritarian elites in post-authoritarian political institutions and organizations, in business, as well as their appearance before criminal courts. These data were collected by tracking the fate of every member of a country's authoritarian elite from the time of regime transition through 2018. I focused on tracing their presence in five sectors: in political parties, in state administration, in the military, in business, and in courts, facing criminal charges.

The key feature of these data is that for each type of presence (state, party business elite, and facing criminal responsibility), they provide us with a single observation for each country. Consequently, cross-sectional analysis of this type can tell us little about the causal relationship between the severity of TJ mechanisms and the fate of authoritarian elites. Yet, given the close conceptual proximity of the dependent and independent variables, I will offer an interpretation of these patterns that suggests a causal connection even though the patterns in question are based on correlations alone.

Figure 8.1 previews the results of the regressions where authoritarian elite presence in sectors is modeled as a linear function of the severity of my four TJ mechanisms.

Each of the boxes on the left represents an independent variable: specifically, the severity of each transitional justice mechanism. Each of the boxes on the right represents a dependent variable: specifically, the weighted proportion of former authoritarian elites in different sectors of the post-authoritarian state. The lines linking the boxes represent significant correlations, and the plus and minus signs represent the direction of the association.[1]

8.2 HOW TRANSITIONAL JUSTICE AFFECTS FORMER AUTHORITARIAN LEADERS

There exists a large literature in political science on the survival of autocrats in public office, but most of it is concerned with the survival within the authoritarian regime itself, and not beyond it. For instance, Adam Przeworski and Jennifer Gandhi, in their seminal article, show that political institutions that "solicit the cooperation of the opposition" by giving it a voice can aid autocratic survival. In their empirical analysis, they single out one particular strategy – giving opposition parties representation in the legislature – as most conducive to prolonging the life of dictatorships (Gandhi & Przeworski 2007).[2]

---

[1] As remarked above, although the lines are marked with arrows, the analysis I present below cannot be used to infer causality.

[2] For more examples of institutional reforms that extend the persistence of autocrats see Blaydes (2010, 2018), Weeks (2014) and Svolik (2012).

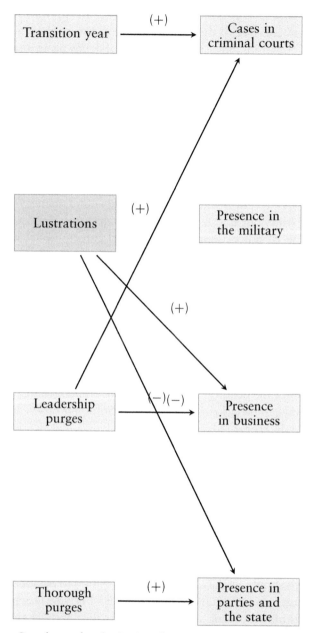

FIGURE 8.1. Correlates of authoritarian elite presence in sectors of public life in post-authoritarian states

Milan Svolik (2012) takes an inside-the-regime approach, attributing authoritarian survival to the way in which dictators share power with their ruling coalitions. Since the typical way of deposing an autocrat is via a coup d'état, sharing power with an elite made up of potentially threatening competitors not only keeps a dictator in check, but simultaneously ensures the survival of the regime beyond the life of the leader. Although they focus on different mechanisms, both Svolik's and Przeworski and Gandhi's research point to the same by-product of securing authoritarian survival: institutionalization of the regime. The expectation implicit in Svolik and explicit in Gandhi is that when equipped with power-sharing institutions, authoritarian regimes survive longer.

In some very recent work, Anne Meng adds more nuance to this argument. She points out that a legislature and elections alone are no more an indication of power sharing than formal constitutional rules are of actual constraints on executive power. True authoritarian institutionalization manifests itself in staffing key regime positions with competitors to power and not figureheads. Only dictators that place de facto and credible institutional limits on their survival can build regimes that will outlive them. Yet, not all dictators have the same incentives to institutionalize. Because some autocrats are strong enough to stave off challenges to their power without institutionalization, they may stay in power just as long as weaker autocrats who do place such limitations upon themselves. Consequently, since the decision to institutionalize is endogenous, when measured properly, the relationship between institutionalization and survival rates should disappear (Meng 2020).

While fascinating in its own right, the primary interest of this scholarship lies in the survival of autocrats *under the same* authoritarian regime. My objective, however, is to examine the autocrats' endurance prospects beyond the regime of their origin. This question has been addressed for instance by Alexandre Debs (2016). In search of an answer to the question "What makes certain dictatorships more likely than others to democratize?," he argues that since military dictators are most threatening to their successors (unless they are chosen by democratic elections), these military dictatorships should be the most likely to transition to democracy swiftly. Also, because former military dictators are less likely to face punishment at the hands of democratic successors than at the hands of authoritarian successors, they are less reluctant to step down. An alternative interpretation to the question of authoritarian survival has been provided more recently by Albertus and Menaldo (2018b), who argue that dictators in general only concede to democratization on conditions that are beneficial to them. However, Albertus and Menaldo are predominantly interested in the terms under which autocrats concede to a democratic transition. They research neither the specific career trajectory of post-authoritarian elites nor the nature of the TJ process that may have been used against them. Indeed, all of their independent variables predate the transition itself.

Anna Grzymala-Busse (2002) has examined how successor authoritarian parties as organizations fare under new democratic conditions. Although her research is limited to the postcommunist world, she finds that the degree to which a party's organization was technocratic – as opposed to ideological – prior to the transition is a very strong predictor of its success. Grzymala-Busse's (2017) newer work extends this argument to a global universe of cases, but finds that although the strategy of reinvention leads successor authoritarian parties to do better in the short term than non-reformed successor parties, eventually their advantage dwindles and they die out (Grzymala-Busse & Nalepa 2022).

Finally, my earlier book, also restricted to post-communist Europe, developed the idea that former authoritarian elites may be harder to punish in the aftermath of transitions to democracy. This may be the result of negotiations that convince the opposition that TJ may reveal skeletons in the opposition's closet by exposing collaborators who worked for the communist secret police and straining the fragile reputation of the new democratic elites (Nalepa 2010*b*).

This literature has convincingly established that authoritarian elites have a better shot at surviving the transition when the opposition is inclined to tolerate them for their skills, because of sharing a past in the same legislative assembly, or because the opposition committed itself to respecting the former autocrats when negotiating the terms of the transition.

8.3 MEASURING AUTHORITARIAN ELITE SURVIVAL

I build on these important contributions in examining how specific TJ mechanisms – transparency regimes on the one hand and purges on the other – influence the career trajectories of individual members of the authoritarian elite. This variable is limited to known members and collaborators of the former authoritarian elite, as I cannot trace the career trajectory of secret collaborators of the authoritarian regime whose identities have not yet been revealed.

The measure I developed codes information about the fate of former authoritarian elites following the transition to democracy. Specifically, to collect these data, I compiled information on authoritarian rulers from seventy-one regimes. To determine which regimes were authoritarian, I followed the same criteria as for the Global Transitional Justice Dataset, but I excluded – for obvious reasons – post-conflict societies. With a few additions, this set of cases largely overlaps with the Geddes et al. (2014) dataset (GWF). The additions include small countries and those that transitioned to democracy after the publication of GWF. I include countries that, as indicated by GWF, are currently democratic and transitioned from a military, party-based, or personalist authoritarian regime in the post-1946 period.[3] One complication I had to deal with when collecting these data is not coding as the authoritarian elite the outgoing leaders who were sometimes liberal figureheads put in place by the actual autocrats who seeing the writing on the wall began to preemptively liberalize. To address this, instead of coding information on the set of authoritarian elites who were in office right before the regime collapsed, I coded information on elites in office within a year of the transition. This strategy ideally avoids bias associated with coding more liberal authoritarian leaders appointed just before the transition to appease the opposition. These more liberal autocrats are frequently innocent of grave human rights violations and have no reason to be subjected to purges, lustrations, or suffer from the operation of truth commissions. A rigorous measure of authoritarian elite reproduction ought to focus on the leaders these transitional elites replaced.

To compile the lists, members of the Transitional Justice and Democratic Stability Lab and I relied on sources that included *Historical Dictionaries* from the *Countries of the World* series, the rulers.org database, Keesing's Record of World Events, and numerous other secondary sources.[4] We identified, on average, twenty-two members of the authoritarian elite for each country. The countries with the largest sets of authoritarian rulers were party-based authoritarian regimes, particularly in the communist world. In the last year of the Soviet Union, the combined number of cabinet and politburo members was over thirty people. The countries with the shortest lists of elites are the post-authoritarian Latin American countries recovering from junta rule (Guatemala, for example, only has fifteen people on the positions list. Some of the Middle Eastern

---

3   This list of countries is slightly shorter than the list discussed in Chapter 4 because it omits countries that experienced conflict in this period but did not have an authoritarian regime. For a complete list see data appendix.

4   A complete list of sources is provided in the raw data appendix.

dictatorships that collapsed over the course of the Arab Spring, like Tunisia and Egypt, had even smaller ruler sets totaling seven to eight people.).

For a measure of *de facto* transitional justice, our key interest is in the presence of these former authoritarian leaders in new democratic governments. However a second complication that arises with measuring this presence is that the governments in post-authoritarian states vary in size. The World Bank has been collecting the data on government size since 2000, calculating measures such as "public sector employment as a percentage of total employment." Their data indicate that thus measured, the size of the public sector in democracies varies 1.4 percent (Senegal) to 17.8 percent (Norway). Taking advantage of the fact that the World Bank reports size of government data since 2000, I take the value of this variable that is closest to the country's transition year. For countries that transitioned to democracy before 2000, I impute the size of the public sector by estimating a regression that predicts public employment from public expenditures on such employment; these data are available from 1990 in the International Monetary Fund's World Economic Outlook (WEO) dataset.[5] The specific procedure is described in Appendix F.1.

In order to adequately account for these two limitations and be able to compare and contrast the reproduction of former authoritarian elites, I propose the following measure:

$$ERP_c = \frac{k_c}{m_c}(1 - g_c), \tag{8.1}$$

where k_c represents country c's size of the post-authoritarian elite, g_c is the size of the country's democratic government using as a proxy the World Bank "public sector employment as total percent of the population"; m_c is size of the authoritarian elite. This measure takes values between 0 and 1 because $k_c \geq m_c$ (the number of authoritarian elites in public positions following the transition cannot be larger than the number of authoritarian elites) and because $g_c < 1$.

In order to see how this measure works, consider the following four highly stylized hypothetical scenarios, all pertaining to a country with a population of 1,000.

---

[5] Available at www.imf.org/external/pubs/ft/weo/2018/02/weodata/index.aspx

1. 4 out of 20 former autocrats survived the transition to hold a position in a post-transition government of 100.
2. 1 out of 20 former autocrats survived the transition to hold a position in a post-transition government of 100.
3. 1 out of 20 former autocrats survived the transition to hold a position in a post-transition government made up of 10.
4. 4 out of 20 former autocrats survived the transition to hold a position in a post-transition government made up of 10.

In Case 1, the measure returns $ERP_1 = .18$. In the country described in Case 2, which is identical to the first, except that only one autocrat survived, the measure returns $ERP_2 = .045$, exactly a quarter of the value of the first country. In the third country, the authoritarian survival rate is the same, but the post-transition government is smaller. This means that it is *harder* for autocrats, holding constant any personnel TJ measures, to survive the transition and remain in political office. The measure for Case 3 is $ERP_3 = 0.0045$ – a tenth of the value of the second country – to reflect the fact that it is ten times harder to survive the transition and assume a political position in a smaller government. Finally, in the country described in Case 4, the survival rate is back up to what it was in the first country, but the government is still small. This time, the measure of authoritarian elite reproduction returns $ERP_4 = .0225$. This is higher than four times the measure of Case 3, which reflects the fact that the rate of survival is weighed by the measure more heavily than government size. This is an arbitrary decision and one could modify the measure to reverse it. The cost would be, however, a more complicated algebraically formula, which is why I decided against it.

Figure 8.2 presents a histogram of the state (left) variable and party (right) variable for the seventy-one former authoritarian countries in the dataset. It is quite apparent from the histograms that the data is not distributed normally, which may pose problems with using OLS regressions. For this reason, as a robustness check, I also used the raw count of former autocrats as this measure's distribution is close to normal. However, I also apply some available solutions, such as robust standard errors, to the heteroscedasticity problem these histograms are a symptom of.

I am interested in the presence of former authoritarian elites in institutions of the state, in political parties, but also in the military, in the business sector, and in court settings, facing criminal responsibility. Here too, measures adjusting the raw number of former authoritarian elites in

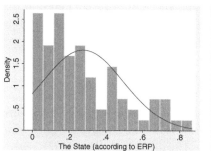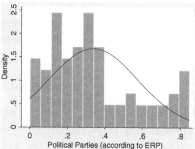

FIGURE 8.2. The presence of former authoritarian elites in the state (left) and in political parties (right) in seventy-one former autocracies of the GTJD

positions of power are called for because some countries have a smaller military, fewer opportunities for being active in business and/or are more or less prone to develop organized crime. For business presence and facing court proceedigs, however, it was not easy to come up with appropriate weights and I resorted to using raw proportions. For measuring presence of former authoritarian elites in the military, I changed the weights in expression 8.1 to (1- percentage of GDP devoted to military spending) in order to reflect the proportion of military spending.

8.4 PRESENCE OF AUTHORITARIAN ELITES IN PARTIES, THE STATE, AND BUSINESS

In Appendix F.1, I regressed the presence of former authoritarian elites in the post-authoritarian state, political parties, and in business on the severity of four TJ mechanisms used in this book. I included all possible combinations of these mechanisms along with two control variables (the year of the transition and whether the country in question had a history of conflict[6]). These regressions were used to derive the associations in Figure 8.1. Yet the number of observations in these regressions is very low, because only one observation of the dependent variable is available for each country. Therefore although I will mention the significant

---

[6] Note, that by excluding from the dataset countries that were in the GTJD solely because of their conflict history, I am not eliminating states that had *both* a history of conflict and an authoritarian history.

associations between the TJ mechanisms and authoritarian elites, in the discussion below, I focus on showing descriptive statistics and illustrative cases instead of regression tables themselves.

8.4.1 Reproduction of Authoritarian Elites

Figures 8.3 and 8.4 illustrate my the ERP measure applied to elite reproduction in political parties and in the state in seventy-one post-authoritarian countries in the GTJD. Unsurprisingly, the states where former autocrats were categorically removed from office, either because of the breakup or unification of a federal state (Bosnia, Germany) or far-reaching purges (Greece, Latvia) have the fewest former leaders in their political parties. In contrast, former authoritarian African states appear to have a considerable representation of former elites in political parties. This is somewhat surprising because a large share of these former autocracies were ruled by leaders who stood at the helm of weak parties that one would expect to disintegrate immediately upon the dictator's death or ousting from office (Meng 2020). Surprisingly, it is the postcommunist countries – those that had vibrant ruling authoritarian parties that survived well into the democratic transition (Grzymala-Busse 2002) – where the elite reproduction is at its lowest. Although postcommunist states made a name for themselves in extensive lustration policies, instances of banning entire parties due to their former authoritarian status were few and far between. The regressions in Appendix F.2 shed some light on the mechanism of authoritarian elite withdrawal from political parties.

Specifically, the results in Table F.2 indicate that lustration severity is significantly associated with decreased presence of former authoritarian elites in political parties. The effect is consistent and robust to including other TJ mechanisms, interaction terms between them, and controls, although none of these terms achieves significance. Both the dependent and independent variables are normalized between 0 and 1. A change in lustration severity from the most lenient lustration law to the most stringent, holding all other variables we control for constant, would lower the presence of authoritarian elites in political parties by almost 34 percent. According to the same table, a thorough purge, paradoxically, increases elite presence in parties significantly, though only at the 10 percent level and only for one specification (Model 2). Based on Model 4, where I inter-

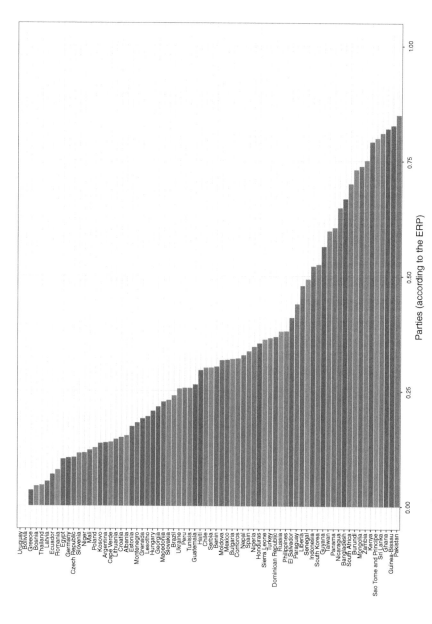

FIGURE 8.3. Elite reproduction in political parties in seventy-one post-authoritarian states in the GTJD

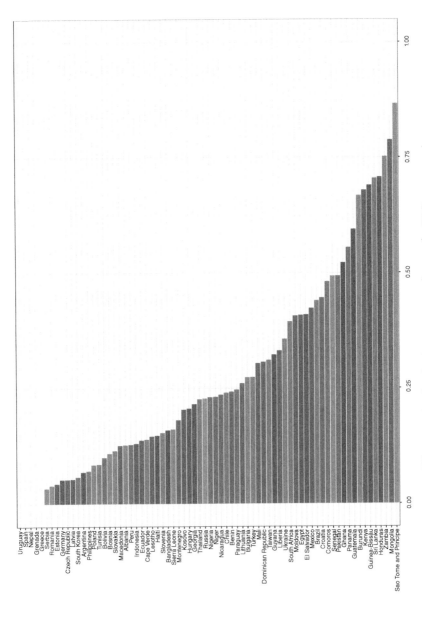

FIGURE 8.4. Elite reproduction in the state according to the ERP measure in seventy-one post-authoritarian states in the GTJD

act thorough purges with post-conflict settings, it seems that this positive effect of thorough purges on the reproduction of former authoritarian elites is driven by post-authoritarian countries that also witnessed a civil war.

What is quite puzzling in these results is that lustration is the mechanism intended to uncover clandestine collaborators of the *ancien régime*. Hence, one would not expect it to have an effect on the open leadership of the regime. Though with the empirical data at hand here, we can at most speculate about a direct causal association, this evidence is consistent with the theory presented here, according to which lustration indirectly weakens networks of former authoritarian elites.

Consider next the presence of authoritarian elites in the state presented in Figure 8.4 and Table F.2.

The stacking of countries from those where former authoritarian elites in the state reproduce least to those where they reproduce most in key institutions of the state, largely paints a similar picture to the previous figure. States with almost no former authoritarian elites, aside from those who transitioned long ago (as Spain did), are mostly postcommunist states (Romania, Estonia, and the Czech Republic). There are also a number of military regimes in the bottom part of the figure, which is surprising because one would expect former military leaders to just return to the barracks (Geddes et al. 2014; Debs 2016). Since the former are states where lustration was more common and the latter are states where it was less common, it is hardly surprising that the weighted proportion of former authoritarian elites in the state is also negatively and significantly associated with lustration severity (see Table F.3 in Appendix F).

It is important here to highlight that although ERP_S, my measure of elite presence in political parties, and ERP_P, my measure of elite presence in the state, tap into similar aspects of the new democracy, they are also different in important respects. For instance, the party measure would increase if the presence of all former authoritarian elites in the state were restricted to successor authoritarian parties even if those parties were not in a position to enter any government coalitions or occupy positions of responsibility in the state. Such a situation is not only a theoretical possibility. In Bangladesh, for instance, the weighted proportion of former authoritarian elites in political parties is .66855654, while the weighted proportion in the state is only .15918013. In addition to these, Nicaragua and South Africa have scores above .6 for presence in parties but below .4 for presence in the state. This situation is consistent with a post-authoritarian "regime divide" described by Anna Grzymala-Busse

(2001) and Herbert Kitschelt (1999), where the main cleavage dividing a post-authoritarian party system is the one between former supporters and former opponents of the former authoritarian regime. In postcommunist states, the divide was so acute that successor communist parties found themselves unable to form governing coalitions even after winning pluralities of seats in the legislature because former dissident parties refused to join cabinets led by former communist (Grzymala-Busse 2001).

Yet despite this theoretical possibility, the patterns of association between lustration severity and presence of authoritarian elites in the state largely resemble those of elite reproduction in political parties, and lustration severity is the only significant effect in the regressions reported in Appendix F.[7]

8.4.2 Reproduction of Authoritarian Elites in Business

Finally, I consider elite presence in the business world. Here the trend appears to be reversed relative to the party and state presence, with considerably more post-socialist states in the lower part of the figure. This comports well with anecdotal evidence from the region, where in some countries the transfer of former authoritarian elites into business was prominent enough to coin the term "oligarchs." Theoretically, purges could extend to the business sphere, but only Bulgaria attempted this. The mechanism (which we do not have evidence for here) is intuitive: When former authoritarian elites are banned from politics and their networks control former state-owned enterprises, exit into business may present a very viable option. There are few theories in the literature predicting the impact of TJ on business, though one could extrapolate from the work of Earle and Gehlbach (2015) who write about the productivity of firms following regime change after the Orange Revolution in the Ukraine. This research finds that in regions that supported the outgoing autocratic incumbent, the productivity of firms is lower than in regions that supported his democratic opponent. This suggests the following logic: Where business is controlled by post-authoritarian networks, exit into business following purges may be easier. At the same time, however, there is less profit to gain in regions that used to be controlled

---

7 The sign on the leadership purge variable is consistently negative and the sign on the thorough purge variable is consistently positive. The latter does switch to negative after being interacted with post-conflict states, again suggesting that what is driving the positive effect are post-conflict states.

by now-purged networks than in regions where purges have left networks intact. If lustration eliminates authoritarian networks while purges put former authoritarian elites out of political office, we might expect the interaction terms between lustration and purge severity to be a significant predictor of authoritarian reproduction in business; their effect should be negative.

A different mechanism is suggested by the work of Tim Frye (2010), who wrote about the linkages between party system polarization and successful economic reform. Frye theorizes and finds that higher levels of polarization, associated with greater executive turnover, lead to less successful economic reform. Here, the TJ interpretation would be as follows: Polarization could be reduced by eliminating former authoritarian elites from political office through leadership or thorough purges. However, this also increases the supply of elites who are ready to move into business. If these technocrats have usable skills (Grzymala-Busse 2002) that can be put to work in business ventures, economic reforms may result in greater success than in states where the supply of well-trained technocrats is lower because they are allowed to remain in politics. This would lead us to expect a positive relationship between purges and elite reproduction in business.

This logic finds supportive evidence in Table F.3 in Appendix F, which suggests that leadership purges are quite consistently associated with lower presence of authoritarian elites in business (except for in some models with leadership purge interactions). Meanwhile, lustration is positively and almost significantly associated with elite reproduction in business (note that the t-statistic is very close to 2). What this suggests is that removing secret networks of former authoritarian elites makes them move to business, where – perhaps via the logic suggested by Grzymala-Busse (2002) – they can capitalize on their usable skills.

At the same time, leadership purges cause them to not enter the business world, perhaps because there is nobody to offer them protection while they are there. This is most likely because the networks that former authoritarian elites have in the business world are swept away by a severe purging campaign that ensures that only token representatives of the former authoritarian elite can become businessmen.

An analysis not shown here also reveals that purges and leadership purges are positively associated with criminal court cases, which is very intuitive, as in order to be put on trial, authoritarian leaders must first be purged from their positions of power.

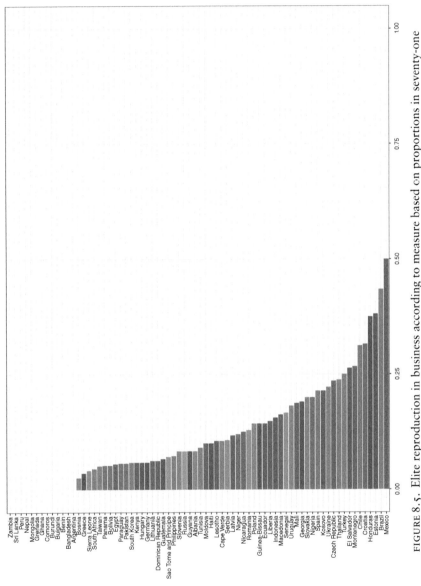

FIGURE 8.5. Elite reproduction in business according to measure based on proportions in seventy-one post-authoritarian states in the GTJD

8.5 SEVERAL EXAMPLES

In order to supplement these conjectures about the mechanism connecting lustrations and purges to authoritarian elite survival, I turn to cases of specific countries. Figures 8.6, 8.7, and 8.8 show the scores of all the countries in my dataset on lustration and purge severity, first using the aggregate purge measure and then breaking it up into leadership and thorough. I have singled out for illustrative purposes four countries: Brazil and Paraguay, as instances of high lustration severity, and Greece and Serbia, as instances of high purge severity.[8] All four countries experienced at least a moderate degree of lustration indicated by the fact that even Serbia and Greece are at .5 of the lustration severity score. A comparison between Figure 8.5 and 8.6 indicates that the purge severity score of Serbia is driven by leadership purges, while the high purge score of Greece is driven by both leadership and thorough purges. Brazil and Paraguay, while similar in lustration severity, differ in their TJ policies concerning purges: While Brazil avoided both leadership and thorough purges, Paraguay experienced a moderate number of thorough purges. It also experienced leadership purges, but because they took place prior to the first free elections, they are not reflected in the GTJD.[9]

In the following, I briefly discuss the circumstances of these countries' democratic transition and the fate of former authoritarian elites.

8.5.1 High Lustration Severity: Brazil and Paraguay

Brazil

Brazil's dictatorship began in 1964 with a military coup that ousted the elected government and established the rule of a military junta (McCann 1997). The coup lasted through 1985, when an electoral college, mostly made up of members elected in competitive elections, elected a civilian president from the opposition (*New York Times* 1985). There was some tension immediately following the elections, when the initially elected president – a member of the opposition – died before his inauguration.

---

[8] I depart here from examining archetypal cases used in my book because I wish to explore extremes on lustration and purges. The countries chosen here bottom out the graph summarizing purge severity (1.2) and the table summarizing lustration severity (4.1).

[9] In constructing the GTJD, I decided to only focus on events recorded after the transition to democracy in order to avoid coding instances of preemptive or victor's justice.

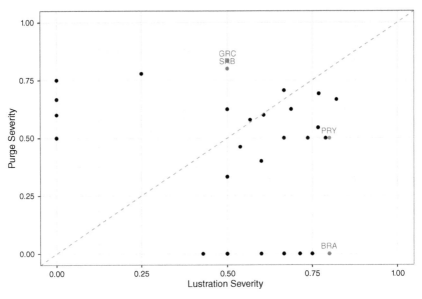

FIGURE 8.6. Severity of lustrations and purges

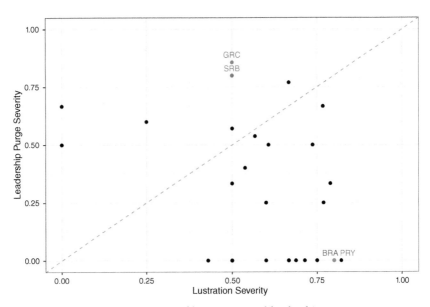

FIGURE 8.7. Severity of lustrations and leadership purges

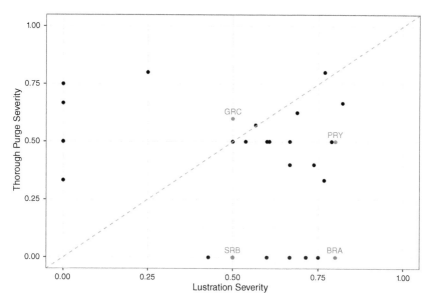

FIGURE 8.8. Severity of lustrations and thorough purges

However, in accordance to the constitution, the outgoing military junta allowed him to be succeeded by his civilian vice president, Jose Sarney, also selected by the electoral college. When the vice president took office, the military returned to the barracks, although General Leonidas Pires Gonsalves was appointed to lead the Ministry of Defense, assuring former junta members that the amnesty agreement would be honored by the new democratic government.[10] Five years before the transition, the junta shielded itself from criminal proceedings for human rights committed by its members by passing a law (Law 6683) that granted immunity for crimes committed between 1961 and 1979.

One of the first legislative acts of the new democratic government was a constitutional act granting every citizen the right to access their files kept by the National Intelligence Agency (*The Guardian*, October 1988).

A good illustration of the effects of the lack of criminal proceedings mandated by the amnesty combined with an early lustration law is the fate of the ministers of finance and agriculture in the Baptista de Oliveira Figueiredo cabinet, the last cabinet before democratic elections

[10] Although Jose Sarney had been a leader of the party that supported the military regime, he was a member of a faction that had defected from the regime support party during the year prior to the transition; he governed in coalition with the party that had led the opposition to the military government [250–60] (Skidmore 1989).

were held. Ernane Galvéas had held the finance portfolio for four years before the junta-supported government stepped down. Following the transition, Galvéas began working in economic consulting. He joined the boards of directors of highly valued companies including Aracruz Celulose, the Lorentzen Group, and Fundacao Getulio Vargas. He eventually became General Secretary of the Brazilian Committee of the International Chamber of Commerce. The authoritarian minister of agriculture, Angelo Amaury Stábil, started working for the Sharp cooperation immediately after the transition and eventually moved to New York City. Another member of the former authoritarian elite who moved to the business sector following the Brazilian transition was the trade and industry secretary, Joáo Camilo Penna, who first became energy advisor to President Jose Sarney in 1989, and then became President of Furnas Electric Power Plants. He then presided over the Brazilian-United States Cultural Institute of Belo Horizonte, the sixth largest (and extremely wealthy) city in Brazil. He also presided over the Dom Cabral Foundation. Finally, some elites, such as the former labor secretary, Murillo Macedo, switched back and forth between business and politics. In 1986, he became president of the Companhia Energaotica de São Paulo (CESP); in 1988, he was offered the opportunity to become a member of the Brazilian Labor Party (PTB) but ended up declining; in 1990, he became secretary of housing and urban development in the government of Orestes Quarcia although there is no evidence that he joined a political party; he held this position until March 1991 at which point he worked in succession for a number of companies in the private sector: In 1991, he was president of Nossa Caixa (a bank), in 1993, he was president of Banespa (the State bank of Sao Paulo), in 1994, he was vice-president of Cofap (an automotive company), and in 1995, he was a consultant for his own company.

The Brazilian case illustrates our statistical findings well: Harsh lustration was effective at removing former authoritarian leaders from positions in the state and political parties, yet it facilitated their transfer into the business world. The limited purge activity, as illustrated in Figures 8.7 (leadership) and 8.8 (thorough) did not prevent the exodus into business world, which is also consistent with the statistical model reported in Table F.3.

Paraguay

Paraguay's authoritarian regime commenced with a coup led by General Alfredo Stroessner. Stroessner ousted the civilian president, Tomas

Romero, and was elected president two months later in an election where Stroessner was the only candidate (Roett & Sacks 1991, p. 53–54; Leon-Roesch 1993, p. 514). The dictatorship ended in September 1993 with competitive elections that came as the culmination of a series of democratizing reforms initiated by the Rodriguez administration between 1989 and 1993. The reforms included, for example, putting an end to the compulsory party affiliation of officers, prohibiting the military and police from political engagement, and electoral reforms toward greater proportional representation that did not discriminate against opposition parties. All of these reforms became part of the new constitution (Leon-Roesch 1993, p. 505). Rodriguez himself was a Stroessner regime insider who had taken office via a palace coup.[11]

Despite this, a surprising number of these former elites briefly remained politically active in the successor authoritarian "Colorado" party, but then transferred their activity to business, not always conducted in a manner that was fair and square. Among them was Carlos Augusto, who found himself at the center of a corruption scandal in 2002. Similarly, Juan Antonio Cáceres was convicted of skimming proceeds from the country's toll road system. He was accused of corruption and convicted shortly after the transition. Delfín Ugarte Centurion, former minister of Industry and Commerce, was arrested and imprisoned for two years after the dictatorship for reportedly having 24 million US dollars in Swiss bank accounts.[12] Adan Godoy Jiménez Carlos Antonio Ortiz Ramarez, Jose Eugenio Jacquet, Cesar Romeo Acosta, Mario Abdo Benitez, Alberto Buenaventura Cantero, and Pastor Coronel all faced criminal charges but only the last two – who served as minister of the police and chief of police investigations, respectively – faced additional charges for human rights violations. All others were charged with criminal corruption.

As remarked earlier, a limitation of the GTJD is that TJ events preceding the first free democratic elections are not recorded and coded. Consequently an important leadership purge that took place in February 1989 is not reported in Figure 8.7: Just one year prior to the first free elections, over 100 of Stroessner's associates were first purged, then arrested and then tried. As suggested by Figure 8.1, purges often open a pathway to criminal trials. Hence, even while scoring high on lustration

---

[11] Abente-Brun (1999, p. 93) calls this "an internal adjustment made by the ruling coalition."

[12] After paying 5 million US dollars to the Paraguayan treasury, he went into exile in Argentina, where he remained until 2011.

severity, Paraguay more closely resembles a high leadership purge country, illustrating well the associations from Model 3 of Table F.3, which show how the leadership purge and lustration severity effects cancel each other out.

8.5.2 High Leadership Purge Severity: Serbia and Greece

Among the two highest purge severity cases coded by the Global Transitional Justice Dataset, are Serbia and Greece, which I discuss briefly in the following.

Greece
Greece's most recent authoritarian intervention commenced in 1967 with a coup led by Colonel Papadopoulos and the so-called Holy Bond of Greek Officers (IDEA) military faction.[13] This regime came to an end when the military peacefully transferred power to Konstantinos Karamanlis, who proceeded to prepare the country for competitive elections and a transition to democracy (Veremis 1985, p. 41).

Leadership purges started almost immediately and continued throughout the transition. According to Sotiropoulos (2007), "legislation for vetting the judiciary was first issued on August 7, 1974, that is, almost immediately after the collapse of the junta on July 23, 1974." The August 1974 legislation was a constitutional act. It created a body called the Highest Disciplinary Council, responsible for carrying out purges (the rules governing the organization and functioning of this council were not specified until late September 1974). Purges started in earnest in August 1974, when the banking sector, followed by public utilities, was purged. Because only the top leadership of these institutions was purged the corresponding events are classified by the GTJD as a leadership purge (Alivizatos & Diamandouros 1997). Purges in other sectors, including police, armed forces, the central intelligence agency, the security forces, and even academia followed.

Temporally, purges were concentrated in the immediate aftermath of the transition but extended to 1977. How effective were they at removing authoritarian elites from parties, the state, and business? Of Greece's former top twenty-eight authoritarian elites, only Ilias Balopoulos, a minister with no portfolio, moved into the business sector. Another minister went into voluntary exile to Switzerland (Orestis Giakas, the minister of communication) and another went into academia (Ioannis Cholevas). Of the

---

[13] For details, see Feit (1973) and Veremis (1985).

remaining leaders, the activities of several were impossible to trace, while ten ultimately faced criminal charges. All but two (Nikolaos Efessios and Ioannis Agathangelou) served prison sentences, several of them for life (these include Ioanis Ladas, Nikolas Makarezos, Konstantin Papadopoulos, Styllanos Pattakos).

The Greek case illustrates the consequences of extensive purges both leadership and thorough: by removing former authoritarian elites from positions of power and undermining their secret networks as well as open administrative networks, they are unable to install themselves in powerful positions. Eventually, those from the top political leadership face themselves criminal responsibility, either for their acts under authoritarian rule or for economic transgressions committed shortly after the transition. A final, more recent, illustration of the effect of leadership purges comes from Serbia.

Serbia

The beginning of authoritarianism in Serbia dates back to June 25, 1991, when Slovenia declared independence. Next to secede were Croatia and Macedonia, followed by Bosnia in 1992, leaving what remained of Yugoslavia dominated by Serbs with Slobodan Milosevic, the leader of the Serbian Communist Party, at its helm. Geddes et al. (2014) use this as the marker of a decidedly authoritarian regime, as the secession of these former republics changed the composition of the state's decision making body. Where previously, Milosevic and the Communist Party were but one of many veto players in a collective leadership, following the secessions, decision-making concentrated in Milosevic himself (Sekelj 2000, p. 63).

The authoritarian regime ended on October 5, 2000 after Milosevic resigned in response to massive demonstrations, which broke out after he refused to allow the party that had won the election to take office (Binnendijk & Marovic 2006).

It is difficult, if not impossible, to write about authoritarian rule in Serbia without mentioning the Balkan wars that elevated Milosevic to a position where he could concentrate so much power. The wars started in July 1991 (with the secession of Slovenia). Although the war with Slovenia lasted eleven days, a series of secession conflicts followed, which included conflicts with Croatia in August – December 1991, a conflict with Bosnia in 1992–1995, and a final conflict with Kosovo in 1998–1999 (Binningsbø et al. 2012b). The last two were most violent and brought about the most human rights violations. The three-way war in Bosnia began as a conflict between the Yugoslav Army, which then renamed itself to "Army of the Republika Srpska" and the Army of the Republic of Bosnia and Herzegovina on the one hand, and the Croatian Defense Council (HVO) on the other. However, by 1993, tensions between Croats and Bosniaks became heightened enough to bring about an independent Croat–Bosniak War in 1993. In the meantime, the war with Serbia escalated after Pakistan defied the United Nations weapons' embargo and airlifted missiles to the Bosnian Muslims, matching their arsenal to that of Serbia. After the Srebrenica and Markale massacres, NATO intervened in 1995 with "Operation Deliberate Force," targeting the positions of the Army of the Republika Srpska; This proved key in ending the war. The three-way war concluded with the signing of the General Framework Agreement for Peace in Bosnia and Herzegovina in Paris on December 14, 1995.

One final conflict took place between 1998 and 1999, when Kosovars from the Ushtria Clirimtare Kosoves (UCK), assisted by NATO, rebelled for independence. A peace agreement terminating that conflict was signed by UCK, but not by Yugoslavia in Rambouillet (France) on February 23, 1999 (Binningsbø et al. 2012*b*).

The breakup of Yugoslavia was accompanied by numerous acts of repression against the civilian populations of the former republics. Most abominable were the concentration camps near Prijedor (Nalepa 2012*a*), the massacre in Srebrenica,[14] and, in Kosovo, the Massacre at Racak.[15] The latter two events brought international attention to the Balkan wars.

Although this book is not preoccupied with international TJ, all of Serbia's TJ events took place in the shadow of the International Tribunal for Former Yugoslavia, an ad hoc tribunal established in 1993 by the United Nations Security Council with a mandate to prosecute war crimes committed in the region since 1991 (Bates 2021). By 2013, when the ICTY officially ended its mandate, the tribunal had indicted 161 persons and had finished proceedings against over 100 defendants.[16]

However, the ICTY could only deal with criminal responsibility for crimes committed during the Balkan wars and was not tasked with dealing with human rights violations committed by Milosevic, the autocrat. Hence, as soon as Milosevic was ousted from power in December 2000,

---

[14] In Srebrenica, according to the most recent estimates, over 7,000 Bosniak men and boys were summarily executed and buried in mass graves; see (Nalepa 2012*a*; Subotic 2010) for details.

[15] Serbian forces massacred 45 civilians. See Vickers and Pettifer (2006).

[16] See www.ictj.org/sites/default/files/ICTJ-Brookings-Displacement-Criminal-Justice-Yugoslavia-CaseStudy-2012-English.pdf.

the new democratic leader, President Emir Kostunica, began wide-scale purges, starting with diplomats and generals who had been loyal to the Milosevic regime. On December 16, 2000, The *Independent* reported that the president had recalled seventeen ambassadors and diplomats from their posts in embassies in a number of different countries including Russia, Macedonia, Israel, and the Czech Republic. Those dismissed included Milosevic's brother, the ambassador to Moscow, Borislav Milosevic, and the ambassador to the United Kingdom, Rade Drobac.[17] That same month, three generals, who had been allies of Milosevic, were dismissed from their positions in Montenegro. In a further move against Milosevic loyalists, Kostunica retired fourteen other generals, including the former defense minister under the Milosevic regime, Dragoljub Ojdanic. Also included in the purge were General Aleksandar Vasiljevic and the head of Milosevic's army intelligence service (KOS), Geza Farkas.

In another move, this time closing in on members of the legal profession still loyal to Slobodan Milosevic, the legislature enacted a bill firing judges and prosecutors who had blindly followed the former Yugoslav president (this act is classified as lustration in the GTJD, as it required the disclosure of acts committed by the judiciary). They were replaced with judges and prosecutors believed to have no impediments to prosecuting the former leader and his allies in the war for war crimes. The purges continued well into 2003, with the Supreme Defense Council dismissing (on August 7th of that year) 16 of 51 active generals or admirals in a purge of officers believed to be loyal to former President Milosevic. Several hundred lower-ranking officers were also dismissed. This purge of the army was believed to have removed from the armed forces the remnants of its conservative and Milosevic-loyalist core, responsible for cooperation with members of the Bosnian Serb army during and after the 1992–95 war in Bosnia.

Scanning the fate of former authoritarian leaders, we uncover that only Marko Marjanovic, who filled the post of prime minister from March 1994 through 2001, went into the business sector right away; he was eventually appointed president of the board of directors of the company "Progres." Jorgovanka Tabakovic, the privatization minister, eventually became the Head of the Central Bank, and Branislav Ivkovic (a former Science and Technology minister) went into academia. The former

[17] See Keesing's Record of World Events (Formerly Keesing's Contemporary Archives 1931–1988) Volume 46 (2000), Issue No. 12 (December), Page 43922.

minister of finance, who would naturally be most suitable for a business exit option and was even part of the transitional government, was later arrested for embezzlement. Eventually, however, he served as Chairman of the supervisory board of Serbian companies. All remaining elites, however – and there were 24 more – were either prosecuted, or assassinated (like Zika Petrovic), or committed suicide (like Stojijkovic).

The Serbian case is broadly consistent with findings discussed in the large-n analysis and summarized in Figure 8.1. Leadership purges, offsetting potential effects of lustration, prevent elites from moving into business at a high rate because their support network in business ventures is disrupted over the course of purges (given that the business leaders are, for the most part, known collaborators). At the same time, a disproportionate number of former elites were charged by the ICTY with responsibility for criminal acts committed during the war and were not in a position to follow their "natural trajectory."

Serbia's strategy of implementing a broad purge policy in combination with minimal thorough purges and moderate lustrations paints an informative picture of where former elites go, following autocracies that have experienced conflict periods as well.

The discovery of a link between lustration and the weakening of former autocrats' positions in state administration and political parties is suggestive that this TJ mechanism weakens the secret authoritarian networks former dictators rely on. Yet, because the analysis I show is solely based on correlations, it could be criticized. For instance, it could be pointed out that the correlation is consistent with the reversed causal direction: With no former autocrats in positions of power, nothing stops new democratic leaders from engaging in the harshest forms of TJ. Note however, that since the target of lustrations are secret and not open collaborators, one would sooner expect a causal arrow to flow from purges to presence in parties and the state, especially from leadership purges. Yet, this correlation is not detected and in the case of thorough purges runs in the opposite direction.

Now, in order to boost my argument that lustration has the indirect effect suggested above of weakening authoritarian networks, I turn to the statistical tools used in Chapter 5 and the dependent variable most keenly focused on the strength of authoritarian networks: Power distributed by Socioeconomic Status. In Section 8.6 of this book, I explore the relationship between all four TJ mechanisms, measured over time and this V-Dem variable.

8.6 LUSTRATION ALSO UNDERMINES AUTHORITARIAN
NETWORKS: EVIDENCE FROM HLM

The upshot of the empirical chapters of this book is that in independent tests, transparency regimes contribute more to the overall health of new democracies than purges. But each chapter has presented evidence for the effects of TJ in isolation. Now, I consider all mechanisms jointly using one of the original outcome variables – Power distributed by Socioeconomic Status. First I present two arguments for why such an analysis helps relax certain limitations of the previous analysis.

8.6.1 Using the Entire Data Range

Consider again the analysis performed in Chapter 6. The indicator format of the treatment variable required to carry out the difference-in-difference design is very stringent. It ignores potentially relevant information about the unfolding over time of TJ mechanisms. Most notably, the negative and/or negligible effects of lustration relative to truth commissions could be attributed to a threshold of severity that lustration must reach in order to be beneficial to democracy. Over and above a severity threshold, lustration's effectiveness could also hinge on a temporal threshold. In order to examine if these limitations are indeed affecting our results, I return once again to the measures of severity developed in Chapter 4, which used the entire TJ trajectory to assess how severe a given mechanism has become.

Chapter 4 of the book developed three new ways to measure aspects of personnel transitional justice: urgency, severity and volatility. The measures succeeded at capturing intuitions about specific countries' TJ trajectories that we know from case studies. At the same time, all three of these measures assign only one value per country. Consequently, they can only be used in static models similar to the HLM framework from Chapter 5 that was used to test the model from Chapter 2.

This problem was addressed somewhat in Chapters 6 and 7 where I modified the severity measures to account for time. Despite allowing me to work with the models that are capable of causal identification this exposed me to a range of limitations associated with using fixed effects. Because each country receives its own "fixed effect," one can be certain that no characteristics of the country have been omitted from the regression. The only problematic source of bias would be country characteristics that change over time and lead to changing the level of personnel TJ *with the intention* of affecting political corruption or power associated with socioeconomic status. It is hard to imagine what such a factor would be. Fixed effects regressions, however, are extremely taxing on the data as they can only detect effects based on within-group variation. This justifies yet another alternative attempt to demonstrate that TJ has the hypothesized effect on democratic quality.

8.6.2 A Fully Structured HLM Model of the Effects of TJ on Democratic Quality

In this section,[18] I walk readers through a series of HLM regressions, beginning with the most basic random effects model (similar to the one used in Chapter 5). Recall, that hierarchical models are constructed to account for the nested (hierarchical) structure of the data. In Chapter 5, this hierarchy was organized as parties within countries. Here, data is collected at the level of countries; however, V-Dem disaggregates quality of democracy scores across time since transition. Hence, the hierarchy I will exploit here is years (since transition) within countries.

I present a series of regressions using PdSES as the dependent variable and my measure of severity of the four TJ mechanisms as the independent variables. PdSES is the variable that I used to examine if TJ mechanisms are effective at eliminating secret authoritarian networks from playing a role in politics. In addition, I make use of the information I collected on years of transition and years lapsed since the transition took place. Recall from Chapter 6 that to create the dependent variable PdSES, the V-Dem team converted the ordinal expert answers to an interval scale.[19] Hence, the format of the dependent variable would permit using OLS. The nested structure of the GTJD data, however, suggests that this would bias the results. The GTJD, recall, is a panel containing all the years since transition for eighty-seven countries. OLS, due to the homoscedasticity assumption, produces unbiased results only when errors are distributed independently across observations (Raudenbush & Bryk 2002). However, in our case, the errors are clustered by country. Hence, when forgoing fixed effects, a multilevel model is most appropriate.

---

[18] Results reported in this section rely on analysis prepared for work published with Ipek Cinar and Genevieve Bates that appeared as "Accountability by Numbers: A New Global Transitional Justice Dataset (1946–2016)" in *Perspectives on Politics*, Volume 18, Issue 1, March 2020, pp. 161–184.

[19] See Coppedge et al. (2018).

I begin with an individual level model. (The results of this model are reported as Model 1 in Table 8.1):

$$y_{ij} = \gamma_{oo} + u_{oj} + \epsilon_{ij}, \tag{8.2}$$

where γ_{oo} is the grand mean of PdSES across all countries (and the fixed effect), u_{oj} (a random effect) describes the error of country means around the grand mean, and ϵ_{ij} (also a random effect) describes the deviation of PdSES from year to year from that country's mean. j in this model indexes the country and i here indexes an individual country year. The goal of estimating this model is to see how much of the variation in the dependent variable comes from variation within the same country and how much of it comes from variation across countries. A good way of thinking about this "null model" is that it serves the purpose of verifying whether a hierarchical model is called for in the first place. To evaluate that precisely, one can calculate the Interclass Correlation Coefficient, which captures how much of the variation in the dependent variable is explained by differences between countries instead of differences within countries.

The Interclass Correlation Coefficient of Model 1 from Table 8.1 is 80 percent (put differently, the correlation of PdSES across years in the same country is .8), on average. This means that most of the variation is explained by differences between countries. Hence, a hierarchical model is definitely justified (Finch et al. 2019).

Model 2 from Table 8.1 incorporates one explanatory variable. Because all of our measures of TJ are taken at the country level, I include first only the variable "years since the transition" (yaftr), which is measured at the level of individual country years. To give a better intuition behind the model's hierarchical structure, I first write the individual-level model:

$$y_{ij} = \beta_{oj} + \beta_{1j} yaftr_{ij} + \epsilon_{ij}. \tag{8.3}$$

The level 2 (country level) model, which is a model of the constant term β_{oj} and coefficient β_{1j}, is given by

$$\beta_{oj} = \gamma_{oo} + u_{oj}. \tag{8.4}$$

$$\beta_{1j} = \gamma_{10}. \tag{8.5}$$

The full or "mixed" model is then written by substituting Eqs. (8.5) and (8.4) into Eq. (8.3):

$$y_{ij} = \gamma_{0j} + \gamma_{10}yaftr_{ij} + u_{0j} + \epsilon_{ij}. \tag{8.6}$$

Adding an error term to Eq. (8.5) would produce a random slope model, which is illustrated in Table 8.1 as Model 3. Model 3 is the same as Model 2 in that it only includes one explanatory variable (yaftr); its error structure, however, is different. While Model 2 admits only random intercepts, Model 3 also admits random slopes. This means that in Model 2, only the intercept can vary within countries; the slopes are constrained to the same country-specific slope. In Model 3, *both* the slopes and intercepts can vary within countries. Crucially, none of these models yet contain any of the TJ severity measures. Such a model would have to be written differently because our measures are at the country level and do not vary with year(recall that we are measuring the severity of each TJ mechanism across all post-transition years). The individual-level model would still be written as:

$$y_{ij} = \beta_{0j} + \beta_{1j}yaftr_{ij} + \epsilon_{ij}. \tag{8.7}$$

The level 2 (country level) model is given by

$$\beta_{0j} = \gamma_{00} + \gamma_{01}S_j + u_{0j} \tag{8.8}$$

$$\beta_{1j} = \gamma_{10} + u_{1j}. \tag{8.9}$$

where S stands for the severity of the TJ mechanism. Recall from Chapters 4 and 5 that this measure is defined as:

$$S = \frac{\sum_t (P^t)}{\sum_t (P^t + N^t) + 1}.$$

The full or "mixed" model is then written by substituting Eqs. (8.8) and (8.9) into (8.7):

$$y_{ij} = \gamma_{00} + \gamma_{01}S_j + \gamma_{10}yaftr_j + u_{1j}yaftr_j + u_{0j} + \epsilon_{ij}. \tag{8.10}$$

The results from running the model described in Eq. (8.10) are described in Model 4 of Table 8.1 for lustration severity. Models 5, 6, and 7 show the results for leadership purge severity, thorough purge severity, and truth commission severity, respectively.

TABLE 8.1. *HLM regressions of PdSES on individual transitional justice mechanisms*

		Dependent variable: Power distributed by socieconomic status					
	Model 1	Model 2	Model 3	Model 4	Model 5	Model 6	Model 7
Years since transition		0.002	−0.011**	−0.012**	−0.011**	−0.012**	−0.011**
		(0.001)	(0.005)	(0.005)	(0.005)	(0.005)	(0.005)
Truth commissions							0.126
							(0.268)
Lustration				0.569**			
				(0.238)			
Leadership purges					0.111		
					(0.345)		
Thorough purges						0.630	
						(0.395)	
Constant	0.579***	0.556***	0.652***	0.491***	0.632***	0.566***	0.597***
	(0.092)	(0.093)	(0.112)	(0.128)	(0.131)	(0.123)	(0.163)
Random effects:							
Intercept (var.)	0.589	0.585	0.875	0.820	0.897	0.839	0.896
Years after (var.)			0.002	0.002	0.002	0.002	0.002
Residual (var.)	0.149	0.149	0.077	0.077	0.077	0.077	0.077
Observations	1,594	1,594	1,594	1,594	1,594	1,594	1,594

Note: $* p < 0.1$; $** p < 0.05$; $*** p < 0.01$

The results indicate that lustration severity has a significant and negative effect on the relationship between political power and wealth, as measured by PdSES. This supports my initial hypothesis about the effects of lustration, as higher values of PdSES represent a smaller association between political power and wealth. Furthermore, this effect is not the result of time lapsed since the transition for two reasons. First, I measure severity at the country level as a proportion of positive lustration events over all events, positive and negative. Second, and more importantly, this effect holds even after I account for years lapsed since the transition.

Interestingly, years since transition also have a significant effect on the association between political power and wealth, but the effect is positive. That is, with every year lapsed since the democratic transition, more political power is distributed according to economic wealth and status. The effect, however, is very small. The passage of an additional year lowers the PdSES score only by .01 units on the five-point scale on which PdSES is measured. In the model that tests the effect of lustration severity, 91 percent of the variation is explained by variation between countries instead of within countries, again justifying the use of a hierarchical model.

In contrast, the same model (Model 5) used for predicting the effect of severity of leadership purges on PdSES shows no effect of these kinds of purges, although years lapsed since the democratic transition remain significant. The insignificant effect is also very small – only .11 (compared to .57, the effect of lustration severity on a 0–1 scale). In the case of thorough purges (in Model 6), the effect, at .629, is similar to the effect for lustration, but still insignificant. The small negative effect of years lapsed since transition still remains significant. Finally, Model 7 shows the results for truth commissions: They are also insignificant as predictors of how power is distributed by socioeconomic status.

Although this finding does not offer support for truth commissions working similarly to lustration, it shows just how important it is to measure lustration over the entire span of the post transition era. Recall that in the dif-in-dif framework for exactly the same dependent variable, the effect of truth commissions, and not of lustration, was democracy enhancing.

While truth commissions indeed ought to prevent the possibility of blackmail through threats to reveal secret information, it is possible that over time, their effects dissipate and that in contrast to lustration, more intensive truth commissions do not necessarily have democracy-enhancing effects.[20]

---

[20] I decided to forgo including all the TJ mechanisms in one regression because some of them are highly correlated with one another, as Table F.4 in the appendix indicates.

TABLE 8.2. *Anova tests*

Object	Df	AIC	LogLik	Deviance	Chisq	Pr(> Chisq)
Baseline model 3 (yaftr only)	6	1021.6	−504.81	1009.6		
Model 4 (lustration)	7	1018.1	−502.05	1004.1	5.5113	0.01889**
Model 5 (leadership purge)	7	1023.5	−504.75	1009.5	0.1097	0.7405
Model 6 (thorough purge)	7	1021.2	−503.60	1007.2	2.4097	0.1206
Model 7 (truth commission)	7	1023.4	504.75	1009.4	0.2271	0.6337

As a robustness test, we can compare all the models against one another using an ANOVA test. This test compares the baseline model (Model 3), which uses only years since the transition as a predictor, against each of the models that additionally incorporate the severity of each TJ mechanism. The results indicate that only the model including lustration severity is significantly different (with a p value of .019) from the baseline model in its predictive power.

Table 8.2 also presents the log-likelihood and the Akaike Information Criterion (AIC) of all models. As a general rule of thumb, the smaller these values are, the better the fit of the model. The value AIC corresponding to the model with lustration severity is clearly smaller than the AIC of the three remaining severities.

8.7 CONCLUSION

Until Chapter 8 of this book, I refrained from considering all four TJ mechanisms at once.

This chapter first, cross-sectionally examined the effect of TJ severity on newly collected data on the fates of authoritarian elites. Second, it illustrated the mechanism I proposed to explain the correlations revealed with case studies. Third, it examined the impact of all four TJ mechanisms side by side in a hierarchical model in order to exploit the full gamut of the severity scale. All three of these tasks served the role of illuminating the multifaceted nature of transparency regimes on the one hand and purges on the other.

In the first section of this chapter, I used the original measure of severity to assess the extent to which the four types of TJ mechanisms – lustration, truth commissions, leadership, and thorough purges – limit the presence of authoritarian elites in political parties, in the state, and in business. To measure this presence, I developed a new and direct measure of the authoritarian elite reproduction. For each former authoritarian leader, I trace his or her career path in the new democratic regime.

In the second half of the chapter, I go beyond cross-sectional evidence and find support for the theory that the severity of lustration also improves the quality of democracy measured by the extent to which economic wealth translates into political power (PdSES). I do not find the same support for the effect of purges, nor do I find it for the severity of truth commissions. The effect for purges is most likely confounded by the failure to distinguish between institutionalized and noninstitutionalized regimes, but could also, similarly to truth commissions, be attributed to the decreasing marginal returns from more purges. According to this argument, ratcheting up purges and truth commissions multiple years after the transition has a negative effect on the quality of democracy.

The upshot of this analysis is that lustrations are complex mechanisms which must reach a threshold of intensity before they can bear fruit. This is in sharp contrast to truth commissions, which, as we saw in Chapter 6, even following a small nudge in the positive direction, start improving the quality of democracy. Yet, once this threshold is exceeded, the effect of lustrations goes beyond just removing secret collaborators: It also affects the fates of known authoritarian leaders by making it much harder for them to hold key positions in the post-authoritarian state and in political parties. Subsequently, it seems that these elites go into the private business sector. However, purges (and leadership purges in particular) seem to sometimes prevent them from exiting into business. This is most likely because the networks that former authoritarian elites have in the business world are swept away by a severe purging campaign that ensures that only token representatives of the former authoritarian elite can become business people.

I illustrated these dynamics with countries on the extremes of the purge and lustration dimensions from the GTJD. Two of them – Brazil and Paraguay – are high lustration severity states, while two others – Serbia and Greece – invested highly in purges.

9

Conclusion: Beyond Ritual Sacrifices

This book has argued that new democracies embarking on transitional justice (TJ) ought to tread lightly when it comes to purging their ancien régimes of known collaborators. At the same time, when it comes to dealing with acts of secret collaboration, transparency mechanisms – such as truth commissions, but especially lustrations – can be used without such limitations. By revealing skeletons in the closet of those in office or running for office, TJ mechanisms improve the overall quality of the new democracy. I have presented a theoretical mechanism and documented empirically, using several broad measures of democratic quality, the effectiveness of these TJ mechanisms. Carefully constructed theoretical and empirical models further corroborate these findings.

Yet before using my results as a ringing endorsement of lustration policies and their close cousin, truth commissions, let us pause and briefly discuss the social and personal costs of revealing the truth about secret authoritarian legacies.

9.1 OUT OF THE DOLL HOUSE

Henrik Ibsen's play "A Doll's House" compellingly illustrates the dilemma. The play introduces readers to what on the surface appears to be a perfect family home on the eve of a winter holiday. Gradually, we learn that this perfect picture is built on a lie that is about to be exposed. Nora, the titular "doll" has borrowed a large sum from a usurer. She spent the money on a family trip to Southern Europe, which doctors prescribed as the ultimate cure for her ailing husband, Helmer. She lied to Helmer about how she came by the money, saying she inherited it from her late father. Since she had nothing to offer for collateral of the loan, she forged her father's signature. Alas, the forgery is discovered by her usurer, as she dates it a day *after* her father's passing. Coming into possession of evidence of her crime, the usurer blackmails her.

He starts blackmailing Nora when his employment at the bank where Helmer is the manager is terminated. He threatens to disclose evidence of Nora's forgery unless she pressures Helmer into reemploying the usurer.

Based on what Helmer says about the values of loyalty and truthfulness of his loved ones, Nora is convinced he would want nothing to do with her if he knew of the lies she entangled herself with. Hence, she is determined that he never finds out about her lie. When he does, initially, her greatest fears are confirmed, although Helmer does seem to be concerned more with his reputation than the lie itself. Next, in an unexpected turn of events, the usurer sends the bond with the forged signature back to Nora and Helmer, surrendering evidence of forgery that he used to blackmail her with. This is the moment of the play when the reactions of Helmer and Nora diverge the most. While he is content for things to return to the *status quo ante*, Nora has learned that to preserve his reputation, Helmer was willing to severe all ties with her and deprive his children of a mother. She discovers that he never loved her but merely enjoyed her entertaining presence. Blackmail, thus, and its consequences exposed their relationship in its most raw and vulnerable form.

Post-authoritarian setting abound in such Ibsenesque stories. The post-unification history of Germany offers a couple I will share as additional illustrations. In the first, reported by *The Guardian* newspaper (2020), a journalist and former political prisoner finds out that his own brother informed against him to the Stasi, resulting in his capture when he attempted to flee to the West. Three decades later he reflected "To be betrayed by a family member touches you deeply. It makes me so sad sometimes that I feel exhausted. I have to be careful that I don't end up succumbing to paranoia, thinking everybody back in the former GDR is a spy." Betrayal by someone as close as one's own sibling must tear at the network of trust needed in any society. The trauma of discovering that one cannot even rely on family must make citizens suspicious of everything and everyone, preventing not just happiness but normal life.

A second example comes from a fictional story. Viewers of Florian Henckel von Donnersmarck's award-wining film, *Lives of Others*, are introduced to a theater power couple: playwright Georg Dreyman and actress Christa-Maria Sieland. Unfortunately for both, their relationship comes under strain when GDR's minister of cultural affairs becomes infatuated with Sieland. To break up the couple, the minister has Dreyman and Sieland's flat bugged and a Stasi officer assigned to listen in on the couple's private conversations. Sieland herself, after refusing the minister's erotic advances, is recruited as a secret informer and asked to spy on her boyfriend. Dreyman remains blissfully unaware that his girlfriend conspired against him with the Stasi until many years following the democratic transition. He learns about his past when Germany reunites and creates an archive of Stasi documents that is made accessible to ordinary citizens. This also means that the blissful oblivion about his partner's true loyalties expires.

When lies are uncovered, relationships may be torn, families irreparably broken. What was once said, cannot be undone. The reactions of Nora on the one hand and Helmer on the other to the invalidated usurer's bond, bring into stark relief what surfaces when skeletons in the closet are revealed. And while polities may become more representative and former authoritarian networks undermined, relationships based on trust may be destroyed. At the end of "A Doll's House" Nora leaves her husband. Knowledge does not bring her happiness and because of her initial forgery, the reader cannot feel the triumph of righteousness when she leaves Helmer's home (even though one feels that Helmer got what he deserved). Dreyman's story is short of complete tragedy only because of the redeeming act of the Stasi officer who was originally assigned to eavesdrop on him. The playwright learns that it was the act of a professional spy and not of his loving girlfriend that saved him from Stasi prison. Ibsen's protagonists are shaken to learn that the lives they thought they lived were but a misleading facade.

Living under authoritarianism abounds in morally impossible choices. Instead of selecting between good and evil, persons are faced with situations that are bad and worse. Becoming a secret police collaborator is rarely the result of succumbing to temptation. Most dissidents who turn into collaborators were manipulated into situations where they had no choice but to say "yes" to collaboration.

Perhaps then, certain dogs should be left sleeping? The story of Nora and Helmer suggests that perhaps transparency should be, on account of all these social costs, avoided altogether.

Even if social relations alone were at the center of our focus I would be weary of drawing that conclusion. After discovering the truth about Helmer, it is not possible for Nora to return to the doll's house. But who would wish to see her there even if all the information about the true nature of her relationship were buried away?

Living in democracies does not necessarily make citizens happier than they were in an autocracy. It makes them more responsible for who is in power because regularly held elections afford them the ability to vote dishonest politicians out of office. The findings of this book have clear implications for how TJ impacts this function. In democracies recovering from authoritarian rule or civil war, politicians trying at all costs to prevent their skeletons from coming out of the closet fail at being effective representatives and betray the interests of their voters. In an effort to bury the truth about skeletons in the closet they succumb to blackmail. The advice to "let bygones be bygones," "forgive and forget," or "let sleeping dogs lie" especially when applied to crimes committed secretly under the authoritarian regime may be deadly for a new polity.

At the same time, new democracies' temptation to punish *known* members and collaborators of the former regime is a form of "ritual sacrifice." Although it signals to some voters a clean break with the former regime, it has little beyond symbolic significance and may be equally crippling as the decisions to let sleeping dogs lie.

There is a caveat, however, to the advice of forgoing purges of known collaborators of the authoritarian regime. When the interests of those working for the *ancien régime* depart so much from those of the new democratic politicians that their expertise is worth surrendering, purges should be used. The bottom line is then, that purges should be applied sparingly, while transparency should be used widely.

Whether the transparency regime takes the form of lustration or truth commissions depends on our time horizon. In the short-term, truth commissions are effective. By applying to everyone and not only persons running for office they reveal the skeletons in the closet and prevent blackmail as well as undermine authoritarian networks.

Whether lustrations or truth commissions are advisable also depends on the tenure of the former authoritarian regime and the ways in which it exerted authoritarian control (Nugent 2019; Dragu 2017; Tyson 2018). Repressive regimes that are short lived and rely on violent repression to control their citizens will have fewer secret collaborators. Consequently there is no one to lustrate. The dilemma facing those regimes is whether to engage in purges. But lasting authoritarian regimes that developed sophisticated agencies tasked with spying on their citizens require the collaboration of those close to the targets by spying on their family members, coworkers, and friends. In those circumstances, lustrations can reveal many skeletons in the closet.

Paradoxically, since in openly repressive regimes, entire sectors of experts with usable skills may be left unscathed, the conclusion of this analysis may seem normatively unacceptable: While cynical agents of the ancien régimes are allowed to hold on to their jobs, the small but secret transgressions of regular citizens, sometimes even dissidents, are brought to light, ruining their careers and sometimes lives. Tackling this normative dilemma could be the subject of another book. To end this one on a less grim note, I focus on the three contributions that I have accomplished.

Beyond this summary and recommendations regarding how to deal with the past, this book has broad implications for at least three different literatures, which I discuss in turn in the following.

9.2 DEMOCRATIC BACKSLIDING

In an era of democratic backsliding (Bermeo 2003; Gandhi & Przeworski 2007; Serra 2012), getting TJ right cannot be overstated. When fragile new democracies are at risk of reverting back to dictatorship, the question arises: Can mechanisms set up by new democracies to deal with former authoritarian elites – prevent such backsliding from happening? Or is backsliding occurring despite extensive TJ provisions? To date, scholars' findings about the effects of personnel TJ on democratic consolidation have been ambiguous at best (Olsen et al. 2010). My results suggest that the reason behind this is the pooling together of two very different vetting mechanisms: lustration, which improves the quality of democracy monotonically, and purges, whose effect is contingent on attributes of the ancien régime.

Since the denazification policies in the US zone following World War II, the United States frequently dealt with former perpetrators of human rights violations and authoritarian leaders. More recently, the U.S. backed Iraq's policy to purge new democratic institutions of former Ba'athists to promote societal reconciliation. De-Ba'athification prevented 185 members of Saddam Husseins party, mostly Sunnis, from running for the legislature in 2003 (David 2003, 2006). Many pundits and journalists have argued that such harsh policies alienating a former privileged class are exactly what prevented democratic stability from taking hold in Iraq, but they identify the alternative as "doing nothing." While "doing nothing" may not produce immediate negative consequences, it may strengthen the power of authoritarian networks. In worst-case scenarios, such reproduced networks may pave the way for an authoritarian return. This book suggests that peacemakers in Iraq should have focused on the lustration of unknown collaborators of the former authoritarian regime, the agents who are in fact most threatening to new democracies. Perhaps, however, they should have left those Ba'athists whose transgression were known in the same positions they held under Saddam Hussein, if their expertise was valuable and their loyalties to the former dictator not at all strong.

My theory and argument about how appropriately designed and implemented personnel TJ can remove from political activity the members of former authoritarian parties who are capable of undermining democratic representation has broad impacts for democratization scholars, policymakers, and their advisors around the world. The impact of this research is twofold. First, there is very little research on the effect of TJ on the long-term quality of democracy. Nobody has examined how TJ affects the survival of former authoritarian networks and the ability of former authoritarian elites to leverage the secret information assembled under their tenure to influence policies of new democracies.

In a nutshell, the causal path between lustration policies and the quality of democratic representation had not been theorized before. This book leveraged a newly assembled dataset to expand current knowledge on the quality of democracy with a special focus on the quality of representation and party–voter linkages in new democracies.

9.3 GLOBAL TRANSITIONAL JUSTICE DATASET

To answer questions about democratic backsliding and resilience, scholars need access to temporally organized and disaggregated data on how states deal with outgoing autocrats, their collaborators, and perpetrators of human rights violations. This book, and the associated with it dataset, will allow scholars and policy makers to revisit findings about the role of personnel TJ in preventing authoritarian backlash.

The dataset created for the book has by now taken on a life of its own and become the centerpiece of the Transitional Justice and Democratic Stability Lab, a community of scholars which is now expanding the Global Transitional Justice Dataset (GTJD) to include criminal trial events as well as examples of reparations and memorialization in the United States. The distinctive feature of the dataset is that at the root of it, are detailed chronologies of TJ events that trace any changes at the institutional level in personnel TJ. I have used these chronologies to classify these changes into positive or negative events, but they could be used by other researchers as the source of coding into other categories as well. For instance, in the expansion of the dataset to criminal trial events, not covered in this book, I classify the events into dealing with high-ranking and low-ranking perpetrators.

In addition to criminal trials, it is important to point out another group of TJ mechanisms that this book leaves out. I exclude various forms of victim compensation, which range from the return of expropriated wealth in monetary substitutes or in kind to purely symbolic public apologies. Such formal apologies can be successful or can fail to accomplish reconciliation between nations. As an example of the latter, consider Aleksander Kwasniewski's apology issued during the unveiling of the memorial to Jews murdered in Jedwabne (a Polish town under the occupation of Nazi Germany) on behalf of the Polish people for wartime crimes committed against Jews. Arguably, the reason the apology failed at reconciling Jews and Poles was that Kwasniewski stressed that the truth of what happened in Jedwabne had not yet been established (Keesing's Record of World Events, formerly Contemporary Archives 1931–1988 2001). As a good example of the former, consider Roman Herzog's apology, issued while attending the fiftieth anniversary of the Warsaw Uprising in 1994, for the suffering Germany caused Poland during World War II. This book left out apologies and other forms of victim compensation to focus on how dealing with authoritarian elites and their secret and open collaborators stabilizes new democratic states. At the same time a book-length study of the political economy of victim compensation in former authoritarian regimes is long overdue and this author hopes that someone sooner rather than later fills this gap.

9.4 QUALITY OF DEMOCRACY

The paramount contribution of this book, though, is to the quality of democracy. Even if new democracies do not slide into what Polity or Freedom House would consider autocracy, they may linger in a state, where (1) those who are selected to serve are entangled in former authoritarian networks; (2) where once in office, they are more responsive to preferences of those who blackmail them with kompromat than to preferences of their voters; and (3) where politicians are not able to delegate power to those who at once share their policy preferences and have the competence to implement it.

Long-term democratic stability requires that parties programmatically represent voters, reducing political corruption, and dissociating political influence from economic wealth. This book has traced the impact of TJ on all three of these outcomes. Far from arguing that personnel TJ is the only facilitator of long-term democratic stability, I have shown how strategies of applying lustrations, purges, and truth commissions can impact all three of these outcome variables. Lustrations and truth commissions, their social costs notwithstanding, make democracies healthier. Purges, depending on the skills and loyalties of those who are being purged, may or may not do so. TJ has significance for democracy that goes far beyond ritual sacrifices. It should be carried out but with a careful eye to discriminating among TJ mechanisms. While getting TJ right may not guarantee democratic stability (there clearly are other factors that account for this), getting it wrong may stifle the democratization process. New democracies do not have the luxury of ignoring their authoritarian legacies altogether. If they are to endure, they cannot afford to let sleeping dogs lie.

Appendices

In this appendix, I present the formal analysis to derive the results from the model in Chapter 2.

A.1 Players, Preferences, Strategies, and Beliefs

There are two players in this game: an Officer (O) who has complete information and a Politician (P) who has incomplete information. The player with incomplete information comes in two types: with evidence of skeletons in the closet with probability $(1 - \pi)$ and without (with π). Recall that the players' payoffs are a linear function of the Euclidean distance between the players' respective ideal points and implemented policy as well as the two types of costs characterized before: (1) the cost to the politician of being fired as a result of revealed skeletons in his closet; and (2) the cost of bluffing incurred by the officer if he makes an empty threat. The strategy of the Officer is a pair $d, \sigma_O, d \in D$. Define $T = \{Evidence, \neg Evidence\}$ and $D = \{demand, \neg demand\}$. Let $r(x) \in \{Reveal, \neg Reveal\}$.

The strategy set of the Politician can be defined as $S_P = \{x(d) : D \to [0, a]\}$. In other words, a strategy for the Politician is a proposal $x \in [0, a]$ that P makes in the event that O makes a policy demand. Note that P can simply ignore the demand if he choses $x = 0$.[1] Also to complete the definition of the strategy for the officer, we have $\sigma_O : T \times D \to D \times \{r(x)\}$, where denotes the action taken by O following P's coun-

---

[1] Since P does not observe whether evidence exists or not, but only observes whether a demand was placed or not, we only need a single action to describe his strategy.

teroffer x. This part of O's strategy can best be represented as a reveal region $R = \{x : x \in R \to O \text{ reveals}\}$. The strategy of the Officer is a pair d, σ_O.

This structure resembles that of a signaling game in which O is the sender of the message while P is the receiver. In line with these types of games, the politician may have a chance to update his prior belief about the type of Officer he is facing – that is, about whether it is an Officer equipped with evidence of collaboration or not – after observing the Officer's action. Depending on the relative magnitudes of a, c, and F, this might be a signaling game or a cheap talk game. The solution concept we use is that of Perfect Bayesian Equilibrium (PBE). This means that strategies are best responses to each other, that I have to specify the Politician's beliefs, and that those beliefs must be consistent with what is observed in equilibrium play. As explained in Section 2.4, in solving this model, to ensure that all equilibria are unique, I assume that

1. The Officer does not use weakly dominated strategies.
2. The Officer rejects all but the highest counteroffer the politician is willing to make.

Below is a formal Proposition that summarizes the results from the main text:

A.2 Proposition

Proposition A.1.   1. *Suppose $F < c$. There is a pure separating PBE in which the Officer makes a demand if and only if evidence exists and in response, the Politician makes a counteroffer $x^* \equiv F$. The Officer's rejection region in this equilibrium is defined by $R^* \equiv [0, F)$, so he accepts the counteroffer and does not reveal the evidence in his possession. The posterior beliefs of P are described by $Pr(E|\text{no demand}) = 0, Pr(\neg E|\text{no demand}) = 1, Pr(E|\text{demand}) = 1, Pr(\neg E|\text{no demand}) = 0$.*

2. *Suppose $F > \frac{c}{(1-\pi)}$. There is a pure pooling PBE in which the Officer always makes a demand, and the Politician responds with a counteroffer $x'' \equiv (1 - \pi)F$. The officer's rejection region in this equilibrium is defined by $R'' \equiv [0, (1 - \pi)F)$; thus, he accepts the counteroffer and does not reveal the evidence is his possession. The posterior beliefs of P are described by $Pr(E|\text{demand}) = (1 - \pi), Pr(\neg E|\text{demand}) = \pi$.*

3. *Finally, suppose $c \leq F < \frac{c}{(1-\pi)}$. There is a semi-separating PBE in which the Officer always places a demand when evidence exists but if evidence does not exist, he places a demand with probability λ^* and refrains from placing a demand with probability $1 - \lambda^*$. In response to the demand, the Politician makes a counteroffer $x' \equiv c$. Since the Officer's rejection region is defined by $R' \equiv [0, c)$, the Officer accepts the counteroffer and does not reveal the evidence in his possession. The posterior beliefs of P are described by $Pr(E|\text{no demand}) = 0, Pr(\neg E|\text{no demand}) = \lambda^*, Pr(E|\text{demand}) = 1, Pr(\neg E|\text{demand}) = 1 - \lambda^*$, where $\lambda^* \equiv \frac{(1-\pi)(F-c)}{\pi c}$.*

Proof

I first prove the part of Proposition A.1, pertaining to the pure separating equilibrium in which the officer equipped with evidence always places a demand, while the Officer not equipped with such evidence never places a demand.

Pure Separating Equilibrium

Since it is never rational for O to not make a demand when he has evidence against the politician,[2] the only possible separating equilibrium is: (*demand, R^*, no demand, x^**). The requirement for this to be a PBE is that the posterior beliefs are $Pr(E|\text{no demand}) = 0, Pr(\sim E|\text{no demand}) = 1, Pr(E|\text{demand}) = 1, Pr(\sim E|\text{demand}) = 0$. The following four steps uncover the conditions for this equilibrium.

1. First, suppose x^* is the proposal accepted in equilibrium. P knows that if he proposes $x < x^*$, evidence against him will be revealed with certainty. Therefore, on the one hand, if he makes a proposal, in equilibrium, it must be accepted because if it were to be rejected, P should propose $x = 0$. On the other hand, if a demand is placed and P makes a counteroffer $x \neq a$, P's utility must be greater from having his proposal accepted than from proposing his ideal point, that is,

$EU_P(x|demand, \text{no demand}) \geq EU_P(0|demand, \text{no demand})$, which is equivalent to $-x \geq -F$. The last expression simplifies to

$$x \leq F.$$

---

[2] Note that P cannot make a counterproposal x when o has not made a demand. Thus, the worst O can do when making a demand is $-a$, which would be his payoff if P's counterproposal were $x = 0$ – that is, if P made no concession at all. Without making any demand, O is guaranteed to receive $-a$ and no more.

2. Second, note that the highest x^* that the politician should be willing to issue is $x^* = F$. Therefore, O's optimal rejection region is $R = [0, F)$.

3. Third, note that to prevent O from bluffing (and making demands when there is no evidence), it has to be the case that $EU_O(\text{demand}|x^*, \sim E) \leq EU_O(\text{no demand}|x^*, \sim E)$, which is equivalent to $-|a - x^*| - c \leq -|-a|$. This last expression simplifies to $x^* \leq c$, which after substituting x^* from above gives:

$$F \leq c.$$

4. Fourth, for x^* to be a feasible proposal, it has to be the case that $x^* \geq 0$ (that is, $F \geq 0$); otherwise, P should just propose 0. Given the assumption that $F > 0$, this always holds.

I conclude that a pure separating equilibrium exists only when the cost of being fired (F) relative to the cost of bluffing (c) is quite low. In this pure separating equilibrium, blackmail is effective with probability $(1 - \pi)$, and the level of misrepresentation (F) is directly proportional to the cost of firing. In the next two sections, I show how this departure from perfect programmatic representation compares with the effectiveness of blackmail under the pure pooling and semi-separating equilibria.

Pure Pooling Equilibrium

In pooling equilibria, Officers with and without evidence will choose the same action, implying that the Politician cannot update his prior beliefs to posterior beliefs by conditioning on the Officer's action. In the previous analysis, I established that the Officer never refuses to place a demand when evidence is present. Thus, the only possibility of a pooling equilibrium in this game is $(demand, R, demand; x'')$ with accompanying beliefs: $Pr(E|demand) = (1 - \pi), Pr(\sim E|\text{no demand}) = \pi$.[3] In this equilibrium, the Officer always places a demand and the Politician always offers the same counterproposal, x''.

1. For such an equilibrium to hold, the politician has to prefer having his proposal accepted to having it rejected, which may lead to his getting fired (if the proposal were to be rejected, he would rather propose his ideal point, 0). Thus, it must be the case that $EU_P(x''|demand, demand) \geq EU_P(0|demand, demand)$, which is

---

[3] Note that paths that involve the officer not making a demand are off the equilibrium path, and we do not have to specify the beliefs there. We can assume that if the Politician observes no demand, he assumes he is dealing with an officer with no evidence.

equivalent to $-|-x| \geq (1 - \pi)(-|0 - 0| - F) + \pi * 0.$[4] The last expression simplifies to :

$$x \geq \pi F.$$

2. Since $x'' = (1 - \pi)F$ is the highest counterproposal the Politician will issue, given his beliefs, the Officer's optimal rejection region is $R = [0, (1 - \pi)F)$.

3. To ensure that the Officer always has an incentive to place a demand, it has to be the case that $EU_O(demand|x'', \sim E) \geq EU_A(\text{no demand}|x'', \sim E)$, which is equivalent to $-|a - x''| - c \geq -| - a|$. This last expression simplifies to $x'' \geq c$, which after substituting x'' from above gives

$$F \geq \frac{c}{\pi}.$$

4. Finally, as before, to be feasible, x'' has to lie between 0 and a, that is, $(0 < \pi F < a)$. The first part of the inequality is ensured by my assumption $0 < F$, and the second is ensured by $F < a$.

Summing up, a pure pooling equilibrium exists only when the cost of being fired (F) relative to the cost of bluffing c is quite high. In this pure pooling equilibrium, lustration blackmail is always effective (takes place with probability 1). The distortion it causes relative to the Politician's ideal point is $(1 - \pi)F$. It is directly proportional to the cost of firing and the extent to which evidence exists. The final subsection of my equilibrium analysis looks at the effectiveness of lustration blackmail under the semi-separating equilibrium.

Semi-separating Equilibrium
In addition to the pure separating equilibrium discussed earlier, I also derive conditions of a semi-separating equilibrium (and verify their plausibility). In this equilibrium, the Officer plays a mixed strategy. He always makes a demand when evidence is present, but he also, with

---

[4] Note that since the Politician cannot tell which type of Officer – with or without evidence – he is facing any better than he could before the Officer took an action, his expected utility from making a proposal outside of the acceptance region is weighted by his priors about the probability that evidence exists.

some probability λ, makes a demand if evidence does not exist (and with probability $1 - \lambda$ does not make a demand). Consequently, any semi-separating equilibrium must fit the format (*demand, R, λ; x'*).[5]

Note that the beliefs consistent with this semi-pooling equilibrium are: $Pr(E|\text{no demand}) = 0$, $Pr(\sim E|\text{demand}) = \frac{\lambda^* \pi}{\lambda^* \pi + (1-\pi)}$, $Pr(E|\text{demand}) = \frac{(1-\pi)}{\lambda^* \pi + (1-\pi)}$, $Pr(\sim E|\text{no demand}) = 1$. These beliefs will be used in the calculation of the expected utilities. I proceed in six steps.

1. First, to find the equilibrium value of λ^*, I calculate the expected utility of the Politician from responding with x to the Officer's demand ($EU_P(x'|\text{demand}, \lambda)$) and set it equal to the expected utility of the Politician's choosing an x which is outside of the Officer's acceptance region ($EU_P(0|\text{demand}, \lambda)$. This yields the equality $(1 - \pi)(-|-x'|) + \pi\lambda(-|-x'|) + 0 = (1 - \pi)(-|0 - 0| - F) + \pi\lambda(-|0 - 0| + 0 - (1 - \pi)F)$.

2. Next, assuming that x' is the equilibrium proposal that falls into O's acceptance region, I require that $(1 - \pi)(-|-x'|) + \pi\lambda(-|-x'|) = -(1 - \pi)F$, which in terms of λ can be stated as:

$$\lambda = \frac{(1 - \pi)(-x') - (1 - \pi)F}{\pi[-(-x')]}. \qquad (A.1)$$

3. To ensure that $0 < \lambda < 1$ and that λ is a probability, F must satisfy:

$$x' < F < \frac{x'}{(1 - \pi)}. \qquad (A.2)$$

4. Next, to pin down x', we make use of the fact that when evidence does not exist, O must be indifferent between placing a demand and not placing one, that is: $EU_O(\text{demand}|x', \sim E) = EU_O(\text{no demand}|x', \sim E)$, which reduces to: $-|-a| = |-a-x'|-c$. The last equality can be written in terms of x' as $x' = c$.

5. Finally, substituting x' into Eq. (A.1):

$$\lambda = \frac{(1 - \pi)(F - c)}{\pi c}. \qquad (A.3)$$

---

[5] This means that the Officer makes a demand with probability 1 if evidence exists and with probability λ if evidence does not exist.

6. To get scope conditions for the semi-separating equilibrium, we can substitute x' into Condition (A.2):

$$c < F < c(1 - \pi).$$

And to ensure that the equilibrium proposal is between a and 0, I need $0 < c < a$.

I will also prove a result about the expected misrepresentation under all three equilibria. It is described again by the following proposition:

Proposition A.2. *The expected level of misrepresentation in any PBE meeting the assumptions described in Section A.1, is given by the same formula across all three equilibria:* $(1 - \pi)F$.

Proof In order to derive the expected level of misrepresentation, I weigh the PBE outcome in each equilibrium by the frequency of its occurrence. In the case of the pure separating equilibrium, it is simply $(1-\pi)F+\pi 0$, as the officer only proposes $x^* = F$ when evidence exists, which is $1-\pi$ of the time. The remaining π of the time, he reverts to 0. In the case of the pure pooling equilibrium, the average policy is implemented at $1 * ((1 - \pi)F)$, as the officer always places a demand and the politician always responds with $x'' = (1-\pi)F$. In the case of the semi-separating equilibrium, the calculation of the policy implemented is somewhat more complex, because the Officer always places a demand when evidence exists (with probability $1 - \pi$), and also does so λ^* of the time when it does not exist. Hence, the total frequency of placing a demand is given by $(1 - \pi) + \pi \frac{(1-\pi)(F-c)}{\pi c}$. The Politician responds to this demand with x', bringing the expected policy outcome to $(c)((1 - \pi) + \pi \frac{(1-\pi)(F-c)}{\pi c}) + \pi(1 - \frac{(1-\pi)(F-c)}{\pi c})0$, which, as in the previous two cases, reduces to $(1 - \pi)F$. These expected policy outcomes are presented in Figure 2.3 and described in Proposition 2.1, in the Chapter 2. □

B.1 Baseline Model

Let $S \subset \Re$ be the unidimensional policy space. Players are the Politician, P and the Agency Officer, A, with ideal points $0 \epsilon S$ and $x_A \epsilon (0, 1) \subset S$, respectively. The strategy set of P, who moves first is given by $S_P = \{P, \sim P\}$. Following the move of the Politician, Nature introduces a shock that represents uncertainty: $\omega \epsilon \{\varepsilon, -\varepsilon\}$. I assume that either policy shock is equally likely: that is, $Pr(\omega = -\varepsilon) = Pr(\omega = \varepsilon) = \frac{1}{2}$. A observes the shock and chooses his strategy, which associates with each type of shock a policy p. Hence, $S_A = \{s_A : \{\varepsilon, -\varepsilon\} \rightarrow S\}$, where an example of a strategy is a pair $(p_\varepsilon, p_{-\varepsilon})$.

The strategy set of the Politician is given by $S_P = \{Purge, \sim Purge\} \times S$.

Since the final outcome is modeled as $x = p + \omega$, the utility functions are written as a function of the policy choice, p, as follows:

$U_P(p) = -|p + \omega|$,
$U_A(p) = -|x_A - (p + \omega)|$.

This game is solved by backward induction as follows. Assume that in the first stage, the Politician choses "$\sim Purge$." Since the Agency Officer observes ω, he can implement a policy to "perfectly absorb" the exogenous policy shock and bring the final outcome to his ideal point. That is, for $\omega = \varepsilon$, he will choose $BR_A(\varepsilon) = p^* = x_a - \varepsilon$ and for $\omega = -\varepsilon$, he will choose $BR_A(-\varepsilon) = p^* = x_A + \varepsilon$. In light of this, the Politician's expected outcome from a leadership purge is given by:

$$U_P(Leadership, BR_A(Leadership)) = -x_A. \qquad (B.1)$$

Assume now that the Politician choses "Purge" in the first stage. Since he cannot observe the policy shock, the Politician's loyalist with identical policy preferences as the Politician chooses the same best response the politician would. Given the symmetry of ω, it is $p = 0$. (Note that actually, any $p \in [-\varepsilon, \varepsilon]$ is a best response; however, $p = 0$ is robust with respect to changing the utility functions from "tent" to quadratic. Gehlbach (2013) and Bendor and Meirowitz (2004) show that changing the players' preferences in this way does not change the end result of the analysis.) As a result, $EU_P(Thorough, 0) = -\varepsilon$.

B.2 Model with Discretion

The players and preferences in this version of the model are just as before. The game tree in Figure B.1 to summarizes it.

As reflected in the game tree, the only modification of this model relative to the previous one is that the strategy set of the Politician is now $S_P = \{P, \sim P\} \cup \mathfrak{R}^+ \subset S$ to reflect that if the Politician chooses to purge, he also sets the discretion limit.

The game is solved for the optimal discretion limit by examining potential limits that appear to be focal. I start here with limit $r = \varepsilon$.

1. If $\omega = -\varepsilon$, A's utility is maximized at $p^* = x_A + \varepsilon$. However, because $x_A > 0 x_A + \varepsilon > \varepsilon$. Given this, whenever $\omega = -\varepsilon$ and $r = \varepsilon$, A will propose $p = \varepsilon$. This will result in A's expected utility of $-|x_A - \varepsilon|$.

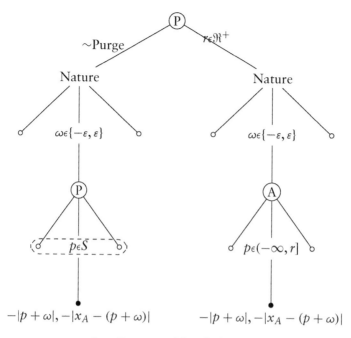

FIGURE B.1. Purges model with discretion limits

2. If $\omega = \varepsilon$, A's utility is maximized at $p^* = x_A - \varepsilon$. A will therefore propose $p = x_A - \varepsilon$ whenever $x_A - \varepsilon < \varepsilon$ or, in other words, when $x_A < 2\varepsilon$. When $x_A > 2\varepsilon$, he will propose $p = \varepsilon$. This will result in an expected utility of 0 when $x_A < 2\varepsilon$, and of $-|x_A - 2\varepsilon|$ when $x_A > 2\varepsilon$.

3. The corresponding utilities for P will $-(\varepsilon + x_A)/2 x_A < 2\varepsilon$, and $-\varepsilon$ when $x_A > 2\varepsilon$.

To show that when $x_A < 2\varepsilon$, P will set the discretion limit to $r = \varepsilon$ and choose not to purge, we consider two cases. First, suppose (1) that r is set higher than ε. If the discretion limit is set higher, to some $r = \varepsilon + \delta$, A would have to set policy to $min\{\varepsilon + \delta, x_A \varepsilon\}$ for $\omega = -\varepsilon$ and to $min\{\varepsilon + \delta, x_A - \varepsilon\}$ for $\omega = \varepsilon$. Consequently, assuming that the term on the left in each bracket is binding, P's expected utility would be given by: $EU_P(r = \varepsilon + \delta) = -\frac{1}{2}|\varepsilon + \delta - \varepsilon| - \frac{1}{2}|x_A - \varepsilon + \varepsilon| = -\frac{x_A + \delta}{2}$.

Now, suppose thar r is set lower than ε. If the discretion limit is set lower, to some $r = \varepsilon - \delta$, A would propose $p = min\{\varepsilon - \delta, x_A + \varepsilon\}$ for $\omega = -\varepsilon$ and $p = min\{\varepsilon - \delta, x_A - \varepsilon\}$ for $\omega = \varepsilon$, leading to (under the same assumptions as before) P's expected utility of:

$$EU_P(r = \varepsilon - \delta) = -\frac{1}{2}|\varepsilon - \delta - \varepsilon| - \frac{1}{2}|x_A - \varepsilon + \varepsilon| = -\frac{\delta}{2} - \frac{x_A}{2}.$$

In both instances, the expected utility of the Politician is lower than with a discretionary limit set at ε. The analysis of these two cases demonstrated that as long as $x_A < 2\varepsilon$, P will set the discretion limit to $r = \varepsilon$ and choose "no purge."[6]

B.3 Model with Imperfect Expertise

This game is analogous to the baseline, save for the institutionalization parameter that characterizes the technology of the signal received by the Agency Officer. This parameter is defined as:

$$s = \frac{Pr(-\varepsilon|\varepsilon)}{Pr(\varepsilon|\varepsilon)} = \frac{Pr(\varepsilon| - \varepsilon)}{Pr(-\varepsilon| - \varepsilon)}, \tag{B.2}$$

where

$$Pr(s = i|\omega = j) \text{ is the probability that A receives a signal } i$$
$$\text{when the signal is i } \forall i, j\epsilon\{-\varepsilon, \varepsilon\}. \tag{B.3}$$

Formally, the strategy set of the Politician is $S_P = \{s_P : (0, 1) \rightarrow \{Purge, \sim Purge\}\}$. That is, the Politician's strategy must assign to every value of $s\epsilon(0, 1)$ one of two actions: purging or refraining from purging. The strategy set of the Agency Officer is given by $S_A = \{s_A : (0, 1) \rightarrow \{(p(\varepsilon), q(-\varepsilon))$ such that p is response to high signal and q is response to low signal$\}\}$.

In order to solve the game for subgame perfect equilibrium, I proceed as follows:

First, assume that the Politician refrains from a purge. Then, in the final stage, given the Officer's limited shock absorption, the Officer will choose p to maximize:

$$EU_A(s, p, q; .) = -(x_A - (p + \varepsilon))^2 * P(\varepsilon|\varepsilon)$$
$$- (x_A - (p - \varepsilon))^2 * P(\varepsilon| - \varepsilon)$$

and simultaneously choose q to maximize:

$$EU_A(s, p, q; .) = -(x_A - (q + \varepsilon)^2 * P(-\varepsilon|\varepsilon)$$
$$- (x_A - (q - \varepsilon))^2 * P(-\varepsilon| - \varepsilon).$$

[6] For an alternative proof, see Gehlbach (2013)'s textbook presentation. I am grateful to Eli Rau for pointing this out and for making comments on my proof. I note that one additional assumption needed to complete the second step of this proof – that increasing the limit relative to ε only decreases P's expected utility – is that $\delta \geq x_A - 2\varepsilon$. Without this assumption, the Politician's expected utility simply does not change relative to $r = \varepsilon$.

Moreover,

$$\frac{P(\varepsilon| - \varepsilon)}{P(\varepsilon|\varepsilon)} = s \implies P(\varepsilon| - \varepsilon) = sP(\varepsilon|\varepsilon), \tag{B.4}$$

and

$$\frac{P(-\varepsilon|\varepsilon)}{P(-\varepsilon| - \varepsilon)} = s \implies P(l(\varepsilon)) = sP(-\varepsilon| - \varepsilon). \tag{B.5}$$

Using condition (2) from Section 3.3.3, we thus have:
$sP(\varepsilon| - \varepsilon) + P(\varepsilon|\varepsilon) = 1$ leading to $P(\varepsilon|\varepsilon) = \frac{1}{(s+1)}$, and $sP(-\varepsilon|\varepsilon) + P(-\varepsilon| - \varepsilon)) = 1$, leading to $P(-\varepsilon| - \varepsilon) = \frac{1}{(s+1)}$.

These transformations allow us to write A's expected utility following a high signal as:

$$EU_{A|H} = -(x_A - (p + \varepsilon))^2 * \frac{1}{(s+1)} - (x_A - (p - \varepsilon))^2 * \frac{s}{(s+1)}.$$

$argmax_p EU_{A|H}$ can be found by solving the first-order condition:

$$\frac{\delta EU_{A|H}}{\delta p} = 0,$$

equivalent to:

$$\frac{\delta EU_{A|H}}{\delta p} = \frac{x_A}{s+1} + \frac{sx_A}{s+1} - \frac{(p+\varepsilon)}{(s+1)} - \frac{s(p-\varepsilon)}{(s+1)} = 0.$$

After solving for p, we arrive at:

$$p^* = x_A - \frac{\varepsilon(1 - s)}{1 + s}. \tag{B.6}$$

Similarly,

$$EU_{A|L} = -(x_A - (q + \varepsilon))^2 * \frac{s}{(s+1)} - (x_A - (q - \varepsilon))^2 * \frac{1}{(s+1)}.$$

And the optimal choice of q in response to the low signal is the q that solves:

$$\frac{\delta EU_{A|L}}{\delta q} = 0. \tag{B.7}$$

Since $\frac{\delta EU_{A|L}}{\delta q} = 0$ if and only if $\frac{x_A s}{s+1} + \frac{x_A}{s+1} - \frac{s(q+\varepsilon)}{s+1} - \frac{(q-\varepsilon)}{(s+1)} = 0$, this q is given by:

$$q^* = x_A + \frac{\varepsilon(1 - s)}{(1 + s)}. \tag{B.8}$$

APPENDIX C QUANTITATIVE SUPPLEMENT TO CHAPTER 5

C.1 Programmaticness (*cosal_3*)

I begin this appendix by explaining the creation of the dependent variable, *cosal_3*, for the analysis conducted in Section 5.4. Recall that it draws on Herbert Kitschelt et al.'s measure of programmaticness from the Democracy and Accountability and Linkages Project (DALP). Of the three components used to produce Kitschelt and Freeze (2010)'s measure, I use only two, cohesion and salience, skipping polarization. The reason for omitting polarization is that it is potentially correlated with distance between parties' ideal points, the independent variable on the right-hand side of the regression in Section 5.4.

My new variable programmaticness, was constructed using Kitschelt and Freeze (2010)'s raw data recording experts' responses to questions characterizing the features and behavior of 535 parties in my sample. Specifically, following Kitschelt and Freeze (2010), I rely for the dimensions of programmaticness on the following questions from the expert survey:

- d1: Party policy position on social spending, measured on a 1–10 scale
- d2: Party policy position on the state role in economy, measured on a 1–10 scale
- d3: Party policy position on public spending, measured on a 1–10 scale
- d4: Party policy position on national identity, measured on a 1–10 scale
- d5: Party policy position on traditional authority, institutions, and customs, measured on a 1–10 scale

The different *cosal* measures are composed of cohesion and salience based on different combinations of the variables above.

Following Kitschelt et al., I measure cohesion for each of the five issues above by calculating the standard deviation for the responses on that issue. The standard deviation of those issues that received less than 5 expert responses and had a higher score than 3.5 have been removed. The reason responses are capped at 3.5 is to avoid outliers resulting from a low response rate. Next, the scores were transformed to translate higher standard deviations into lower values for cohesion. Finally, I normalized the scores to range from 0 to 1. The salience for issue i of party p in country k is simply the proportion of experts that gave a valid answer to the question on issue i. The specific measure *cosal_3* used here is created by taking the average of three values. The first two values are $cosal_{d4}$

TABLE C.1. *Summary statistics for country-level variables*

	Min.	1st Qu.	Median	Mean	3rd Qu.	Max.	N
lustration severity	0.00	0.00	0.00	0.30	0.60	0.82	59
Years Sine Transition	0.02	0.35	0.53	0.50	0.57	1.00	59
Freedom of the Press	0.54	0.72	0.79	0.78	0.84	1.00	59
Opposition Status	0.00	0.00	1.00	0.54	1.00	1.00	59
No Succ	0.00	0.00	0.00	0.24	0.00	1.00	59

and $cosal_{d5}$, and the third is the maximum value of $cosal_{d1}$, $cosal_{d2}$, and $cosal_{d3}$.

There are, of course, many different ways to create the measure of programmaticness . I chose this one for its affinity with the original (Kitschelt & Freeze 2010).

Table C.1 presents summary statistics of all variables used in the cross-sectional models – that is, all non-time varying variables.

C.2 Additional Robustness Checks

In this section, I present a series of robustness checks of the analysis in Chapter 5. The main result showing a positive effect of lustration on programmatic representation is robust to these different specifications and perturbations to the statistical model.

Subset of countries with no missing successors

Recall that in Chapter 5, not all countries had successor authoritarian parties. I used an imputation method to assign a successor to each country, which may be problematic for a variety of reasons not picked up by the missingness dummy. Given this, I also estimated models from Table 5.1 using only countries that had a non-imputed successor authoritarian party. These results are in Table C.2.

Distance normalized by country

Next, I replicate the results from Table 5.1 using a modified version of the *party distance* variable. I normalize this variable so that the maximum distance of any party in country k to the authoritarian successor party in country k is 1, and the minimum distance of any party in country k to the authoritarian successor party in country k is 0. These results are presented in Table C.3.

TABLE C.2. *Programmaticness, countries with a successor party only*

	Model 1	Model 2	Model 3	Model 4	Model 5
Party distance	−0.086*	−0.090**	−0.092**	−0.094**	−0.095**
	(0.044)	(0.044)	(0.044)	(0.044)	(0.044)
Severity		0.200**	0.163*	0.160*	0.159*
		(0.080)	(0.090)	(0.091)	(0.093)
Years since transition			0.148	0.082	0.072
			(0.163)	(0.183)	(0.200)
Press freedom				0.254	0.263
				(0.312)	(0.325)
Opposition status					−0.009
					(0.061)
Constant	0.374***	0.302***	0.247***	0.077	0.080
	(0.032)	(0.042)	(0.074)	(0.222)	(0.226)
Country intercepts	Y	Y	Y	Y	Y
Observations	153	153	153	153	153
Log likelihood	83.746	85.065	84.581	84.667	82.794
Akaike inf. crit.	−159.492	−160.130	−157.162	−155.333	−149.588
Bayesian inf. crit.	−147.370	−144.977	−138.979	−134.120	−125.345

Note: $^*p < 0.1$; $^{**}p < 0.05$; $^{***}p < 0.01$

TABLE C.3. *Programmaticness, party distance normalized by country*

	d_party normalized by country				
	Model 1	Model 2	Model 3	Model 4	Model 5
Party distance (normalized)	−0.019	−0.019	−0.020	−0.020	−0.020
	(0.023)	(0.023)	(0.023)	(0.023)	(0.023)
Severity		0.199**	0.165*	0.162*	0.161*
		(0.080)	(0.090)	(0.090)	(0.092)
Years since transition			0.138	0.089	0.085
			(0.160)	(0.181)	(0.198)
Press freedom				0.189	0.192
				(0.311)	(0.322)
Opposition status					−0.004
					(0.060)
Constant	0.354***	0.279***	0.227***	0.101	0.103
	(0.030)	(0.041)	(0.073)	(0.219)	(0.224)
Observations	152	152	152	152	152
Log likelihood	80.913	82.248	81.708	81.642	79.747
Akaike inf. crit.	−153.825	−154.496	−151.417	−149.283	−143.494
Bayesian inf. crit.	−141.730	−139.377	−133.273	−128.116	−119.303

Note: $^*p < 0.1$; $^{**}p < 0.05$; $^{***}p < 0.01$

Using imputed values for successors

Table C.4 presents the HLM regressions of programmaticness on lustration severity and distance to successor authoritarian parties when all countries in the GTJD are included with imputed values for countries without successors.

Using log(years since transition)

he next robustness check explores the possibility of a nonlinear effect of *years since transition*. I estimate all of my models using *log(years since transition)* instead of *years since transition*, and include an interaction term between *log(years since transition)* and severity of lustration. The results are provided in Table C.5.

Using original outcome variable cosalpo_4

In addition, I present the same set of models as in Table 5.1, but instead of using *cosal_3*, my programmaticness measure constructed for the analysis in Chapter 5, I use DALP's *cosalpo_4*, the measure that also includes polarization (Table C.6). Recall that in Section 5.4, I dropped polarization from the measure because *party distance* was one of the covariates implied by the model from Chapter 2. These results are in Table C.6

TABLE C.4. *Robustness check: imputed successors*

	Model 1	Model 2	Model 3	Model 4
Lustration severity	0.257***	0.195***	0.286	0.200***
	(0.061)	(0.066)	(0.230)	(0.068)
Party distance	−0.084**	−0.081**	−0.081**	−0.082**
	(0.035)	(0.036)	(0.036)	(0.036)
Years since transition		0.096	0.120	0.116
		(0.097)	(0.114)	(0.109)
Press freedom		0.350*	0.369*	0.340
		(0.212)	(0.218)	(0.215)
Years*severity			−0.176	
			(0.427)	
Opposition status				0.019
				(0.044)
Constant	0.306***	0.002	−0.024	−0.012
	(0.030)	(0.156)	(0.169)	(0.161)
Observations	307	307	307	307
Log likelihood	180.504	180.680	180.830	178.570
Akaike inf. crit.	−351.008	−347.359	−345.661	−341.140
Bayesian inf. crit.	−332.374	−321.272	−315.846	−311.325

Note: *$p < 0.1$; **$p < 0.05$; ***$p < 0.01$

TABLE C.5. *Robustness check: replication using years since transition logged*

	Model 1	Model 2	Model 3	Model 4	Model 5
Lustration severity	0.278***	0.260***	0.214***	0.213***	0.109
	(0.062)	(0.065)	(0.070)	(0.071)	(0.152)
Party distance	−0.107***	−0.108***	−0.110***	−0.111***	−0.112***
	(0.034)	(0.034)	(0.034)	(0.034)	(0.034)
log(Years since transition)		0.031	0.009	0.007	0.021
		(0.036)	(0.038)	(0.039)	(0.043)
Press freedom			0.410*	0.412*	0.452**
			(0.222)	(0.223)	(0.230)
Opposition status				−0.006	−0.006
				(0.037)	(0.037)
Severity*log(years since transition)					−0.152
					(0.198)
Constant	0.278***	0.313***	−0.016	−0.014	−0.032
	(0.036)	(0.054)	(0.186)	(0.188)	(0.190)
Country intercepts	Y	Y	Y	Y	
Missing successor	Y	Y	Y	Y	
Observations	313	313	307	307	307
Log likelihood	184.327	182.293	178.196	175.841	175.436
Akaike inf. crit.	−356.654	−350.586	−340.393	−333.682	−330.871
Bayesian inf. crit.	−334.177	−324.362	−310.578	−300.140	−293.603

Note: $^*p < 0.1$; $^{**}p < 0.05$; $^{***}p < 0.01$

TABLE C.6. *Robustness check: replication using DALP's cosalpo_4*

	Model 1	Model 2	Model 3	Model 4
Lustration severity	0.200***	0.186***	0.140***	0.144***
	(0.045)	(0.045)	(0.049)	(0.049)
Years since transition		0.125*	0.098	0.118
		(0.071)	(0.072)	(0.078)
Press freedom			0.319**	0.313**
			(0.155)	(0.155)
Opposition status				0.019
				(0.028)
Constant	0.182***	0.121***	−0.101	−0.118
	(0.020)	(0.040)	(0.113)	(0.116)
Country intercepts	Y	Y	Y	Y
Observations	313	313	307	307
Log likelihood	286.689	286.497	280.789	278.365
Akaike inf. crit.	−565.377	−562.995	−549.578	−542.730
Bayesian inf. crit.	−550.393	−544.264	−527.216	−516.642

Note: $^*p < 0.1$; $^{**}p < 0.05$; $^{***}p < 0.01$

APPENDIX D QUANTITATIVE SUPPLEMENT TO CHAPTER 6

As a first step, I present summary statistics in Table D.1.

In a next step, as a baseline, I present the results of a pooled linear regression model. Table D.2 shows my estimates of the association

TABLE D.1. *Descriptive statistics*

	Min.	1stQ.	Med.	Mean	3rdQ.	Max.	Obs.
Political corruption	0.05	0.26	0.44	0.48	0.69	0.99	1923
PdSES+	0.04	0.51	0.62	0.60	0.68	0.98	1923
Minimalist truth commission events	0.00	0.00	0.00	0.48	1.00	1.00	1923
Net truth commission events	0.00	0.00	0.00	0.08	0.00	1.00	1923
Net cumulative truth commission events	0.00	0.00	0.00	0.45	1.00	1.00	1923
log(GDPpc)	5.39	7.40	8.43	8.33	9.28	10.73	1923
Year since transition	1.00	6.00	13.00	14.15	21.00	49.00	1923
Public sector corruption	0.05	0.33	0.53	0.54	0.77	0.99	1923
Executive corruption	0.04	0.31	0.51	0.54	0.76	0.99	1923
Legislative corruption	0.08	0.31	0.40	0.43	0.54	0.90	1923
Judicial corruption	0.09	0.36	0.45	0.49	0.63	0.94	1923

TABLE D.2. *Effect of TCE on democractic quality: pooled models*

	PC	PC	PC	PdSES	PdSES	PdSES
Minimalist TCE	0.0509***			0.0206***		
	(5.35)			(3.63)		
Net TCE		0.0329			0.00529	
		(1.91)			(0.52)	
Net cumulative TCE			0.0648***			0.0110
			(6.80)			(1.92)
Log(GDPpc)	0.136***	0.138***	0.135***	0.0396***	0.0403***	0.0397***
	(34.90)	(35.26)	(34.55)	(16.98)	(17.29)	(16.93)
Constant	−0.682***	−0.677***	−0.675***	0.259***	0.262***	0.263***
	(−20.77)	(−20.43)	(−20.68)	(13.20)	(13.31)	(13.37)
Observations	1,747	1,747	1,747	1,747	1,747	1,747

t statistics in parentheses
PC- political corruption
PdSES - Power distributed by Socioeconomic Status
$*p < 0.05$, $**p < 0.01$, $***p < 0.001$

between truth commissions and the political corruption index and PdSES, including GDP logged as a covariate. The results below show a positive association between the minimalist measure of truth commission events and the net cumulative measure and political corruption and PdSES. When we use the measure of net truth commissions, however, the association is negative although statistically indistinguishable from 0. Of course, these results use a panel dataset without proper fixes to account for nonindependence, and without controlling for selection into treatment. As such, they are illustrative of a general trend but cannot be treated as conclusive (Tables D.1 and D.2).

Recall that a dif-in-dif design restricts the independent variables to a dummy format and thus forces me to reduce the rich data collected on transitional justice (TJ) to the mere occurrence of lustration, purge, or truth commissions. Nevertheless, as a robustness check, it may be useful to rerun the regressions from Chapter 6 using a continuous severity measure defined as follows:

$$\frac{\Sigma_1^t P_t}{\Sigma_1^t P_t + N_t + 1}. \tag{D.1}$$

This measure is a direct extension of the severity measure from Chapter 4, which assigns to each country the ratio of positive events to the total number of that country's post-transition years. Since my measure has to vary over time, instead of using the total post-transition history, I use use the years leading up to year t to create the adjusted severity measure in year t. Table D.3 shows the results from running the robustness checks with this adjusted measure of severity, for political corruption and for PdSES status.

D.1 Fixed Effects Regressions

The goal of this section is to replicate the results from the main text but using fixed effects regressions. I first examine the impact of truth revelation procedures on several corruption indicators discussed in Chapter 6. The model I estimate takes the following form:

$$QDI_{it} = TJ_{it}\gamma + x_{it}\beta + c_i + \epsilon_{it}. \tag{D.2}$$

Here, QDI_{it} is the quality of democracy indicator (political corruption or PdSES) measured at time t in country i; TJ_{it} is my measure of severity for either of the transparency mechanisms – lustration or truth commissions;

TABLE D.3. *Dif-in-dif regressions on continuous measures, country-clustered standard errors*

	(1) Political corruption	(2) PdSES
Net Cummulative Truth Commission Events	0.00742* (2.20)	0.000925 (0.06)
logGDP	0.00798 (0.21)	0.304 (1.07)
Constant	−1.143 (−1.26)	−6.486 (−0.96)
Observations	1,747	1,747

t statistics in parentheses
*$p < 0.05$, **$p < 0.01$, ***$p < 0.001$

x_{it} is a $1 \times k$ vector of time-varying independent variables that could predict the quality of democracy indicator in question.[7] γ is the coefficient on our main independent variable of interest; it represents the effect TJ mechanisms have on the quality of democracy indicator; β is the vector of coefficients on the time-varying covariates; c_i represents the sum of all time-invariant characteristics that affect the quality of democracy indicator in question.

All regressions in the following are performed on "demeaned" variables; this produces consistent estimates of β and γ even when the covariance between the country-fixed effects and time-varying covariates is nonzero (that is, when $Cov[x_{it}, c_i] \neq 0$). Table D.4 shows the relationship between Truth Commissions and PdSES using the three measures of transitional justice.

In the next step, I look a bit closer at the relationship between lustration and political corruption using fixed effect regressions (Table D.5).

Since country-fixed effects capture all the time-invariant causes of quality of democracy in each country, I need not worry about these potential determinants of political corruption in this model. The estimator predicting the effect of the transparency mechanism will be biased, however,

---

[7] Throughout all of my regressions, I use log GDP and years since transition; the only exceptions are instances where the measure of TJ severity already accounts for time lapsed since the transition.

TABLE D.4. *Power distributed by Socioeconomic Status and truth commissions events*

	Power distributed by Socioeconomic Status		
	(1)	(2)	(3)
Minimalist truth commission	0.196*** (0.037)		
Net truth commissions		0.052 (0.032)	
Cumulative net truth commissions			0.186*** (0.035)
GDP per capita (logged)	−0.177** (0.061)	−0.176** (0.062)	−0.176** (0.061)
Country FE	Y	Y	Y
Year FE	Y	Y	Y
Observations	1,759	1,759	1,759
R^2	0.067	0.052	0.067

Note: $^*p < 0.05$; $^{**}p < 0.01$; $^{***}p < 0.001$
All truth commission events are lagged

if I fail to include all *time-varying* determinants of the dependent variable. In both the lustration regressions and the truth commissions one, I include log GDP, obtained from the World Bank and a variable of my own construction that counts the years lapsed since the transition took place. The fixed effects estimations of the effect of truth commission events on PdSES largely corroborate earlier findings. Whether truth commissions are measured according to the minimalist or cumulative measure, they enhance democratic quality as reflected by PdSES.

Moving on to Table D.5, Model 1 shows the effect of the minimalist measure of lustration severity, which indicates whether a progressive event occurred at all. The effect is weak and negative but insignificant. As far as the count measures of lustration severity are concerned, we see that net lustration (in model 2) is still negative and insignificant, as is net cumulative lustration (in model 3).

Net cumulative lustration becomes positive and significant in models that do not cluster standard errors by country. I ran such models for both fixed and random effects (Models 4 and 5, respectively). The coefficients from Models 4 and 5 on net cumulative lustration seem similar in magnitude, but a Hausman test fails to produce a chi-square high enough to justify a random effects design; thus, I can only rely on fixed effects here.

TABLE D.5. *Effect of lustration on political corruption*

	(1) v2x_corr	(2) v2x_corr	(3) v2x_corr	(4) v2x_corr	(5) v2x_corr	(6) v2x_corr
Minimalist lustrations	−0.0124 (−0.78)					
Net lustrations		−0.00519 (−1.25)				−0.00443 (−1.29)
Net cumulative lustrations			0.00202 (1.03)	0.00202* (2.48)	0.00226** (2.80)	0.00218 (1.17)
log GDP	0.0156 (0.36)	0.0156 (0.36)	0.0228 (1.21)	0.0228*** (4.68)	0.0237*** (5.24)	0.0176 (0.97)
Years since transition	0.000346 (0.19)	0.000242 (0.14)				
Constant	−0.906 (−0.87)	−0.909 (−0.87)	−1.086* (−2.37)	−1.086*** (−9.14)	−1.131*** (−10.07)	−0.957* (−2.15)
Observations	1,759	1,759	1,826	1,826	1,826	1,759
Clustered std. errors	yes	yes	yes	no	no	yes
Fixed/random effects	Fixed	Fixed	Fixed	Fixed	Random	Fixed

t statistics in parentheses
*$p < 0.05$, **$p < 0.01$, ***$p < 0.001$

My fixed effects models yield barely significant results, and only yield these results before I account for clustered errors within countries. Finally, Model 6 includes both the net lustration events from the preceding year and the cumulative net lustration effects. Here, too, lustration does not seem to affect political corruption in any significant way.

Hence, in general, the relationship between lustration and political corruption is weak at best. An analysis of truth commissions, however, reveals an entirely different story (Table D.6).

First, Model 1 in Table D.6 looks at the effect of the minimalist measure of truth commissions, analyzing whether a single positive event occurring affects corruption. It does not, although the coefficient is positive and almost significant at the 10 percent level.

Model 2 uses net truth commission events and shows that these events have a positive and statistically significant effect on political corruption. Net truth commission events are not bounded by 0 and 1. The way to interpret these results is that an additional positive truth commission event relative to the mean net events each year decreases political corruption by almost 1 percent. This effect alone is not substantially large, but no doubt, there are other factors behind transitional justice influencing political corruption. Moreover, it is clear that political corruption responds to a multitude of stimuli and that truth commission procedures are but one corruption-reducing factor.

Model 3 uses net cumulative truth commissions in a fixed effects setting and Model 4 in a random effects model (here, a Hausman test supports the use of random effects). The variable "net cumulative truth commissions" varies from 1 to 22, and the coefficient .007 indicates that an additional progressive event relative to the mean number of events increases the corruption index by .7 percent. This finding is significant at the .001 level. Finally, in the model with both net events from the previous year and cumulative events up to that year, the coefficient on net cumulative events is positive, almost significant, and indicates that close to half of a percent in the corruption index can be attributed to a progressive truth commission event. The multilevel structure of these data allows me to comment on the portion of the variation in the model that comes from differences between countries and not within countries. In this case, an overwhelming percentage – around 93 percent – of the variance is explained by differences between countries.

Overall, there is strong support for the general hypothesis that transparency regimes improve the quality of representation and that within transparency regimes, truth commissions are particularly significant in

TABLE D.6. *Effect of truth commissions on political corruption*

	(1) v2x_corr	(2) v2x_corr	(3) v2x_corr	(4) v2x_corr	(5) v2x_corr
Minimalist truth commissions	0.0223 (1.52)				
Net truth commissions		0.00822* (2.52)			0.00431 (1.30)
Net cumulative truth commissions			0.00669*** (5.86)	0.00649*** (5.78)	0.00565 (1.77)
log GDP	0.0127 (0.29)	0.0156 (0.36)	0.0123* (2.37)	0.0150** (3.10)	0.0109 (0.56)
Years since transition	0.000110 (0.06)	0.000272 (0.15)			
Constant	−0.846 (−0.81)	−0.911 (−0.87)	−0.836*** (−6.60)	−0.924*** (−7.73)	−0.797 (−1.68)
Observations	1,759	1,759	1,826	1,826	1,759
Fixed/random effects	Fixed	Fixed	Fixed	Random	Fixed
Clustered std. errors	yes	yes	no	no	yes

t statistics in parentheses
*$p < 0.05$, **$p < 0.01$, ***$p < 0.001$

reducing political corruption. Interestingly, at least among the fixed effects models, the evidence favoring lustration is not very strong. This is likely because truth commissions have much wider coverage than lustration laws; this is supported by the fact that lustration laws became more marginally significant in the random effects model, where power could be obtained from countries with much richer lustration trajectories. Note that this finding only partially supports my hypotheses, where I predicted that while all transparency regimes would reduce political corruption, the effects would be stronger for truth commissions than for lustrations. I expected this precisely because lustrations focus on political elites and not on the broader population, they should have a narrower impact on reducing corruption.

APPENDIX E QUANTITATIVE SUPPLEMENT TO CHAPTER 7

In this Appendix, I provide additional tables to the ones in the main text. In addition, I propose, as a robustness check, a two-stage selection model to test the effect of purges, after accounting for institutionalization, that determines which countries select into purges in the first place. This robustness check rests on assumptions that cannot be demonstrated empirically, so the results from it can at most serve as supportive evidence.

E.1 Regressions of PdSES Split Sample by Institutionalization with Pooled Purges

The first table uses the same specifications as Table 7.4 in Chapter 7, but substitutes pooled purges for leadership purges as the independent variable. The results largely corroborate our expectations from Chapter 7: in states with low institutionalization, purges improve democratic quality, whereas in states with high institutionalization, purges have no effect on democratic quality.

E.2 Robustness Check: Two-Stage SLS

The discussion from Chapter 7 implies that in regressing the quality of democracy on purges, we must account for the process through which states "select into" purges. An alternative approach to this is through the use of a two-stage regression, or selection model, which accounts for

TABLE E.1. *Split sample (by capacity) regressions of PdSES on pooled purges: country-fixed effects and country-clustered standard errors*

	Pooled low inst.	Pooled high inst.
Lagged net purge	0.146**	−0.00125
	(2.76)	(−0.03)
Log GDP	0.227	0.109
	(0.84)	(0.31)
Years after transition	−0.00232	−0.00675
	(−0.17)	(−0.53)
Constant	−4.899	−1.798
	(−0.79)	(−0.21)
Observations	760	998

t statistics in parentheses
$^{*}p < 0.05, ^{**}p < 0.01, ^{***}p < 0.001$

the effect purges have on quality of democracy. Structurally, this model is identical to an instrumental variable approach. Therefore, we have to consider the following:

1. The *first stage* regression, where institutionalization is used to predict the occurrence of purges:

$$Purge_{it} = \pi_0 + \pi_1 Inst_i + \epsilon_{FS} + \epsilon_i, \tag{E.1}$$

where $Inst_i$ is the measure of authoritarian institutionalization within a year of transition (using the Hanson–Sigman capacity score), x_{it} is the set of control variables, including log GDP per capita and years lapsed since transition, and ϵ_i is the country-specific error term.

2. The *second stage* regression, where I establish the relation between purges and the quality of democracy:

$$QDI_{it} = \alpha_0 + \alpha_1 Purges_{it} + x_{it}\alpha + \epsilon_{it}^{SS}. \tag{E.2}$$

3. The reduced form OLS where the predicted level of purges from the first stage is used as an independent variable to predict the ultimate

TABLE E.2. *Effect of institutionalization on net cumulative purges, random effects, country-clustered standard errors*

	(1) All purges	(2) Thorough purges	(3) Leadership purges
Institutionalization	1.182***	0.573***	0.391
	(4.48)	(3.46)	(1.34)
Log GDP	−0.122	−0.0727	−0.0467
	(−0.85)	(−1.19)	(−0.42)
Years after transition	0.0150	0.00952*	0.00538
	(1.76)	(2.21)	(1.01)
Constant	3.600	1.939	1.622
	(1.07)	(1.37)	(0.62)
Observations	1,665	1,665	1,665

z scores in parentheses
$*p < 0.05, **p < 0.01, ***p < 0.001$

variable of interest, the quality of democracy indicator:

$$QDI_{it} = \alpha_0 + \alpha_1(\pi_0 + \pi_1 Inst_{io} + \epsilon_{FS}) + \epsilon_{it}^{SS}. \qquad (E.3)$$

Equation (E.3) simplifies to:

$$QDI_{it} = (\alpha_0 + \alpha_1\pi_0) + \alpha_1\pi_1 Inst_{io} + \alpha_1\epsilon_{FS} + \epsilon_{it}^{SS}, \qquad (E.4)$$

which can be conveniently rewritten as:

$$QDI_{it} = \gamma_0 + \gamma_1 Inst_{io} + x_{it}\gamma + \epsilon_{it}^{RF}. \qquad (E.5)$$

after allowing $\gamma_0 = \alpha_0\pi_0, \gamma_1 = \alpha_1\pi_1$, and $\epsilon_{it}^{RF} = \alpha_1\epsilon_{FS} + \epsilon_{it}^{SS}$.

The assumptions required in this analysis resemble those in the instrumental variable approach. One has to be convinced that:

1. The exclusion restriction holds: authoritarian institutionalization affects the quality of democracy only through purges, or in other words, $Cov(Purge_{it}, \epsilon_{it}|x_{it}) = 0$

2. Institutionalization affects the endogenous regressor: purges , that is $\pi_1 \neq 0$.

As far as item (1) is concerned, one can plausibly argue that whether institutionalization has an effect on the quality of democracy must depend on the extent to which the staff of the *ancien régime* was purged or allowed to continue in office. Without accounting for purges, it is difficult to imagine how prior institutionalization would impact the quality of the subsequent democracy.

An argument for the second assumption is easiest to make by showing the results of the first-stage regression, where the expectation is that institutionalization will be a significant predictor of purges. Note that purges here, as in the remainder of the analysis, are measured using cumulative net purges. Consider the results in Table E.2.

Institutionalization of the former authoritarian regime is indeed a strong predictor of purges, but the effect is largely driven by thorough purges. This is consistent with the analysis from the previous section and can be explained by the fact that thorough purges are typically purges of the authoritarian security apparatus, the purging of which is most urgent when its capacity had previously been high.

E.3 Two-Stage Regression Analysis: Political Corruption

Table E.3 presents the results of the regression described in equation E.5 along with the simple OLS for comparison in model (1).[8]

Table E.3 contains four models. Model 1 is a simple OLS regression similar to the one in Table 7.1, but using net cumulative purges for the sake of more effective comparison with two-stage least squares.[9] In the OLS regression, purges did not appear as a significant predictor of political corruption: the coefficient is close to zero and insignificant. As argued earlier, this is likely a result of the fact that this model did not take into account the institutionalization of the former authoritarian state when deciding to purge its administrative apparatus. The following three models account for this by using state capacity as a predictor of purges in a first-stage regression. They use pooled, thorough, and leadership purges to predict political corruption. The results indicate that each positive purge event on average improves the Political Corruption Index by .15. Models in the third and fourth column, however, reveal that this effect is driven predominantly by thorough purges where, on average a positive event improves the Political Corruption Index by .318. These results take into account the change in political corruption owed to economic development

---

[8] Note here that I am using for consistency the same measure that is used in the remaining two-stage models – the net cumulative purges.

[9] Also, for the sake of transparency, I only use the pooled purges result.

TABLE E.3. *Two-stage regression of political corruption on purges via institutionalization*

	(OLS) All Purges	(2SLS) All Purges	(2SLS) Leadership	(2SLS) Thorough
Lagged net cum purge	−.0002124	0.151***	0.130***	0.318***
	(.0104479)	(9.12)	(8.60)	(10.67)
Log GDP	.0199464	0.0133*	0.0184***	0.0395***
	(.043007)	(2.05)	(3.33)	(8.69)
Years after transition	−.0000354	−0.00333*	−0.00134	0.000375
	.0017801	(−2.39)	(−1.17)	(0.38)
Constant	−1.007282	−0.963***	−1.052***	−1.595***
	(1.033945)	(−6.32)	(−8.03)	(−14.70)
Observations	1,758	1,603	1,603	1,603
Under identification test (LM)		107.149	120.921	175.629
Weak identification test (Wald F)		114.538	65.189	98.629

t statistics in parentheses
*$p < 0.05$, **$p < 0.01$, ***$p < 0.001$
Note: In the OLS, standard errors are reported in parenthesis, while in the 2SLS, I record Z scores in parentheses. A Stock-Yogo weak ID test in the pooled purge regression yielded critical values 16.38 (10 percent maximal IV size), 8.96 (15 percent), 6.66 (20 percent), and 5.93 (25 percent); for the leadership and thorough Purge regression, critical values were 19.93 (10 percent maximal IV size), 11.59 (15 percent), 8.75 (20 percent), and 7.25 (25 percent).

(measured by log GDP), which is also a significant predictor of political corruption and years lapsed since the transition to democracy, which is not significant in any of the four models.

It is also useful to look at the components of the Political Corruption Index to see if these are affected differently by purges in the two-stage regression. I look at four indicators in particular. Recall that I conducted a similar disaggregation exercise in Figure 6.7 in Chapter 6. The first is the indicator for public sector corruption, which is constructed out of answers to: "To what extent do public sector employees grant favors in exchange for bribes, kickbacks, or other material inducements, and how often do they steal, embezzle, or misappropriate public funds or other state resources for personal or family use?"

The second component is an indicator of executive corruption, which codes answers to: "How routinely do members of the executive, or their agents grant favors in exchange for bribes, kickbacks, or other material inducements, and how often do they steal, embezzle, or misappropriate public funds or other state resources for personal or family use?" As

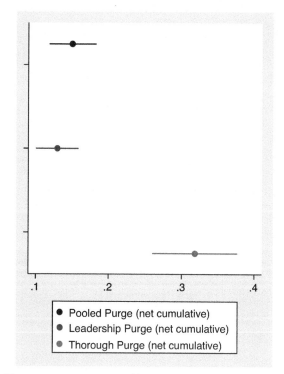

FIGURE E.1. Two-stage regression coefficients on political corruption: Three different kinds of purges (lagged net cumulative purge measures)

expected, this indicator is highly correlated with the public corruption indicator.

The next component is judicial corruption, which is constructed out of answers to: "How often do individuals or businesses make undocumented extra payments or bribes in order to speed up or delay the process or to obtain a favorable judicial decision?" The judicial corruption index is scaled from 4 (which codes the answer "Always") to 0 (which codes the answer "Never").

A similarly reversed scale appears also in one other component of political corruption. Legislative corruption codes answers to: "Do members of the legislature abuse their position for financial gain?" In my analysis, both of these indicators have been normalized and the scales reversed to match political corruption, so that higher values reflect more democratic outcomes.

Appendices

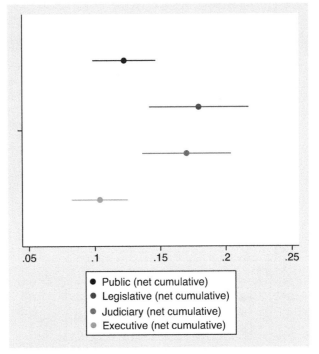

FIGURE E.2. Components of the Political Corruption Index in two-stage least squares regressions predicting pooled purges

This makes them directly comparable to the public corruption and executive corruption indicators. It also leads me to expect a positive effect of purges on these indicators. Finally, the executive corruption index codes answers to: "How routinely do members of the executive, or their agents grant favors in exchange for bribes, kickbacks, or other material inducements, and how often do they steal, embezzle, or misappropriate public funds or other state resources for personal or family use?"

Figure E.2 shows point estimates and confidence intervals from two-stage regressions for all four components of the Political Corruption Index. I focus on the effects for pooled purges. We see, in particular, that purges best predict the absence of judiciary corruption, followed closely by legislative corruption. The effects on public and especially executive corruption are smaller, although still significant. Hence, it appears that purges are most effective at eliminating corruption in the highest, or elite, echelons of power. This is perhaps not surprising as purges may scarcely

TABLE E.4. *Two-stage regression of Power distributed by Socioeconomic Status on purges via institutionalization*

	(OLS) All purges	(2SLS) All purges	(2SLS) Leadership	(2SLS) Thorough
Lagged net cumulative purge	−.0772936	0.397***	0.463***	0.849***
	(.0499759)	(11.16)	(9.92)	(9.45)
Log GDP	.1902241	−0.0238	−0.0325	0.0451**
	(.247786)	(−1.48)	(−1.90)	(3.29)
Years after transition	−.0053344	−0.00613	−0.00501	0.00350
	(.0100296)	(−1.78)	(−1.42)	(1.17)
Constant	−3.833734	0.932*	1.206**	−0.732*
	(5.936925)	(2.46)	(2.98)	(−2.24)
Observations		1,603	1,603	1,603
Under identification test (LM)		107.149	120.921	175.629
Weak identification test (Wald F)		84.056	65.189	98.312

t statistics in parentheses
*$p < 0.05$, **$p < 0.01$, ***$p < 0.001$
Note: In the OLS, standard errors are reported in parenthesis, while in the 2SLS, I record Z scores in parentheses. Stock-Yogo weak ID test in the Pooled Purge regression critical values are 16.38 (10 percent maximal IV size), 8.96 (15 percent) 6.66 (20 percent), 5.93 (25 percent); For the Leadership and Thorough Purge regression critical values were 19.93 (10 percent maximal IV size), 11.59 (15 percent) 8.75 (20 percent), and 7.25 (25 percent).

be carried out for a sufficiently long period of time and persistently enough to trickle down to the levels at which petty corruption and corruption in local government occur.

Setting aside varieties and components of political corruption, I now turn to using the same two-stage least squares to predict PdSES.

E.4 Two-Stage Regression: PdSES

As explained earlier, in Chapter 6, PdSES is a V-Dem variable that operationalizes expert assessments about the degree to which political and economic power are correlated with each other. To the extent that a high concentration of economic assets and political power are symptomatic of authoritarian regimes, this variable can be regarded as a good proxy for the extent to which vestiges of the former authoritarian regime persist and former authoritarian networks succeed at perpetuating themselves.

Recall from Table 7.2 in Chapter 7 that before controlling for institutionalization of the prior regime, purges had a negative effect on Power distributed by Socioeconomic Status. Table E.3 in Appendix E.1 indicates that the sign of this coefficient remained unchanged, although it lost significance when alternative measures of purges were used.

As the results in Table E.4 show, using institutionalization to predict purges helps better uncover the actual effects of purges. Moreover, in the two-stage regression, the effect of purges is positive. Recall that PdSES is measured on a four-point scale, while political corruption is measured on a one-point scale. After taking this into account, it seems the size of the effects is not necessarily larger than in the case of political corruption and its components. Once more, the effects are considerably stronger for thorough purges than for leadership purges. This is most clearly portrayed in the last column of Figure E.4.

APPENDIX F QUANTITATIVE APPENDIX TO CHAPTER 8

F.1 Deriving Public Employment

This appendix explains the steps taken to extrapolate the Public Employment Data from public expenditures as a percentage of GDP. The advantage of using this source as opposed to World Bank data on public employment is that it covers all authoritarian countries in the GTJD and the trend starts in 1990.[10]

1. First, we regress public employment in the year 2004 on public expenditures as a percentage of GDP. (Using 2004 was a reasonable choice because it provided entries for nearly all autocracies in the Global Transitional Justice Data). The graph of the regression with a correlation coefficient of 0.603 and an $r^2 = 0.364$ is provided in Figure F.1.

2. Removing just three near outliers (Russia, Georgia, and Lithuania) greatly improves the fit, increasing the correlation coefficient to 0.782 ($r^2 = 0.612$), with the graph in Figure F.2.

3. To measure this regression's predictive power, in the third step I used it to predict the Public Employment data and compare it to the actual World Bank Employment data. To see if the difference was statistically significant, I used the regression equation and the public expenditures data from 2000. A paired two-tailed t-test to test

---

[10] Several data sources were used. GDP per Capita comes from the World Bank and is available at data.worldbank.org/indicator/ny.gdp.pcap.cd. Public employment data is also from the World Bank and available at www.worldbank.org/en/topic/governance/brief/size-of-the-public-sector-government-wage-bill-and-employment. Finally, public expenditures as a percentage of GDP comes from the International Monetary Fund's World Economic Outlook and comes from www.imf.org/en/Publications/WEO/weo-database/2021/April/select-country-group.

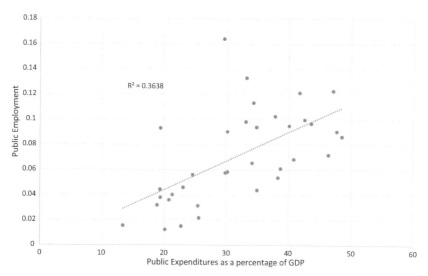

FIGURE F.1. Linear regression of Public Employment on Expenditures in 2004

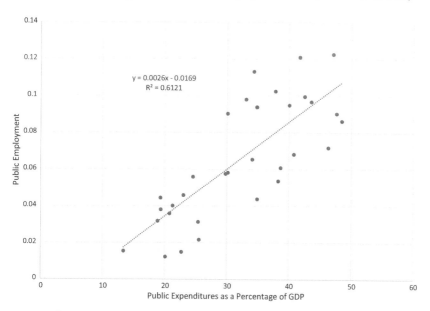

FIGURE F.2. Linear regression of Public Employment on Expenditures in 2004

the significance of the difference between the real and the predicted public employment data for 2000 revealed a p-value of 0.158, indicating that the difference was not statistically significant. Repeating the same process for the year 2009 revealed a similar result: the *p*-value for that year was 0.154. That is to say, the public employment data predicted by the model for 2000 and 2009 did not have a statistically significant difference from the actual public employment data in those years.

4. Given these results, I used the regression above (with coefficient .782) to predict the public employment data for all the former autocracies in the Global Transitional Justice Dataset with transition dates after 1980 (because public expenditures data only goes back that far). The WEO dataset lacked public expenditures data for thirty-eight countries for the exact year in which they provided data for the years relatively proximate to the transition date allowing to run regressions on thirty-four countries using the ten years nearest to the transition to estimate their public expenditures for their actual transition year (e.g., Cape Verde transitioned in 1991 but did not have data till 1994, so data from 1994 to 2003 was used to estimate the public employment expenditures in 1991). Each of these country regressions, took the form: $PE_t = \beta_0 + \beta_1 * t$, allowing to recover coefficient that allowed to predict public expenditure for the transition year.

5. There were also four countries (Dominican Republic, Ecuador, Turkey, Uruguay) for which WEO had no public expenditures data within fifteen years of the transition. Here, estimating public employment from public employment expenditures data was inferior to simply taking the closest year where the World Bank provided data. In some instances, this created considerable gaps between the transition year and the public employment weight. For instance, in the case of Ecuador, which transitioned in 1979, public expenditures as a percentage of GDP come from 1995.

F.2 Correlates of Authoritarian Elite Presence

Since this analysis is cross-sectional alone, I conducted these investigations systematically by examining first a baseline model with just the severity of every mechanism; next, for each sector, I analyzed all pairwise interactions between mechanism severities and the two other control variables. That is, I ran 6! *5 regressions – decidedly too many to report in a book. Therefore, below, I only report those that caused instability of initially significant coefficients in relation to the baseline regression. All of the results reported include robust standard errors (according to STATA).

TABLE F.1. *Regressions of party elite reproduction on transitional justice mechanisms*

	(1)	(2)	(3)	(4)
Lustration	−0.359***	−0.327***	−0.364***	−0.340***
	(−4.82)	(−3.85)	(−5.02)	(−4.68)
Thorough purge	0.127	0.132	0.231*	−0.00933
	(1.21)	(1.22)	(2.07)	(−0.08)
Leadership purge	−0.0933	−0.0267	0.0216	−0.0692
	(−1.00)	(−0.15)	(0.16)	(−0.72)
Truth commission	0.0787	0.0743	0.0698	0.0832
	(1.03)	(0.97)	(0.93)	(1.09)
Post conflict	−0.00699	−0.0101	−0.0160	−0.0502
	(−0.13)	(−0.19)	(−0.29)	(−0.75)
Years of transition	0.00407	0.00398	0.00347	0.00388
	(1.15)	(1.14)	(0.99)	(1.09)
Lustration * leadership purge		−0.224		
		(−0.71)		
Thorough * leadership purge			−0.490	
			(−1.45)	
Thorough purge * post conflict				0.300
				(1.61)
Constant	−7.714	−7.549	−6.515	−7.319
	(−1.09)	(−1.08)	(−0.93)	(−1.03)
Observations	71	71	71	71

t statistics in parentheses
*$p < 0.05$, **$p < 0.01$, ***$p < 0.001$
Note: Transitional justice variables are measured as severity over all post-transition years

Table F.1 starts with a Model 1 that only includes these controls and the severity of each of the four TJ mechanisms. Models 2 through 4 include interaction terms between pairs of mechanisms to examine whether there is a reinforcing effect between them, and whether jointly they are more effective at removing authoritarian elites from key sectors of public life.[11] The results indicate that lustration severity is significantly associated with decreased presence of former authoritarian elites in political parties. The effect is consistent and robust to including interaction terms, although none of these terms achieves significance. Both the dependent and

---

[11] Although I ran regressions with all pairwise interactions, I only include the ones where the effect was stronger than .2.

TABLE F.2. *Regressions of state elite reproduction on transitional justice mechanisms*

	(1)	(2)	(3)	(4)	(5)
Lustration	−0.248*	−0.146	−0.329**	−0.324**	−0.232*
	(−2.43)	(−1.25)	(−2.75)	(−2.80)	(−2.29)
Thorough purge	0.0726	0.323	0.0949	0.0942	−0.0468
	(0.59)	(1.72)	(0.75)	(0.79)	(−0.38)
Leadership purge	−0.103	−0.125	−0.0991	−0.100	−0.0815
	(−1.17)	(−1.39)	(−1.12)	(−1.14)	(−0.97)
Truth commission	0.00893	−0.00734	−0.0228	0.0136	0.0129
	(0.12)	(−0.10)	(−0.23)	(0.19)	(0.18)
Post conflict	−0.0371	−0.0516	−0.0343	−0.0790	−0.0748
	(−0.73)	(−1.03)	(−0.67)	(−1.13)	(−1.21)
Year of transition	0.00407	0.00370	0.00383	0.00433	0.00391
	(1.36)	(1.21)	(1.26)	(1.43)	(1.33)
Lustration * leadership purge		−0.622			
		(−2.00)			
Lustration * truth commission			0.156		
			(0.79)		
Lustration * post conflict				0.168	
				(1.08)	
Thorough purge * post conflict					0.262
					(1.46)
Constant	−7.760	−7.024	−7.257	−8.256	−7.416
	(−1.30)	(−1.15)	(−1.19)	(−1.37)	(−1.26)
Observations	71	71	71	71	71

t statistics in parentheses
*$p < 0.05$, **$p < 0.01$, ***$p < 0.001$
Note: Transitional justice variables are measured as severity over all post-transition years

independent variables are normalized between 0 and 1. A change in lustration severity from the most lenient lustration law to the most stringent, holding all other variables we control for constant, would lower the presence of authoritarian elites in political parties by almost 34 percent. A thorough purge, paradoxically, increases elite presence in parties significantly, though only at the 10 percent level and only for one specification (Model 2). Based on Model 4, where I interact thorough purges with post-conflict settings, it seems that this positive effect of thorough purges on the presence of former authoritarian elites is driven by post-authoritarian countries that also witnessed a civil war Table F.1.

Table F.2 indicates that the weighted proportion of former authoritarian elites in the state is also negatively and significantly associated with

TABLE 3. *Regressions of authoritarian elite transfer to business on transitional justice mechanisms*

	(1)	(2)	(3)	(4)	(5)	(6)
Lustration	0.116	0.143	0.140	0.116	0.122*	0.113
	(1.93)	(1.82)	(1.98)	(1.90)	(2.03)	(1.90)
Thorough purge	−0.0966	−0.0310	−0.0928	−0.0912	−9.707	−0.0981
	(−1.73)	(−0.49)	(−1.70)	(−1.25)	(−1.13)	(−1.82)
Leadership purge	−0.0766*	−0.0826*	−0.0255	−0.0706	−0.0677	−0.0782*
	(−2.02)	(−2.19)	(−0.44)	(−1.29)	(−1.72)	(−2.11)
Truth commission	−0.0314	−0.0357	−0.0347	−0.0319	−0.0361	0.0326
	(−0.97)	(−1.11)	(−1.06)	(−0.97)	(−1.11)	(0.64)
Post conflict	0.00239	−0.00142	0.0000376	0.00191	0.000381	0.0566
	(0.10)	(−0.06)	(0.00)	(0.07)	(0.02)	(1.74)
Year of transition	−0.000730	−0.000827	−0.000795	−0.000761	−0.00134	−0.000825
	(−0.53)	(−0.60)	(−0.56)	(−0.53)	(−0.79)	(−0.58)
Lustration * thorough purge		−0.163				
		(−0.93)				
Lustration * leadership purge			−0.172			
			(−1.27)			
Thorough * leadership purge				−0.0259		
				(−0.16)		
Thorough purge * Year					0.00482	
					(1.12)	
Truth commission *Post conflict						−0.132
						(−1.88)
Constant	1.586	1.779	1.713	1.649	2.795	1.752
	(0.58)	(0.65)	(0.61)	(0.57)	(0.82)	(0.61)
Observations	71	71	71	71	71	71

t statistics in parentheses

*$p < 0.05$, **$p < 0.01$, ***$p < 0.001$

TABLE F.4. *Correlation matrix of severity of personnel transitional justice mechanisms*

	lustration	Leadership purge	Thorough purge	Truth commissions.
Lustration	1.00	−0.16	−0.22	−0.14
Leadership purge	0.16	−1.00	−0.48	−0.13
Thorough purge	0.22	−0.48	−1.00	−0.03
Truth commissions	0.14	−0.13	−0.03	−1.00

lustration severity. Patterns of association between lustration severity and presence of authoritarian elites in the democratic state largely resemble those of elite presence in political parties. While lustration severity is the only significant effect, the sign on the leadership purge variable is consistently negative and the sign on the thorough purge variable is consistently positive. The latter does switch to negative after being interacted with post-conflict states, again suggesting that what is driving the positive effect are post-conflict states.

To examine authoritarian elite reproduction in business, I use raw proportions – that is, $ERP_c = \frac{k_c}{m_c}$, where k_c represents the size of country c's post-authoritarian elite, and m_c is the size of the authoritarian elite. We see in Table F.3 that leadership purges are quite consistently associated with lower presence of authoritarian elites in business (except for in some models with leadership purge interactions). At the same time, lustration is positively and almost significantly associated with higher elite presence in business (note that the t-statistic is very close to 2).

Finally, Table F.4 provides the correlation coefficient for the severities of all four mechanisms analyzed jointly in Chapter 8.

APPENDIX G GIS APPENDIX

The following appendix presents a GIS coded version of our dataset with all three measures applied to each of the TJ mechanisms. The first map presents GIS coded data on the severity of lustration in countries making up our universe of cases. The second map presents the severity of leadership purges for the same group of countries. The third map presents the severity of thorough purges and the fourth map presents the severity of truth commissions. This order is repeated for volatility and urgency/delay.

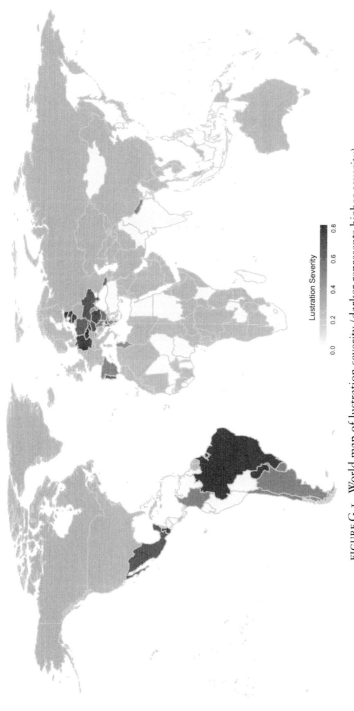

FIGURE G.I. World map of lustration severity (darker represents higher severity)

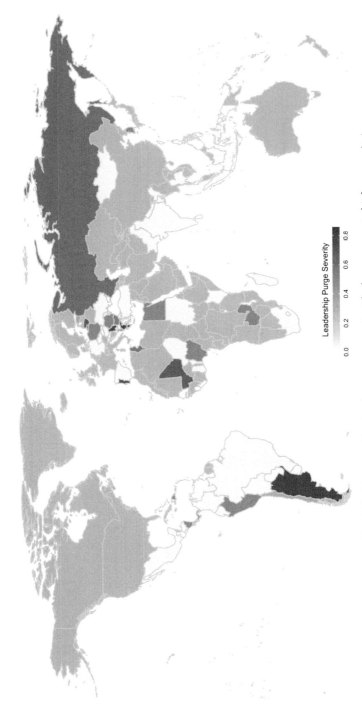

FIGURE G.2. World map of leadership purge severity (darker represents higher severity)

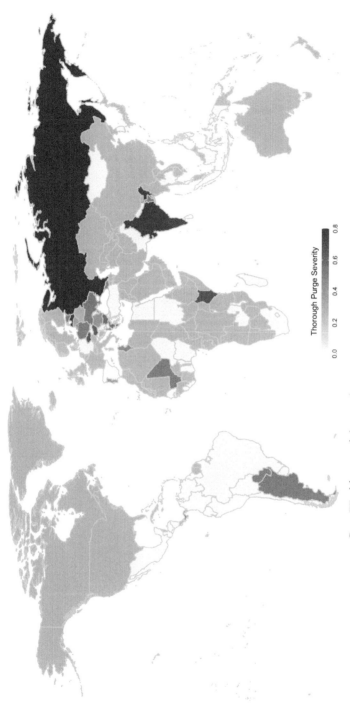

FIGURE G.3. World map of thorough purge severity (darker represents higher severity)

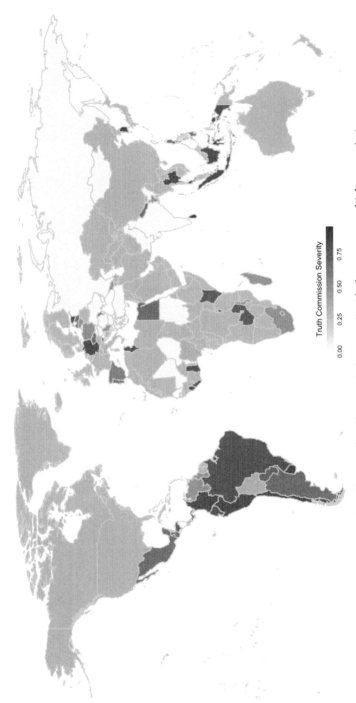

FIGURE G.4. World map of truth commission severity (darker represents higher severity)

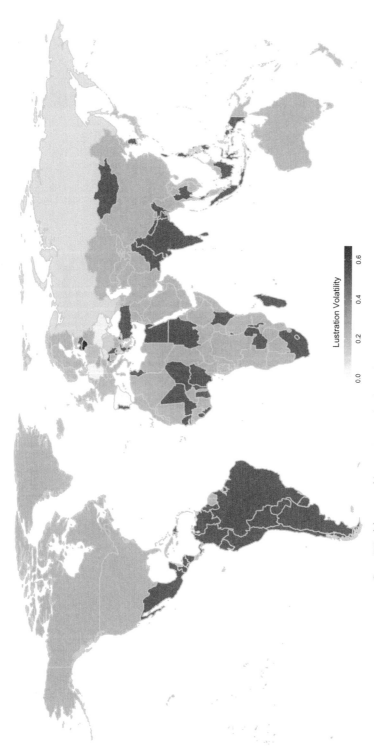

FIGURE G.5. World map of lustration volatility (darker represents higher polarization)

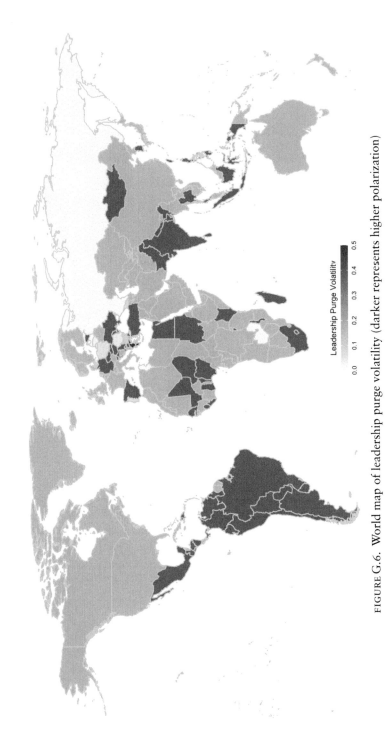

FIGURE G.6. World map of leadership purge volatility (darker represents higher polarization)

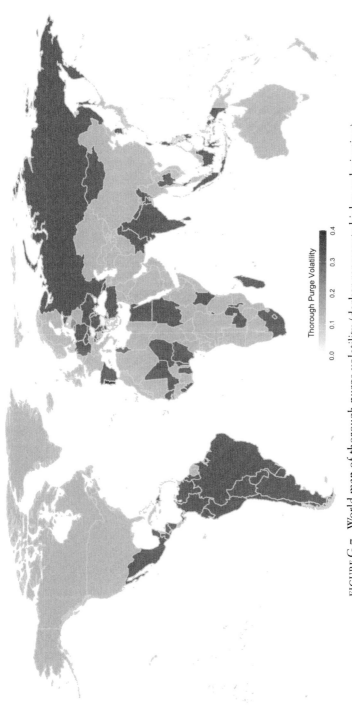

FIGURE G.7. World map of thorough purge volatility (darker represents higher polarization)

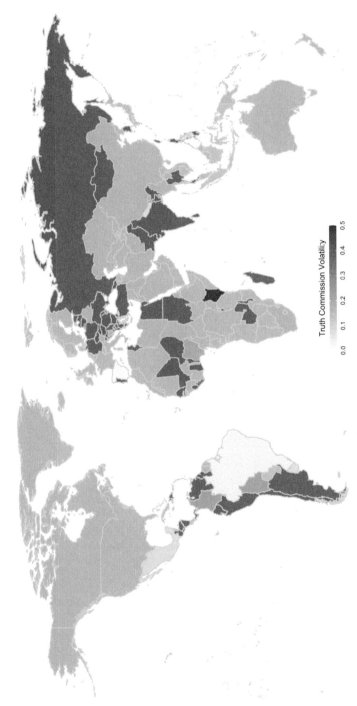

FIGURE G.8. World map of truth commission volatility (darker represents higher polarization)

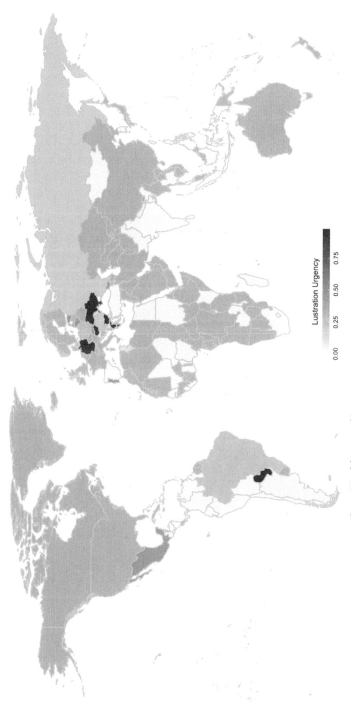

FIGURE G.9. World map of lustration urgency (darker represents higher delay)

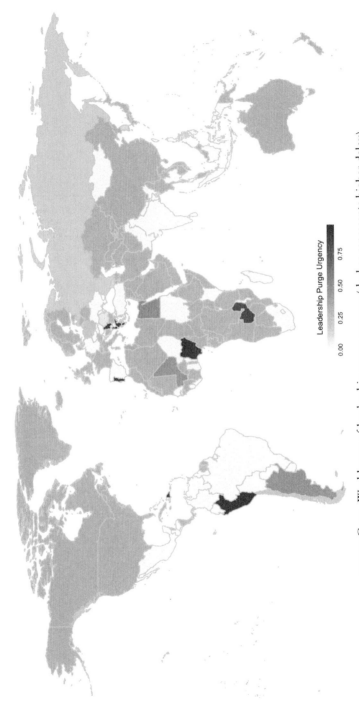

FIGURE G.10. World map of leadership purge urgency (darker represents higher delay)

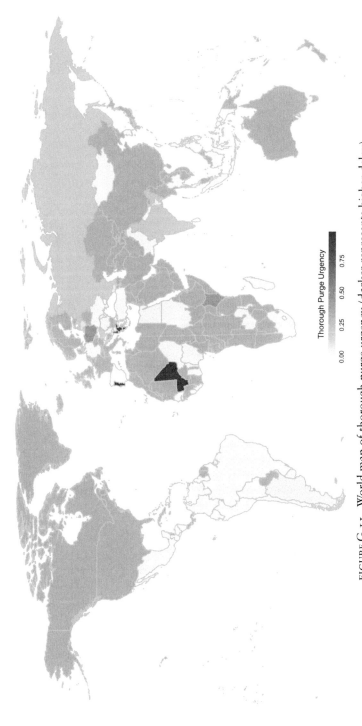

FIGURE G.II. World map of thorough purge urgency (darker represents higher delay)

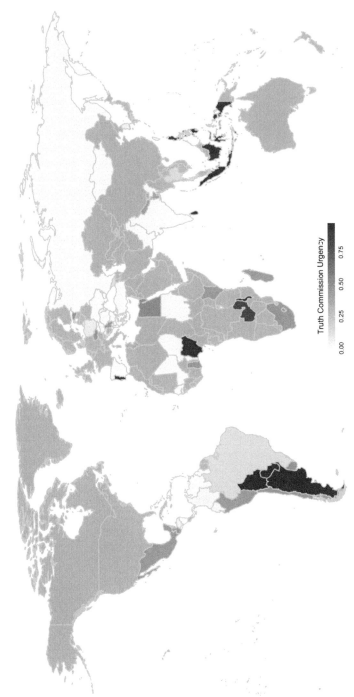

FIGURE G.12. World map of truth commission urgency (darker represents higher delay)

References

Abadie, A., Diamond, A., & Hainmueller, J. (2015), 'Comparative politics and the synthetic control method', *American Journal of Political Science* 59(2), 495–510.

Abente-Brun, D. (1999), 'Latin America's imperiled progress: "People power" in Paraguay', *Journal of Democracy* 10(3), 93–100.

Albertus, M. & Menaldo, V. (2014), 'Gaming democracy: Elite dominance during transition and the prospects for redistribution', *British Journal of Political Science* 44(3), 575–603.

(2018), *Authoritarianism and the Elite Origins of Democracy*, Cambridge University Press.

(2018b), *Authoritarianism and the Elite Origins of Democracy*, Cambridge University Press.

Alivizatos, N. C. & Diamandouros, P. N. (1997), 'Politics and the judiciary in the Greek transition to democracy', *Transitional Justice and the Rule of Law in New Democracies*, pp. 27–60.

Ang, M. (2019), Corrupting Accountability: Crime, Orphaned Bureaucracies, and the Failure of the Democratic State, University of Chicago, May 2018, Unpublished manuscript.

Ang, M. & Nalepa, M. (2019), 'Can transitional justice improve the quality of representation in new democracies?', *World Politics* 71(4), 631–666.

Angrist, J. D. & Pischke, J. S. (2008), *Mostly Harmless Econometrics: An Empiricist's Companion*, Princeton University Press.

Ansell, B. & Samuels, D. (2010), 'Inequality and democratization: A contractarian approach', *Comparative Political Studies* 43(12), 1543–1574.

Archive, f. t. (February 1992), 'War's end in El Salvador. But peace needs time to grow', United Press International.

Auerbach, A. M. & Thachil, T. (2018), 'How clients select brokers: Competition and choice in India's slums', *American Political Science Review* 112(4), 775–791.

Baik, C. J. (2011), *The Park Chung Hee Era*, Harvard University.

Bakiner, O. (2016), *Truth Commissions: Memory, Power, and Legitimacy*, University of Pennsylvania Press.

Balcells, L., Valeria P., & Elsa V. (2022), 'Do transitional justice museums persuade visitors? Evidence from a field experiment',. *The Journal of Politics* 84(1), 496–510.

Barahona de Brito, A., González-Enríquez, C., & Aguilar, P., eds. (2001), *The Politics of Memory: Transitional Justice in Democratizing Societies*, Oxford University Press.

Bates, G. (2021), Holding Their Feet to the Fire: Negotiated Accountability in the Shadow of the International Community, PhD thesis. The University of Chicago.

Bendor, J. & Meirowitz, A. (2004), 'Spatial models of delegation', *American Political Science Review* 98(2), 293–310.

Beres, W. & Skoczylas, J. (1991), *General Kiszczak mowi–prawie wszystko*, Polska Oficyna Wydawnicza "BGW."

Bermeo, N. G. (2003), *Ordinary People in Extraordinary Times: The Citizenry and the Breakdown of Democracy*, Princeton University Press.

Bernhard, M. & Kubik, J. (2014), *Twenty Years after Communism: The Politics of Memory and Commemoration*, Oxford University Press.

Besley, T. & Burgess, R. (2004), 'Can labor regulation hinder economic performance? Evidence from India', *Quarterly Journal of Economics* 119(1), 91–134.

Binnendijk, A. L. & Marovic, I. (2006), 'Power and persuasion: Nonviolent strategies to influence state security forces in Serbia (2000) and Ukraine (2004)', *Communist and Post-Communist Studies* 39(3), 411–429.

Binningsbø, H. M., Loyle, C. E., Gates, S., & Elster, J. (2012a), 'Armed conflict and post-conflict justice, 1946–2006: A dataset', *Journal of Peace Research* 49(5), 731–740.

(2012b), 'Post-conflict justice dataset codebook', available at: chrome-extension://efaidnbmnnnibpcajpcglclefindmkaj/viewer.html?pdfurl=https%3A%2F%2Fwww.justice-data.com%2Fpcj-dataset%2FPCJ%2520codebook%2520-%2520Binningsb%25C3%25B8%2520et%2520al%2520JPR_49(5).pdf&clen=450960&chunk=true.

Blaydes, L. (2010), *Elections and Distributive Politics in Mubarak's Egypt*, Cambridge University Press.

(2018), *State of Repression: Iraq under Saddam Hussein*, Princeton University Press.

Borchert, J. (2006), *Die Zusammenarbeit des Ministeriums fur Staatssicherheit (MfS) mit dem sowjetischen KGB in den 70er und 80er Jahren: ein Kapitel aus der Geschichte der SED-Herrschaft*, LIT Verlag Munster.

Bouguerra, B. (2014), *Reforming Tunisia's Troubled Security Sector*, Atlantic Council, Rafik Hariri Center for the Middle East.

Brehm, J. O. & Gates, S. (1999), *Working, Shirking, and Sabotage: Bureaucratic Response to a Democratic Public*, University of Michigan Press.

Brun, D. A. & Diamond, L. (2014), *Clientelism, Social Policy, and the Quality of Democracy*, Johns Hopkins University Press.

Callander, S. (2008), 'A theory of policy expertise', *Quarterly Journal of Political Science* 3(2), 123–140.

Capoccia, G., & Pop-Eleches, G. (2020), 'Democracy and retribution: Transitional justice and regime support in postwar West Germany', *Comparative Political Studies* 53(3–4), 399–433.

Carey, J. M. & Shugart, M. S. (1995), 'Incentives to cultivate a personal vote: A rank ordering of electoral formulas', *Electoral Studies* 14(4), 417–439.

Carroll, R. & Nalepa, M. (2014), 'Can parties represent after communism? The dissipation of the regime divide cleavage in post-communist party systems', in *21st International Conference of Europeanists*, CES, Washington, DC.

(2020), 'The personal vote and party cohesion: Modeling the effects of electoral rules on intraparty politics', *Journal of Theoretical Politics* 32(1), 36–69.

Cepl, V. (1992), 'Ritual sacrifices', *East European Constitutional Review* 1, 24.

Chapman, A. R. (2009), 'Truth finding in the transitional justice process', in eds. Van der Merwe, Hugo, Victoria Baxter, and Audrey R. Chapman *Assessing the Impact of Transitional Justice: Challenges for Empirical Research*, Publisher is US Institute of Peace Press, pp. 91–114.

Cheibub, J. A., Gandhi, J., & Vreeland, J. R. (2010), 'Democracy and dictatorship revisited', *Public Choice* 143(1–2), 67–101.

Cheibub, J. A., & Nalepa, M. (2020), 'Revisiting electoral personalism', *Journal of Theoretical Politics* 32(1), 3–10.

Childs, D. & Popplewell, R. (2016), *The Stasi: The East German Intelligence and Security Service*, Springer.

Chiopris, C., Nalepa, M., & Vanberg, G. (2022), 'A wolf in sheep's clothing: Citizen uncertainty and democratic backsliding', Harvard University, Unpublished manuscript.

Chodakiewicz, M. J. (2009), 'Agent Bolek', *Intelligencer: Journal of US Intelligence Studies* 17(2), 108–110.

Chromiak, L. (2019), 'Cracks in Tunisia's democratic miracle', published as issue 292/3 (Fall/Winter 2019), available at: https://merip.org/2019/12/cracks-in-tunisias-democratic-miracle/.

Chromiak, L. & Salman, L. (2016), 'Refusing to forgive: Tunisia's Maneesh M'Sameh campaign' Lana Salman, Laryssa Chomiak In: 281 (Winter 2016), available at: https://merip.org/2017/05/refusing-to-forgive/.

European Commission, Directorate-General for Justice, Closa Montero, C., Study on how the memory of crimes committed by totalitarian regimes in Europe is dealt with in the Member States, European Commission, 2014, https://data.europa.eu/doi/10.2838/62564

Cohen, S. (1995), 'State crimes of previous regimes: Knowledge, accountability, and the policing of the past', *Law & Social Inquiry* 20(1), 7–50.

Congreso de los Diputados, Comisión de Cultura (2013), '161/002111', *Boletín Oficial de Las Cortes Generales* D(360), 27–28.

Coppedge, M. (2012), *Democratization and Research Methods*, Cambridge University Press.

Coppedge, M., Gerring, J., Knutsen, C. H., Krusell, J., Medzihorsky, J., Pernes, J., ... & Lindberg, S. I. (2019), 'The Methodology of "Varieties of

Democracy" (V-Dem)', *Bulletin of Sociological Methodology/Bulletin de Méthodologie Sociologique* 143(1), 107–133.

Coppedge, M., John, G., Staffan, I. L., Svend-Erik, S., Jan, T., David, A., Michael, B., M. Steven Fish, Adam, G., Allen, H., Carl, H. K., Kyle, L. M., Kelly, M., Valeriya, M., Pamela, P., Daniel, P., Laura, S., Brigitte, S., Rachel, S., & Jeffrey S., (2017). 'V-Dem Codebook v7.1' Varieties of Democracy (V-Dem) Project.

Dancy, G. & Montal, F. (2017), 'Unintended positive complementarity: Why International Criminal Court investigations may increase domestic human rights prosecutions', *American Journal of International Law* 111(3), 689–723.

Dancy, G. & Thoms, O. T. (2022), 'Do truth commissions really improve democracy?', *Comparative Political Studies* 55(4), 555–587.

Dancy, G. & Wiebelhaus-Brahm, E. (2018), 'The impact of criminal prosecutions during intrastate conflict', *Journal of Peace Research* 55(1), 47–61.

Darden, K. A. (2001), 'Blackmail as a tool of state domination: Ukraine under kuchma', *European Constitutional Law Review* 10, 67.

David, R. (2003), 'Lustration laws in action: The motives and evaluation of lustration policy in the Czech Republic and Poland (1989–2001)', *Law & Social Inquiry* 28(2), 387–439.

(2006), 'From Prague to Baghdad: Lustration systems and their political effects', *Government and Opposition* 41(3), 347–372.

(2011), *Lustration and Transitional Justice: Personnel Systems in the Czech Republic, Hungary, and Poland*, University of Pennsylvania Press.

De Brito, A. B., Enríquez, C. G., & Aguilar, P. (2001), *The Politics of Memory and Democratization: Transitional Justice in Democratizing Societies*, Oxford University Press.

De Greiff, P. & Mayer-Rieckh, A. (2007), Justice as prevention: Vetting public employees in transitional societies, SSRC.

Debs, A. (2016), 'Living by the sword and dying by the sword? Leadership transitions in and out of dictatorships', *International Studies Quarterly* 60(1), 73–84.

Deming, M. (2020), The strategic foundations of Authoritarian successor parties, PhD thesis.

Dragu, T. (2017), 'On repression and its effectiveness', *Journal of Theoretical Politics* 29(4), 599–622.

Dragu, T. & Lupu, Y. (2018), 'Collective action and constraints on repression at the endgame', *Comparative Political Studies* 51(8), 1042–1073.

Dragu, T. & Przeworski, A. (2019), 'Preventive repression: Two types of moral hazard', *American Political Science Review* 113(1), 77–87.

Dudek, A. & Gryz, R. (2003), *Komunisci i Kosciol w Polsce: 1945-1989*, Znak.

Earle, J. S. & Gehlbach, S. (2015), 'The productivity consequences of political turnover: Firm-level evidence from Ukraine's Orange Revolution', *American Journal of Political Science* 59(3), 708–723.

Egorov, G. & Sonin, K. (2011), 'Dictators and their viziers: Endogenizing the loyalty–competence trade-off', *Journal of the European Economic Association* 9(5), 903–930.

Ellis, M. S. (1996), 'Purging the past: The current state of lustration laws in the former communist bloc', *Law and Contemporary Problems* 59(4), 181–196.

Elster, J. (1998), 'Coming to terms with the past. A framework for the study of justice in the transition to democracy', *European Journal of Sociology/Archives Européennes de Sociologie* 39(1), 7–48.

(2004), *Closing the Books: Transitional Justice in Historical Perspective*, Cambridge University Press.

(2005), 'Preference formation in transitional justice', *Katznelson, Ira/Weingast, Barry R*, pp. 247–278.

Encarnacion, O. G. (2014), *Democracy without Justice in Spain: The Politics of Forgetting*, University of Pennsylvania Press.

Epstein, D. & O'Halloran, S. (1999), *Delegating Powers: A Transaction Cost Politics Approach to Policy Making under Separate Powers*, Cambridge University Press.

Escriba-Folch, A. & Wright, J. (2015), 'Human rights prosecutions and autocratic survival', *International Organization* 69(02), 343–373.

Europe: A Rude Awakening; Spain's Past (2007).

Europe: Painful Memories; Spain's Civil War (2006).

Feit, E. (1973), 'Greece: The military coup of april, 1967', in eds. Feit, Edward *The Armed Bureaucrats; Military-Administrative Regimes and Political Development*, Boston: Houghton Mifflin Go.

Felli, L. & Hortala-Vallve, R. (2015), 'Collusion, blackmail and whistle-blowing', *Quarterly Journal of Political Science* 11, 279–312.

Finch, W. H., Bolin, J. E., & Kelley, K. (2019), *Multilevel Modeling Using R*, Crc Press.

Frye, T. (2010), *Building States and Markets after Communism: The Perils of Polarized Democracy*, Cambridge University Press.

Gandhi, J. & Lust-Okar, E. (2009), 'Elections under authoritarianism', *Annual Review of Political Science* 12, 403–422.

Gandhi, J. & Przeworski, A. (2007), 'Authoritarian institutions and the survival of autocrats', *Comparative Political Studies* 40(11), 1279–1301.

Gasiorowski, M. J. (1995), 'Economic crisis and political regime change: An event history analysis', *American Political Science Review* 89(4), 882–897.

Geddes, B., Wright, J., & Frantz, E. (2014), 'Autocratic breakdown and regime transitions: A new data set', *Perspectives on Politics* 12(2), 313–331.

Gehlbach, S. (2013), *Formal Models of Domestic Politics*, Cambridge University Press.

Gibson, J. L. (2006), 'Overcoming apartheid: Can truth reconcile a divided nation?', *The Annals of the American Academy of Political and Social Science* 603(1), 82–110.

Ginsburg, T. & Simpser, A. (2013), *Constitutions in Authoritarian Regimes*, Cambridge University Press.

Goertz, G. (2006), *Social Science Concepts: A User's Guide*, Princeton University Press.

Goodman-Bacon, A. (2021), 'Difference-in-differences with variation in treatment timing', *Journal of Econometrics* 225(2), 254–277.

Dudek, A. (2020), Od Mazowieckiego do Suchockiej. (From Warszawa, Wydawnictwo Otwarte).

Grzymala-Busse, A. (2001), 'Coalition formation and the regime divide in new democracies: East central Europe', *Comparative Politics*, pp. 85–104.

(2007), *Rebuilding Leviathan: Party Competition and State Exploitation in Post-Communist Democracies*, Cambridge University Press.

(2019), 'Hoist on their own petards? The reinvention and collapse of authoritarian successor parties', *Party Politics* 25(4), 569–582.

Grzymala-Busse, A. M. (2002), *Redeeming the Communist Past: The Regeneration of Communist Parties in East Central Europe*, Cambridge University Press.

Grzymala-Busse, A., & Nalepa, M. (2022), How illiberal populists gain and stay in power: programmatic cohesion and government performance. Unpublished Manuscript, The University of Chicago.

Haggard, S. & Kaufman, R. R. (2012), 'Inequality and regime change: Democratic transitions and the stability of democratic rule', *American Political Science Review* 106(3), 495–516.

(2016), *Dictators and Democrats: Masses, Elites, and Regime Change*, Princeton University Press.

Hanson, J. K., & Sigman, R. (2021), 'Leviathan's latent dimensions: Measuring state capacity for comparative political research', *The Journal of Politics* 83(4), 1495–1510.

Hayner, P. B. (1994), 'Fifteen truth commissions-1974 to 1994: A comparative study', *Human Rights Quarterly* 16, 597.

(2001), *Unspeakable Truths: Confronting State Terror and Atrocity*, Psychology Press.

Henry, C. (2007), 'Tunisia's 'sweet little' regime', in *Worst of the Worst: Dealing with Repressive and Rogue Nations*, pp. 300–323.

Hicken, A. & Martínez Kuhonta, E. (2011), 'Shadows from the past: Party system institutionalization in Asia', *Comparative Political Studies* 44(5), 572–597.

Hoekstra, Q. (2021), 'Helping the contras: The effectiveness of Us support for foreign rebels during the Nicaraguan Contra War (1979–1990)', *Studies in Conflict & Terrorism* 44(6), 521–541.

Hollenbach, F. M. (2019), 'Elite interests and public spending: Evidence from Prussian cities', *The Review of International Organizations*, 1–23.

Holmes, S. (1994), 'The end of decommunization', *European Constitutional Law Review* 3, 33.

Horne, C. M. (2017a), Vetting, purges, and lustration: Measurement choices and empirical implications. In *Conference Proceedings of the American Political Science Association Meeting*, September (Washington, DC, September 2, 2017).

(2017b), *Building Trust and Democracy in Transition: Assessing the Impact of Transitional Justice in Post-Communist Countries*, Oxford University Press.

Horne, C. M. & Levi, M. (2004), 'Does lustration promote trustworthy governance? An exploration of the experience of Central and Eastern Europe', in Kornai, J., & Rose-Ackerman, S. (Eds.). (2004). *Building a Trustworthy State in Post-Socialist Transition*. New York: Palgrave Macmillan. pp. 52–74.

Huber, J. D. & McCarty, N. (2004), 'Bureaucratic capacity, delegation, and political reform', *American Political Science Review* 98(3), 481–494.

Huber, J. D. & Shipan, C. R. (2002), *Deliberate Discretion?: The Institutional Foundations of Bureaucratic Autonomy*, Cambridge University Press.

Hübert, R., & Little, A. T. (2021), 'Kompromat Can Align Incentives but Ruin Reputations'. *American Journal of Political Science*. First published: 13 May 2021 https://doi.org/10.1111/ajps.12620

Huntington, S. P. (1991), *The Third Wave: Democratization in the Late Twentieth Century*, University of Oklahoma Press.

(1993), *The Third Wave: Democratization in the Late Twentieth Century*, Vol. 4, University of Oklahoma Press.

Jensen, N. M., Malesky, E., & Weymouth, S. (2014), 'Unbundling the relationship between authoritarian legislatures and political risk', *British Journal of Political Science* 44(3), 655–684.

Jiang, J. & Yang, D. L. (2016), 'Lying or believing? measuring preference falsification from a political purge in china', *Comparative Political Studies* 49(5), 600–634.

Kaminski, M. M. & Nalepa, M. (2006), 'Judging transitional justice: A new criterion for evaluating truth revelation procedures', *Journal of Conflict Resolution* 50(3), 383–408.

(2014), 'A model of strategic preemption: Why do post-communists hurt themselves?', *Decyzje* (21), 31–66.

Kaminski, M. M., Nalepa, M., & O'Neill, B. (2006), 'Normative and strategic aspects of transitional justice', *Journal of Conflict Resolution* 50(3), 295–302.

Keefer, P. (2007), 'Clientelism, credibility, and the policy choices of young democracies', *American Journal of Political Science* 51(4), 804–821.

Keesing's Record of World Events. (1974), 'Announcement of general election date. – resumption of party politics. – other internal developments.', vol. 20, p. 26781.

Keesing's Record of World Events. (1998), 'South Africa', vol. 44, p. 42536.

Kim, Byung-Kook and Ezra F. Vogel, *The Park Chung Hee Era: The Transformation of South Korea*, Harvard University Press, 2011.

King, G., Pan, J., & Roberts, M. E. (2013), 'How censorship in China allows government criticism but silences collective expression', *American Political Science Review* 107(2), 326–343.

Kitschelt, H. (1999), *Post-communist Party Systems: Competition, Representation, and Inter-party Cooperation*, Cambridge University Press.

Kitschelt, H. & Freeze, K. (2010), Programmatic party system structuration: Developing and comparing cross-national and cross-party measures with a new global data set, in *APSA Annual Meeting*, Washington, DC, Vol. Available at https://goo.gl/xhxeyj.

Kitschelt, H. & Singer, M. (2018), 'Linkage strategies of authoritarian successor parties', in *Life after Dictatorship: Authoritarian Successor Parties Worldwide*, pp. 53–83.

Kitschelt, H. & Wilkinson, S. I. (2007), *Patrons, Clients and Policies: Patterns of Democratic Accountability and Political Competition*, Cambridge University Press.

Koehler, J. O. (1999), *STASI: The Untold Story of the East German Secret Police*, Basic Books.

Kovras, I. (2013), 'Explaining prolonged silences in transitional justice: The disappeared in Cyprus and Spain', *Comparative Political Studies* **46**(6), 730–756.

Krauss, C. (2000), 'New Argentine president orders purge of 'dirty war' remnants', *New York Times*, p. 6.

Laplante, L. J. & Phenicie, K. (2009), 'Mediating post-conflict dialogue: The media's role in transitional justice processes', Available at https://goo.gl/tvDDs6.

Leon-Roesch, M. (1993), 'Paraguay', in *Handbuch der Wahldaten Lateinamerikas und der Karibik*, Springer, pp. 631–650.

Leskiewicz, R. (2016), 'Od sluzby bezpieczenstwa do urzedu ochrony panstwa', *Dzieje Najnowsze* **48**(1), 165–188.

Lessing, B. (2017), 'Counterproductive punishment: How prison gangs undermine state authority', *Rationality and Society* **29**(3), 257–297.

Letki, N. (2002), 'Lustration and democratisation in East-Central Europe', *Europe-Asia Studies* **54**(4), 529–552.

Levitsky, S. & Way, L. A. (2010), *Competitive Authoritarianism: Hybrid Regimes after the Cold War*, Cambridge University Press.

Linz, J. J., Stepan, A., & Valenzuela, A. (1978), *The Breakdown of Democratic Regimes*, Vol. 1, Johns Hopkins University Press.

Loyle, C. E. & Appel, B. J. (2017), 'Conflict recurrence and postconflict justice: Addressing motivations and opportunities for sustainable peace', *International Studies Quarterly* **61**(3), 690–703.

Lundy, P. & McGovern, M. (2008), 'Whose justice? Rethinking transitional justice from the bottom up', *Journal of Law and Society* **35**(2), 265–292.

Macdonald, G. & Waggoner, L. (2018), 'Dashed hopes and extremism in tunisia', *Journal of Democracy* **29**(1), 126–140.

Magaloni, B. (2006), *Voting for Autocracy: Hegemonic Party Survival and Its Demise in Mexico*, Vol. 296, Cambridge University Press.

Mainwaring, S. (1999), *Rethinking Party Systems in the Third Wave of Democratization: The Case of Brazil*, Stanford University Press.

Mallinder, L. (2008), *Amnesty, Human Rights and Political Transitions: Bridging the Peace and Justice Divide*, Bloomsbury Publishing.

Malloy, J. M. & Gamarra, E. (1988), *Revolution and Reaction: Bolivia, 1964–1985*, Transaction Books.

Masri, S. M. (2017), *Tunisia: An Arab Anomaly*, Columbia University Press.

Mattingly, D. C. (2019), *The Art of Political Control in China*, Cambridge University Press.

McCann, F. (1997), 'The military republic 1964-85 in a country study: Brazil', available at: www.country-data.com/cgi-bin/query/r-1700.html Washington: The Library of Congress.

Medina, L. F. & Stokes, S. (2007), 'Monopoly and monitoring: An approach to political clientelism', *Patrons, Clients, and Policies*, pp. 68–83.

Meng, A. (2020), *Constraining Dictatorship: From Personalized Rule to Institutionalized Regimes*, Cambridge University Press.

Miller, J. (1998), 'Settling accounts with a secret police: The German law on the Stasi records', *Europe-Asia Studies* 50(2), 305–330.

Montagnes, B. P. & Wolton, S. (2019), 'Mass purges: Top-down accountability in autocracy', *American Political Science Review* 113(4), 1045–1059.

Muller, J. W. (2002), *Memory and Power in Post-war Europe: Studies in the Presence of the Past*, Cambridge University Press.

Naff, K. C. & Capers, K. J. (2014), 'The complexity of descriptive representation and bureaucracy: The case of South Africa', *International Public Management Journal* 17(4), 515–539.

Nalepa, M. (2008), 'To punish the guilty and protect the innocent comparing truth revelation procedures', *Journal of Theoretical Politics* 20(2), 221–245.

(2010a), 'Captured commitments: An analytic narrative of transitions with transitional justice', *World Politics* 62(2), 341–380.

(2010b), *Skeletons in the Closet: Transitional Justice in Post-communist Europe*, Cambridge Studies in Comparative Politics, Cambridge University Press.

(2012a), 'Reconciliation, refugee returns, and the impact of international criminal justice: The case of Bosnia and Herzegovina', *Nomos* 51, 316–359.

(2012b), 'Tolerating mistakes: How do popular perceptions of procedural fairness affect demand for transitional justice?', *Journal of Conflict Resolution* 56(3), 490–515.

(2020), 'Transitional justice and authoritarian backsliding', *Constitutional Political Economy*, pp. 1–23.

Nalepa, M. & Sonin, K. (2022), 'How does kompromat affect politics? A model of transparency regimes' University of Chicago, Becker Friedman Institute for Economics Working Paper, 2020–29.

Nedelsky, N. (2013), 'From velvet revolution to velvet justice: The case of Slovakia', *After Oppression*, pp. 390–417.

Nugent, E. (2020), 'The Psychology of Repression and Polarization', *World Politics* 72(2), 291–334. doi:10.1017/S0043887120000015

Nugent, E. R. (2020), *After Repression: How Polarization Derails Democratic Transition*, Vol. 24, Princeton University Press.

O'Donnell, G., Schmitter, P. C., & Whitehead, L. (2013), *Transitions from Authoritarian Rule: Tentative Conclusions about Uncertain Democracies*, Johns Hopkins University Press.

of World Events (Formerly Keesing's Contemporary Archives 1931-1988), K. R. (2001), 'Life expectancy'.

Olimpieva, E. (2021), Putin's Prosecutors: How Law Enforcement Helps Build Authoritarian States, Unpublished manuscript.

Olsen, T. D., Payne, L. A., & Reiter, A. G. (2010), 'The justice balance: When transitional justice improves human rights and democracy', *Human Rights Quarterly* 32(4), 980–1007.

Otis, J. (1992), 'Chamorro backers warn of 'new dictatorship' in Nicaragua'. URL: www.upi.com/Archives/1992/06/05/Chamorro-backers-warn-of-new-dictatorship-in-Nicaragua/5442707716800/

Paine, J. (forthcoming). Reframing the Guardianship Dilemma: How the Military's Dual Disloyalty Options Imperil Dictators, *American Political Science Review.*

Payne, S. G. (2011), *The Franco Regime, 1936–1975*, University of Wisconsin Press.

Pemstein, D., Marquardt, K. L., Tzelgov, E., Wang, Y.-t., & Miri, F. (2017), 'The v-dem measurement model: Latent variable analysis for cross-national and cross-temporal expert-coded data', University of Gothenburg, Varieties of Democracy Institute: Working Paper No. 21, 2nd edition.

Perkins, K. (2014), *A History of Modern Tunisia*, Cambridge University Press.

Pettai, E.-C. & Pettai, V. (2014), *Transitional and Retrospective Justice in the Baltic States*, Cambridge University Press.

Pinto, A. C. (2001), 'Settling accounts with the past in a troubled transition to democracy: The portuguese case', in *The Politics of Memory: Transitional Justice in Democratizing Societies*, pp. 65–91.

   (2008), 'Political purges and state crisis in portugal's transition to democracy, 1975-76', *Journal of Contemporary History* 43(2), 305–332.

   (2010), 'The authoritarian past and South European democracies: An introduction', *South European Society and Politics* 15(3), 339–358.

Pop-Eleches, G. (2007), 'Historical legacies and post-communist regime change', *Journal of Politics* 69(4), 908–926. URL: www.journals.uchicago.edu/doi/abs/10.1111/j.1468-2508.2007.00598.x

   (2010), 'Throwing out the bums: Protest voting and unorthodox parties after communism', *World Politics* 62(2), 221–260.

Pop-Eleches, G. & Tucker, J. A. (2011), 'Communism's shadow: Postcommunist legacies, values, and behavior', *Comparative Politics* 43(4), 379–408.

   (2013), 'Associated with the past? Communist legacies and civic participation in post-communist countries', *East European Politics and Societies* 27(1), 45–68.

Powell, J. M. (2014), 'Trading coups for civil war: The strategic logic of tolerating rebellion', *African Security Review* 23(4), 329–338.

Preysing, D. (2016), *Transitional Justice in Post-revolutionary Tunisia (2011–2013): How the Past Shapes the Future*, Springer.

Price, R. M. (1991), *The Apartheid State in Crisis: Political Transformation in South Africa, 1975-1990*, Oxford University Press.

Prorok, A. K. (2017), 'The (in) compatibility of peace and justice? the international criminal court and civil conflict termination', *International Organization* 71(2), 213–243.

Przeworski, A. (1991), *Democracy and the Market: Political and Economic Reforms in Eastern Europe and Latin America*, Cambridge University Press.

Rauch, J. E. & Evans, P. B. (2000), 'Bureaucratic structure and bureaucratic performance in less developed countries', *Journal of Public Economics* 75(1), 49–71.

Raudenbush, S. W. & Bryk, A. S. (2002), *Hierarchical Linear Models: Applications and Data Analysis Methods*, Vol. 1, Sage.

Remmer, K. L. (1990), 'Democracy and economic crisis: The Latin American experience', *World Politics* 42(3), 315–335.

Renewed Threats to Peace Process Purge of Army Officers Keesing's Record of World Events (1993) vol 39, page 39265, January 2,1993. (1993).

Rev, I. (2005), *Retroactive Justice: Prehistory of Post-Communism*, Stanford University press.

Riedl, R. B. (2014), *Authoritarian Origins of Democratic Party Systems in Africa*, Cambridge University Press.

Roett, R. & Sacks, R. S. (1991), *Paraguay: The Personalist Legacy*, Westview Press.

Rosenfeld, M. (1997), 'Constitution-making, identity building, and peaceful transition to democracy: Theoretical reflections inspired by the Spanish example', *Cardozo Law Review* 19, 1891.

Sang-Hun, C. (2015), 'Kim Young-Sam, South Korean president who opposed military, dies at 87', *New York Times*.

Sekelj, L. (2000), 'Parties and elections: The Federal Republic of Yugoslavia-change without transformation', *Europe-Asia Studies* 52(1), 57–75.

Serra, G. (2012), 'The risk of partyarchy and democratic backsliding: Mexico's electoral reform', Repositorio digital CIDE: http://repositorio-digital.cide.edu/handle/11651/1356.

Sikkink, K. (2011), *The Justice Cascade: How Human Rights Prosecutions Are Changing World Politics (The Norton Series in World Politics)*, WW Norton & Company.

Sikkink, K. & Walling, C. B. (2007), 'The impact of human rights trials in Latin America', *Journal of Peace Research* 44(4), 427–445.

Simon, H., Smithburg, D., & Thompson, V. (1950), *Public Administration*, Knopf.

Skidmore, T. E. (1989), *The Politics of Military Rule in Brazil, 1964-1985*, Oxford University Press.

Skocpol, T. (1979), *States and Social Revolutions: A Comparative Analysis of France, Russia and China*, Cambridge University Press.

Snyder, J. & Vinjamuri, L. (2004), 'Trials and errors: Principle and pragmatism in strategies of international justice', *International Security* 28(3), 5–44.

Sotiropoulos, D. A. (2007), 'Swift gradualism and variable outcomes: Vetting in post-authoritarian Greece', *Justice as Prevention: Vetting Public Employees in Transitional Societies*, pp. 121–145.

Southall, R. (2020), 'Flight and fortitude: The decline of the middle class in Zimbabwe', *Africa* 90(3), 529–547.

Stan, L. (2006), 'The vanishing truth? politics and memory in post-communist Europe', *East European Quarterly* 40(4), 383–409.

(2012), 'Witch-hunt or moral rebirth? Romanian parliamentary debates on lustration', *East European Politics and Societies* 26(2), 274–295.

(2013), 'Reckoning with the communist past in Romania: A scorecard', *Europe-Asia Studies* 65(1), 127–146.

Stan, L. & Nedelsky, N. (2015), *Post-communist Transitional Justice: Lessons from Twenty-five Years of Experience*, Cambridge University Press.

Stan, L. et al. (2009), *Transitional Justice in Eastern Europe and the Former Soviet Union: Reckoning with the communist Past*, Routledge.

Stokes, S. C., Dunning, T., Nazareno, M., & Brusco, V. (2013), *Brokers, Voters, and Clientelism: The Puzzle of Distributive Politics*, Cambridge University Press.

Subotic, J. (2010), *Hijacked Justice: Dealing with the Past in the Balkans*, Cornell University Press.

Svolik, M. W. (2012), *The Politics of Authoritarian Rule*, Cambridge University Press.

Szczerbiak, A. (2002), 'Dealing with the communist past or the politics of the present? lustration in post-communist Poland', *Europe-Asia Studies* 54(4), 553–572.

Tavits, M. (2005), 'The development of stable party support: Electoral dynamics in post-communist europe', *American Journal of Political Science* 49(2), 283–298.

Teitel, R. G. (2003), 'Transitional justice genealogy', *Harvard Human Rights Journal* 16, 69.

The Economist, j. (2021), 'The world must not accept the jailing of Alexei Navalny', pp. 39–40.

The Guardian (2020), "Experience: my brother spied on me for the Stasi" (by Peter Keup September 18, 2020.)

Thoms, O. N., Ron, J., & Paris, R. (2010), 'State-level effects of transitional justice: what do we know?', *International Journal of Transitional Justice* 4(3), 329–354.

Tillack, H.-M. (n.d.), 'A tale of gazoviki, money and greed', *Stern Magazine*, p. 192.

Tilly, C. et al. (1992), *Coercion, capital, and European States, AD 990-1992*, Blackwell Oxford.

Todd, S. C. et al. (2007), *A Commentary on Lysias, Speeches 1-11*, Oxford University Press on Demand.

Todd, S. C. (2000), *Lysias* (Vol. 2). University of Texas Press.

Tyson, S. A. (2018), 'The agency problem underlying repression', *The Journal of Politics* 80(4), 1297–1310.

UN Integrated Regional Information Networks (Nairobi) (2011), 'Comoros; missing guns delay demobilization process', *Africa News*.

United States Institute of Peace (2011a), 'Truth commission: Ecuador 07'.

(2011b), 'Truth commission: Ecuador 96'.

(2011c), 'Truth commission: Germany 92'.

(2011d), 'Truth commission: Germany 95'.

(2011e), 'Truth commission: Kenya'.

(2011f), 'Truth commission: Liberia'.

(2011g), 'Truth commission: Paraguay'.

(2011h), 'Truth commission: Peru 01'.

Van der Merwe, H., Baxter, V., & Chapman, A. R. (2009), *Assessing the Impact of Transitional Justice: Challenges for Empirical Research*, US Institute of Peace Press.

Veremis, T. (1985), 'Greece: Veto and impasse, 1967–74', *The Political Dilemmas of Military Regimes*, pp. 27–45.

Vickers, M. & Pettifer, J. (2006), *Albanian Question: Reshaping the Balkans*, IB Tauris.

Vilasi, A. C. (2015), *The History of the Stasi*, AuthorHouse.

Vinjamuri, L. & Snyder, J. (2004), 'Advocacy and scholarship in the study of international war crime tribunals and transitional justice', *Annual Review of Political Science* 7, 345–362.

Waldmeir, P. (1997), *Anatomy of a Miracle: The End of Apartheid and the Birth of the New South Africa*, WW Norton & Company.

Weber, M. (1968), 'Economy and society (G. Roth & C. Wittich, eds.)', *New York: Bedminster*.

Weeks, J. (2014), *Dictators at War and Peace*, Cornell University Press.

Wilde, A. (1999), 'Irruptions of memory: Expressive politics in chile's transition to democracy', *Journal of Latin American Studies* 31(02), 473–500.

Williams, K., Fowler, B., & Szczerbiak, A. (2005), 'Explaining lustration in central Europe: A 'post-communist politics' approach', *Democratization* 12(1), 22–43.

Wilson, J. Q. (2019), *Bureaucracy: What Government Agencies Do and Why They Do It*, Basic Books.

Woldense, J. (2018), 'The ruler's game of musical chairs: Shuffling during the reign of Ethiopia's last emperor', *Social Networks* 52, 154–166.

Wright, J. (2008), 'Do authoritarian institutions constrain? how legislatures affect economic growth and investment', *American Journal of Political Science* 52(2), 322–343.

Yarhi-Milo, K. (2013), 'Tying hands behind closed doors: The logic and practice of secret reassurance', *Security Studies* 22(3), 405–435.

Zakharov, A. V. (2016), 'The loyalty-competence trade-off in dictatorships and outside options for subordinates', *The Journal of Politics* 78(2), 457–466.

Zvobgo, K. (2019a), 'Demanding truth: The global transitional justice network and the creation of truth commissions' PhD Dissertation, University of Southern California, Unpublished manuscript.

(2019b), 'Designing truth: Facilitating perpetrator testimony at truth commissions', *Journal of Human Rights* 18(1), 92–110.

Index

Printed by Printforce, United Kingdom